DOMESDAY STUDIES

THE UNIVERSITY OF
WINCHESTER

Martial Rose Library
Tel: 01962 827306

2 2 MAY 2014	

To be returned on or before the day marked above, subject to recall.

DOMESDAY STUDIES

*Papers read at the Novocentenary Conference
of the Royal Historical Society and
the Institute of British Geographers
Winchester, 1986*

EDITED BY J. C. HOLT

THE BOYDELL PRESS

© Contributors 1987

First published 1987
for the Royal Historical Society
by The Boydell Press
an imprint of Boydell & Brewer Ltd
PO Box 9, Woodbridge, Suffolk IP12 3DF
and Wolfeboro, New Hampshire 03894-2069, USA

ISBN 0 85115 477 8

British Library Cataloguing in Publication Data
Domesday studies: papers read at the NOVO-centenary
   conference of the Royal Historical Society and the
   Institute of British Geographers, Winchester, 1986.
   1. Domesday book
   I. Holt, J. C.   II. Royal Historical Society
   III. Institute of British Geographers
   333.3'22'0942   DA190

   ISBN 0-85115-477-8

Library of Congress Cataloging in Publication Data
Domesday studies.
   Includes index.
   1. Domesday book—Congresses.   2. England—
Historical geography—Congresses.   3. Great
Britain—History—Norman period, 1066–1154—
Congresses.   4. England—Economic conditions—
Medieval period, 1066–1485—Congresses.
   I. Holt, James Clarke.   II. Royal Historical Society
(Great Britain)   III. Institute of British Geographers.
DA190.D7D68   1987   333.3'22'0942   87–895
ISBN 0-85115-477-8

Photoset by Galleon Photosetting and
printed in Great Britain by St Edmundsbury Press,
Bury St Edmunds, Suffolk

CONTENTS

PREFACE

The essays in this volume fulfil various functions. Some distil the wisdom accumulated over years of research. Some assemble hard-won information to which scholars will turn for years to come. Many shed new light on Domesday data affecting a whole range of problems from towns, mints and rural settlement, to financial matters, the incidence of the geld, and the structure of English government. Some are concerned with the re-examination of old Domesday problems; some with the motives and methods of the Survey and the making and function of Domesday Book. Not unnaturally the contributors differ both in approach and opinion. That is an inevitable consequence of bringing together in a single conference scholars who were given no target, no constraints, except to say something original about the single great work which has cast its spell over each one of them. In editing the collection I have not sought to resolve differences, still less impose uniformity. It has even proved impossible to encumber the book with a system of cross-references directing the reader to differences, wide or narrow, between one contributor and another. The index has been designed to serve this purpose so that those interested in controversy, intended or accidental, can happily pursue the trail. They will be rewarded not only by diversity, even occasional discordance, but also by some striking coincidences of opinion which will surprise them no less than the contributors.

Centenaries allow no choice of occasion. The last centenary of Domesday was celebrated by the Royal Historical Society at a time when Round was beginning his great work and within a dozen years of the publication of Maitland's immortal *Domesday Book and Beyond*. Few now read, or need to read, the work of that earlier celebration apart from Round's own contribution. This centenary coincides with the first major statistical analysis of the Domesday of two counties and with the maturing of three major efforts at computerising Domesday data. In this as much else Maitland got it right. His prophecy of 1897 that 'a century hence the student's materials will not be in the shape in which he finds them now . . . the substance of Domesday Book will have been rearranged. Those villages and hundreds which the Norman clerks tore into shreds will have been reconstituted and pictured in maps . . .' is now on the point of fulfilment. And the new databases will provide much more than even Maitland could see. They will illuminate language, social classification, jurisdiction, rights of tenure, the old question of 'continuity', and many other problems in ways still only barely perceptible.

So in this sense this volume comes too early. But all the contributors were conscious of this; some have exploited the new opportunities; others are concerned with matters which are unlikely to be affected by them. Yet much will change in the next few years and it may be that at the millenium some future general editor will look back and reflect in patronising style on his predecessors of 1986. To him, across the years, I send a message and a challenge. May his contributors change the study of Domesday Book as much as these have done.

I am grateful to the Officers and Council of the Royal Historical Society and the Officers of the Institute of British Geographers for all the encouragement and help which they have given in the preparation of this volume. All those who attended the Conference at Winchester in July 1986 would wish me to express our thanks to Dr Brian Golding who acted as our Secretary and to Mrs Jean Chapman, the Executive Secretary of the Royal Historical Society. Mrs Chapman also helped at many stages in the planning of the Conference and the preparation of this volume. Finally I wish to thank my wife, Dr Elizabeth Holt, who has helped with the proofs and prepared the index.

December 1986

J. C. HOLT
FITZWILLIAM COLLEGE
CAMBRIDGE

LIST OF PLATES

between pages 332 and 333

LIST OF MAPS

LIST OF DIAGRAMS AND TABLES

ABBREVIATIONS

Note Here and throughout the footnotes all items are published in London unless otherwise noted.

AN Infl	R. E. Zachrisson, *A Contribution to the Study of Anglo-Norman Influence on English Place-names* (Lund, 1909).
ASC	*Anglo-Saxon Charters: an annotated list and bibliography*, ed. P. Sawyer (Royal Historical Society, 1968).
Balzani, *Farfensi*	*Chronicon Farfensi di Gregorio di Catino*, ed. Ugo Balzari, 2 vols. (*Fonti*, xxxiii–iv, Rome, 1903).
BCS	W. de Gray Birch, *Cartularium Saxonicum*, 3 vols. (1885–93).
Beyer, *mittelrhein*	*Urkundenbuch zur Geschichte der mittelrheinischen Territorien*, ed. H. Beyer, L. Eltaster and A. Goerz, 3 vols. (Koblenz, 1860–74).
Bishop and Chaplais	*Facsimiles of English Royal Writs to A.D. 1100*, ed. T. A. M. Bishop and P. Chaplais (Oxford, 1957).
BL	British Library.
CDF	*Calendar of Documents preserved in France*, ed. J. H. Round (HMSO, 1899).
Clarke (1985)	H. B. Clarke, 'The Domesday Satellites', *Domesday Reassessment*, 50–70.
Darby (1977, 1979)	H. C. Darby, *Domesday England* (Cambridge, 1977, 2nd edn, 1979).
DB	*Domesday Book seu Liber Censualis Wilhelmi Primi Regis Angliae*, ed. Abraham Farley, 2 vols. (1783); vols. iii, iv, ed. Henry Ellis (1816).
DB, ed. Morris	*Domesday Book*, ed. J. Morris, 35 vols. in 40 pts (Chichester, 1974–).

Déléage, *Vie rurale* A. Déléage, *La vie rurale en Bourgogne jusqu'au début du XI siècle*, 2 vols. (Académie de Macon: Annales d'Ige en Maconnais, iv–v, 1942, 1943).

DEPN E. Ekwall, *The Concise Oxford Dictionary of English Place-Names* (Oxford, 1936, 4th edn, 1960).

Dialogus Richard fitz Nigel, *Dialogus de Scaccario*, ed. Charles Johnson (1950), rev. F. E. L. Carter and Diana E. Greenway (1983).

DM *The Domesday Monachorum of Christ Church, Canterbury*, ed. D. C. Douglas (Royal Historical Society, 1944).

Docs. inédits *Collection de documents inédits sur l'histoire de France* (Paris, 1835–).

Dolley (1966) R. H. M. Dolley, *The Norman Conquest and the English Coinage* (1966).

Dollinger, *L'Evolution* P. Dollinger, *L'Evolution des classes rurales en Bavière* (Paris, 1949).

Domesday Gazetteer H. C. Darby and G. R. Versey, *Domesday Gazetteer* (Cambridge, 1975).

Domesday Reassessment *Domesday Book: a reassessment*, ed. P. Sawyer (1985).

Douglas (1964) D. C. Douglas, *William the Conqueror* (1964).

Duby, *Rural Economy* G. Duby, *Rural Economy and Country Life in the Medieval West*, trans. Cynthia Postan (London, 1968).

Early Yorkshire Charters *Early Yorkshire Charters*, 13 vols., i–iii, ed. William Farrer, iv–xii, ed. C. T. Clay (Yorkshire Archeological Society, Record Ser., Extra Ser., 1914–65).

Econ. HR *Economic History Review.*

EHD *English Historical Documents*, 12 vols., general ed. D. C. Douglas (1953–); i, ed. Dorothy Whitelock (1955, 1979); ii, ed. D. C. Douglas and G. W. Greenaway (1953, 1981).

EHR *English Historical Review.*

Ellis (1833) Henry Ellis, *A General Introduction to Domesday Book*, 2 vols. (1833).

EPNS English Place-Name Society.

xvi

Exon	Liber Exoniensis.
Finn (1961)	R. Welldon Finn, *The Domesday Inquest and the Making of Domesday Book* (1961).
Finn (1963)	R. Welldon Finn, *An Introduction to Domesday Book* (1963).
Fonti	*Fonti per la storia d'Italia* (Rome, 1887–).
Fossier, *Polyptyques*	R. Fossier, *Polyptyques et censiers* (Turnthout, 1978).
Galbraith (1942)	V. H. Galbraith, 'The Making of Domesday Book', *EHR*, lvii (1942), 160–77.
Galbraith (1961)	V. H. Galbraith, *The Making of Domesday Book* (Oxford, 1961).
Galbraith (1974)	V. H. Galbraith, *Domesday Book: its Place in Administrative History* (Oxford, 1974).
Gesetze	F. Liebermann, *Die Gesetze der Angelsachsen*, 3 vols. (Halle, 1898–1916).
Guérard, *Irminon*	*La Polyptyque de l'Abbé Irminon*, ed. B. Guérard, 2 vols. (Paris, 1844).
Guérard, *Reims*	*La Polyptyque de l'Abbaye de Saint Rémi de Reims*, ed. B. Guérard (Paris, 1853).
Gullick and Thorn (1986)	M. Gullick and Caroline Thorn, 'The Scribes of Great Domesday Book: a preliminary account', *Journal of the Society of Archivists*, viii (1986), 78–80.
Hallam (1986)	Elizabeth M. Hallam, *Domesday Book through nine centuries* (1986).
Harvey (1971)	Sally P. J. Harvey, 'Domesday Book and its predecessors', *EHR*, lxxxvi (1971), 753–73.
Harvey (1975)	Sally P. J. Harvey, 'Domesday Book and Anglo-Norman governance', *TRHS*, 5th ser., xxv (1975), 175–93.
Harvey (1980)	Sally P. J. Harvey, 'Recent Domesday Studies', *EHR*, xcv (1980), 121–33.
Harvey (1985)	Sally P. J. Harvey, 'Taxation and the ploughland in Domesday Book', *Domesday Reassessment*, 86–103.
HMSO	Her Majesty's Stationery Office.
ICC	*Inquisitio Comitatus Cantabrigiensis, Subjicitur Inquisitio Eliensis*, ed. N. E. S. A. Hamilton (1876).

Inventari	*Inventari Altomedievali di terra, coloni e redditi*, ed. A. Castagnetti, M. Luzzati, G. Pasquali and A. Vasini (*Fonti*, civ, 1979).
JEPNS	*Journal of the English Place-Name Society.*
Kötzschke, *Rhein urbare*	*Rheinische Urbare*, ii and iii, ed. R. Kötzschke (*Publikationen der Gesellschaft für Rheinische Geschichtskunde*, xx, 1906).
KPN	J. K. Wallenburg, *Kentish Place-Names* (Uppsala, 1931).
Maitland	F. W. Maitland, *Domesday Book and Beyond* (Cambridge, 1897, London, 1960, New York, 1966).
Martin (1985)	G. H. Martin, 'Domesday Book and the Boroughs', *Domesday Reassessment*, 143–63.
MGH	*Monumenta Germaniae Historica* (Hannover, etc., 1826–).
MGH, DRK	*MGH, Diplomata Regum Germaniae a stirpe karolinorum*, 3 vols. (1906–66).
MGH, SRG	*MGH, Scriptores Rerum Germanicarum in usu scholarum seperatim editi*, 62 vols. (1839–1965).
MIOG	*Mitteilungen des Instituts für Osterreichische Geschichtsforschung.*
Monasticon	William Dugdale, *Monasticon Anglicanum*, ed. J. Caley, H. Ellis and B. Bandinel, 6 vols. in 8 parts (1817–30).
Mon Boica	*Monumenta Boica* (München, 1763–).
MPL	J. P. Migne, *Patrologia Latina*, 222 vols. (Paris, 1844–64).
Orderic	*The Ecclesiastical History of Orderic Vitalis*, ed. Marjorie Chibnall, 6 vols. (Oxford, 1969–80).
Percival (1985)	J. Percival, 'The Precursors of Domesday: Roman and Carolingian Land Registers', *Domesday Reassessment*, 5–27.
Perrin, *Recherches*	C.-E. Perrin, *Recherches sur la seigneurie rurale en Lorraine* (Strasbourg, 1935).
PNDB	O. von Feilitzen, *The pre-Conquest Personal Names of Domesday Book, Nomina Germanica*, iii (Uppsala, 1937).

PNK	J. K. Wallenberg, *The Place-Names of Kent* (Uppsala, 1934).
PRO	Public Record Office.
Recueil Charles II	*Recueil des Actes de Charles II le Chauve*, ed. A. Giry, M. Prou, F. Lot, Cl. Brunel and G. Tessier, 3 vols. (*Collection Chartes et Diplômes*, Paris, 1943–55).
Recueil Charles III	*Recueil des Actes de Charles III le Simple*, ed. F. Lot and P. Lauer (*Collection Chartes et Diplômes*, Paris, 1940).
Regesta	*Regesta Regum Anglo-Normannorum*, 4 vols., i, ed. H. W. C. Davis; ii, ed. Charles Johnson and H. A. Cronne; iii and iv, ed. H. A. Cronne and R. H. C. Davis (Oxford, 1913–69).
Rev. belge	*Revue belge de philologie et d'histoire.*
RHF	*Recueil des historiens des Gaules et de la France* (Paris, 1783–1904).
RS	*Rolls Series.*
Rumble (1985)	A. R. Rumble, 'The Palaeography of the Domesday Manuscripts', *Domesday Reassessment*, 28–49.
SCBI	*Sylloge of Coins of the British Isles.*
TRHS	*Transactions of the Royal Historical Society.*
VCH	*Victoria County History.*
WS	*Winchester Studies*, ed. M. Biddle (Oxford, 1976–); i, F. Barlow, M. Biddle, Otto von Feilitzen and D. J. Keene, *Winchester in the early Middle Ages: an edition and discussion of the Winton Domesday* (1976); ii, D. J. Keene, *A Survey of Medieval Winchester*, in 2 parts (1985).

The Beyond of Domesday Book

H. R. Loyn

TO CHOOSE A title for this paper was not difficult. A tribute to F. W. Maitland was appropriate and heartfelt; and what better tribute than to make allusion to his great work, published in 1897, *Domesday Book and Beyond*.[1]

It has not, however, been quite so easy to give content to the title. False starts have been made and paths retraced. Indeed, if I may extend the image further, I quickly found that Domesday Book lies at the centre of a crossroads as far as the beyond is concerned and that none of the four tracks leads us cleanly and safely through the maze.

Yet the tracks themselves are all worth exploring. Two of them are obvious, chronological guides to and from the record. Much vital and creative work in this last generation has dealt with the immediate background to the administrative effort needed to create Domesday Book, Anglo-Saxon and Norman.[2] Some of the liveliest work of the present generation treats the impact and use of Domesday Book in succeeding centuries.[3] We look before and after. The beyond along these tracks is clear cut.

Not quite so obvious is the sideways route to contemporary Europe. Domesday scholarship has tended to be insular, somewhat possessive, though with honourable exceptions.[4] Least obvious but perhaps most fruitful of all is the fourth path, contemporary but insular, that leads us through the Domesday text or through the satellites to the places where material was collected and sifted, the localities, the reeves and estate-managers, the courts of the hundreds and wapentakes, above all to the shire-court itself. We shall look more at this later. It is enough for the moment to comment on the awakening of interest in what can truly be called the side-effects and side-products of the administrative efforts that led to the creation of Domesday Book.

My main interest, and the main weight of the paper runs naturally to the

---

[1] Reprinted with introduction by Edward Miller (1960).

[2] Galbraith (1942, 1961); outstanding among more recent contributions are the works of Sally Harvey, especially Harvey (1971), and Harvey (1975); Clarke (1985).

[3] Hallam (1986).

[4] J. Campbell, 'Observations on English Government from the Tenth to the Twelfth Century', *TRHS* 25 (1975), 39–54, is the most valuable and helpful of recent examples.

beyond in Maitland's sense, to the back-track, so to speak. Thanks to the work of the late Professor Galbraith some of this track was well cleared early on for my generation.[5] We were taught to recognise a society in 1086 with a firmer inheritance of administration than we had realised, a society more used to the written record than we had appreciated, a society well on the way to creating a permanent if rudimentary central bureaucracy, a writing-office that deserved the name of Chancery with a Chancellor, a Treasury moving towards the complexities of the Exchequer, commissioners with some of the attributes of royal justices on circuit. Other scholars were stimulated to deeper investigation. R. S. Hoyt, already well known among Domesday Book specialists for his work on the ancient demesne and the *Terrae Occupatae* of the South-West, published in the early 1960s an essay under the title 'A Pre-Domesday Kentish Assessment List'.[6] He based his paper on Lambeth MS 1212 which he showed to be a taxation list, pre-Domesday but not long before Domesday, arranged by tenants-in-chief with a consistent order of lathes, giving some assessments to tax that were higher than those of Domesday Book. His analysis helped further to confirm that the Normans inherited from the Anglo-Saxons an administration at shire level that was literate, active and continuous. An element of massive common sense entered into the discussion. A society capable of standardising writs addressed to shire-courts and controlling coinage did not lack the basic skills to make a land-tax work. One remembered that fine passage from Asser which tells us that almost all the ealdormen, reeves and thegns who had been untaught from childhood gave themselves to the toilsome study of letters rather than resign their office.[7]

Seizing on these clues and others a younger generation of scholars, notably Dr Sally Harvey and more recently H. B. Clarke, have further illumined the situation.[8] Internal evidence from Domesday Book itself and even more so from the so-called satellites makes it likely that at every shire headquarters in the charge of the sheriff and his officers there existed a body of documentation, kept up to date as far as human frailty would permit, that would give:

1. a list of the hundreds of lathes or wapentakes and their answerability to the geld
2. the basic tenurial pattern of the shire, lordship by lordship
3. the answerability of the lordships to the geld.

All this was to be provided for the reign of King William and also (else the demands made by the terms of reference in the Ely Inquisition would be nonsense) for the day on which King Edward was alive and dead and for the

---

[5] See above n. 2 and also Galbraith (1974).
[6] *A Medieval Miscellany for Doris Mary Stenton*, ed. Patricia Barnes and C. F. Slade (Pipe Roll Soc. N.S. xxxvi, 1960), 189–202.
[7] *Asser's Life of King Alfred*, ed. W. H. Stevenson with an article on recent work by Dorothy Whitelock (1959), 92–5.
[8] See n. 2, especially Harvey (1971).

day when the new lord took over.[9] Evidence for the existence of formal land-registers at shire level is strong: and my guess – it is no more – is that they existed in roughly this tripartite form from the reign of the maligned Ethelred and probably earlier as soon as the administrative functions of the shire were closely defined.

But now for the complication, partly of our own making. Two strands run through discussion of the background to Domesday Book, the territorial and the tenurial, or, simply in terms appropriate to 1086-7, the territorial and the feudal. To treat the two strands separately courts danger. Administration depended on territorial structures but the administrators depended on the feudal hierarchy. The sheriffs themselves in 1086 tended to be great men, powerful tenants-in-chief and, as Eleanor Searle reminded us forcefully from her Battle Abbey evidence, great landlords maintained an abiding interest in the organisation and collection of geld.[10]

Significant advance in understanding has come recently from the West Midlands, building on the seminal work of Professor Sawyer.[11] H. B. Clarke, supported by John Moore and Caroline and Frank Thorn, has offered an intelligible explanation of that most difficult of all body of material relating to Domesday Book – the Evesham evidence. In simplified form which does no justice to the subtlety of his argument the outline of his case is as follows: Evesham A represents a stage in the assembly of Domesday Book material prior to the hundredal inquiry, Evesham M a post-Domesday hidage schedule arranged according to fiefs and, most important, indeed vital, for our argument, Evesham K, an account of Gloucestershire arranged according to fiefs, provides an outline draft prepared after the hundredal inquiry at the shire-court in preparation for the provincial draft.[12] The nature of Evesham K (together with a fragmentary account relating to Worcestershire – Evesham Q) points to the existence at shire headquarters of documents that enabled the routine administrators to transform territorial into feudal and feudal into territorial, and points also to a surprising degree of consistence and continuity among our local administrators. The Yorkshire summaries fit perfectly into this new picture.

Elsewhere other evidence suggests similar flexibility. Well-known basic facts about central documentation take on new meaning. The *Inquisitio Eliensis* and the *Inquisitio Comitatus Cantabrigiensis* nestle together in the same manuscript, the product of the same archive though not of course of the same administrative process.[13] The great men, the abbot of Ely in this instance, needed to know at both levels, territorial and feudal, the pattern of

[9] ICC, 97.

[10] Eleanor Searle, *Lordship and Community: Battle Abbey and its Banlieue 1066-1538* (Toronto, 1974).

[11] Peter Sawyer, 'Evesham A, a Domesday Text' (Worc. Hist. Soc. *Miscellany*, i. 1960), 3–36.

[12] Clarke (1985), 62–5; also John Moore, *Gloucestershire* (*Domesday Book*, vol. 15, ed. John Morris 1982), Appendix on the Evesham MSS, BL Cotton *Vespasian*, Bxxiv and BL Harleian 3763, and Frank and Caroline Thorn, *Worcestershire* (*Domesday Book*, vol. 16, ed. John Morris 1982), Appendix IV. Good comment on Hemming's Cartulary also appears in these volumes.

[13] BL Cotton *Tiberius* Avi, fos. 71–98v and fos. 36–69: a point made by Clarke (1985), 53.

holdings and obligations in the shires in which they had interest. We multiply written evidence but not beyond reason.

So in this sense, in the immediate beyond in the England of William I there has been advance in understanding. We recognise the work not only of the master craftsmen who created the final record at regional and national level but also that of a number of competent literate clerks in the shires with a volume of written and continuous record at their disposal. The Geld Roll from Northampton illustrates the point vividly: to Witchley East hundred belong 80 hides as was the case in King Edward's time and of these 15 hides have paid geld and there are 34 hides in demesne and 31 hides waste.[14] The groans of the chronicler lamenting the heavy taxes, 6s a hide in 1083, came from the heart and the pocket.[15] Reorganisation of the mechanics of taking royal profit from coinage, associated with the imposition of the new and hateful *monetagium* tax both from town and country, demanded literate support. Professor Grierson has recently discovered indications that place this innovation in a context that would lead to the run-up to Domesday Book.[16] Politics, trouble in the north, the death of the queen, unrest in the ruling house, the threat of Danish invasion, difficulties in quartering the great crowd of Frenchmen and Bretons imported to meet the threat, and possible unease on the part of the West Saxon survivors, Edgar Atheling and his sister Christina:[17] all these provide possible spurs for action, but the great Survey stands, unique in completed achievement but perfectly intelligible and practicable in the light of what we now know of the administrative activities of the shires and the nation in the reign of William I.

Fine, we recognise activity with implications at both tenurial and fiscal levels, but why in this form and what lay further beyond? What after all is the essence of Domesday Book?

In the simplest terms it is a Survey of the landed wealth of England, organised nationally, created through the hierarchy of existing governmental structures, hundreds, shires, regions (an innovation that had no future) and then at headquarters at Winchester: all of it was arranged feudally, boroughs, royal land and then the land of tenants-in-chief. In its totality and in its survival there is no precedent in medieval Europe. It is truly unique, the product and function of a unique occasion, the conquest of a much governed Christian kingdom by a Christian prince who exercised sometimes brutally and sometimes subtly the dual role of conqueror and legitimate successor to his kinsman, Edward the Confessor. Domesday Book revealed the facts and

---

[14] *Northamptonshire Geld Roll*, conveniently accessible in A. J. Robertson, *Anglo-Saxon Charters* (Cambridge, 1939) with translation and annotation, pp. 231–7 and 481–4; also *EHD* ii. no. 61.
[15] Anglo-Saxon Chronicle, s.a. 1083: *Two of the Saxon Chronicles Parallel*, ed. Charles Plummer (1982), 215 – *twa 7 hundseofenti peanega* from each hide.
[16] Philip Grierson, 'Domesday Book, The Geld *De Moneta* and *Monetagium*: a forgotten minting Reform', *British Numismatic Journal* 55 (1985), 84–94.
[17] Anglo-Saxon Chronicle, s.a. 1083; s.a. 1085, *swa mycclan here ridendra manna 7 gangendra of Francrice and of Brytlande*; s.a. 1086 (falsely 1085 in the MS) for the references to Edgar and Christina whose movements (Edgar because he had received no great honour from King William, Christina to enter the monastery at Romsey) are associated by the chronicler with King William's departure from England to Normandy in the late summer.

the legal basis of the Norman settlement.

If this is true of the totality, a national survey limited only by the extent of the existing shire organisation, what of the parts, the nature of the inquiry, the type of information required? In this respect, the route south, so to speak, to the more remote beyond splits into two, England and the Continent. On the English side we have partial precedents, even some central documentation associated with tax, the Tribal Hidage (though that is truly remote and generalised), the Burghal Hidage of the early tenth century, and the eleventh-century County Hidage. Laws, charters, wills, late Anglo-Saxon surveys, above all the tracts known as the *Rectitudines Singularum Personarum* and its allied *Gerefa*, enrich the scene and enable us to formulate some basic ideas as we grope for precedent.[18] Some of these ideas are inevitably general. We recognise, for example, that kingship with its basic association of royal authority and defence and the right to tax carried an associated duty to find out the resources of a community and what it could bear. Again we recognise the force of the simple fact that standardisation of units of assessment in terms of hides was commonplace by the eleventh century; though this is not of course to deny an element of reality and even possible areal extent (at least on a shire basis) to the hide of Domesday Book. Above all we recognise that the arrangements for territorial government, refined in the course of the tenth and eleventh centuries, were such as to make detailed and standardised surveys possible. Emphasis is rightly falling on the shire-court, and it seems increasingly likely that the bulk of the effort needed to construct the Domesday record was the product of two separate meetings of that court, possibly in the rhythm of Easter and Whitsun assemblies. Norman concentration on defence of the shire towns, the building of castles, the fostering of urbanisation of bishoprics becomes intelligible in the context of the reality of power, influence and accumulation of traditional mechanics of government that made the shire-court the most powerful institutional heritage, next to the monarchy, to pass into new Norman hands in 1066.

This is not all. Kingship, geld and the shire-court may properly stand as the obvious products of Anglo-Saxon heritage. Lower down in the effective administrative scale we have also our smaller units, the hundreds and tithings. The key answers to the detailed manorial inquiries were given according to the testimony of the hundred jurors given on oath. Domesday hundreds are not matter for the investigation by the faint-hearted.[19] Many were substantially in private hands in 1086; and our dichotomy, feudal and

[18] H. R. Loyn, *The Governance of Anglo-Saxon England 500–1087* (1984), pp. 34–8 (Tribal Hidage), pp. 70–2 (Burghal Hidage) and p. 120 (County Hidage). Peter Sawyer, *From Roman Britain to Norman England* (1978) gives the best modern account of the County Hidage. Evidence of surveys may be found in some of the surviving documents in A. J. Robertson, *Anglo-Saxon Charters. EHD*, ii. no. 172 provides a good translation of the *Rectitudines* under the title 'Rights and Ranks of People'. For the tract *Gerefa* it is still necessary to consult *Gesetze*, i. 453 ff.

[19] H. M. Cam, '*Manerium cum Hundredo*', *EHR*, xlvii (1932), 353–76 with a revealing distribution map facing 370; reprinted in *Liberties and Communities in Medieval England* (1944). F. E. Harmer, *Anglo-Saxon Writs* (Manchester, 1952), 127, where she points out that at least 130 hundreds were in private hands by 1087.

territorial, proves false at ground level. Lords of hundreds were vitally concerned with investigations into the wealth of rural communities in all manifold variety of hundreds attached to manors, of hundreds in sole ownership, and in hundreds diversified in lordship with patterns as complex as those which obtained in towns. This, of course, was again an inheritance direct from the Anglo-Saxon past with the element of private ownership intensified but still in direct continuity of institutional life. We may conclude then that the apparatus and the traditions, the potential to realise Domesday Book, was present in native English structures.

What can we draw in similar vein from the continental side? Institutionally there are two features of outstanding importance. The use of great men from the court sent out as Commissioners has a continental ring to it. We think instinctively of Charles the Great and the *missi dominici*.[20] The employment of the sworn jury for administrative purposes takes us to Frankish precedent as well as to English: but we note that the jurors are drawn from both communities and appear to represent no break with custom on the English scene. But most of all we turn to personalities and there we are on solid ground that brings us to the second path I want to explore, a path which might be described inelegantly as a sideways lurch to the Continent, a sideways lurch with a backward thrust.

The simplest scheme of analysis of Domesday Book ascribes the territorial side to Anglo-Saxon roots, the feudal to the Norman, administrative procedures to English precedent and use, personal energy and initiative that gave the Survey its characteristic nature and feudal direction to Norman vigour. Certainly the Norman bishops were vigorous enough and one of the delights of the anniversary celebrations of Domesday Book has been the way in which scholars have been forced to move to a reappraisal of episcopal activities as they have examined the principal key texts. Perhaps the most familiar of all these texts in relation to the making of Domesday Book is correctly the fine purple passage from the Chronicle describing the scene at Gloucester where the book was planned.[21] We have all pondered it, noted the divisions, the emphasis, the tone, the content. It was indeed a great occasion, a Christmas feast, a solemn court that lasted five days, an ecclesiastical synod that went on for a further three and finally the deep speech itself. The archbishop, Lanfranc himself, presided over the synod and at it there were elected three bishops, all described as king's clerks, Maurice, bishop of London, William of Thetford, and Robert of Chester. The most interesting of the three was Maurice, who had been archdeacon of Le Mans, had served as royal chancellor, and in his twenty-two years as bishop came to reorganise the chapter, the revenues and the building plans of St Paul's in an arbitrary dogmatic legalistic manner.[22] His chief monument to posterity consists of the lists of prebends, thirty canons, thirty stalls set up at St Paul's,

[20] Campbell, 'Observations on English Government' draws cautious but powerful attention to Carolingian analogies, especially 43–51.
[21] Anglo-Saxon Chronicle, s.a. 1085.
[22] *Early Charters on the Cathedral Church of St Paul, London,* ed. Marion Gibbs (Camden 3rd Ser. lviii, 1939), xxii–xxv; F. Barlow, *The English Church 1066–1154* (1979), 64.

a record unique in its way as Domesday Book itself for that age. It is hard to believe that such a mind can have been inactive at the deep speech which fomented Domesday Book. Maurice was, of course, only one among many, joining one of the most formidable groups of prelates England has ever possessed, the great Archbishop Lanfranc himself (1070–89), his fellow archbishop, Thomas of Bayeux (1070–1100), Wulfstan of Worcester (1062–95) in whose diocese the Gloucester assembly was held, Robert of Hereford (1079–95), Giso of Wells (1061–88), Osborn of Exeter (1072–1103), Osmund of Salisbury (1078–99), Walkelin of Winchester (1070–98), Remigius of Lincoln (1067–92), Gundulf of Rochester (1077–1108), William (of St Calais) of Durham (1080–96), to say nothing of Geoffrey, bishop of Coutances (1047–93), perhaps the most active of all William's legal agents and advisers. Abbots such as Baldwin of Bury St Edmunds (1065–98) or Paul of Caen at St Albans (1077–93) were far from negligible.[23] William had about him men qualified to give the best up-to-date advice on aims and strategy, discreet men of business, of great energy and success. As a point of antiquarian interest nearly all of them enjoyed over twenty years in office and nearly all were remembered as organisers, administrators and builders.

The question has to be asked what advice could they offer William? Was there anything in their collective experience that might help us in our search for the beyond of Domesday Book? A key man was surely Lanfranc himself, and it would be wrong not to reflect a little on his attitude. Modern scholars have rightly stressed the complexity of this extraordinary man and are not happy with any interpretation that lays too much emphasis on the law. Even so his early reputation and family background at Pavia, his concern with and personal use of legal manuscripts and anxiety shown in Councils to clarify the law of the Church remind us of the type of man we deal with. The old and familiar refrain comes heavily to mind. What is the law of the Church but the law of Rome?[24] For we all recognise the second half of the eleventh century as one of the most dynamic periods in recorded Western European history, the age of the Investiture disputes, of the extension of the boundaries of Western Christendom north, east and south, the age of the First Crusade. The Norman Conquests in Southern Italy and Sicily as well as in England are properly read in the context of the revitalisation and reshaping of the West, part of the move from epic to romance.[25] We all recognise, too, that new attitudes were being formulated precisely during the decades of the 1070s and 1080s to Roman Law. Primarily these new attitudes are connected with new discovery and appraisal of Justinian's work. The Florentine

[23] Barlow, *The English Church*, 56–67; Douglas (1964), 325–31. Margaret Gibson, *Lanfranc of Bec* (1979), 153–4, makes the valuable observation that a concern for estate records and the maintenance of archives was the hallmark of the progressive bishop and reminds us that three of the prelates, Wulfstan of Worcester, Giso of Wells and Abbot Baldwin of Bury St Edmunds were well placed and qualified to see to the conversion of Anglo-Saxon records into Latin.

[24] W. Ullmann, *Law and Politics in the Middle Ages* (1975), 53, draws attention to the tag embodied in Ripuarian law *ecclesia vivit iure Romano*.

[25] R. W. Southern, *The Making of the Middle Ages* (1953), accurately entitles his final analytical chapter 'Epic to Romance' and with equal accuracy leads us to consider as central elements in the story the work of Anselm and of Bernard of Clairvaux.

manuscript of the Codex was known in Italy from about 1070 and provided suitable armoury for the papal monarchy as it shaped new forms in the stressful days of Gregory VII and his successors.[26] Some ninety-three excerpts from the Digest have been noted in the surviving work of Pope Victor III (Desiderius d. 1087).[27] Most agree that knowledge was patchy and slow in dissemination though in some areas this may not have been so. The school of Bologna was certainly flourishing by the end of the century and the reputation of Irnerius reminds us of the forceful and rapid impact of new ideas expressed by a powerful group. As always among modern scholars Stephen Kuttner provides a useful guide, as we approach this delicate matter of the reintroduction of 'Roman Law'. Echoing von Savigny he argues that any continuity of Roman jurisprudence between the sixth and eleventh centuries remains a dream if 'by jurisprudence we understand an intellectually coherent discipline, a mastery of the sources which can give rational guidance to legal thinking, as distinct from professional routine'.[28] But again in one sense it is professional routine we look for, and a professional routine that was found in Carolingian Europe and especially in Italy, based not on Justinian but on pre-Justinian laws, some of which were incorporated in Barbarian codes. Chris Wickham in a recent essay has stressed the importance of legal activity in eleventh-century Italy. The Italy in which Lanfranc spent his boyhood, youth and early manhood was well blessed with notaries, *iudices, defensores, legisperiti* who looked after everyday business;[29] and to come firmly to the point, it was precisely this everyday business we have in mind when we think of Domesday Book. Men thought themselves Roman when they attempted general themes; and who more so than a group of conquerors among whom there was a leaven of very able curial prelates, masters of the Romanesque, aware of the heady new legal thought of Northern France, Lorraine and even Pavia. Their *descriptio* could provide an efficient national land register, a fiscal monument of the first order, dripping with money; and also an effective instrument by which both myth and reality of the kingdom could be perpetuated.

It is proper to ask if this type of legal thinking was a product of the brave New World, the Second Feudal Age, as Marc Bloch delighted to call it, or are the roots deeper? Ten years ago my colleague, as he then was, John Percival and I published a book on Charles the Great. Chief among our interests were the Capitularies, and chief among them the two splendid documents we know as *De Villis* and the *Brevium Exempla*.[30] Both deal with detailed surveying on great estates. Both deal with the links between

---

[26] Stephen Kuttner, 'The Revival of Jurisprudence', *Renaissance and Renewal in the Twelfth Century*, ed. R. L. Benson and Giles Constable (1982), 299–323, provides the best concise introduction.

[27] Kuttner, 302–3.

[28] Kuttner, 299–300.

[29] Chris Wickham, 'Lawyers' Time: History and Memory in Tenth- and Eleventh-Century Italy', *Studies in Medieval History Presented to R. H. C. Davis*, ed. H. Mayr-Harting and R. I. Moore (1985), 53–71: perceptive comments also appear in the same author's *Early Medieval Italy* (1981), especially on the Lombard kingdom, 28–63.

[30] H. R. Loyn and John Percival, *The Reign of Charlemagne* (1975), 64–73 and 98–105.

landowners and the state. We found ourselves involved here in our discussion with yet another Mr Facing Both Ways problem. How Roman were the Carolingians? What did they in turn transmit? The simple answer to that last question was the polyptyques and, *a fortiori* it might be argued, Domesday Book, described by the most influential of nineteenth-century investigators as the most extensive and remarkable of the polyptychs.[31]

The first problem was not so open to simple answers and yet great advance has been made both by Walter Goffart and by John Percival himself; and though their conclusions differ in detail the general tenor is much in line with Kuttner's. The Carolingians did in fact possess some general idea of the Roman register and *census*; and also specific ideas of what information was required in the *professio* a landowner or his reeve would make to a public authority in terms of real estate, livestock, slaves, and of what safeguards such a *professio* could give him. The analogies present in the Theodosian Code in theory and in the sprinkling of documents papyri and parchment from the sub-Roman period are striking, notably when one grasps the basic concept that *capita* refer not to heads but to headings in tax registers.[32] Some of the echoes ring deep to those of us familiar with the evidence of Domesday Book. Tenant farmers, for example, are divided into two categories, the first that pays its own taxes, the second, the collection of whose taxes rests with the landlord or his agent. The *iugum* was equated with the land of one family but developed into a unit of assessment and, as Goffart comments, is more than an accountants' abstraction; it indeed constitutes an index by which the historian may trace the devolution of tax responsibility from person to land.[33]

This is encouraging, and in many ways the line of continuity from Rome is proving stronger than expected, more than just a reflection of the problems faced by any powerful authority faced with the need to levy permanent tax on an agrarian community. The backward-look from Charles the Great is yielding results; and the forward look towards Domesday Book?

This has not proved so successful. There are two dozen or so well-known surveys, polyptychs that survive from the late Carolingian days. The best-known and closest studied is the polyptych of Irmino, abbot of St Germain des Prés, of the early ninth century, but others are almost equally well known, from Bobbio, Montier-en-Der or Prüm, for example. There is variety in detail. Some emphasise the nature of tenure, some of the yield, and others again give minute detail such as the names of peasants and their children, reminiscent of some of our Anglo-Saxon wills or the Hatfield

---

[31] B. Guérard, *Polyptyque de l'abbé Irminon*, 2 vols. (Paris, 1844), i. 25: *le plus étendu et le plus remarquable sans contredit, quoiqu'il ne soit pas des plus anciens.*

[32] W. Goffart, *Caput and Colonate: towards a history of late Roman Taxation* (Toronto, 1974), 57. Percival (1985), 5–27, especially 13 for comment on polyptychs and 25 for reference to a recently published fragment of a land register of the late seventh or early eighth centuries from St Martin of Tours.

[33] Goffart, *Caput and Colonate*, 35; also 63ff. for discussion of his major arguments that the division of tenant farmers into those responsible for paying their own taxes and those who were not, contributed to the creation of the bound colonate.

records. Duby notes accurately that they were practical documents used in the courts to defend ownership in troubled times.[34]

If however the group is studied as a whole some of the basic features we recognise in Domesday Book readily emerge. Firstly it is clear that initiative came from central government in prompting great landlords to make known the resources of their estates. In one instance, in 843, we are told that no fewer than 120 commissioners were employed, touring the country in order to make the *descriptio per descriptas mansas*. Then again elements of standard procedure appear, well calculated to provide a systematic description of land and its taxable capacity. Finally the detail itself often strikes chords to anyone familiar with Domesday Book: the name of the manor, the yield of the arable, the mills, the fisheries, the yield of the vineyards.[35] In weighing the evidence of the polyptychs we must, of course, make allowance for the fact that they are survivors, drawn exclusively from sources that are royal or associated with great ecclesiastical houses. There are implications too in the tenacity of their survival, no matter in what small proportion: our main texts had a long life, treasured in archives for centuries after their initial production. Even so we face a difficulty. The production of polyptychs appears to fade away in the late tenth century, probably for simple political reasons. In themselves they represent documentary evidence of a conscious Romanising policy on the part of Carolingian administrations exercising broad general authority. France closes in during the tenth century on to smaller units, and *census* declines into local feudal imposts. The polyptychs were the product of central pressure forcing the landlords for their own good to make local defence possible and looking to Roman precedent. The Norman Conquest neatly created a situation which made England amenable to accept such activity. The payment of Danegeld had been followed by Danish Conquest under Sweyn Forkbeard and his son, Cnut, in the early years of the eleventh century. The Benedictine revival of the tenth century had been followed by grants of extensive estates to great monasteries, permanent and relatively efficient institutions. Experience on general tax and in local surveying was gained along converging tracks. All this was reinforced by the Norman Conquest and by Norman activity. The new men gained enormous wealth and quickly showed the will and capacity to use it: *census*, geld, Peter's Pence, currency reforms, but (and this is the point to emphasise from the path that leads sideways and backwards) many of the bishops surrounding Lanfranc had been exposed to the fervour of legal investigation that marked the vital decades of growth in curial power at Rome. The *Collectio Britannica*

---

[34] G. Duby, *Rural Economy and Country Life in the Medieval West*, trs. Cynthia Paston (1968), 366.

[35] Duby, *Rural Economy*, 366–71, and Percival (1985), 13ff. give good modern introductions with full reference to the voluminous literature on the polyptyques. F. L. Ganshof, *The Carolingians and the Frankish Monarchy*, trs. Janet Sondheimer (1971), 292–5, refers to the survey of 843. Percival reminds us that the polyptyque of Abbot Irminon should not be taken as typical. Attention should also be drawn specifically to the polyptyques of Prüm, ed. H. Beyer (Coblenz, 1860), of Montiérender, ed. C. Lalore (Paris, 1878) and of Bobbio, ed. C. Cipolla (Rome, 1917).

may rest by chance in the British Library but it is quite in accord with the general spirit of the seventies and eighties of the eleventh century; and the creation of an effective *Descriptio* is distinctly Romanic in inspiration, its emphasis on the overriding majesty of the king. In this sense Domesday Book is truly a symbol.[36]

There remain two further paths to explore in our efforts to discover what lay beyond Domesday Book. If the one sideways path leads us south to the Continent and to Romanic influence and Rome, the other leads us obliquely and widespreading into the shires of England. We have touched on this briefly but I would now like to return to it with extra emphasis. Galbraith in fine phrases referred to the Survey as indicating the introduction of feudal law to England and also as a harbinger so to speak of literate bureaucratic effort.[37] It does indeed seem clear that the impact of the Survey and techniques used in the Survey were heavy and permanent in the English shires. This was a full-scale effort, involving virtually all the literate administration of the realm. A mass of people were involved in the collection of material, the framing of written evidence, the formulation of current returns. It is wrong to think of such activity as a one-off passing phase. Not all effects, of course, were permanent. At Gloucester, as we can tell from internal evidence, the kingdom was divided into seven circuits, each the province of a set of commissioners bearing marked resemblance to Carolingian *missi dominici*. As far as I know the circuits were *ad hoc* and not used either before or after.[38] The shires were a very different matter. It was Lennard who long ago told us to look to the shire-court as the institution which best explains the success of the Norman settlement, and Domesday studies help to reinforce the validity of his judgement. There at the solemn meeting of the shire the sheriff exercised his royal authority and the great men sorted out the working balance of interest without which permanent

[36] Z. N. Brooke provides an effective guide to English manuscripts containing a collection of ecclesiastical law from Lanfranc's collections to Ivo of Chartres *The English Church and the Papacy* (1931), Appendix, 231–45. Among much important modern general discussion attention should be drawn to Paul Fournier, 'Un Tournant de l'Histoire du Droit, 1060–1140', *Vouvelle Revue Historique de Droit Français et Etranger*, 41 (1917), 129–86, who points to the importance (144) of Edmund Bishop's discovery of the Collectio Britannica (BL Add. MS 8873), a collection of papal records of the late eleventh century containing ninety-three recognised excerpts from the Digest; W. Senior, 'Roman Law in England before Vacarius', *Law Quarterly Review*, 46 (1930), 191–206; Eleanor Rathbone, 'Roman Law in the Anglo-Norman Realm', *Studia Gratiana* 11 (1967), 255–71; and R. V. Turner, 'Roman Law in England before the time of Bracton', *Journal of British Studies* XV (1975), 1–25. Peter Stein, *From Juristic Rules to Legal Maxims* (1966), and Walter Ullman, *Law and Politics in the Middle Ages* (1975), give valuable guides to current thought on the major problem of transmission of Roman ideas of law through the central Middle Ages.
[37] Galbraith (1961), 160, 'the formal written record of the introduction of feudal tenure, and therefore of feudal law into England': acute comments on the importance of written evidence are to be found throughout Galbraith's work.
[38] A. Ballard, *The Domesday Inquest* (1906), 12–13, suggested the division into seven circuits, and the researches of historical geographers embodied in H. C. Darby's *The Domesday Geography of England* (7 vols., 1952–77) substantiate the accuracy of the division.

political structures would be unthinkable.[39] Great Domesday Book is principally a feudal document but, and we should never forget, within a shire.

Lower down the intensive use of hundredal jurors gave extra strength to institutions at a time when it was most needed. The *Leges Henrici Primi* is no starry-eyed tract. It is well aware of the corruption of judges and rapacity of lawyers; but one notes the echoes of Domesday procedures when it lays down that courts are to be attended at fixed times and at fixed places by a reeve, a priest and four *de melioribus ville* on behalf of those not summoned in their own name.[40] The Domesday inquiry used and strengthened customary procedures. And if this is true on the territorial side, it is equally true on the tenurial. Assessments were not always equitable, far from it.[41] Domesday Book gave opportunity to modify, but also in some areas, notably Nottinghamshire and the West Midlands, helped to consolidate as discrete estates were moulded into financial units, ripe for the Exchequer.[42]

Last of all one should attempt a glimpse along, scarcely a comment on, the fourth of the routes I mentioned, the route forward, the glimpse into the future.[43] Hard thought about the many references in cartularies, about the Herefordshire partly updated Domesday Book of 1162, about the thirteenth-century records, the Breviate and the *Abbreviatio*, leads to one firm proposition. Domesday Book was well known in the central Middle Ages not only in itself but in the guise of copies and extracts. To the landowners and managers of the twelfth and thirteenth centuries Domesday Book was the record of the Norman Conquest. For central government anxious about escheats and vacancies, minorities and dowers it was an essential work of reference. The Exchequer assumed permanent interest and perpetual possession. The *Dialogus* did not exaggerate. The prestige of the Book could be compared to the day of judgement from which there was no appeal. Later in the Middle Ages concern over ancient demesne, villein status and borough rights presented practical concern. We can be happy about the importance and continued use of Domesday Book, its satellites, its abstracts and copies. The residue of the Survey at regional and shire level remained fruitful. The path forward is clear.

These then are the four paths which open up as we contemplate the 'Beyond the Domesday Book'. What conclusions can fairly be drawn?

[39] R. Lennard, *Rural England, 1086–1135* (Oxford, 1959), especially 34–9 and 61–2.

[40] *Leges Henrici Primi*, ed. L. J. Downer (Oxford, 1972), 7, 76: *prepositus et sacerdos et quattuor de melioribus ville*, if the lord or his steward (*dapifer*) is unavoidably absent.

[41] Recent investigation is, however, establishing a good commonsense point that the values of Domesday manors bear a positive correlation to the geld assessments: J. McDonald and G. D. Snooks, 'How Artificial were the Tax Assessments of Domesday England? the Case of Essex', *Econ. HR*, 2nd Ser., XXXVIII (1985), 352–72.

[42] Della Hooke, 'Pre-Conquest estates in the West Midlands: preliminary thoughts', *Journal of Historical Geography* (1982), 227–44, indicates suggestion of continuous development from Anglo-Saxon days in the emergence of coherent fiscal units. D. R. Roffe, introduction to *The Nottinghamshire Domesday* (Alecto Historical Editions, forthcoming (1987), stresses rightly the complexity of estate organisation but gives cautious grounds for believing that lordship was beginning to express itself in terms of economic manorialisation in the classic sense.

[43] Hallam (1986).

Nothing very startling I am afraid. I would suggest an emphasis on its unique nature which is more than just a question of uniqueness in survival. Nothing of the scope of Domesday Book has survived from the central middle ages in Western Europe; and my strong suspicion is that nothing quite like Domesday Book was ever made. The Carolingian surveys were more specific or more limited. *Landnamabok* was different.[44] Feudal records such as the *Catalogus Baronum* of Apulia were different.[45] The other contemporary western kingdoms lacked the machinery of local territorial and feudal authority which both made Domesday Book possible and at the same time obscured the processes by which it was made. In our attempts to explain it we fall back on the two traditional refuges of the desperate historian, the immediate circumstances and the nature of the times. The main immediate circumstances are so familiar that we have to make conscious effort to see them in their proper light: the conquest of a Christian kingdom by an alien group, speaking an alien tongue, also Christian and imposing a settlement in the name of legality. The nature of the times, the age of the Investiture disputes, is also familiar, though not always brought into full focus on Domesday Book. Let us think again of the men who held the deep speech at Gloucester, of their varied background, and of their exposure to new Roman ideas of law, the magistracy, the *census*, Peter's Pence. Let us think most of all of the two towering figures in age and majesty, the king himself and Archbishop Lanfranc, monk, administrator, theologian, and no mean lawyer. The raid into the beyond of Domesday Book has left me to my surprise with the emphasis not on continuity but on novelty, not on mere use of what was available but on a new sense of purpose behind the use. Clarification of tenure and finance in a brave new world may be taken as a primary objective behind the plan and the execution.

I finish this paper, as I began it, with a tribute to a fine historian. John Le Patourel in the last decades of his life made great advance in modern interpretation of the role of the Normans and the significance of the Norman Conquest. He stressed three special attributes of the Norman conquerors: their gift for colonisation, their skill at assimilation, and above all their dynamism.[46] The second half of the eleventh century was indeed one of the most dynamic periods in Western European history; and Domesday Book is a product of the dynamism of one of the most extraordinary of the new dominant groups.

---

[44] *Islendingabok, Landnamabok* (Íslenzk Fornrit I, 1: 1968), ed. J. Benediktsson. Benediktsson has contributed an important article on 'Landnamabok: some remarks on its value as a historical source' to *Saga-Book of the Viking Society*, xvii (1969), 275–92.

[45] *Catalogus Baronum*, ed. Evelyn Jamison (Rome, 1972).

[46] The fruits of his analysis, presented in a series of papers during the preceding decade, were brought together authoritatively in *The Norman Empire* (Oxford, 1976), especially ch. 8 on 'The Dynamic and the Mechanics of Norman Expansion'.

Domesday Book: Continental Parallels

R. H. C. Davis

THE CONTINENTAL PARALLELS of Domesday Book can be divided into two classes, those which were made before 1086 and those which were made after. The first could have influenced the making of Domesday Book, the second could have been influenced by it. Both enable us to see more clearly those features of Domesday Book which are unique.

To start with the first class, we must observe that most of Domesday's predecessors, like Domesday Book itself, were known as *descriptiones*. The English word 'description' does not do justice to them, and we would do better to translate *descriptio* as an assessment or survey, which is the sense in which it was used from the first century AD to the eleventh. One reason why it retained this technical use is probably to be found in the Vulgate's version of Luke 2: 1, 'there went out a decree from Caesar Augustus that all the world should be taxed', *ut describeretur universus orbis*.[1]

If Domesday Book is in some sense a tax register, it is even more obviously a land register, recording ownership. Both aspects are discussed by Professor John Percival in the important paper on 'The Precursors of Domesday Book', which he has contributed to Peter Sawyer's *Domesday Book: a reassessment*.[2] It should be noticed that in writing of Roman and Carolingian land registers, Professor Percival deliberately avoids two misleading terms which have hitherto been in common use – Roman 'census rolls' and Carolingian 'polyptychs'. It is always unsatisfactory when records are classified simply by their physical appearance, but it is particularly misleading when it is found that physical appearance is not always correct. A 'polyptych' means literally a book ('many leaves'), but some of the so-called Carolingian 'polyptychs' were not written in books but on scrolls; while outside Egypt (where everything was different) the only census 'rolls' that have survived are neither scrolls nor books but inscriptions in stone. Walter Goffart cites nine of them, five from the Greek islands and four from Asia Minor, commenting that stone seemed an unsuitable material on which to

---

[1] Cf. Numbers, 33: 1-2: 'Hae sunt mansiones filiorum Israel . . . quas descripsit Moyses juxta castrorum loca. . . .'
[2] Percival (1985), 5–27.

record facts which would be 'bound to change from year to year'.[3] The Romans did not see matters in this way. They often preserved and publicised important records by displaying them as inscriptions in public places. Many cities followed the example of Rome itself which maintained a *tabularium publicum* with a curator in charge of it; examples in Southern Gaul were at Aix-en-Provence, Vienne, Vaison and Orange. At Orange (*Arausio*) there were also three separate stone *cadasters* or land surveys; archaeologists have discovered 269 fragments of them and have made considerable progress in fitting them together again. There now seems no doubt that the earliest of the three was erected for the Emperor Vespasian in AD 77, in order to record in perpetuity the recovery of public lands from the hands of private usurpers. Though it could well have had some use for taxation, it was primarily a public title-deed. It was erected in a prominent place in the town and covered quite a large wall; when complete it would have measured about 4.35 m by a little more than 4 m.[4] Though it was concerned only with the territory of *Arausio* it can be compared with Domesday Book because of the way in which it attempted to establish titles to land in perpetuity, particularly when they were lands which had only recently been recovered by the state. Though archaeologists have been unable to date the period at which the wall and its inscription collapsed, it seems probable that this monumental *cadaster* did not in fact survive quite as long as Domesday Book has done. Walls cannot be protected quite as easily as books.

It has been established that the Roman *census* records originally covered two sorts of tax, a poll or head tax (*tributum capitis*) and a tax on land (*tributum soli*), but by the time of Diocletian (284–305) the two seem to have been combined and to have become a fixed customary payment, bearing little or no relation to changing monetary values. Diocletian introduced the assessment of land by *jugera*, a *jugum* (pl. *jugera*) being, like the later *mansus* or hide, not a fixed area but a notional value. If vines were cultivated, the area of a *jugum* would be much smaller than in the case of arable land, which in its turn would be less extensive than land which could hardly be cultivated at all. According to the law codes, the assessments were made by an official called a *censitor*, who had to enter on the register the names of the farms concerned and the *civitas* and *pagus* to which they belonged, together with the amount of arable, vines, olive-trees, meadowland and pasture.[5] The ideal tax register would therefore have borne some resemblance to Domesday Book. The same general sort of questions were being asked, and they were being asked by a government official who recorded the answers and kept the record as public property. On the other hand, the information was arranged not by the holdings of particular landowners but according to the geographical lie of the land. This was presumably because the imperial govern-

---

[3] Goffart, *Caput and Colonate*, 121. The inscriptions are from Lesbos, Mylasa, Hypaepa, Thera, Cos, Chios, Astypalaea, Magnesia-on-the-Meander, and Tralles. Goffart thought that the use of stone for them might have been 'a momentary fad'.

[4] For both the surveys at Orange and for *tabularia publica* in general, see André Piganiol, 'Les Documents cadastraux de la colonie romaine d'Orange' (xvi supplement to *Gallia*, Paris, 1962).

[5] Percival (1985), 12.

ment did not levy its taxes on individual landowners but on the land itself, imposing a lump sum on each district such as a *colonia* or *civitas*, and requiring its *curiales* to collect it in detail.[6]

There is nothing to suggest that the Roman tax registers came to an end with the collapse of the Roman Empire in the West. No ruler likes to forgo an opportunity of receiving taxes, and the barbarian kings who took over the government of the various parts of the Empire would have found it in their interest to take over the tax registers. There is some evidence that they did so in Italy, and even more in Gaul.

In Italy the continued existence of the tax registers under the Ostrogothic kings is attested by Cassiodorus in the first quarter of the sixth century.[7] We know also that the papacy maintained land registers, either in its own name or in that of the empire, till the time of Pope Gregory the Great (590–604).[8] As public authority declined, many landowners may have usurped the rights of government and deliberately confused taxes with rent. The Land Register of the Church of Ravenna may well be a case in point. Part of it has survived on a papyrus fragment known as 'P. Ital. 3'. It dates from some time in the sixth century and is concerned with estates in the region of Padua; it gives the name of each estate, the names of the *coloni* on it, their dues payable in money or kind, and the number of day-works owed in each.[9] In South Italy the authority of the Empire lingered on through the Byzantine period to the eleventh century. Though it is impossible to prove complete continuity, it is known that the Normans who occupied S. Italy and Sicily made use of survey records called *dafâtir* which were written in Arabic but probably originated from διφθέρα (rolls or pells), which would have been the *cadasters* of the Byzantine Empire.[10] As a result there has been a temptation for historians to jump to the conclusion that the idea of making a Domesday Survey could have come to the Normans in England from their relatives in Italy, but Miss Dione Clementi, the leading English authority on Norman Italy, has explained why this is improbable. Indeed it is much easier to demonstrate how the Normans could have found prototypes of Domesday earlier and more directly in Normandy and the adjacent parts of France.

The Roman tax registers continued to be used or renewed in Merovingian Gaul. Gregory of Tours (d. 594) has several references to them, one being an account of how (*c.* 587–9) King Childebert II was asked to revise those of Poitiers, since many of those named on the lists had died, 'and the weight of the tribute pressed heavily upon their widows and the orphans and the infirm'.[11] The oft-quoted reference to an official land register (*tabula fiscorum*)

---

[6] Ibid., 7.

[7] *Cassiodorii Senatoris Variae*, ed. Th. Mommsen (MGH, *Auct. Antiq.*, xii, 1894), v. 14 (pp. 150–1), *tabularius*; v. 39 (pp. 164–6), *polypticis publicis* and vii. 45 (p. 225).

[8] *Gregorii I Papae Registrum Epistolarum*, ed. P. Ewald and L. M. Hartmann (2 vols. MGH, *Epistolarum*, ii, Berlin, 1883–93) ii, 188 (ix. 199), 433–4 (xiv. 14). Cf. the *Life* of Gregory the Great by John the Deacon, Book ii, Chs. 24 and 30, MPL, 75, cols. 96–8.

[9] J.-O. Tjäder, *Die nichtliterarischen lateinische Papyri aus der Zeit 445–700* (Lund, 1955), 184–9.

[10] Dione Clementi, in Galbraith (1961), 55–8.

[11] Gregory of Tours, *History of the Franks*, Bk ix, Ch. 30, trans. O. M. Dalton (Oxford, 1927), ii. 40.

under King Dagobert (629–39) is of less value because it occurs in the book of *The Miracles of St Martin of Vertou* which was not written till near the end of the ninth century.[12] But we do know that Bishop Rauracius of Nevers had a *descriptio mancipiorum* made on his lands in the bishopric of Cahors, *c.* 630–50.[13] Better still, fragments of an original seventh-century *census* list have been found in the binding of a medieval manuscript. It names some 900 *coloni* and the amount of *agrarium* and *lignaticum* which they paid on estates belonging to Saint Martin de Tours, an abbey whose estates were to be surveyed again in 856.[14]

In the eighth and ninth centuries, references to, and texts of, surveys become frequent. When Pepin III was raised to the throne in 751, he immediately ordered the property of the Church to be described and divided (*res ecclesiarum descriptas atque divisas*). This command must have been received by the churches with mixed feelings. On the one hand the mention of dividing their lands could only suggest that the king intended to take a portion of them as benefices for his vassals. On the other hand, those estates which were left to the churches would have their titles re-enforced.

To take the first point first, we know that in 787 Charlemagne ordered Landric Abbot of Jumièges and Count Richard to enumerate the property of the abbey of Fontanelle (Saint-Wandrille), and we are also told that immediately afterwards some of the abbey's lands were given to the king's men. The actual survey has not survived, but a summary of it was included in the *Gesta Abbatum Fontanellensium* some fifty years later, indicating that on the demesne there were 1569 manses occupied (and 158 unoccupied) with 39 mills, and also 2395 occupied manses (and 156 unoccupied) with 24 mills given out as benefices. But we are also told that there were other (unspecified) manses which had been handed over to royal vassals, or given to others on lease, by Wido, a layman who had been put in charge of the abbey for two years;[15] as in the case of the Emperor Vespasian's *cadaster* of the territory of *Arausio*, the effect of this survey was to confirm a partial redistribution of the land by the state. It is important for our present purpose, because the abbey of Fontanelle was situated on the lower Seine in what was later to become the heartland of Normandy. Under the name of Saint-Wandrille, it was to become one of the most venerable abbeys of the duchy, and its traditions would have been well known to the Normans.

Once a survey had been made by public authority, the advantage to those left in possession would soon be apparent, because the effect of it would be to validate their title. In 780, for example, the bishop of Marseilles won a lawsuit at Digne because he was able to produce in court the survey (referred

[12] MGH, *Scriptores Rerum Merovingicarum*, ed. B. Krusch (Hannover, 1896), iii. 571–2.
[13] MGH, *Epistolae Merowingici et Karolini Aevi*, i, 206–7 (letter of Bishop Rauracius to Desiderius Bishop of Cahors).
[14] Ed. P. Gasnault, *Documents comptables de Saint Martin de Tours a l'époque merovingienne* (*Documents inédits*, Paris, 1975).
[15] *Gesta Abbatum Fontanellensium*, ed. S. Loewenfeld (Scriptores Rerum Germanicarum, Hannover, 1886), 45.

to as both *descriptio* and *poleticum*) of the estate in question.[16] Similarly, in 828 the abbot of Cormery discomfited his *coloni* of Chasseneuil (Vienne) by producing in court a survey (*descriptio*) of 801–2, which had been drawn up in accordance with the evidence of these same *coloni* or their predecessors.[17] The public nature of such surveys gave them an authority far greater than that of any private document. In the same way, one of the greatest values of Domesday Book was that it confirmed titles to land, because they had been recognised by the sworn testimony of the hundred and shire in the presence of the commissioners of the king.

There is evidence to suggest that Charlemagne may have contemplated the idea of having the whole of his kingdom surveyed. In 807 he ordered his *missi* to send him inventories of the benefices (i.e. fiefs) and allods of the churches in every county.[18] In 811–13 he ordered his *missi* diligently to hold inquests and describe (*diligenter inquirere et describere faciant*) what everyone had in the way of a benefice and how many tenants (*homines casatos*) were in it; how these benefices had been agreed upon (*condicta*), and who had bought or constructed an allod out of his benefice. The benefices to be described were those not only of the bishops, abbots, abbesses, counts or vassals of the king, but also of the fisc (or royal demesne), so that the king could know how much he had delegated to everyone (*quantum etiam de nostra in uniusquisque delegatione habeamus*).[19] Such a survey embracing the whole kingdom or empire would have been far larger than Domesday Book, if ever it had been executed. In the event it proved little more than wishful thinking – Robert Fossier, for one, believes that it was never more than a pious exhortation – and it is difficult to know what, if anything, resulted from it. Some scholars have thought that the well-known *Brevium Exempla* may have been produced as models for this exercise, others that they were a result of it, but there is nothing like agreement on this point.[20] A large fragment of a roll (now 25 cm × 216 cm) from S. Victor–de–Marseille contains part of a survey of about the right date; it records the abbey's *colonica* estate by estate, naming the *coloni*, their wives and children, and stating the ages of those under sixteen.[21] Also of approximately the right date (811 × 29) is the well-known *Polyptych of Abbot Irmino of Saint-Germain-des-Prés*, outside Paris. It is probably the fullest of all Carolingian surveys, and it also is careful to name the *coloni* and their wives and children.

The period with the greatest number of these surveys was undoubtedly the forty years from 830 to 870, in which we know of at least twenty-two. The most important reason for this concentration is probably the fact that one of the main preoccupations of this period was the partition of the

---

[16] *Cartulaire de l'abbaye de Saint-Victor-de-Marseille*, ed. B. Guérard, 2 vols. (vols. viii and ix of *Collection des Cartulaires de France*, in *Documents inédits*, Paris, 1858), i. 45 (no. 31).

[17] *Polyptyche de l'Abbé Irminon*, ed. Guérard, ii. 344–5.

[18] *Capitularia Regum Francorum*, ed. A. Boretius (MGH, Hannover, 1883), i. 136.

[19] Ibid., i. 177, 'capitulare de justiciis faciendis', Chs. 5–7.

[20] Ibid., i. no. 128. Translation and commentary in H. R. Loyn and J. Percival, *The Reign of Charlemagne* (London, 1975), pp. 98–105.

[21] Guérard, *Cartulaire de Saint-Victor-de-Marseille*, i. pp. xi–xiii; ii. 633–54. The probable date is *c.* 814–18.

Empire amongst the sons and grandsons of Louis the Pious, particularly in 843 (the Partition of Verdun) and 870 (the Partition of Meersen). The *Annals of Saint Bertin* relate how in 842, the three brothers, Lothar I, Louis the German and Charles the Bald, eventually agreed to send *missi* throughout the kingdom, to make a survey (*descriptio*) which would make it possible for the land to be divided equally between them.[22] In the event these *missi* did not succeed in their task because, as Nithard would have it, they were impeded by Lothar.[23] It is possible, however, that some of the extant surveys are the result of their activities; O. P. Clavadetscher and F. L. Ganshof certainly made a strong case for the survey of the estates of the see of Chur being made in this context, and it is possible that the Freising fragment may also be connected with it.[24]

None the less, if these surveys were the result of deliberate royal policy, it has to be admitted that they are a very heterogeneous lot. Whereas the Domesday commissioners were given a detailed set of questions to ask about every manor, those who made the Carolingian surveys can have received only the most general instructions from their superiors. Some include the churches' treasures (chalices, vestments, books, etc.), others do not. Some include the land given out as benefices, others not. Some enumerate only the units of land, *mansus*, *huben* or *modia*, the equivalents of our English hides or carucates; others give also the numbers of *coloni* or cultivators, others give also their names, and yet others give also the names of their wives and children. The variety is enormous, but not surprising when it is appreciated what disparate lands the surveys come from – North France, South France, Belgium, different parts of Germany, Switzerland and Italy.

The distinctions which can most often be made are four in number. The first is between those surveys which we can call 'public' because they were drawn up by order of the king or emperor, as opposed to the private surveys which were drawn up by the landlords on their own initiative. In the case of a public survey, commissioners (*missi*) would come from the king or emperor and (as in the Domesday Survey) either collect their information from inquests held on the spot, or alternatively use local inquests to verify the information which had already been provided by the landlord. We have an instructive example of this latter method in a letter from Archbishop Hincmar of Reims to the monk Anselm at the abbey of Hautvillers (Marne), instructing him to make an inventory of his monastery, including all its possessions both before and after Hincmar's consecration (845), the number of monks and servants, the details of the properties disposed of in his own time, the people to whom they were transferred, and the reasons for having

[22] *Annales de Saint Bertin*, ed. Felix Grot, Jean Viellard and Suzanne Clemencet, with introd. and notes by Leon Levillain (Soc. de l'histoire de France, Paris, 1964, 43–5 and 172–4 (*annis* 842, 843 and 870).

[23] *Nithard: Histoire des fils de Louis le Pieux*, ed. P. Lauer (Les classiques de l'histoire de France, 1962), Bk iv, Ch. 5. Translation in Bernhard W. Scholz, *Carolingian Chronicles* (Ann Arbor, 1972), 171.

[24] F. L. Ganshof, 'Zur Entstehungsgeschichte und Bedeutung des Vertrags von Verdun (843)'. *Deutsches Archiv*, 12 (1956), 313–30.

done so. All this was to be done so exactly that the king's commissioners (*missi dominici*) would be unable to find any mistakes in it.[25] Such a survey, endorsed by public authority, would presumably have provided a title as effective as any entry in Domesday Book, but the preparations necessary before it was completed must have given the landlord a very anxious time, since one of the implications of the questions could have been that the land in question was held at the pleasure of the king and could be resumed by him if he thought it desirable to do so.

The distinction between public and private surveys is so basic, that it is strange to find that one cannot always be certain as to which of the two types a particular survey belongs. Those of which we can be certain start with an account of the circumstances in which the survey was made and give the names of the bishops, abbots or counts who made them. It sometimes happens, however, that the opening passages of a survey are missing, the first and last folios of a manuscript being the most easily lost or damaged, as in the case of the polyptych of the Abbot Irmino. But in these cases, it may still be possible to classify a survey as 'public' if it gives clear reference (as in *Irmino*) to the sworn inquests on which its evidence was based, so that the survey could be seen to have some independent authority at law.

The second distinction is between those surveys which give details of the lands distributed as benefices to vassals, those which merely record the names of the places and vassals concerned, and those which give no information about benefices at all. These variations are in sharp contrast with the regular pattern of Domesday Book, whose compiler took enormous pains to arrange his material for each county under the entry or *breve* of the correct tenant-in-chief. He was able to do this because William the Conqueror, having conquered the whole country, had rewarded his followers with the lands of the dispossessed Anglo-Saxons, who were not given any opportunity to get a protest entered in the text of Domesday Book. In the Carolingian empire, however, many churches felt that they had been despoiled by the king or emperor in order to provide for his vassals, and (as we have already seen) their continued resentment could show through even in a survey.

The third distinction concerns the details given of the individual estates surveyed. Some surveys state no more than the name of each villa or manor and the number of *mansus* or *huben* (the continental equivalents of the English hide) in it. Usually, but not always, there will also be a statement of the dues (in money or kind) and services owed. Such entries, though not similar, are more or less in the same category as the entries for individual manors in Domesday. In other surveys, however, we are given not only the services and payments due from each *mansus* but also the names of the peasants (*coloni*) who held them, together with the names of their wives, and the names and ages (if under sixteen) of their children, so that there is none of the difficulty experienced by Domesday scholars of determining the size of the average family. In this detailed counting of heads it is tempting to see,

<hr>

[25] Flodoard: 'Historia Remensis Ecclesie', in *MGH*, *Scriptores*, xiii. 552.

as many historians have tried to see, a continuation of the Roman *census* system through the Merovingian period.[26] If this were so, the differences in the types of information given in the various Carolingian surveys might theoretically reflect various regional forms of taxation in the Roman Empire. Professor Percival has shown that such regional differences existed, but he has also demonstrated convincingly that any continuity in this respect from the Roman to the Carolingian period, though theoretically possible, cannot be proven.[27]

The fourth distinction is between surveys which are concerned exclusively with landed property and those which include moveable goods also. Very occasionally these moveable goods include animals, as in Little Domesday,[28] but more usually they are confined to the treasures of churches. In Hariulf's account of the survey of the abbey of Saint Riquier, made on the orders of Louis the Pious in 831, he considered the details of landholding too tedious for his attention, but copied out in full the inventory of church treasures and books, which occupies almost seven pages of the printed edition.[29] He probably regarded it as a useful catalogue of what the abbey ought still to possess. One cannot help wondering about the extent to which the emperor or his agents regarded it with covetous eyes. The imperial commissioners of the Carolingian emperors may well have seemed as alarming to the churchmen of the time as were the Domesday commissioners to Robert Bishop of Hereford when he wrote that 'the land was plagued with many disasters because of the collection of the royal taxes'.

Though it has been convenient to distinguish four ways in which Carolingian surveys might differ from each other, it is far from easy to say what those differences signify. It would have been neat if it could have been claimed that the surveys which named the *coloni* and their families were inevitably public and vice versa; or that there was a necessary connection between the public surveys and the treatment given to benefices or moveable goods; or that any of the differences could be pinned down to a particular date. Unfortunately no such claims can at present be made, but this may be because our knowledge of the surviving surveys is still too haphazard. What is needed, above all, is a complete list of the documents concerned in all parts of the countries which formed the Carolingian Empire. In the appendix to this paper I have made a start by listing those which I have been able to find, but I am under no illusion about its failings. Quite apart from the difficulty of tracking down the printed texts and references, there is often a major difficulty in deciding which documents should, and which should not, be classified as surveys. The words 'polyptych' *Urbar* and *Saalbuch* have been

[26] Walter Goffart, 'Merovingian Polyptychs: reflections on two recent publications', *Francia*, 9 (1981), 57–78, and 'Old and New in Merovingian Taxation', in *Past and Present*, 95 (1982), 3–21.
[27] Percival (1985), 26–7.
[28] E.g. Fulda, in *Traditiones et Antiquitates Fuldenses*; ed. E. F. Dronke and W. Metz (Fulda, 1844), 125–9.
[29] *Hariulf: Chronique de Saint-Riquier*, ed. Ferdinand Lot (Collection de Textes, Paris, 1894), 87–93.

used loosely by historians to describe surveys which are particularly long and bulky. But there are other surveys, to be found embedded in the texts of charters, and in these cases it is always difficult to be sure how much should, or should not, be included.

This last difference becomes very much greater in the tenth and eleventh centuries, for though the ninth-century surveys were varied in form, those of the tenth and eleventh centuries were very much more so. Looking back from the later centuries one can see that though Charlemagne and his successors had failed to impose a uniform pattern or questionnaire for their surveys, they had nevertheless promoted a general idea. Like the idea of empire itself, it survived longer in the Germanic regions than the French, with surveys embedded in charters for S. Glossinde de Metz (963), S. Arnoul de Metz (967) and Gorze (984), and larger surveys for S. Emmeran of Regensburg (1031) and Corvey (c. 1060). In general, however, even these surveys are more suggestive of private feudal enterprise than a survival of the Carolingian Empire. If, as Mr Campbell has rightly suggested, they were known and imitated in the reformed monasteries of tenth-century England,[30] they could hardly have prepared anyone for the fact that the greatest and most systematic of all surveys was to be made in England in 1086.

Domesday Book gives a vast amount of information in a relatively short space. It is unique because it surveys almost every inch of the kingdom, whether it was royal demesne or not. The survey follows the pattern of royal administration, each county being given a separate section of its own. Within the counties the lands are arranged in *breves* under the heads of those who held them, those held by the king himself coming first, followed by his tenants-in-chief, ecclesiastical and lay. We are given no details of knight-service. Instead we are told the name of each manor, who held it in the time of King Edward, subsequently and now (1086), the number of hides in it, the number of ploughs both on demesne and otherwise, the number of villeins, cottars, slaves, freemen and sokemen; the amount of woodland, meadow and pasture; the number of mills and fisheries; what had been added to, or taken away from, the estate; and its annual value in the time of King Edward, subsequently and now (1086). The consistency is such that one has to believe that there was a standard questionnaire from which individual commissions diverged only slightly.

At first sight it is remarkable that the Domesday formula was not immediately copied elsewhere. Such an enormous achievement must have been noticed very widely, and one might have expected other rulers to attempt similar surveys based on a similar set of questions, carried out by similar inquests, and reduced to order in a similar way. In fact no one copied Domesday Book. After 1086 surveys were made at various times, particularly between 1150 and 1300, in various parts of Europe, but they are basically different because they do not address themselves to the same questions. Presumably their compilers considered that Domesday Book provided

[30] Campbell, 'Observations on English Government', 39–54, esp. 49–51.

information which for them would have been irrelevant.

In the first place they would have noticed that whereas their own surveys usually stated by whom the various estates had been granted, Domesday Book did not specifically state this at all. Instead it merely stated who held the land in the time of King Edward, afterwards, and in 1086. The assumption is that after the Conquest all land had been at King William's disposal, and that he had given it to whomsoever he wished. True, some Normans might have seized land which had not been granted to them, but Domesday Book provided a check on these by naming the person who had held the land in King Edward's day. If that person was not the current Norman's official *antecessor*, there was trouble in store, as the sections of *clamores*, *invasiones* and *terrae occupatae* show.[31] But in the case of church lands there is no information as to how they had been acquired in the first place; it is stated merely that the church had held them 'then' (in King Edward's day) as well as 'now'. The assumption must be that since William the Conqueror had formally regranted them to the various churches, no other information was required. This would not have satisfied a continental ruler, but then no continental ruler had acquired his whole kingdom by conquest and as the result of a single battle.

Secondly, the Domesday Survey asked no questions about knight-service. In one sense this seems surprising, because a list of knights' fiefs might have seemed a basic requirement for a feudal king. But though we know that in the ninth century both Louis the Pious and Charles the Bald attempted to make lists of those who owed military services in the various counties,[32] and though we have a summary *indiculus loricatorum* for the Italian expedition of Otto II in 981,[33] no systematic list of fiefs can be found in any country before the middle of the twelfth century. The earliest known comes from Norman Sicily and is the earliest part of the *Catalogus Baronum* which was made in 1149–50 and revised in 1167 and 1168.[34] It is followed by our own King Henry II's *Cartae Baronum* in England (1166) and Normandy (1172) and by the so-called *Scripta de Feodis* of Philip Augustus and his successors in France.[35] No detailed account of them need be given here because they are not parallels to Domesday Book, but quite a different sort of record.

[31] R. H. C. Davis, 'The Norman Conquest', *History*, 51 (1966), 279–86, esp. 285–6.

[32] F. L. Ganshof, 'A propos de la politique de Louis le Pieux', *Revue belge d'Archeologie et d'histoire de l'Art*, 37 (1968), 48.

[33] 'Indiculus loricatorum Ottoni II in Italiam mittendorum (981)'. This is preserved on a single tenth-century membrane, bound up with the works of St Augustine (Bamberg, B. iii. 11) and is printed in *MGH Constitutiones et Acta publica*, ed. L. Wieland (1983), 632–3.

[34] *Catalogus Baronum*, ed. E. Jamison (*Fonti*, 101, Rome, 1972). The catalogus contains three documents of which the most important is the *quaternus magne expeditionis*, drawn up in 1149–50 and revised in 1167 and 1168.

[35] The English *Cartae Baronum* (1166) are printed in *The Red Book of the Exchequer*, ed. H. Hall (3 vols. *RS*, London, 1896), i. 186–445. The *Infeudationes Militum* of Normandy (1172) are printed ibid., ii. 624–45, but see also the comments of F. M. Powicke in *EHR*, xxvi (1911), 89–93. For Philip Augustus in France, see 'Scripta de feodis ad regem spectantibus et de militibus ad exercitum vocandis', ed. De Wailly, Delisle and Jourdan in *RHF*, 23 (Paris, 1894), 608–728. See also the comments by Sivéry in the article cited in n. 44 below.

Thirdly, Domesday Book is not a record of royal revenue. There are some places where it records rents, renders or customary services, but it does so incidentally. In this respect it stands in sharp contrast to some foreign documents which have sometimes been thought parallel, such as the list of payments due to the emperor as king of the Lombards, c. 1027,[36] or the twelfth-century list of food-rents due to the king of the Romans from Saxony, Franconia, Bavaria and Lombardy.[37] These documents, short enough (one would think) to have been written originally on a single sheet of parchment, are more like memoranda than a survey and cannot be compared to Domesday Book in any way. The nearest one can get to a parallel is in Catalonia, where the counts of Barcelona made a full survey of their demesnes, rights and revenues in 1151–2.[38] It is like Domesday inasmuch as the information was recorded on the spot from named bailiffs and notables who gave their evidence on oath and declared (in those districts which had already been divided into manses) the number of manses on each estate and the revenues and services due to the count. On the other hand, it gives no information about ploughs, villeins, sokemen, freemen, cottars, meadow, pasture, mills, fisheries or previous holders of the land. The survey is restricted to the count's own demesne and reads more like a rental than a land survey. The same is true of the thirteenth-century surveys of the dukes of Bavaria,[39] and of the rulers of Upper and Lower Austria,[40] as also of the early fourteenth-century survey of the lands of the House of Habsburg in Switzerland, Swabia and Alsace;[41] they are all demesne surveys and are concerned primarily with rents and renders.

The contrast with Domesday Book is important, because it stands alone in its insistence on values. In every manor we are told what it was worth (*valuit*) in the time of King Edward, what it was worth subsequently, and

---

[36] 'Instituta regalia et ministeria camerae regum Langobardorum et honorantiae civitatis camerae regis', ed. A. Hofmeister in *MGH, Scriptores*, xxx. 2 (1934), 1444–60. The oldest part of it is c. 1027, but the prologue and epilogue are fourteenth-century additions. No authority for the survey is stated, and there is no suggestion of a jury or sworn inquest.

[37] Printed by Aloys Schulte, 'Das Verzeichnis der Königlichen Tafelgüter und Servitien von 1064/5' in *Neues Archiv*, 41 (1919), 572–4. Schulte's date is no longer accepted. Various dates from 1131–2 to 1185 are now suggested; see refs. in R. C. van Caenegem, *Guide to the Sources of Medieval History* (Amsterdam, New York and Oxford, 1978), 95, n. 4. The document is simply a list of food-rents due to the king of the Romans in Saxony, Franconia, Bavaria and Lombardy.

[38] Thomas N. Bisson, *Fiscal Accounts of Catalonia under the early Count-Kings* (2 vols., Berkeley/Los Angeles/London, 1984), ii. 3ff.

[39] 'Urbarium ducatus Baiuwarium antiquissimum' which should be dated c. 1221–8 (not c. 1240), the 'urbarium secundum' which should be dated c. 1262–7 (not 1180–1), and the 'urbarium tertium jussu Ludovici bavari of 1326. The oldest of these surveys is in German, the two later ones in Latin. All three are printed in *Monumenta Boica*, 36 (1852).

[40] Alfons Dopsch and W. Levec (eds.), *Die Landfürstlichen Urbare Nieder und Oberösterreichs aus dem 13 und 14 Jahrhundert* (Wien und Leipzig, 1904) includes a survey of the Babenberg period (c. 1220–40) in Latin (1–114), of Ottokar of Bohemia (1251–76) also in Latin (115–227) and of the Habsburgs (before 1297) in German (229–52), as well as a fourteenth-century survey of Steiermark (253–332).

[41] R. Maag (ed.), *Das Habsburgische Urbar* 2 vols. in 3, vol. ii. 2 being by P. Schweizer and W. Glättl (*Quellen zur Schweizer Geschichte*, 14 and 15, Basel, 1894–1904). The main survey, which is in German, dates from 1303–8, but there are parts of thirteenth-century lists also.

what it is worth (*valet*) now (1086). There are occasions when Domesday mentions rents and renders, but they are mainly in the 'preliminaries' for each county, the county borough and in some (but not all) of the more important manors of the royal demesne. When Domesday gets to the lands of the tenants-in-chief, it says nothing about their renders, but displays their values prominently at the end of each section.

The purpose of recording the values was presumably to enable the king to assess how much he could charge one of his barons' heirs as a relief, and how much for licence to marry a daughter. The values would also make it possible for him to estimate the amount of profit he could expect when the land of a tenant-in-chief reverted to him, either temporarily (as during a vacancy or wardship) or permanently through forfeiture or escheat. In these cases the king would use his sheriff or other agents to manage the lands and account for the profits at the Exchequer. This, presumably, was one of the reasons why the lands of the tenants-in-chief were not surveyed as single nation-wide honours, but divided into their constituent parts in each county. Each sheriff made his audit separately at the Exchequer, and when he was accounting for lands which had recently come into the king's hands, his statements could be checked against Domesday Book, which was kept in the Exchequer for that purpose. The *Dialogus de Scaccario* explains how the correct entry can be found by turning to the list of the holders of land which comes at the beginning of each county.

> The King's name heads the list, followed by those of the nobles who hold of the King in chief, according to their order of dignity. The list is then numbered, and the matter in the actual text of the book relating to each tenant is easily found by the corresponding number.[42]

The attention paid to the lands of the tenants-in-chief, which account for much the greater part of Domesday Book, was one of the main reasons for the alarm expressed by notables such as Robert Bishop of Hereford when the Survey was being made.[43] It also helps to explain how it was that the Domesday Survey was neither extended to Normandy, nor imitated in any other country. No tenant wants his landlord to make a fresh valuation of his property, and if the new valuation is accompanied by a thorough survey, he is likely to fear that his tenancy may be terminated. We have already seen that the Carolingian surveys often led to a partial redistribution of the land, and that abbeys and churches awaited them with apprehension. But in 1086 the situation in England was different. A vast redistribution of the land had just been completed, and a full survey was more likely to endorse it than undermine it. The very fact that many, if not most, of the jurors on the inquests were Anglo-Saxons, implied a legal recognition by the conquered of the redistribution that had taken place, and the Normans were likely to consider that the advantages of the Survey were greater than its disadvantages. In Normandy, on the other hand, they would almost certainly have

---

[42] *Dialogus*, 63–4.
[43] Printed in W. Stubbs, *Select Charters . . . of English Constitutional History*, ninth ed. by H. W. C. Davis (Oxford, 1913), 95.

objected to a ducal survey of their lands, for there their titles were old, and it would have been difficult to see what purpose a new survey could have had, except to facilitate some future distribution.

The point is important because it underlines the fact that the Domesday Survey could not have been made without the co-operation of the barons. The royal administration was astonishingly efficient in its use of sworn inquests in the hundreds and shires, but it could have been brought to a standstill if the barons had been determined to obstruct it. They might have refused to provide the king with information about their own holdings, prevented their own tenants from doing so, and delayed the judicial proceedings by every legal device. But in the circumstances of 1086 it was not in their interest to do so. Because the Conquest was so recent, they had more to gain than lose by co-operating in the Survey, so co-operate they did. At other times and in other countries the circumstances were different. Philip Augustus did not dare to make a 'Domesday Survey' of Normandy after he had conquered it in 1204, and part of his reason for not doing so was that it would have been impolitic. Instead he simply collected such information as he could find in the ducal archives, out of date though much of it was.[44] Similarly the papacy, when it required a record of the payments due to it from churches far or near, did not attempt a series of inquests in the provinces concerned, but merely researched in its own archives (1192), sometimes with strange results.[45]

However one looks at Domesday Book, one is driven to the conclusion that the essential circumstance which made it possible was the Norman Conquest, and that not because of some extraordinary genius of the Normans, but because of the extraordinary nature of the Conquest itself.[46] No other conquest except the Arab conquests of the seventh century had been so speedy, so complete or so permanent, and as a result of it the Normans adopted a superior attitude to the natives. No matter what the language used in the course of the Domesday inquests, the final verdict was written down in Latin by men who spoke French and knew little, if any, English. From their superior viewpoint they attempted to fit the English

[44] G. Sivéry, 'La description du royaume de France par les conseillers de Philippe Auguste et par leurs successeurs', Le Moyen Age, 90 (1984), 65–84, esp. 84, 'l'insuffisance d'agents bien formés et les résistances recontrées dans plusieurs des territoires annexes au domaine ou en voie de l'être suffisant à inciter la prudence'.

[45] Le Liber censuum de l'Eglise Romaine, ed. Paul Fabre, L. Duchesne and G. Mollat, 3 vols. (Bibliothèque des écoles françaises d'Athènes et de Rome, 2e serie, 1889–1952). Most errors were the result of the lack of local knowledge, as when the church of Florentia was placed in the bishopric of London instead of Liège (i. 224). Nonetheless the Liber Censuum was repeatedly revised and remained a working document till the fifteenth century.

[46] The nearest approach to similar conditions was in Spain where, in addition to the survey of the demesne of the counts of Barcelona (above, p. 25) there were several repartimientos recording the resettlement of land reconquered in the thirteenth century, as at Jerez and Seville. Curiously enough the Kingdom of Jerusalem, which was also the result of a conquest, seems to have had no land-surveys, though John of Jaffa's 'Livre des Assises de Hautcour' (c. 1266) includes lists of those who had their own courts of justice, lists of knight-service owed, arranged by baronies, lists of aids owed by churches and townsmen, and the number of sergeants owed. Recueil des historiens des croisades: Lois, i. 419-27.

into categories which they understood, and they succeeded so well that the great majority of people were classified as freemen, sokemen, villeins, bordars, cottars or slaves. Only on one circuit were the conditions so complex, or the commissioners so lacking in confidence, that the elegant pattern failed to emerge,[47] so much so that the master-mind who supervised the text of 'Big Domesday', made no attempt to reduce these three counties to the normal formulae, but left them alone as 'Little Domesday'. The English probably found 'Little Domesday' much more accurate than 'Big Domesday' which reduced their society to the terms which could be understood by a foreign conqueror.

In comparing Domesday Book with surveys made on the continent, one is constantly struck by the immensity of the book; it is so very much larger than any of its rivals. In consequence some scholars have found it difficult to believe the colophon of Little Domesday which states that the Survey was completed for all counties in 1086. When one considers the immensity of the work one begins to realise that if it had not been completed quickly, it would never have been completed at all. The longer the time spent on the work, the more difficult it would have been to resist the temptation to start again whenever an important tenant died, land changed hands, the whole of one circuit forgot about churches, a town was entered on the wrong folio, or the text was in a muddle. Everything had to be done at speed so that the Survey could be completed before it was out of date. Hence the rapid editorial judgements and the way in which unresolved doubts were parcelled away neatly as *clamores*, *invasiones* or *terrae occupatae*.

As a result Domesday Book is not only immense but also monumental. Folio after folio is laid out in two columns with apparent uniformity, with neat headings and rubrications which make the logical order clear at a glance. Everything about it looks final. In this respect one cannot fail to be impressed by the contrast in the physical appearance of Great Domesday Book with any other medieval survey. Even Little Domesday, neat though it is, lacks the air of finality. In part this is because it includes too many details, particularly the numbers of animals, which detract from the impression of timelessness, but apart from that, all it needs is to be written on a much larger page, divided into two columns, and written in a decisive hand which is, or at any rate seems to be, the same all the way through. Dr Rumble has remarked on the air of finality given by that hand, and it is indeed monumental, giving the same impression of timelessness as the stone inscriptions of the Emperor Vespasian's land survey at Orange. Both were public statements of land settlements which were new but were intended for perpetuity.

Domesday Book is the title-deed of all the Norman conquerors of England. We know that when they first received their lands from King William they were given writs which they showed to the relevant county

---

[47] A good example of their confusion is their account of the sokemen of Earsham Hundred, *DB*, ii. 138b–139b.

courts, but the fact that no such writ has survived suggests that the new landowners had to surrender their writs to the king as part of their Domesday returns. Thenceforward they had no title but Domesday Book. That is why Domesday Book is unique.

APPENDIX

A list of Continental Surveys, 751–1086

751	Pepin III orders church property to be described and divided (*res descriptas atque divisas*. Ref. only. *Annales Guelferbytani*, *Annales Alamannici, Annales Nazariani s.a.* 751, in *MGH, SS*, i. 26–7.
c. 760 (?)	Abbey of Wessobrünn (Bavaria); a short list of services and renders allegedly of this date, but more probably composed retrospectively in the twelfth century. 'Monumenta Wessofontana', in *Mon. Boica*, 7 (1776), 337–8.
7 Oct. 777	Abbey of Fulda; estate at Hammelburg (*et descriptus atque assignatus inde locus undique hiis terminis, postquam iuraverunt nobiliores terrae illius, ut edicerent veritatem de ipsius fisci quantitate*). Two counts and twenty-one witnesses were involved in the transfer of the land, but what is described is only the bounds of the estate. Edmund E. Stengl (ed.), *Urkundenbuch des Klosters Fulda*, i. 153–4. (*Veröffentlichen der historischen Kommission Hessen und Waldeck*, x. pt. i. (Marburg, 1913)).
768 × 814	Abbey of Fleury (Saint-Bénoît-sur-Loire). Ref. to the *libri politici a temporibus Magni Caroli* (but possibly a mistake for Charles the Bald, 838–77) by Abbo of Fleury (d. 1003). *MPL*, 139, col. 442B.
775	Abbey of Prüm. Charlemagne invites the *fiscalini* of the abbey to answer to the *missi* instructed by him to make an *inquisitio publica*. Fossier, *Polyptyques*, 26 and n, but his ref. to Böhmer–Mühlbacher, *Die Regesten des Kaiserreichs unter den Karolingen*, second ed., 1908, no. 198 (194), is incorrect, and I have failed to find his real source.
before 780	Abbey of Saint-Victor de Marseille. The *poleticum* produced with great effect in a lawsuit, 20 Feb. 780, but now lost. B. Guérard, *Collection des Cartulaires de France*, vols. viii and ix: *Cartulaire de l'abbaye de Saint-Victor-de-Marseille* (2 vols. Docs. inédits, 1858), i. 45 (no. 31).
780 × 800	Abbey of Lorsch. Survey of, *c.* 780–800, ed. K. Glöckner, *Codex Laureshamensis* (3 vols. Darmstadt, 1929–63), iii. nos. 3651–62. But see also 830 × 50. For the date(s) see K. Glöckner in *MIOG*, xxxviii (1919), 381–98; also D. Neundorfer, *Studien zur ältesten Geschichte des Klosters Lorsch* (Berlin, 1920), 93–110.
May 787	Abbey of San Vincenzo al Volturno, ed. Vincenzo Federici, *Chronicon Volturnensi del Monaco Giovanni*, 3 vols., Fonti 58–60 (1929–30), i. 204–11, Public survey. No benefices. Peasants named. No *trésor* or moveable goods.

787   Abbey of Saint-Wandrille (Fontanelle). Public survey. Text lost
        but summarised in W. Loewenfeld (ed.), *Gesta Abbatum
        Fontanellensium MGH, SRG*, 1886, 45. Benefices included.
        Manses enumerated but unknown whether or not peasants were
        named or *trésor* or moveable goods included. (But see refs. to
        losses of *trésor* on p. 44).

790   Bishopric of Salzburg. *Notitia Arnonis* and *Breves Notitiae*
        compiled by inquest of monks and laymen with the 'consent and
        licence' of Charlemagne, P. Willibald Hauthaler (ed.), *Salzburger
        Urkundenbuch* (four vols., Salzburg, 1898–1933), i. 3–16. Only
        benefices listed. Names of donors of the lands given, but no
        peasants named. No *trésor* or moveable goods. See also F. Prinz
        in *Frühmittelalterliche Studien*, 5 (1971), 10–36.

799 × 832   Abbey of Farfa. List of slaves of the abbey, in Balzani, *Farfensi*,
            i. 258–77. Probably a private survey. No benefices. Peasants and
            their sons named, but usually not their wives. No *trésor*. Dated
            by reference to two items which Duke Winigis (of Spoleto,
            789–822) holds.

800 × 811   Abbey of Saint-Bavon, Ghent. Two fragments of a survey,
            apparently public, ed. A. Verhulst, in *Frühmittelalterliche Studien*
            (1971), 193–234 (text on 231–4). Two benefices mentioned.
            Manses listed but peasants not named. Inventory of *trésor* and
            demesne animals.

800 × 820   *Brevium Exempla* a) *Staffelsee* (Worth). Public survey. No
            benefices. Manses and their services listed, but no peasants
            named. Inventory of *trésor* and demesne animals. b) *Abbey of
            Wissembourg*. Public survey. Benefices included. Manses listed
            and their (peasant) tenants named. No inventory of *trésor* or
            animals. c) *Annapes* and four other estates in N. France. Public
            survey. No benefices, no manses and no *trésor* listed, but full
            inventory of farm buildings, animals and crops. A. Boretius
            (ed.), *MGH, Capitularia*, i. no. 28. For discussion see
            K. Verhein in *Deutsches Archiv*, 10 (1954), 313–94, and 11 (1955),
            333–92. For identification of estates, P. Grierson in *Rev. belge*,
            28 (1939), 437–61. English translation in H. R. Loyn and
            J. Percival, *The Reign of Charlemagne* (London, 1975), 98–105,
            and Duby, *Rural Economy*, 363–6.

801–2   Abbey of Cormery (Indre-et-Loire). Ref. in a lawsuit of 828 to a
        descriptionem of 801–2 which specified the dues from each manse
        in Attoigné as evidenced on oath by the *coloni* of that time.
        Guérard: *Irminon*, ii. 344–5.

811 × 29   Saint-Germain-des-Prés (Paris). Polyptych of the abbey's
           widespread estates under the Abbot Irmino. Public survey.
           Survey of the benefices now lost. Peasants named, together with
           their wives and children (in the case of the free manses). No
           trésor or animals. Ed. Guérard: *Irminon*. Extracts transl. in Duby,
           Rural Economy, 366–70.

31

before 814   Archbishopric of Lyon. Refs. to lists of *colonica*, now lost, in a letter of Archbishop Leidradus to Charlemagne. *MGH, Epistolae Karolinae Aevi*, ii. 544.

814 × 18   Abbey of Saint-Victor de Marseille. A list of the unfree (*mancipia*) who are also called *coloni*. No benefices. *Coloni* listed by estate, and named, as also are their wives and children (whose ages also are stated). No *trésor* or moveable goods. The original doc. is a roll of which part (25 cm × 216 cm) survives in the Archives départementales of Bouches du Rhône. *Cartulaire de Saint-Victor de Marseille*, ed. B. Guérard, ii. 633–54, with introduction in i. xi–xiii.

c. 820   Abbey of Saint Eugendus (*alias* Jurakloster or Saint-Claude-sur-Bienne (Jura)). Text lost, but ref. in *MGH, SS*, xiii. 744, 'Zmaragdus abbas et Teutbertus capellanus, missi dominici domni nostri Ludovici imperatoris, in anno vi imperii eius imbreviarunt res monasterii Sancti Eugendi et invenerunt colonicas vestitas 840, absas 17', i.e. public survey listing manses.

822   Survey for the monastic cells of Saint-Pierre-le-vif, Saint-Jean and Saint-Rémi in Sens to rectify depredations by bishops at the expense of the monks. The *libellus* (now lost) mentioned in a diploma of Louis the Pious (18 May 822) (*RHF*, vi. 529 (no. cvii)) in a passage repeated *verbatim* in a charter of Charles the Bald (*Recueil Charles II*, i. 275–9 (no. 104)), which latter text is cited by Fossier, *Polyptyques*, 31, as a simple list of revenues. The survey was confirmed by a synod of bishops.

830 × 50   Abbey of Lorsch, ed. K. Glöckner, *Codex Laureshamensis* (as in 780 × 800 above), nos. 3671–5 which cover an imperial fisc given to Lorsch at this time. List of manses or *huben*. No benefices, no named peasants, no *trésor* or moveable goods.

831   Abbey of Saint Riquier. Full text lost, but summary in F. Lot (ed.), *Hariulf: Chronique de Saint Riquier* (Paris, 1894), 87–97 and 306–8. Public survey including benefices. Summary includes no named peasants, but Hariulf gives full text of the inventory of the *trésor*.

834 × 45   Abbey of Montier-en-Der (Haute Marne). Private(?) survey of the lands allotted for the monks' food and clothing. No benefices as such, but pp. 110–15 are concerned with *precaria* or *prestaria* of persons who look like benefice-holders. No named peasants. No *trésor* or moveable goods. *Collection des principaux cartulaires du diocèse de Troyes*, iv, ed. Charles Lalore: *Cartulaire de Chapelle-aux-Planches, Chartes de Montier-en-der*, etc. (Paris, 1878), 89–115.

before 835   Sant'Ambrosio of Milan. Public survey of Limonta; no benefices; no named peasants; no *trésor* or moveable goods, *Inventari*, 21–5. One paragraph translated in G. Duby, *Rural Economy*, 376.

839   Cathedral of Urgel. List of dues from the parishes of the diocese to the cathedral church, discussed in P. Bonnassie, *La Catalogne du milieu du Xe à la fin du XIe siécle* (Toulouse, 1975), 86–7. Drawn up on orders of the Bishop Sisebut.

840   Abbey of Farfa. Remains of a survey listing estates without stating whether they are benefices or divided into manses. No *trésor*. Balzani, *Farfensi*, i. 198–206 (the actual survey, 200, l. 33–205, l. 1).

c. 840   Cathedral of Saint Vincent, Le Mans. *Summa de poleticis vel plenariis*. Full text lost, but summary of renders in money and kind survives. Guérard, *Irminon*, i. 922–3 (no. xvii) from *Gesta Aldrici Cenomanensis episcopi*, *c.* 52. *MPL*, 115 (1852), 92.

c. 841   Abbey of Niederaltaich. Fragment, or summary of a fragment of a survey of a benefice at Ingolstadt, in a diploma of Louis the German, converting the benefice *in propriam*. *MGH, DRK*, i. 37 (no. 30). No mention of public inquest. No peasants named. No *trésor*.

842   Bishopric of Freising, fragment of a survey relating to Bergkirchen. Unknown whether public or private; no benefices; no peasants named; no *trésor*. Printed, Dollinger, *L'Evolution*, 12, n. 23 from ed. Theodor Bitterauf, *Die Traditionen des Hochstifts Freising* (2 vols., Munich, 1905–9), i. no. 652.

842–3   Bishopric of Chur. Public survey, *Die Bündner Urkundenbuch*, ed. E. Meyer Marthaler und Franz Perret (Chur, 1955), i. 373–96. For the date, see O. P. Claverdetscher in *Zeitschrift Schweizer Geschichte*, 30 (1950) and F. L. Ganshof in *Deutsches Archiv*, 12 (1956), 313–30.

844 × 59   Abbey of Saint-Bertin. *Breviarium villarum monachorum victus*, partial text embodied in Folcuin's 'Gesta Abbatum' and ed. F. L. Ganshof, F. Golding-Ganshof and A. de Sinet in *Méms. de l'Académie d'Inscriptions et Belles-Lettres*, 45 (Paris, 1975), 75–86. Private survey on orders of Abbot Adalard, covering 20 vills; no benefices; peasants named on some (but not all) estates; no *trésor* or moveable goods.

847 × 57   Notre-Dame de Soissons. Public survey (now lost) made by the bishops of Soissons and Laon and the abbot of Saint-Médard-de-Soissons, ref. in lost diploma of Charles the Bald, cited in *Recueil Charles II*, i. 509, no. 109.

c. 850   Abbey of Saint-Rémi de Reims, Guérard, *Reims*. Public survey of twenty-four fiscs and five groups of benefices. Peasants named but normally not their wives or children. No *trésor* or moveable goods. Extracts transl. in Duby, *Rural Economy*, 370–1.

c. 850   Abbey of Hautvillers (Marne). Public survey, now lost. In a letter Archbishop Hincmar orders the monk Anselm to make a full inventory of his monastery including details of properties disposed of (as benefices, presumably) and the numbers of monks and servants, *Flodoard, Hist. Remensis Ecclesie, MGH, SS*, xiii. 552.

856   Abbey of Saint-Martin de Tours. Orders for a survey (now lost) in ed. André Salmon, *Recueil des Chroniques de Touraine* (Soc. archéologique de Tours, coll. de documents, t. 1, Tours, 1854), 43.

858 × 83   Abbey of Montecassino. Private survey lost but quoted by Leo of Ostia, *MGH, SS*, vii. 610–12. Made in the time of Abbot Bertharius. Lands and churches described, but no mention of their inhabitants or of their dues or services. No benefices described as such, no peasants named or enumerated. No *trésor* or moveable goods.

862   Abbey of Saint Columbanus, Bobbio. Public survey. No benefices. No peasants named. No *trésor*. Written on a parchment roll. See 883 for another roll; ed. *Inventari*, 127–44. Excerpt (from p. 200) trans. in Duby, *Rural Economy*, 377.

866   Abbey of Saint-Vaast d'Arras. Public survey made by Guillebertus, Ordericus and Eurebertus, *missi* of Charles the Bald. Text lost, but the monk Aimer who compiled the cartulary in 1170 had it before his eyes. *Cartulaire de l'Abbaye de Saint-Vaast d'Arras*, ed. A. van Drival (Arras, 1875), 2.

866 × 924   Priory of Saint-Symphorien d'Autun, *poleticus de rebus canonicorum et abbatis ipsius loci*, now only a fragment with (private?) surveys of five estates; no benefices; no named peasants; no *trésor* or moveable goods. *Recueil des Actes du Prieuré de Saint-Symphorien d'Autun, de 696 a 1300*, ed. André Déléage (Autun, 1936), 15–16 (no. 4). For comment, Déléage, *Vie rurale*, ii. 1199–1205.

868   Abbey of Lobbes. Public survey by authority of Lothar II at request of John Bishop of Cambrai, to restore the monks' share (for food and clothing) which had been despoiled by the lay abbot, Hubert d'Agaune; ed. J. Warichez, 'Une "descriptio villarum" de l'abbaye de Lobbes a l'époque carolingienne', *Bull. de la Commission royale d'Histoire*, 78 (1909), 249–67. No benefices. No named peasants. No *trésor*, but inventories of livestock.

c. 870 (?)   Abbey of Wissembourg. Fragment of a public survey, included in the *Brevium Exempla* (above, 800 × 820, item b), but dated to 870 by Willhelm Metz, 'Das Kloster Weissenburg und der Vertrag von Metz', *Speculum Historiale*, ed. C. Bauer, L. Böhm and M. Müller (Freiburg/München, 1965), 458–68, esp. 461.

c. 870   Abbey of Saint-Trond. Ref. to lost survey and inventory of *trésor*, in Fossier, *Polyptyques*, 32, n. 36.

before 872   Abbey of Saint Amand. One leaf only of (?public or private) survey covering four benefices in detail, no peasants named; no *trésor* or moveable goods; ed. Guérard, *Irminon*, i. 925–6.

878   Cathedral Chapter of Mâcon. *Memoratorium de mansis que sunt Ymitherii* of 878 with additions of tenth–thirteenth centuries. Public(?) or private(?) survey, mentioning one benefice. No peasants named. No *trésor* or moveable goods; ed. Déléage, *Vie rurale*, i. 1219–20.

878 × 938   Abbey of Saint-Bénigne de Dijon. 'Breve commorantium quod Ademarus rogavit facere' for Etourvy (Aube), Melisey (Yonne) and seven other places. Public(?) survey (*invenimus*); no benefices; no peasants named; no *trésor*; ed. Déléage, *Vie rurale*, i. 1214–19.

879–906   Abbey of Santa Giulia di Brescia. Private survey (beginning and end missing); no benefices; no peasants named (free or slaves); *trésor* of dependent churches and chapels; animals. *Inventari*, 53–94. Extract transl. in Duby, *Rural Economy*, 377–8.

883   Abbey of Saint Columbanus of Bobbio. New survey updating that of 862 (q.v.); ed. *Inventari*, 145–65.

c. 893   Abbey of Prüm. Public survey made soon after Viking incursion of 892; includes list of fief-holders but not of their fiefs (or benefices); no named peasants; no *trésor* or moveable goods. Ed. Beyer, *mittelrhein*, i. 142–201 from the cartulary into which it was transcribed with a running commentary by the ex-abbot Caesarius in 1222. K. Lamprecht argued that the basis was a survey of *c*. 810, revised in 854 and 893, but Perrin, *Recherches*, no. 1, has established that the survey was made soon after 892 by nine commissions working simultaneously in different geographical areas.

899   Abbey of Gorze. Text lost, but ref. to *Hubenliste* in an act of 899. Fossier, *Polyptyques*, 31, n. 34.

ninth cent.   Abbey of Hersfeld. (a) *Breviarium Sancti Lulli* or *Breve Compendium*, *Urkundenbuch der Reichsabtei Hersfeld*, ed. Hans Weirich (Marburg, 1936, Veröffentlichungen der Hist. Komm. für Hessen und Waldeck, xix, pt. 1), i. 68–74 (no. 38). Private survey; no benefices; no peasants named; no *trésor* or moveable goods. (b) A possible survey may also be embedded in a charter of 835 × 63 (ibid., 61–3, no. 35), in which the donor gives his family lands to the abbey. No benefices included. Peasants and their wives named, their children enumerated. No *trésor* or moveable goods. (c) A list of places rendering tithes to the abbey, *c*. 880–99 (ibid., 65–7, no. 37).

ninth cent.   Abbey of Saint Maur de Fossés. Polypticum, ed. Guérard, *Irminon*, ii. 283–8 (no. 1). Public(?) survey; no benefices; many peasants named (with numbers of their children) in sections 17–22; no *trésor* or moveable goods.

ninth cent.   Abbey of San Tommaso di Reggio. Private survey of agricultural equipment, stock and renders of five manors and one benefice; no *trésor*; ed. *Inventari*, 196–8.

ninth cent.   Cathedral of San Lorenzo di Tortona. Record of gifts by the lady Teberga; no benefices; six peasants named; no *trésor* or moveables; ed. *Inventari*, 115–17.

late ninth cent.   Abbey of Werden. Composite private survey. Usually peasants named. No *trésor* or moveable goods; ed. Kötschke, *Rhein Urbar*, ii. 4–87. The passage relating to the lordship of Friemersheim (ii. 15–18) translated in Duby, *Rural Economy*, 374–6.

late ninth cent.   Bishopric of Lucca. Two related surveys, ed. Luzzati in *Inventari*, 211–46. (i) (pp. 211–25) is a public(?) survey (*invenimus*) of the bishop's demesnes. No benefices. Many peasants named. *Trésor* included. Apparently second half of ninth cent. (ii) (pp. 225–46) a private(?) survey of the benefices of twenty-seven of the bishop's men; some named peasants; no *trésor* or moveable goods (890–900).

ninth–tenth cents.   Abbey of Saint Columbanus at Bobbio, private survey, ed. *Inventari*, 169–75, incl. a few benefices, no named peasants, no *trésor* or moveable goods.

913–14   Abbey of Gorze. Survey of demesne at Quincy embodied in a charter by the donor, Count Boso. Text in *Histoire de Metz par les religieux Bénédictins de la congrégation de Saint-Vanne* (6 vols., Metz, 1769–90), iii. 14. Comment in Perrin, *Recherches*, 171–9 (no. 5). Private(?) survey; no benefices; no peasants named; no *trésor* or moveable goods.

before 921   Verberie (Oise) ref. in diploma of Charles the Simple, 25 April 921 – 'tres mansos in Vermeria, quos ipse Hadegerus in beneficii jure ex nostro tenebat dare. Et haec sunt eorum nomina qui eosdem incoluerunt mansos ex antiquo, ut est scriptum in polipdico de Vermeria.' *Recueil Charles III*, i. 263 (no. cix).

925 × 50   Abbey of Saint Peter at Ghent (Blandinium). Private survey, *Liber Traditionum Sancti Petri Blandiniensis*, ed. A. Fayen (Ghent, 1906), 15–21. No benefices; all peasants named; no *trésor* or moveable goods. F. L. Ganshof in *Rev. belge*, 26 (1948), 1021–41 thinks that some sections go back to the first half of the ninth, eighth, or even to the second part of the seventh century.

after 926   Verdun Cathedral. Public survey (*pulepium*) compiled after Hungarian invasion by Evrard the provost, Bertier the dean, and Lanfred and Odilo, archdeacons, with the testimony of a few villeins. Demesne manors of the chapter only; ed. Waitz in preface to 'Gesta Episcoporum Verdunensium' in *MGH, SS*, iv. 38; it includes refs. to earlier surveys. Comment in Perrin, *Recherches*, 101–7 (no. 2).

937   Autun Cathedral. Public survey by the bishop, dean, canons, Robert the judge and five other named jurors, of seven vills in their lordship of Champdôtre (C. d'Or). No benefices. No peasants named. No *trésor*; ed. Déléage, *Vie rurale*, ii. 1207–8. Excerpt trans. in Duby, *Rural Economy*, 373–4.

c. 940   Abbey of Fulda. Private survey, *Traditiones et Antiquitates Fuldenses*; ed. Ernst F. J. Dronke (Fulda, 1844), 125–9 (no. 44); one benefice mentioned; no peasants named; no *trésor* or moveable goods. Excerpts Guérard, *Irminon*, i. 927–9.

945   Bishopric of Tivoli. List of 257 estates given by named individuals and now confirmed by papal authority; ed. *Inventari*, 253–75.

949   Abbey of Saint-Père de Chartres. Private survey transcribed by
Paul the monk in the cartulary which he began after the fire of
1078, *Cartulaire de l'Abbaye de Saint-Père de Chartres*; ed.
B. Guérard, i. 35–45 (Collections des Cartulaires de France, t i,
Docs. inédits, 1840). No benefices; no peasants named; no *trésor*
or moveable goods.

c. 950   Abbey of Metlach. Private survey to replace a (?public)
polyptych destroyed *c.* 915 × 30. Text in thirteenth-cent.
transcript (on a roll), the transcriber adding his own
observations, but often unable to decipher the original's
abbreviations; ed. Beyer, *mittelrhein*, ii. 338–51 (no. 10). Some
excerpts in Guérard, *Reims*, 122–3. Perrin, *Recherches*, 108–40
(no. 3), claims that chapters 1, 3, 4, 5, 7, 9, 18, 21 and 23 are
from *c.* 950, the rest being added at various dates into the
eleventh cent. No benefices. No peasants named. No *trésor* or
moveable goods.

950 × 75   Abbey of Remiremont. Public(?) survey, ed. Perrin, *Recherches*,
693–703. No benefices. Peasants named. No *trésor* or moveable
goods. Discussed, ibid., 141–69.

950 × 75   Abbey of Gorze. Survey of Count Boso's lands in Wormsgau,
embedded in a charter allegedly of 766 but really a twelfth-cent.
forgery; *Gallia Christiana*, xiii, instrumenta, 372. Perrin,
Recherches, 196–217 (no. 7) thinks that though the charter is a
forgery, the survey it quotes is genuine.

before 959   S. Maria di Monte Velate. Private survey of rents and renders
(only); no benefices, named peasants or *trésor*; ed. *Inventari*,
14–16.

before 963   Abbey of Saint Glossindis (previously Saint Sulpicius) at Metz.
Ref. to the existence of public polyptychs (now lost) when the
history of the translation of Saint Glossindis was written, *c.* 963.
'Edicta quoque publica de possessionibus ejusdem monasterii in
cunctis scriptis vel polipticis vetusto stylo et calamo editis.'
Perrin, *Recherches*, 212, n. 2.

967   Abbey of Saint-Arnoul de Metz. Fragment of a public survey
(soon after 942) relating to Morville-sur-Seille, embodied in a
charter of 967; ed. H. V. Sauerland, *Die Immunität von Metz*
(Metz, 1877), 142 and (facs). *Musée des archives departementales*
(Paris, 1878), Pl. 10, no. 14. No benefices. No named slaves.
No *trésor* or moveable goods. See Perrin, *Recherches*, 225–39
(no. 8).

968 × 80   Abbey of Saint Vanne de Verdun. Private register compiled in
part from records 'in antiquo scripto regali et apostolico', ed.
Hermann Bloch in *Jahrbuch der Gesellschaft für lothringische
Geschichte und Altertumskunde*, 10 (1898), 447–9, and also
Guérard, *Reims*, 115–23. No benefices. No names of peasants.
No *trésor*.

975 × 1092   Chapter of Saint-Dié. Survey (on a single sheet of parchment), ed. Chr. Pfister, 'Les revenus de la collégiale de Saint-Dié au Xe siècle, *Annales de l'Est*, ii (1888), 515–17 and iii (1889), 407. Discussed, Perrin, *Recherches*, 269–317 (no. 10). Two benefices included. No tenants named. No *trésor* or moveable goods.

984   Abbey of Gorze. Survey of Brouch in a charter of Count Boso, listing manses and services but no named peasants, no benefices and no *trésor* or moveable goods; ed. Guèrard, *Irminon*, ii. 351–2 (no. 18). Comment in Perrin, *Recherches*, 180–96 (no. 6).

tenth cent.   Abbey of S. Giulia di Brescia. Inventory of the estate at Migliarina (in Carpi, Modena) when given as a benefice; no named peasants or *trésor*; ed. *Inventari*, 203–4.

second half of tenth cent.   Bishopric of Verona. Private(?) survey (beginning lost); no benefices; peasants not usually named; *trésors* of dependent churches; ed. *Inventari*, 101–11.

end of tenth cent.   S. Cristina di Corteolona. Private survey of estates, with bounds; no named peasants, *trésor* or moveable goods; ed. *Inventari*, 31–40.

before first half of eleventh cent.   S. Lorenzo di Oulx. Private survey; no benefices; peasants named, and their wives and children either named or mentioned; no *trésor*, but some agricultural equipment and animals; ed. *Inventari*, 5–9.

tenth–eleventh cent.   Abbey of S. Columbanus, Bobbio. Private survey (*breviarium*); benefices included; some peasants named; no *trésor* or moveable goods; ed. *Inventari*, 178–98.

c. 1027   Pavia. Verbose account of the renders in money or kind due to the kings of the Lombards at Pavia, from tolls, criminal jurisdiction, taxes on trade, crafts and fishing rights, etc., but excluding land. Prologue and epilogue fourteenth-cent. additions; ed. A. Hofmeister in *MGH, SS*, xxx, pt. 2 (1934), 1444–60 as 'Instituta regalia et ministeria camerae regis Langobardorum et honorantiae civitatis camerae regis'.

1031   Abbey of St Emmeran, Regensburg. Private survey made on orders of Abbot Burchard, Arnold the reeve and all the brethren in 1031. No benefices. No peasants named. No *trésor* or moveable goods; ed. Dollinger, *L'Evolution*, 504–12.

1040 × 50   Abbey of Saint-Vanne de Verdun. Private survey with no benefices, no peasants named and no *trésor* or moveable goods, but renders in kind or money from the various manses. Lands of the parish churches included; ed. H. Bloch in *Jahrbuch der Gesellschaft für lothringische Geschichte und Altertumskunde*, 14 (1902), 123–30. Discussed in Perrin, *Recherches*, 243–68 (no. 9).

1052 × 76   Abbey of S. Père de Vilamajor en Vallès. Fragments of a rental said to have followed on from a tenth-cent. survey and to have been ed. (in roneo) by A. Mundo in *Bull. du Musée Fidel Fita d'Arenys de Mar*, Circulaire no. 9, 1961. Information from P. Bonnassie, *La Catalogne du milieu du Xe siècle a la fin du XIe siècle* (Toulouse, 1975), i. 243, n. 109.

1056 × 76   Cathedral Church of Urgel. Unpublished survey parts of which
            survive in the cathedral cartulary, e.g. for estates at Méranges.
            Alàs, Err and Ayguatebic. See P. Bonnassie, *La Catalogne*, i. 87,
            243–50.

c. 1060   Abbey of Corvey. Private survey by Abbot Saracho. No
            benefices, but peasants are named. No *trésor* or moveable goods.
            Extracts in Guérard, *Irminon*, i. 926–7 from Paul Wigand in
            Archiv für Geschichte und Alterthumskunde Westphalen (Hamm,
            1826 et seq.).

1086

J. C. Holt

ON 1 AUGUST 1086 William the Conqueror held court at Salisbury and there received homage and fealty from his men. This was the central event of the year and is the pivot on which my argument will turn. To quote Stenton's translation of an oft-repeated passage from the Peterborough version of the Anglo-Saxon Chronicle, William:

> came at Lammas to Salisbury, and his council came to him there, and all the landholding men of any account throughout England, whosesoever men they were, and they all bowed to him and became his men, and swore oaths of fealty to him that they would be faithful to him against all other men.[1]

For the present purpose many of the details of the translation do not matter: 'council' or 'counsellors', 'men' or 'vassals';[2] nor is the definition of the much debated phrase 'landholding men of any account' of great moment. It perhaps matters more that on that day William accepted from his men both fealty and homage, for they swore their oath and also 'bowed down to him and became his men'. The obvious and generally accepted interpretation of the phrase is that this was an act of homage.

The passage is a historiographic curiosity. It is enshrined in Stubbs's *Charters*.[3] More than forty years ago I sat at the feet successively of Edwards, Jolliffe and May McKisack: none of them suggested that the Salisbury oath had anything to do with the Domesday Survey. It came under a different heading, 'liege homage'; no one asked whether one famous event of 1086 was related in any way to the other. Years later, some time after 1974, when the present argument was beginning to take shape, I put the question directly to Galbraith, only to receive a downright if perhaps rueful dismissal: his two books on Domesday contain only one casual reference to the Salisbury oath.[4] Galbraith was no exception. In an important and influential historical revision devoted to the Salisbury oath in *History*, 1934, H. A. Cronne commented: 'the fact that the Salisbury Council met about that time

---

[1] F. M. Stenton, *The First Century of English Feudalism 1066–1166*, 2nd edn (Oxford, 1961), 112.
[2] Cp. *EHD*, ii. 161–2.
[3] Stubbs, *Select Charters*, 96.
[4] Galbraith (1974), 25.

is a mere coincidence'.[5] Since then in book after book on the Norman Conquest or the reign of William I historians have treated the Salisbury oath quite separately from the Domesday Survey, all of them in one way or another commenting on the oath in discussions of the superiority of the Crown, or the particular characteristics of English feudalism, on the external threats to William's rule in 1085–6.[6] The pedigree of these views is not in doubt. They stem from Stubbs and Freeman; they are a quaint survival from the wreck caused by Round, repaired rather than jettisoned through all the subsequent revisions in the study of the Conquest which he began.[7]

There was a still older view, scathingly denounced by Freeman, more judiciously criticised by Stubbs.[8] This was derived from Martin Wright's *Introduction to the Law of Tenures* of 1730,[9] and was given full expression in Blackstone's *Commentaries*.[10] It amounted to nothing less than an argument that Domesday and the Salisbury oath marked the introduction of feudal tenures, that Domesday described the terms of such tenure and that at Salisbury homage was performed for the terms so described. Wright commented:

> as this general homage and fealty was done about the time that Domesday Book was finished, and not before, we may suppose that the Survey was taken upon or soon after our ancestors' consent to tenures in order to discover the quantity and to fix his homage.[11]

Ellis summarised Blackstone and quoted Wright in 1833, but he also noted the opposite views of Coke and Selden that such tenures were of ancient English origin. He added preceptively that 'the internal evidence of Domesday itself bears no reference whatever to any simultaneous surrender of former tenures and re-grant of the same as feudal'.[12] There matters rested until Freeman launched his assault.

No one now accepts Blackstone's argument. We seem no longer to

---

[5] H. A. Cronne, 'The Salisbury Oath', *History*, xix (1934–5), 248–52, especially 251.

[6] See, for example, F. W. Maitland, *The Constitutional History of England* (Cambridge, 1908), 161; G. B. Adams, *The Origin of the English Constitution* (New York, 1912), 186–7; H. W. C. Davis, *England under the Normans and Angevins* (1905), 36–7; H. R. Loyn, *The Norman Conquest* (1965), 127–8; Frank Barlow, *William I and the Norman Conquest* (1965), 110–11; R. Allen Brown, *The Normans and the Norman Conquest* (1969), 240–1.

[7] W. Stubbs, *The Constitutional History of England*, 3 vols. (Oxford, 1874–8), i. 288–90; E. A. Freeman, *The History of the Norman Conquest*, 6 vols. (Oxford, 1867–79), iv. 694–6. For comment see Cronne.

[8] Freeman, v. 366–7; Stubbs, i. 289nn.

[9] Martin Wright, *An Introduction to the Law of Tenures* (1730), 52–8.

[10] W. Blackstone, *Commentaries on the Laws of England*, 4 vols. (Oxford, 1770), ii. 49–50.

[11] Wright, 56. Wright continues: 'This supposition is the more probable because it is not likely that a work of this nature was undertaken without some immediate reason, and no better reason can be assigned why it was undertaken at this time or indeed why this Survey should have been taken at all' (56–7). See also his note: 'And this was the reason why almost all the historians of those times join the account of this Survey and of the Homage done about that time together, in such a manner that we must needs think they took them to have immediate relation one to the other' (56n.).

[12] Henry Ellis, *A General Introduction to Domesday Book*, 2 vols. (1833), i. 15–18.

believe in feudalism let alone the notion that it was established at a single stroke in 1086. But the case included two cogent points. First the coincidence of the Survey and the oath cannot simply be dismissed. In 1961 Welldon Finn concluded a discussion of the date of completion of Domesday Book with the comment:

> The time-limit is reached, perhaps that of the Lammas gathering at Salisbury, when all the land-owning men of any account in England, no matter whose men they were, did the King homage and swore fealty to him, and at which, perhaps, there were brought to him the 'writings', with each county still separated from its fellows.[13]

Other scholars have followed that view, two within the last year.[14] Meanwhile Sally Harvey has put forward an even closer relationship, namely that the Salisbury oath was a consequence of the Domesday Survey, a means of disciplining undertenants the importance of whom the Survey had just revealed.[15]

Secondly, and more important, Blackstone's case implied a question which no one has asked or answered since. At Salisbury King William's men performed homage to him. For what? No one should rule Blackstone out of court without first answering that.

The chronology of 1086 depends very much on the evidence of the Peterborough chronicler. He tells of a year begun in routine fashion – a court at Winchester for Easter, another at Westminster at Whitsuntide at which William knighted his youngest son, Henry.[16] Then Salisbury on 1 August marked a break, not just in the famous ceremony but also in the rhythm of the year. William left Salisbury for the Isle of Wight with the intention of going to Normandy. He crossed the Channel later in the year; the precise date is unknown. If that is correct, and there is no good reason for rejecting it, it imposes a strict consequence, namely that the Domesday Survey was completed by 1 August and the king's subsequent departure to the Isle of Wight. No king in the eleventh and twelfth centuries went to the Isle of Wight unless to cross to France. William's fortunes in France, in Maine and on the Vexin border, were deteriorating under the combined threat of King Philip, Fulk of Anjou and Robert of Flanders.[17] William can scarcely have crossed without a considerable force; war in France was impending; his

---

[13] Finn (1961), 190; repeated in Finn (1963), 12, 93.
[14] See, for example, D. C. Douglas: 'The Salisbury oath, like the Domesday Inquest of which it was in some sense the counterpart was the king's response to a challenge' [the external threat of 1085–6] (1964), 356. Compare Clarke (1985), 56: 'Indeed there may be a connection between the presentation of "all the writings" to King William and the famous oath of Salisbury' and Elisabeth Hallam: 'The colophon, which states that the survey of England was made by King William in 1086, implies that all the final drafts were completed in that year, perhaps even by 1 August when the king received his oaths of homage from many important under-tenants', Hallam (1986), 24.
[15] Harvey (1975), 190.
[16] *EHD*, ii. 161–2; *The Peterborough Chronicle 1070–1154*, ed. Cecily Clark (Oxford, 1958), 8–9.
[17] Douglas (1964), 356–8.

expedition culminated in his attack on the Vexin and the sack of Mantes Gassicourt in the following year.

There is other evidence to be brought into play in support of this account. First, the Peterborough chronicler himself tells us that after the Salisbury assembly William exacted 'a very great amount of money from his men where he had any pretext for it either justly or otherwise' – which can be read, and may be best read, as an exaction of penalties from individuals charged with the wrongful possessions which the Domesday Survey reported.[18] Secondly, one of the last surviving written instruments of the reign, in favour of the abbey of St Amand of Rouen, indicates beyond reasonable doubt that William Rufus, Robert, count of Mortain, Eudo Dapifer, Robert Dispensator, Hugh earl of Chester, Gilbert de l'Aigle and Walter fitz Richard were all in the king's company in Normandy in 1086–7.[19] Thirdly, and more critically, in a well-known entry in both Exon and Great Domesday, it was recorded that King William had conceded lands in Taunton to St Peter and Bishop Walkelin (of Winchester) 'as he acknowledged at Salisbury in the hearing of the bishop of Durham whom he instructed that the concession should be entered in his *breves*'.[20] The hand of this section occurs nowhere else in Exon Domesday. It is also exceptional in that it did not follow the common practice in Exon Domesday of allotting a quire or quires to each holder of land. Ker concluded that 'it was probably added in a convenient blank space after the rest of Exon Domesday had been completed'.[21] If so, it can scarcely refer to other than the meeting at Salisbury on 1 August 1086, in which case it indicates not only that one item in the Survey was part of the business at Salisbury but also that the king's *breves* were almost certainly in hand at that time. That is undoubtedly the best reading of the passage.

All these points reinforce the simple common-sense argument that William would scarcely have interrupted the work of the Survey in order to hold the meeting at Salisbury. It follows, therefore, that it was complete by 1 August.

The starting point is even more certain: the Domesday Survey was set on foot at Gloucester, Christmas 1085. That left seven months, including the worst of the English winter, for its execution. It was a tall order.

In reality the time available was even less than that. Work could have begun in Gloucestershire immediately after the Christmas festival. It could not have started in Yorkshire, Lincolnshire or Kent much before mid-January, and county courts could scarcely have been assembled in most counties much before the end of the month. At the other end of the process

---

[18] *Peterborough Chronicle*, 8; *EHD*, ii. 162.

[19] Archives Seine-Maritime, 55H, carton 1; a confirmation and attestation by William I of the grant by Maurice, bishop of London, to S. Amand of his tithes from the forests of Aliermont and Eawy. The confirmation was also attested by William, archbishop of Rouen: hence the conclusion that it was issued in Normandy. The document is calendared with an incomplete witness list in *Regesta*, i. no. 285; cp. ibid. no. xlv; and in *CDF*, no. 94. I am obliged to Dr David Bates for a copy of the MS.

[20] Exon, fo. 175v; GDB, fo. 87v. For comment see Galbraith (1961), 207.

[21] N. R. Ker, *Medieval Manuscripts in British Libraries*, 3 vols. (Oxford, 1969–83), ii. 806.

the Salisbury assembly must have required approximately four weeks' notice; William must have known no later than the beginning of July that the work had been completed or would be completed during that month; the circuit commissioners must have reached that conclusion even earlier. These are not guesses. They are based on known facts easily arrayed from parliamentary writs of summons and returns of the thirteenth century.[22] So from the total of seven months available for the completion of the Survey a deduction of some four to six weeks must be made to allow for administrative lag of one kind or another.

The remaining period of less than six months is an even taller order. Into that we have to fit two inquiries, following the evidence of Robert Losinga, bishop of Hereford, and three if the geld inquisition is dated 1086 and distinguished from the other two. There are not many ways of reducing that overloaded schedule. One is to put one inquiry after 1 August as a kind of rounding-off exercise or to allow that some of the business of the Survey dragged on after that date: that only reduces, it does not remove the difficulties outlined above; it is an unlikely option if the king's men were mustering for an expedition overseas. A second is to put the geld inquisition or at least the geld with which the inquisition was concerned, earlier, before the Christmas council of 1085: some have argued for that,[23] but it still leaves two inquiries in the first six months of 1086. A third is to assume that one of Robert Losinga's inquiries and the geld inquisition were one and the same: that is possible, even likely.[24] A fourth does not recover much time, but is much more interesting: it is that the Salisbury assembly required no administrative planning in the spring of 1086 because it was predetermined, because it was known when the Survey was ordered at Christmas 1085 that it would end with the performance of homage and fealty and that all that there remained to do was perhaps to arrange or confirm a place and date, which could easily be done at the Easter court at Winchester (5 April) or at Westminster at Whitsuntide (24 May). That would imply that the Survey was conducted to a strict schedule ending with a dead-line. The generally accepted explanation of Little Domesday is that somehow it missed just such a dead-line.[25]

Consider the implications of such a schedule. Some are well known and require no more than a brief mention here:

1. It is agreed that the Survey involved a complex intermingling of data, some of it derived from landowners, some of it derived from local courts, all of it confirmed by juries of the hundred in the county courts, data which were reduced to order by adopting at an early stage the tenurial pattern of arrangement which is the format of the final book. That

[22] J. C. Holt, 'The prehistory of Parliament', *The English Parliament in the Middle Ages*, ed. R. G. Davies and J. H. Denton (Manchester, 1981), 11–13.
[23] Finn (1961), 147–8.
[24] Gabraith (1961), 94–5.
[25] V. H. Galbraith, *Studies in the Public Records* (1948), 97; Finn (1961), 190; the dead-line usually being assumed to be the death of William I.

depends on an analysis of the so-called satellites, some of them sources, others by-products of the Domesday data. Now there is little difficulty in relating one satellite to another in a logical pattern reflecting the accumulation of the data. But it does not follow that each logical step was also a necessary chronological stage, still less one involving the transcription and redrafting of data or the verification of information. Sally Harvey and others are surely right in seeking to reduce the successive stages to the absolute minimum.[26] 1086 was no time for frills or repetition. Even so, the variety of the satellites demonstrates how complex the procedure was and how tight the schedule is.

2. It is agreed that the collection of data in the county courts could not have been done without drawing on a great deal of written information. Some of this was in the form of pre-Domesday records concerned with the assessment and collection of the geld which recorded hundred by hundred the separate assessment of each vill and landowner. Some of the written information was provided by the landowners themselves, especially by ecclesiastical landowners. This leads in turn to:

3. The Survey could not have been carried out in the time available without the co-operation of landowners. Indeed it could scarcely have been launched at all unless William knew that it would have the support of his barons and ecclesiastical tenants, ready not only to supply information, but also to attend the county courts as the Survey proceeded. Much has occasionally been made of an outcry against the Survey. This depends on a short critical comment in the Peterborough chronicle[27] and on the lengthier statement of Robert Losinga that 'the land was vexed with many calamities arising from the collection of the royal money'.[28] It is to be doubted how far the vexation and calamities extended to the king's barons except to some of those guilty of flagrant *invasiones*. Occasionally a holding might be concealed.[29] Some men failed to answer for their manors,[30] but they constitute a very small proportion of the total and there are many possible explanations of non-attendance other than wilful resistance. Against their example there is that of Robert Malet apparently referring *as a defence* to the day on which he was *inbreviatus*.[31] Then we know the names of the *legati* of the west Midland circuit: Remigius, bishop of Lincoln, Walter Giffard, subsequently earl of Buckingham, Henry de Ferrers, ancestor of the earls of Derby, and Adam, brother of

---

[26] Harvey (1971), 755; Finn (1961), 147–8, 189–90. Cp. Clarke (1985) which assumes a much more lavish provision both of circuits and of preliminary stages in producing the final texts.

[27] 'There was no single hide, nor a yard of land, nor indeed (it is a shame to relate but it seemed no shame to him to do) an ox, nor one cow nor one pig was there left out and not put down in his record', *EHD*, ii. 161.

[28] W. H. Stevenson, 'A contemporary description of the Domesday Survey', *EHR*, xxii (1907), 74; Galbraith (1961), 51–2.

[29] DB, i. 149a; DB, ii. 101a; Exon, 506a; R. Welldon Finn, *Domesday Studies: The Liber Exoniensis* (1964), 72.

[30] Ellis, i. 31, n.

[31] DB, ii. 276b.

Eudo Dapifer.[32] To them William of Saint-Calais may be added for the south-western circuit.[33] Two especially privileged tenants-in-chief, Roger of Montgomery and Hugh of Avranches, must have been responsible for mustering the county courts of their respective earldoms, Shropshire and Cheshire. Many other lords held 'private' hundreds; their stewards and bailiffs must have played their part in mustering the hundredal evidence and the hundred juries. It is unlikely that all these were pressed men. Galbraith rightly commented: 'The ruling class was no more than a few score of great men, each of whom was vitally interested in the results of the Survey'.[34]

What that interest was depends on the object of the Survey and the function of its outcome, Domesday Book. And the purpose of the Book can only be discussed on a common ground of assumption. One assumption which now seems to be generally agreed is that Great Domesday fairly reflects what King William and his men intended, in the information it contains and in its general layout and detailed format. Indeed, the strongest impression which it conveys, apart from the sheer immensity of the achievement, is that of a single controlling mind at work: unable perhaps to eliminate all the variations, for example in systems of measurement, between one circuit return and another; incapable, certainly, of reducing all the vagaries of local tenures to a single coherent scheme;[35] but determined and clear-headed to an astonishing degree, sufficiently so that he arranged his data in so highly organised a fashion that it permits, even invites, sophisticated statistical analysis nine hundred years later.[36] We can only conclude that the result was what was intended. No one now seriously accepts, with Round, that the data was rearranged from a geographic to a tenurial format almost as an afterthought.[37] No one seems to have been convinced by the assertion of Richardson and Sayles that it was all a 'vast administrative mistake'.[38] What we have in Great Domesday is what was intended. Indeed, the purpose of the Book cannot seriously be discussed on any other basis, for once intention and result are detached one from the other, imagination can roam freely over all kinds of predilections.

Therein lies the difficulty. For if we take the Book as an accurate reflection of its purpose it rapidly becomes obvious that it is far easier to determine what it was not than what it was. First, it was clearly not a geld book as

---

[32] *Hemingi Cartularium ecclesiae Wigorniensis*, ed. Thomas Hearne, 2 vols. (Oxford, 1723), i. 288.
[33] Galbraith (1961), 87.
[34] Ibid., 65.
[35] Darby (1977), 9–56, 375–84.
[36] See especially J. McDonald and G. D. Snooks, *The Domesday Economy* (Oxford, 1986).
[37] See the criticism in Galbraith (1961), 12–27; (1974), 1–17. Round's view is perhaps most clearly worked out in *Feudal England* (1895), 123–42 and in 'An early reference to Domesday' in *Domesday Studies*, ed. P. Edward Dove, 2 vols. (1888–91), ii. 539–49. But the old view is best summarised in a few words by F. M. Stenton, *Anglo-Saxon England* (Oxford, 1971), 655.
[38] H. G. Richardson and G. O. Sayles, *The Governance of Medieval England* (Edinburgh, 1963), 28.

Round and Maitland thought; that is to say, it was not designed primarily for the assessment (though it is concerned with that) still less the collection of the geld. The fundamental argument of Galbraith, that the final format is not that of a geld book and that the final format was intended from the start and is in no way accidental, still stands. It is neither invalidated nor weakened by the argument that the crisis of 1085–6 and the consequent drafting of mercenaries into England was good cause for a heavy geld accurately assessed.[39] Nor is it undermined by the survival of an occasional geld record arranged tenurially from before 1066,[40] for Dr Clarke has recently pointed out what should have been obvious for years from the so-called Yorkshire recapitulation, namely that there was no difficulty at all in passing from a territorial to a tenurial order or vice versa.[41] The plain fact is that the data in Domesday Book are inconveniently arranged for geld purposes. They leave no room even for a compromise hypothesis, for example that Domesday was aimed at shifting geld liability from a geographic to a tenurial basis.[42] No attempt was made to total geld liability, whether of landowners, counties, hundreds or vills. In particular, no attempt was made to total the liability of landowners within each hundred. The *inquisitio geldi* for the south-western counties, by contrast, provides totals of hidage, hundred by hundred as a matter of course. It provides a *summa* of geld for Dorset and a *summa* of hides for Devon.[43] Comparing the two documents, and relating them to the evidence of Robert of Hereford, it seems plain that there were two different inquiries, one concerned with the geld and the other with many other matters as well, and two different formats, one arranged geographically, hundred by hundred; the other tenurially or feudally, tenant by tenant within each county. The two formats are not totally distinct; each uses the other. But the documentary duplication for the south-western counties carries one forceful implication: there were two distinct documents with two distinct purposes; and if the geld was the objective of the *inquisitio geldi*, then the objective of Domesday was something else.

As a result Domesday Book does not look like a geld book. It looks like a directory with lists of tenants at the head of each county, each one numbered to correspond with his appropriate entry. But if it is not a geld book it is

---

[39] For recent emphasis of this see Sally Harvey (1975), 181–2; also Douglas (1964), 346–7. The point is at least as old as Blackstone, *Commentaries*, ii. 49.

[40] Harvey (1971), 755–9; (1980), 122–3.

[41] Clarke (1985), 62–4, 67. Dr Clarke's argument establishes that the transfer from a geographic to a tenurial base was done by interlineating the landholders in documents arranged hundredally, from which were drawn up new lists arranged by landholder which necessarily retained a consistent hundredal order. He does not pursue the obvious conclusion that such a documentary change of data-base is likely to lie behind consistent hundredal order wherever it occurs throughout DB. For earlier discussion of the problem see P. Sawyer, 'The "Original Returns" and Domesday Book', *EHR*, lxx (1955), 177–97; Galbraith (1961), 156–65.

[42] In addition to the arguments advanced above see Tait's review of F. W. Maitland, *Domesday Book and Beyond* (Cambridge, 1897) in *EHR*, xii (1897), 768–72, and Maitland's letter in reply thereto in *The Letters of F. W. Maitland*, ed. C. H. S. Fifoot (Cambridge, 1965), nos. 200, cp. 264.

[43] Exon, 24a, 71a.

equally clear that it is not simply a directory or, as Galbraith put it, a feodary. In the first place both the Survey and the Book were concerned with geld assessment; they asked and answered the question – How many hides? Now it may be that they did so because this was the only way of expressing amounts of land; that could be supported by much other documentary evidence. But that would not explain why the data contain many instances where changes in geld assessment are noted. In the second place Domesday is concerned with very much more than geld assessment. It asks and answers questions about resources – how many ploughs? how much meadow? how much woodland? how many mills? and so on; and it assesses values, values in the time of King Edward before the conquest of 1066, values when King William gave the land, values now. It also tells us 'whether more could be had than was being taken'. In short, the Book is very much more comprehensive in its information and very much more concerned with economic resources than we might expect if it were intended as a feodary and nothing more.

We are faced, therefore, with a quandary. Domesday is not a geld book because it is not so arranged and it looks like a feodary. But it is not a feodary either because it contains information more appropriate to a geld book or a survey of resources. Faced with this, most historians have settled for a mixed function and purpose which we might summarise as follows:

1. Domesday is a description of economic resources and fiscal (geld) assessments.
2. It is arranged in a tenurial or feudal format which identifies owners and in so doing resolves disputed ownership.
3. In some way therefore it has to do with recording the total resources of the country, county by county, landowner by landowner.

Each historian may mix these ingredients to his own particular taste, but that is always the resulting mixture, in one form or another.

For various reasons this will not do, not at least without severe qualification. Domesday may contain a vast array of economic data but at the time it must have been a very poor instrument for assessing total economic resources of counties, hundreds or individual tenants. Just as the Book provides no totals of geld so it provides no totals or subtotals of any of these units of calculation. The larger or more complex the unit the more arduous it is to compute them. Where the larger tenancies-in-chief cross the boundaries of counties or of the Domesday circuits such calculations are made more difficult by the different measurements adopted in the different circuits. Ph.D.'s are written on these matters; it took H. C. Darby and his collaborators five large volumes and many years to complete quantitative assessments of this kind. That the Book was intended to enable government officials in the eleventh century to do what Professor Darby needed years to accomplish is beyond belief. And it is easy to demonstrate that this was not the intention. The Exon Domesday does in fact contain totals of this kind: for the abbey of Glastonbury and for Ralph Mortimer, Milo Crispin, Robert fitz Gerold and Robert, count of Mortain.[44] These refer to counties or groups of counties. They are almost certainly fragments of a larger endeavour rather than casual exercises. To give an example:

> The Count of Mortain has in Wiltshire, Dorset, Devon and Cornwall 623 manors comprising 833 hides less 2½ virgates. There is land for 2480 ploughs; it is worth £1409 less 6s 10d. Of these hides the Count has 200 less 2 in demesne which are worth £400 and 1 mark of silver per annum; his men have 655 hides, less ½ virgate which are worth £1000 less 6s 10d:

a total covering four counties and apparently involving all the lands of the count of Mortain in the south-western circuit.[45] The most important point about it is that it was not included in the final text, Great Domesday. Nor were other similar totals which were included in Exon Domesday. Nor were the somewhat similar totals which appear in the Ely Inquest if indeed it derived its arrangement at this point from material preliminary to Domesday.[46] So it is not simply that totals of this kind are difficult to calculate from the final Domesday data: they are not there in the Book: it was not intended that they should be: the opportunity to include them from preliminary material was rejected. Domesday was not to be used in this way. We may use it for what we are pleased to call macro-analysis. King William's men can have had no such intention.

What then was its purpose? Or to rephrase the question significantly, how might it have been used by an official of the Treasury under the Conqueror and his sons? That is to convert the problem into a practical question. It releases us at once from all those sophisticated interpretations which involve the logical error of deriving the purpose of Domesday from the perceived regularities (or irregularities) which modern analysis of its content reveals. It puts the Book on the same footing as a pipe roll, for example. And why not?

At this level the answers are clear and straightforward. First, Domesday Book was concerned with the county and by implication with the sheriff: that depends on the major divisions of the Book, dependent in turn on the original gatherings or groups of gatherings. Before it was bound the Treasury official could move easily, as we ourselves may now move in the new facsimile, from one county to another. Secondly, within each county, the official was guided, as we are, to specific sections, to the county towns and county customs, to the king's lands, and finally through the index of landowners at the head of each county to tenants and under each tenant to individual manors. In this he was helped by the numbering of the index lists and texts, by the use of capitals and by the rubrication. Index lists, numbering, capitals and rubrications were all interlocked; the rubricator himself entered the numbers and usually the name of each landholder in the

[44] Ibid., 527b–528a, 530b–531a.

[45] Ibid., 531b; Galbraith (1961), 137.

[46] Galbraith (1961), 137; ICC, 121, 136. See also the lists of lands in Cambridgeshire, Norfolk and Suffolk arranged by tenants-in-chief which include total values and some totals of amounts of land, the totals usually being prefaced by 'Hoc appreciatum est' or 'Hoc totum appreciatum est', ibid., 175–83.

text. There need be no apology for recounting something so simple. These features have largely been forgotten amidst all the more sophisticated or esoteric explanations of the Book. The crucial point is that the features which I have described were not mere decoration but a frame of reference integral to the whole work and essential to its purpose.

This system is obvious, more obvious once we turn from printed editions to the manuscript. In traditional Domesday scholarship it has frequently been mentioned or described, but it has not been discussed thoroughly enough to resolve all the problems it poses. These arise in the relationship of index lists to texts and in the numbering of both. Galbraith thought that the lists were entered first,[47] but this is not easily reconciled with the entries for Berkshire, Dorset and Warwickshire, all of which are compressed into insufficient space.[48] He also pointed to discrepancies between lists and texts: the many instances of variant personal names, the occurrence of tenants in the text but not in the lists and vice versa, the changes in the grouping of the less important tenants and the mismatches in the numeration.[49] He explained all this by arguing that the lists were based on the circuit returns and that the rubricator who was responsible for the numeration then had to contend with the unforeseen results of editorial amendments of the compiler or abbreviator.[50] This argument is still accepted;[51] if correct, it indicates that the reference system was already intended in the circuit returns as indeed the one survivor, Little Domesday Book, suggests. It matters more for the present argument that the numeration was applied systematically throughout Great Domesday by one man, the rubricator.[52] He scarcely varied in his work.[53] He made errors, certainly, but it is more significant that often when he did, he tried to fudge, or indicate, or correct them.[54] There is no real doubt that the numeration was intended for use. It can still be used.

The rubrication and the use of capitals is equally plain. The rubricator's work included the county headings, the introductory notes to the lists, the heading of each tenant's entry, the numeration and the underlining of hundreds and manors and the decoration of initials. Capitals were used in the main text for hundreds, wapentakes and manors and by the rubricator for

[47] Galbraith (1961), 32, 192–9, especially 193n; (1974), 50–3.

[48] GDB, fos. 56r, 75r, 238r. The Berkshire entry could simply reflect a misjudgement of the space required for the index. This is less adequate as an explanation of the other two. R. W. Eyton considered that the Dorset index was entered after the text, *A Key to Domesday: an analysis and digest of the Dorset Survey* (1878), 74. All these instances were noted by Finn who nevertheless seems to accept Galbraith's conclusion (1961), 169.

[49] Galbraith (1961), 191–2.

[50] Ibid., 192–6.

[51] Rumble (1985), 37–40.

[52] For the sake of clarity I have distinguished here and elsewhere between the rubricator and the main scribe of Great Domesday. They could well have been one and the same person as Galbraith thought (1961), 193n. My argument would be reinforced if this were so.

[53] *Domesday Rebound*, Public Record Office (1954), 32–4. It should also be noted that the rubricator did not usually enter a number against the *terra regis*: there was no need. However, he did so for Huntingdonshire, 203, and Derbyshire, 272. Middlesex lacks the number II in the text and Somerset nos. II–V.

[54] Galbraith (1961), 194; Finn (1961), 169.

the heading of each numbered section. In all this it is easy enough to find variations and lapses; it is well known, for example, that there are no hundredal headings in the Domesday of the south-western circuit; but the purpose is clear: it was to direct our Treasury official from county to landholder and within each unit of landholding to manors. That still leaps to the eye: it is a compliment to the directing genius that for this purpose, still after 900 years, the facsimile is easier to use than any subsequent edition, despite, or perhaps because of, all the typographical experiments they contain.

Consider now what was not done. The rubricator, working under the direction of the compiler, could have highlighted a wide variety of matters. He could have underlined geld assessments: he did not. He could have underlined changes in geld assessment: he did not. He could have underlined values: he did not. He could have underlined changes in value: he did not. All this might have been more difficult than what he did, and for one good reason: the compiler did not have these matters highlighted either. Instead he directed his energies to providing capitals for manors, which greatly facilitated the task of the rubricator. Both could have taken other courses which would have emphasised all these fiscal and economic matters.[55] Why not, for example, a simple marginal indication of changes in assessment or value?[56] Why not a marker or rubric where more could be had? To all appearances there was red ink enough to spare. And why did the compiler not infrequently insert other information after the values which terminate the standard entry, so that the value does not always figure as the bottom line? To be sure all these matters can be excavated by a careful reading of the text, but a busy official had little time for that. He would only do it if for some special reason he had to. Then it would be a particular, perhaps a major, task. I shall turn shortly to the circumstances which might require it.

Now there is plenty of evidence, quite apart from its general appearance and patent utility, to indicate that the reference system was integral to the purpose of the record. First, it broke down where it was inapplicable. On

[55] Once again I distinguish between the rubricator and the main scribe. Once again the point is reinforced if they were one and the same.
[56] An exception which proves the rule is the marginal entry recording a change in the geld assessment of Pyrford in favour of Westminster Abbey, GDB, fo. 32r. This is clearly related to and probably a consequence of a reduction in hidation authorised in the well-known writ of William I dated *post descriptionem totius Angliae*. See Galbraith (1961), 206; Bishop and Chaplais, no. 26. The writ, it should be noted, frees eight hides from all scot, custom and geld, not, as the editors suggest, the whole manor.

The writ and the marginal entry are of critical importance. Taken together they establish that the DB scribe came to know of the writ subsequently to making the Pyrford entry in GDB. Galbraith (1961, 206–7) was uncharacteristically tentative in pursuing the obvious conclusion, namely that this passage in GDB was written before William's death and, since it is likely that the writ was issued in England, before his departure for the continent in 1086. The point is quite independent of the debate over the meaning of *descriptio* (Douglas, DM, 24; Galbraith, 1961, 183–4). Such an early date for the completion of at least part of GDB is inessential to, although coherent with, my argument. It is more important that, if my interpretation is right, Domesday Book must have been a powerful influence in establishing evidentiary as opposed to dispositive documentation in Anglo-Norman practice.

folio 208 the rubricator encountered for the first time in his manuscript a list of *clamores* – for Huntingdonshire. He confined himself to giving the initials some red shading largely coinciding with the paragraph markings. His normal procedures could not contend with exceptional information for which they were not designed, information which was normally excluded from Great Domesday.[57] 167 folios later he encountered the same phenomenon: this time the *clamores* of Yorkshire and Lincolnshire extending over five folios 373–7. On folio 373 he reacted as he had done on folio 208, with red shading of the initials reinforced this time by underlining of the emphatic headings. Then he gave up; there is no rubrication on any of the remaining folios of the *clamores*; the so-called Yorkshire recapitulation which follows is a distinct section, written in yet another format and rubricated for an entirely different purpose.[58]

Secondly, the system of reference was applied to Little Domesday. Here the prefatory lists were based directly on the text and correspond exactly.[59] Unlike Great Domesday, the headings of each tenancy had already been entered when the rubricator set to work; so there were some necessary variations in his procedure, and in general the work here was cruder and less complete. But there is the same numeration in red; the reader is guided by rubricated county headings and initials or abbreviations of the tenant at the head of the folios; the tenant-headings are underlined in the text; the hundreds are highlighted with a touch of red and occasionally with red underlining; the underlining does not extend to manors, which are emphasised simply by a capital. *Mutatis mutandis* and making some allowance for a hastier job, the frame of reference corresponds closely to that of Great Domesday in both inclusions and exclusions. Its purpose was the same.

Finally, from 1179 or thereabouts, less than 100 years after Domesday, there is direct evidence from a user, no less a person than Richard fitz Neal, Henry II's treasurer:

> The Survey is made by counties, hundreds and hides. The King's name heads the list, followed by those of the nobles who hold of the King in chief,

---

[57] I assume here that the *clamores* in Great Domesday represent a residuum of a larger number of cases, a proportion of which had been resolved by the completion of the final record. The assumption rests on a comparison of the *clamores* with the text, chiefly for Huntingdonshire and Lincolnshire. See Finn (1961), 94–5 and below, p. 54, n. 62.

[58] GDB, fos. 379r–82r. The main purpose of the rubrication here was to emphasise the interlineated names of landholders.

[59] Galbraith (1961), 192–3. Galbraith's argument that the lists preceded the text was criticised by Finn who suggested that the lists were done after the text (*Domesday Studies: the Eastern Counties* (1967), 65–7). Rumble takes the same line (1985), 40. There are four short lists at DB, ii. 9a, 17a, 292a, 372a. On the whole the lists at 9a and 17a look like headings of gatherings or groups of gatherings. Those at 292a and 372a, in contrast, are added at the foot of preceding gatherings and are hence more consistent with Galbraith's view. However, the entry concerning S. Stephen of Caen in Essex, 1a, is more likely to be derived from the text, 17a, rather than vice versa. Similarly, in the Suffolk folios, the abbey of Ramsey is missing from the short list, 372a, but is included in the index and text: the short list on 372a cannot therefore have been used, as Galbraith suggests, as a guide to the order of the following entries in the text.

according to their order of dignity. The list is then numbered and the matter in the actual text of the book relating to each tenant is easily found by the corresponding number.[60]

That passage from Richard's *Dialogus* has often been quoted. It still bears repetition.

Now it should be axiomatic that no explanation of the purpose of Domesday Book is worth considering unless it is consonant with its framework and the reference procedure which Fitz Neal described. And given the systematic and deliberate arrangement of the framework of reference, any explanation must not only match what is there but also accept what is not there; we cannot require Treasury officials of the Norman period to engage in the equivalent of Ph.Ds. In one respect Fitz Neal is almost certainly misleading. 'A careful survey of the whole country was made', he tells us, 'in order that every man be content with his own rights and not encroach unpunished on those of others'.[61] That imposes the common law of the twelfth century on the more primitive circumstances of the eleventh. Domesday Book was not constructed as the ultimate resolution of actions between party and party. The determining of such cases was essential to its construction, but they were listed separately as appendices to the main texts. In some counties an attempt was made to resolve such disputes before the final book was drafted.[62]

The evidence of the Book is that it could fulfil three possible functions, and only three at all easily:

1. Within each county it provides a record of the customs of shire and boroughs and of the location, value, potential and assessment of the *terra regis*. It puts the Treasury in a firm and informed position in imposing requirements on the sheriff and others who farmed and accounted for these resources. There is no need to dwell on this aspect of the Book's purpose.
2. It gives a record, county by county, sometimes hundred by hundred, always manor by manor, of the holdings of the king's tenants. It provides a reference work for the settlement of conflicting claims. It enables the king's men to instruct the sheriff of each county to dispossess a tenant or give possession to an heir or claimant.
3. It records, county by county, the location, extent, value and potential of particular tenements, for which the sheriff or some other nominated royal agent will be accountable if the lands come into the hands of the crown.

[60] *Dialogus*, 63–4.
[61] Ibid., 63.
[62] See above, p. 53, n. 57, and Finn (1961), 92–7. The correlation of the DB text with the lists of disputes depends in part on the point or period in the gathering of information at which the lists of disputes were compiled. A comparison of the *terrae occupatae* in LE with Little DB indicates that there were considerable differences in procedure in this matter between one circuit and another. See Finn, *Liber Exoniensis*, 55–81; *The Eastern Counties*, 42–5. The point was reiterated by Galbraith (1961), 21, 38, 60, 73–4, 83–5, 176–8. See also R. S. Hoyt, 'The *terrae occupatae* of Cornwall and the Exon Domesday', *Traditio*, ix (1953), 155–99.

Hence the county arrangement of the Book refers us at once to the relationship between central and local government, between the Treasury or Exchequer and the sheriffs. In its major component, the lands of the king's tenants, it is concerned above all with tenure, with succession, and with royal rights of escheat and wardship. That is the plain evidence of the record. For these purposes there was no immediate need for totals of either geld assessments or values. The Treasury did not need what the Book does not provide. Its concern lay entirely with the county, with the sheriff, through him with the tenants, and hence with data arranged in that format. If there was a dispute over a particular manor, its tenancy or hidage, the Book would settle it at once. Instructions for the dispossession of even the greatest tenant with lands scattered over several counties could be drafted precisely, if necessary, in a few hours in writs to the sheriffs specifying his holdings (if they did not already know them from their own information). Similar action could be taken for the instatement of an heir. If land came into the king's hands on an ecclesiastical vacancy or after the death of a tenant or through more prolonged escheat or by wardship, locations and extent were equally easy to determine. It was only at this stage that it became essential to have further information: tax assessment, value and 'if more could be had'. This characteristic Domesday information was essential to, not separate from, its main feudal purpose, for without it wardships and escheats could not be assessed to farm. That is probably all that was intended in the first instance when the compiler laid down the format. Some have argued that Domesday helped in assessing reliefs or amercements, and it could certainly be used in that way; but other matters entered into these calculations, and while Domesday Book was a very precise instrument, they were somewhat blunt.[63]

To sum up: Domesday presents information at two different levels. As a quick work of reference it is concerned with the location and tenure of manors. At a deeper level it is concerned with resources, values, potential and geld assessment. At this level it was part of the continuing relationship of Treasury and sheriff in the management of counties, boroughs and the royal demesne. For the rest, that is for the tenants-in-chief, this function could be brought into play as and when necessary for ecclesiastical vacancies and the operation of the feudal incidents of wardship and escheat.

This now poses a political question. All the evidence about the procedure of the Survey indicates that it was astonishingly rapid and that it had the active support of William's tenants-in-chief. Why did they co-operate? To revert to the old 'geld-book' hypothesis for a moment, who would want to see his tax return turned into a rubricated manuscript?[64] Or, on the argument outlined above, who would want to strengthen the king's control of succession, escheat and wardship? Yet it is plain that Walter Giffard and

---

[63] In the case of amercements much depended on the seriousness of the offence. In the case of reliefs something depended on the proximity of the heir or the access of the successor to royal favour.

[64] With acknowledgement and apologies for the necessary amendment to Jonathon Sale, '1086 and All That', *Punch*, 18/25 December 1985, 38.

Henry de Ferrers, to name two of whom we can be certain, participated as commissioners in a survey which did just that. So why did they do it? What advantage did they see in it? For advantage there must have been. Blackstone and his predecessors are the only commentators who help in providing an answer. For the response to the question: 'For what did the landholding men of any account perform homage on 1 August 1086?' must surely be: 'for the tenements recorded in the Domesday Survey',[65] and that logic strengthens in its turn the argument that the oath was integral to the Survey, intended from the start at Christmas 1085, because baronial co-operation was available from the start. Hence Domesday Book seems to embody a hard-headed deal. William got a survey of his own and his tenants' resources; he was strengthened in the exercise of his feudal rights. His tenants got a record of their tenure, in effect a confirmation of their enfeoffment. In short, as regards the tenant-in-chief, Domesday Book was a vast land book which put a final seal on the Norman occupation.

The Peterborough chronicler tells us that at the end of the Survey the writings were brought to the king.[66] Some modern historians have suggested that the returns, even the completed Book, were presented to him at Salisbury on 1 August 1086[67] – rather like a prize day. That, indeed, is to impose a modern gloss on the words of the chronicler; the fact is that there was no one else to whom the returns might go and that is probably all he meant. But if we are to think of presentation, it is just as likely to have been in the other direction, from William to his men, for if this reconstruction is approximately right, William's homagers knew that their tenements had been recorded with the king's agreement, that the Survey was complete, that the *breves* and circuit returns were already to hand and that the compilation of a final record, the future Domesday Book, was going forward. So William was both receiving and presenting the consequences of the great survey in which they had all participated.

That this above all was the central purpose of the Book (leaving aside of course the county and borough customs and the *terra regis*) is the plain message of the later evidence. It was used to determine tenure throughout the next two centuries.[68] Ownership, location, amount of land (i.e. hidage), were still the main concern of the Herefordshire Domesday of 1160–70 as of all the later abbreviations.[69] It was as the 'charter of the king', or 'my charter of Winchester', or 'the charter of my Treasury' that the record came to be described as soon as the memory of the *breves* had faded. These terms come from the royal chancery itself.[70] But best of all, perhaps, they come from the earliest collateral evidence of Hemming's cartulary of 1100 or not much later: 'A *descriptio* of the land of the bishopric of the church of Worcester

[65] The point is put most succinctly by Martin Wright, above, p. 42, n. 11.
[66] *Peterborough Chronicle*, 9; *EHD*, ii. 161.
[67] Finn (1961), 190; Harvey (1971) 755; Clarke (1985), 56.
[68] Hallam (1986), 32–51; Galbraith (1974), 100–22.
[69] *Herefordshire Domesday*, ed. V. H. Galbraith and James Tait (Pipe Roll Society, n.s., 25, 1950), xxiv–xxxii; Hallam (1986), 32–51.
[70] *Herefordshire Domesday*, xxvi–xxvii.

according to the *carta regis* which is in the King's Treasury' – thus his title. And even more explicitly: the Domesday commissioners had 'this testimony written in the original (*autentica*) *cartula* of the King', and again – 'In confirmation of this matter the exemplar is written in the original (*autentica*) *cartula* of the King which is kept in the royal treasury with the *descriptiones* of all England'.[71]

What precise advantage did the tenants-in-chief see in such a record? Hemming provides the clue to one such group which had a very special interest. Since the Conquest the Church had suffered depredation at the hands of the new French nobility – and others, for churchmen preyed on churchmen. There had been some notable legal actions seeking the restoration of the lands which had been lost.[72] Less obviously there was a running battle between ecclesiastical lords and laymen seeking and acquiring fiefs which bishops and abbots were forced to concede to meet the new service-quotas which the Conqueror imposed.[73] So great churchmen had a very direct interest in the compilation of an exact and final record. They used the opportunity not only to record their lands but also to advance claims to the lands which they had lost over the last twenty years.[74] So these landowners, a very important group to whom we owe practically all the surviving subsidiary documents of the Survey, had a very close interest in ensuring its success. This necessarily involved the laymen, for a unilateral establishment of title by the Church must have been unthinkable. Hence the bishops and abbots carried the rest.

Nevertheless there were good grounds for the rest to join in. Domesday provided 'warranty' for all tenancies-in-chief – 'warranty' in the simple eleventh-century sense which it enjoyed in Domesday, namely authority for tenure. The lay tenants needed such warranty. Moreover William needed to give them warranty, not just to achieve stability, to put a seal on the settlement, but, as I shall argue shortly, to get from them what he wanted. What warranty did they have already? It is assumed inaccurately in·our text-books that the Norman settlers were relatively secure in their tenures: that they had performed homage to the king for precisely defined fiefs in

[71] *Hemming's Cartulary*, i. 298, 288. See also J. H. Round in *Domesday Studies*, i. 546, criticised by Galbraith in *Herefordshire Domesday*, xxviii, n. 1. On the dating of Hemming's cartulary see N. R. Ker, 'Hemming's Cartulary' in *Studies in medieval history presented to F. M. Powicke*, ed. R. W. Hunt, W. A. Pantin and R. W. Southern (Oxford, 1948), 49–75, and V. H. Galbraith, 'Notes on the career of Samson, bishop of Worcester', *EHR*, lxxxii (1967), 97–101.

[72] See the varied information assembled in Finn (1961), 92–111, and *Liber Exoniensis*, 69–76; also F. M. Stenton, 'St Benet of Holme and the Norman Conquest', *EHR*, xxxvii (1922), 225–35; F. R. H. Du Boulay, *The Lordship of Canterbury* (1966), 36–43; Barbara Harvey, *Westminster Abbey and its estates in the Middle Ages* (Oxford, 1977), 71–4. For the losses of the abbey of Ely see ICC, 184–9, discussed by Finn, *Eastern Counties*, 87–94, and by E. Miller, *The Abbey and Bishopric of Ely* (Cambridge, 1951), 66–7. For a cautionary note see David Knowles, *The Monastic Order in England* (Cambridge, 1963), 117–18.

[73] V. H. Galbraith, 'An episcopal land grant of 1085', *EHR*, xliv (1929), 353–72; Edmund King, *Peterborough Abbey 1086–1310* (Cambridge, 1973), 18–23; Miller, 67–70.

[74] See especially the case of Ely, above, n. 72. For other examples see Finn (1961), 101–9; Barbara Dodwell, 'The Honour of the Bishop of Thetford/Norwich in the late eleventh and early twelfth centuries', *Norfolk Archaeology*, xxxiii, pt. ii (1963), 185–8; Harvey (1980), 124.

return for agreed military service, the arrangements all concluded at one and the same time. This is demonstrably false; to choose only one example at random, Henry de Ferrers received his Domesday holdings in at least five tranches over a considerable period of time.[75] The evidence of the Book itself is somewhat different from the assumptions of the text-book. In most cases, where it tells us anything at all, it is simply that the land was held *de rege*. Sometimes it reveals that Norman tenants were put in seisin by instruction of the king, by writ, or seal (which was the same thing), by his agent or *liberator*, sometimes explicitly by the sheriff, or by his own word of mouth.[76] Occasionally it refers to English *antecessores*; in other cases, where they are not mentioned specifically, some Norman tenancies can be correlated with the holdings of English predecessors. However, much of this evidence is the product of contested possession, and it is by no means clear how far these precise procedures were themselves a consequence of dispute. The main argument that there was some formal process of enfeoffment, involving recognition of seisin, is that the settlement itself was relatively orderly. However, there is no evidence at all that William's vassals were enfeoffed by charter: no such charter survives except as a blatant forgery.[77] Strictly speaking the evidence does not allow us to assume that a grant of land was accompanied by the performance of homage. Most of the companions of the Conqueror must already have been his homagers. Why bother to renew the bond when a vassal received his expected reward in the new English acquisitions? Finally, it does not allow us to assume very much, if anything at all, about terms of tenure. There is no direct evidence about title or succession.

Even so, three reasonable inferences may be drawn from scattered and fragmentary evidence. First, it seems inescapable that by 1086 men had come to think that homage was part of a reciprocal act, that it was not performed *in vacuo* or for the promise of good lordship but in return for something material and real, actual or expected, usually in return for recognised and

[75] Henry de Ferrers acquired the following:

a) probably in 1066–7, lands in Berkshire previously held by Godric the sheriff who fell in battle, probably at Hastings.

b) certainly after 1068 and probably before 1070, lands in Buckinghamshire, Berkshire, Oxfordshire and Essex previously held by Bondi the staller.

c) c. 1070, lands in Derbyshire, Nottinghamshire, Warwickshire, Berkshire, Essex, Gloucestershire and Lincolnshire previously held by Siward Barn.

d) c. 1071, lands in Appletree wapentake, Derbyshire, previously held by twenty-four TRE landholders and contiguous lands in Staffordshire which together came to form the core of the honour of Tutbury, in which Henry was possibly preceded by Hugh of Avranches.

e) other acquisitions in Derbyshire of uncertain date and apparently of miscellaneous origin. I am indebted here to P. E. Golob, 'The Ferrers earls of Derby: a study of the honour of Tutbury 1066–1279' (University of Cambridge, Ph.D., 1985). For more general discussion see John Le Patourel, 'The Norman Colonisation of Britain', *I Normanni e la loro Espansione in Europa nell'alto medioevo* (Settimani di Studi del Centro Italiano di Studi sull'alto Medioevo, xvi, 1969), 409–38; J. C. Holt, 'The Introduction of Knight-Service in England', *Anglo-Norman Studies*, vi (1983), 100–3.

[76] Finn (1961), 100–9.

[77] *Early Yorkshire Charters*, ed. W. Farrer and C. T. Clay, 12 vols. (Yorkshire Archeological Society, Record Series, extra series, 1914–65), iv. 94–5 and frontispiece.

lawful seisin of land. Whatever the personal nature of the act of homage at an earlier date, men's minds must now have been conditioned by the recurrent performance of homage by heirs as they claimed the succession to estates and by bishops as they acquired the temporalities of their sees. Much more often than not, homage and tenure went hand in hand: that was the assumption of both William of Poitiers and Eadmer.[78]

Secondly, Domesday and other evidence indicates that exchanges of land were by no means unusual. Many were effected simply for the mutual convenience of the new Norman tenants.[79] But one well-known case, the so-called exchange of Lewes, which was the most extensive transaction of this kind, demonstrates that William the Conqueror was able to dispossess one newly endowed tenant, William de Warenne, in order to make way for another, William de Braose, and the only indication that Warenne had any kind of claim in what he lost in Sussex is that he got lands in Norfolk which were recorded as an exchange or as the exchange of Lewes.[80] That is extremely frail evidence of any kind of right or title, and whether so or not, Warenne was closer to the king than the run-of-the-mill tenant. The main conclusion to be drawn from this evidence is that the Conqueror could shift his original tenants around if convenience so required.

Thirdly, except for the inherited possessions of the French already established in England under Edward the Confessor and for those held by the residue of the English, all the new tenancies were conquests or acquisitions. By definition there could be no confirmation of a succession until the succession occurred. Certainly such had happened by 1086. It is reasonable to assume for example that Roger de Lacy, who succeeded his father, Walter, less than a year before the Survey,[81] sought the succession, performed homage and was instated in all the lands of his father, perhaps by writs directed to the appropriate sheriffs. His lands were now his patrimony, with such title as that implied. But only a proportion of King William's tenants were in that enviable position. Just to take a few of de Lacy's immediate or not too distant neighbours, Chester, Montgomery and Ferrers were all at the stage of acquisition, warranted solely by the initial grant from the king, whatever its nature, and by the passage of years.

---

[78] See William of Poitier's account of Harold's alleged submission to William in which homage is distinguished from fealty and associated with William's promise to confirm his English possessions, an account all the more telling because of its quasi-fictional nature (*Gesta Guillelmi ducis Normannorum et regis Anglorum*, ed. Raymonde Foreville, Classiques de l'Histoire de France au Moyen Age, Paris, 1952, 104). He also links restitution of lands with the 'obsequium' and 'sacramenta' of the English lords in 1066 (236). For Eadmer's association of homage with episcopal temporalities see the account of Anselm's election in which Eadmer also refers to Lanfranc (*Historia Novorum*, ed. M. Rule, RS, 1884, 41). I am grateful to Dr Marjorie Chibnall for raising these matters with me.

[79] Finn (1961), 20–1; *The Eastern Counties*, 31–2; *Liber Exoniensis*, 71–2. For sales see Ellis, i. 43, nn; Freeman, *Norman Conquest*, v. 778–85.

[80] J. F. A. Mason, *William the First and the Sussex Rapes* (Historical Association, Hastings, 1966; London, 1972), 15–16.

[81] W. E. Wightman, *The Lacy Family in England and Normandy, 1066–1194* (Oxford, 1966), 168.

Amidst these more general uncertainties there was also a more precise difficulty. By 1086 a number of the original tenants-in-chief had withdrawn from England; two, Roger, earl of Hereford and Odo of Bayeux had been dispossessed and the lands of one other, Roger of Poitou, were in the king's hands in whole or in part. How did their tenants stand? What and whose warranty did they enjoy? Are we to assume that on siding with the king against their lords they performed homage and were put into all their holdings just as an heir or someone newly enfeoffed? Dr Wightman assumes so in the case of Walter de Lacy, tenant of Roger, earl of Hereford,[82] but there is no direct evidence that it happened. Indeed in some ways Domesday suggests the opposite. The extent and structure of fitz Osbern's earldom is now controversial. It is no longer possible to accept that the 1086 tenants-in-chief in Herefordshire and Shropshire had all, with certain exceptions, been his tenants.[83] Nevertheless, some of the tenements of the earldom are still apparent in the Domesday record of Herefordshire and most obviously of Oxfordshire where they are listed separately and numbered both in text and index as the lands of Earl William.[84] In both counties the tenants of the old earldom now held in chief either explicitly or in effect. Yet in Herefordshire Earl William still figures as warrantor. Sometimes the Survey simply records that he built a castle – Clifford or Wigmore. Sometimes it is specifically stated that Earl William established a holding for a tenant, that he had given four carrucates of waste land in the castlery of Ewyas to Walter de Lacy, for example.[85] The king certainly intruded his own men into the county after the fall of Earl Roger,[86] but there is singularly little evidence that he set about confirming the tenancies of the earl's tenants who remained. The record mentions the grant by King William of 1½ hides in Wolferflow which completed Walter de Lacy's holding there,[87] a grant by the king to Roger de Pistes,[88] a quittance of geld to King Maredudd[89] and the agreement of the king to grants by Walter de Lacy of land in Acle and Upleadon to the church of Hereford,[90] but only once, in the case of Alfred of Marlborough's tenure of Ewyas castle, does it state specifically that King William confirmed a grant of fitz Osbern.[91] It may well be that in particular terms the Domesday Survey itself provided the first confirmation which many of these tenants enjoyed. The same is even more obviously true of the Oxfordshire list which is scarcely explicable on other grounds.

[82] Ibid., 123–4.
[83] Christopher Lewis, 'The Norman Settlement of Herefordshire under William I', *Anglo-Norman Studies*, vii (1984), 195–213. Cp. the long standing and still arguable view fully developed in W. E. Wightman, pp. 117–34, and 'The palatine earldom of William fitz Osbern in Gloucestershire and Worcestershire 1066–71', *EHR*, lxxvii (1962), 6–17.
[84] DB, i. 161a.
[85] Ibid., i. 184a.
[86] Lewis, 'The Norman settlement of Herefordshire', 209.
[87] DB, i. 185a.
[88] Ibid., i. 186b.
[89] Ibid., i. 187b.
[90] Ibid., i. 184a, 184b.
[91] Ibid., i. 186a.

The fee of Odo of Bayeux, who was arrested and dispossessed in 1082, presents matters at an earlier stage of development. Odo's fee still survived as a separate unit, headed and numbered in Little Domesday.[92] The effect of the record is to confirm the position of his tenants, especially of the greatest of them, Roger Bigod. In Kent the units of undertenancy do not yet appear as tenancies-in-chief, which many of them subsequently became, but the undertenants are consistently named in such a manner as to break up the regular order of lathes characteristic of the Kentish Domesday.[93] Here the Domesday record could well have been the first royal warranty of Odo's enfeoffments. The lands of Roger of Poitou reflect a still earlier stage in this process. Here between Ribble and Mersey, the present tenants are simply listed as enjoying their respective portions by gift of Roger.[94] In all probability Domesday itself was the first royal confirmation of their tenancies. But in this case there was no consistency. The Yorkshire entry for Roger was merely an extract from a geld roll; no tenants were mentioned.[95] In Derbyshire it was simply noted that the lands were in the king's hands; in Norfolk that the lands had been Roger's.[96] In other counties he appears as a sitting tenant. It is probable that he was dispossessed in the course of the Survey.[97]

One further complication is perhaps worth nothing. The Chester Domesday does not follow the rules. Here the lands of Earl Hugh are listed with first the demesne holdings and then the holdings of each undertenant, none of whom appear in the prefatory list of tenants but each one of whom is emphasised by capitals, rubricated lineation and an emphatic space before each tenancy.[98] It is always recorded that these men hold of Earl Hugh, but the compiler is plainly trying to tell us that they are different, and that must be because, apart from the diocesan lands, Earl held the county of the king.[99] The presentation is not accidental. It is repeated only in Shropshire.[100] There too Earl Roger held the county of the king apart from the lands of the church and certain lay tenancies.[101] In both these cases the treatment of undertenancies was exact and intrinsic to the record. It contrasts sharply with the more haphazard treatment of undertenancies elsewhere.[102]

---

[92] Ibid., ii. 18a–26a, 142a–143b, 373a–378b.

[93] Ibid., i. 6a–11b; Harvey (1971) 757.

[94] DB, i. 269b, 270a.

[95] GDB, fo. 332r. The entry is not numbered either in the list or text. It is in the hand of the main scribe and rubricator, but is not rubricated in the usual detail. The heading 'Lands of Roger of Poitou' does not necessarily prove that Roger was still in possession.

[96] DB, i. 273b; ii. 243a–244b.

[97] Galbraith (1961), 187–8.

[98] GDB, fos. 264r–70r.

[99] 'Totam reliquam terram comitatus tenet Hugo comes de rege', GDB fo. 262v.

[100] GDB, fos. 253r–259v.

[101] 'Comes Rogerius quod reliquum est tenet cum suis hominibus', GDB, fo. 252r.

[102] The features noted above are not readily apparent in the printed text, especially of Cheshire. They deserve closer attention than they have hitherto received in the discussion of the 'palatine' status of both counties.

How then might a lay tenant-in-chief gain advantage from the Domesday Survey? To summarise:

1. It provided a single coherent record of tenancies accumulated piecemeal over a period of up to twenty years.
2. It provided a written record which warranted possession which in many cases had not advanced beyond the stage and status of acquisition.
3. It recorded purchases and exchanges, many of which had presumably been made without royal confirmation.
4. It warranted a large number of tenancies originally established by Norman lords who had withdrawn or been dispossessed.
5. It recorded the tenancies held of the two remaining comital earldoms of Chester and Shrewsbury.

All this is quite apart from the fact that it resolved disputes from which a lay tenant might either gain or lose: some of them certainly may not have been all agog about that. Finally, Domesday was a general record. Most important of all, it was a royal record, a great evidentiary certification held in the king's treasury. It was novel. It was unique. That probably gave it all the more prestige in the eyes of men who were familiar with writs and Norman *pancartes* but who knew not the charter of enfeoffment. All that was worth an homage. All that was worth combining with a meticulous survey of resources conducted in the interests of the king. That was the agreement of Christmas 1085 which came to fruition at Salisbury in 1086.

But if that is why king and barons did it, why did they do it precisely then? There is in fact a ready explanation. First, it has long been recognised that in 1085 William had to assemble an army of mercenaries as a defence against the combined threat of King Cnut of Denmark and Count Robert of Flanders. As Dr Harvey has recently emphasised that provided an impetus for the *inquisitio geldi* and for the survey of resources embodied in Domesday Book.[103] Others have linked this crisis with the Salisbury Oath.[104] This seems less convincing and less again if the Survey and the oath were connected in the manner suggested above. But our doubts here, reasonable though they may seem, depend on our understanding of the oath and on William's intentions in the face of external threat. What in fact he did in the last year of his life was cross to France and deliberately attack his liege lord, King Philip of France, invading the Vexin and receiving his fatal injury as he put Mantes Gassicourt to fire and sword.[105] Now it is only our insularity that blinds us to the probability that the oath sworn by William's men at Salisbury which bound them to him 'against all other men' was most likely aimed against the king of France. Far from deterring rebellion in England it underwrote rebellion in France. It was intended not to sustain liege lordship in England but to shatter liege lordship in France. William in short was

[103] Sally Harvey (1985), 103; (1975), 181–2.
[104] Stenton, *The First Century of English Feudalism*, 113–14; H. W. C. Davis, *England under the Normans and Angevins*, 36–7; Douglas (1964), 355–6.
[105] Douglas (1964), 356–8.

bringing all the moral and legal weight of English tenure to bear to support an intended offensive against King Philip. He was reminding his Norman followers that they now had extended resources to support their ancient duty to the dukes of Normandy. He was emphasising his requirements of those who, like the Beaumonts, held their lands immediately both of him and King Philip. He was imposing an entirely novel obligation on those of his tenants in England who, like the Breton, Count Alan, lord of Richmond, or Eustace Count of Boulogne, were not of Norman origin; in so doing he changed the balance of power in France.

That interpretation may seem to involve a lot of guesswork. It certainly requires us to assume that William's campaign in France in 1087 was already in his mind at Christmas 1085. That is not impossible for the necessary springboard had come into Norman hands in 1080–1 when the county of Meulan passed by inheritance to Robert de Beaumont.[106] But it is supported by one crucial fact and one critical piece of evidence. The fact is that the English baronage somehow came to accept that they owed service for their English fees in Normandy. That was rarely questioned: it was admitted even in 1215.[107] It was an unusual arrangement of which England certainly provides the most striking example.[108] It demands explanation. The evidence lies in what may well be another account of the Salisbury oath, which was recognised as such by Blackstone.[109] This is cap. 2 of the so-called Ten Articles of William the Conqueror:

> We lay down that all free men shall affirm by fealty and oath that they are willing to be faithful to King William and preserve his lands and honour in all fidelity and defend him against his enemies *both within and without England*.[110]

That text has received some severe criticism.[111] It certainly cannot be taken, as Blackstone was tempted however cautiously to take it, as a literal statement of the Salisbury oath. But it can scarcely be later than 1135;[112] it has no known source; and in referring to service outside the realm it provides the first statement of an authentic peculiarity of English feudal service. If we accept that immediately or distantly it gives us the precise

---

[106] Ibid., 357; *Complete Peerage*, vii. 524; Orderic, v. 214.

[107] J. C. Holt, *The Northerners* (Oxford, 1961), 88–92; *Magna Carta* (Cambridge, 1965), 151. See also John Le Patourel, *The Norman Empire* (Oxford, 1976), 201–6.

[108] For continental parallels see Holt, *Magna Carta*, 64–6. The service which German vassals of the emperor provided on occasion in Italy was, of course, of more ancient, Carolingian, origin and hence antedated the tenurial arrangements characteristic of the eleventh and twelfth centuries.

[109] Blackstone, *Commentaries*, ii. 49–50.

[110] 'Statuimus etiam ut omnis liber homo foedere et sacramento affirmet, quod infra et extra Angliam Willelmo regi fideles esse volunt, terras et honorem illius omni fidelitate cum eo servare et ante eum contra inimicos defendere', *Gesetze*, i. 486; Stubbs, *Select Charters*, 98; *EHD*, ii. 399.

[111] H. G. Richardson and G. O. Sayles, *Law and Legislation from Aethelbert to Magna Carta* (Edinburgh, 1966), 46–7, 101. See also Stubbs, *Constitutional History*, i. 289n.

[112] *Gesetze*, i. 486; iii. 277–80. See also L. J. Downer, *Leges Henrici Primi* (Oxford, 1972), 6.

intent embodied in the Peterborough chronicler's phrase 'all other men' against whom the Salisbury oath was directed, much falls into place.

If that was the package agreed in 1085–6, it is an intriguing one. It indicates hard bargaining between William and his men, that the 'deep speech' at Gloucester embodied a deal, but a deal firmly set in the proper context of tenure and title such as they were in the late eleventh century. For those who find it hard to swallow there is some sugar to coat the pill. The view that Domesday was intended as a great national review of economic resources has always run into a major difficulty: nothing much happened. Explanations can be found: William and Lanfranc soon died; the data were soon out of date, and so on.[113] Or perhaps something did happen and Ranulf Flambard is used as the villain of the peace, reassessing dues and[114] measuring the lands of England, in Orderic's phrase, 'with a rope'.[115] It is all somewhat unconvincing. If on the other hand Domesday is viewed as it is presented above little of this arises. The adjustment of farms of counties and *terra regis* could go on quietly in the inner sanctum of Treasury or Exchequer; resources could be totalled and farms set as and when other lands came into the king's hands. For the rest the Survey had already achieved its objective. Its end was largely in its beginning. It was not just a *descriptio* but a *carta*. As such it was not intended to 'do' anything. It simply 'was'.

[113] Richardson and Sayles, *Governance of Medieval England*, 28; Galbraith (1961), 19: 'The king's undertaking died with him'. Cp. ibid., 29, 180, 202, 205.
[114] Harvey (1975), 188–9, 190–3; R. W. Southern, *Medieval Humanism and other Studies* (Oxford, 1970), 190–1.
[115] Orderic, iv. 172.

William of Saint-Calais and the Domesday Survey*

Pierre Chaplais

WE ALL MARVEL at the efficiency and speed with which the great Survey of 1086 was conducted and Domesday Book produced. That an operation of such magnitude could have been planned, carried out and its results set down in writing in a final form during the short period which, according to V. H. Galbraith, ran from the Gloucester meeting of Christmas 1085 to the death of William the Conqueror (9 September 1087) seems almost incredible. Some of the credit for this administrative *tour de force* should, of course, be given to the Conqueror himself, whose decision it had been to have the Survey made and who no doubt remained the driving force behind it as long as he remained in England. Given his reputation for determination and impatience, it is not difficult to believe that he would have insisted on the work being completed in record time. More than a passing thought should also be given to the bishops and lay barons who, in the areas allotted to them as circuit commissioners, had been burdened with the invidious task of collecting and checking the required data, as well as to the numerous scribes who had to cope with the vast secretarial work which all this entailed. But we must reserve our admiration for the mysterious figure who, below the king and on his instructions, must have directed the whole Domesday campaign, drawing up the initial plan for the Survey – perhaps in consultation with others, co-ordinating the work of the various groups of commissioners and finally supervising the last all-important stage, namely the digesting of

* I wish to thank the following owners and custodians of manuscripts who have given me permission to reproduce them: the Deans and Chapters of Exeter (Pl. III. a–b), Hereford (Pl. II) and Westminster (Pl. IV. a), the Keeper of Public Records (Pls. III. c–h and IV. b), the President and Fellows of Trinity College, Oxford, and the Curators of the Bodleian Library (Pl. I). I am also very grateful to Mrs M. Bull, Mrs A. M. Erskine, Mr D. J. V. Fisher, Miss B. H. Harvey, Dr R. F. Hunnisett, Professor G. H. Martin, Miss P. Morgan and Mrs E. Nixon for help with photography. My deepest debt is to Mr Michael Gullick and Mrs Teresa Webber, who generously allowed me to use their discoveries ahead of publication and helped with comments and valuable references, to Mr Roger Norris, Dr A. I. Doyle and Mr A. J. Piper, who lent me photographic reproductions from Durham, Miss A. C. de la Mare, who helped with the problem of Exeter manuscripts, and Miss S. Burdell and her staff at the History Faculty Library, Oxford, who gave me assistance of many kinds throughout the preparation of this paper.

the data recorded in the circuit returns. In a later period these duties might have been left to a committee, but one cannot imagine that there was much room for committees in the world of William the Conqueror, who is likely to have preferred individual men of action. 'The man behind the Survey', to use one of Galbraith's favourite expressions,[1] must have been a person of considerable standing, ability and integrity, a man also who could be trusted to maintain the momentum of the Domesday work after the king's departure for Normandy in the last third of 1086. If such a hypothetical personality with vice-regal powers in Domesday matters did really exist, who may he have been? There is no mention of him in any narrative source, but perhaps the Domesday manuscripts themselves may provide us with a clue to his identity.

In *The Making of Domesday Book* Galbraith argued most convincingly that the three manuscripts known as Exon Domesday, Little Domesday and Great Domesday represented three successive stages in the writing of Domesday Book: Exon was a draft of the return for the south-western circuit, Little Domesday the fair copy of the return for East Anglia, and Great Domesday the Survey's final, condensed text, which had been arrived at by abbreviating and partly recasting the circuit returns for the whole of England south of the Tees except East Anglia.

In so far as Exon Domesday is concerned, it is true that the manuscript, with its numerous erasures, corrections and interlineations, looks much less tidy than Little Domesday. Therefore, if Little Domesday can be regarded as typical of all circuit returns, Exon must represent an earlier stage of writing, in other words a draft. But the point should not be pressed too far, since even Great Domesday has its fair share of emendations and additions of various kinds. It is true also that in Exon the lands are listed under tenants-in-chief and then subdivided into counties instead of the other way round as in both Little Domesday and Great Domesday. But if he was a competent editor, the compiler of Great Domesday should have been capable of making the necessary adjustments himself without the help of a fair copy arranged in the correct order, an intermediary step which in any case would have been out of the question if time was of the essence. Working under pressure and from an unsatisfactory exemplar, the compiler might omit an entry here and there, and miscalculate the amount of writing-space he required for each individual section; this would in due course force him to make marginal additions and resort to compression, both of which features are far from rare in the quires of Great Domesday which are devoted to the south-western counties.

There are in fact in Exon itself two groups of scribal memoranda which indicate that its text was used for the compilation of two other manuscripts. The first group consists of ten identical notes, 'Consummatum est', written in a hand contemporary with Exon, on the first recto or last verso of ten quires; an eleventh note, 'Consummatum est usque huc', probably in the same hand as the others, occurs in the margin of fo. 490r, opposite a gap

---

[1] V. H. Galbraith (1974), 50.

between two entries. These notes would in my opinion be best interpreted as cautionary reminders to scribes involved in a copying operation that the quires so marked had already been dealt with. Whether the copy which is thus implied was a rearranged but otherwise more or less *verbatim* transcript of the type postulated by Galbraith as an intermediary between Exon Domesday and Great Domesday, or a drastically revised version such as Great Domesday, we cannot unfortunately say.

Three other scribal memoranda, probably all in one single hand which I now believe to be later than Exon by several decades, give the names of scribes who also copied the manuscript or part of it. One of these notes, 'hoc scripsit Ricardus', at the foot of fo. 316r (the first recto of a quire), probably means that the scribe Richard copied the whole quire. This interpretation is confirmed by the appearance of a similar note, 'usque huc scripsit R.', in the margin of fo. 414r; in this case a caret tells us exactly not only in which line, but also at which point in the line (before the place-name *Hanecheforda*) the scribe R. (probably the *Ricardus* of the previous note) stopped writing; even if the hand of the notes is earlier than I think, the reference cannot be either to Exon or to Great Domesday, since in both manuscripts there is no change of hand or any obvious break in the line in which the name *Hanecheforda* (or *Hancheford* in Great Domesday, fo. 115r) occurs. The meaning of the third and last note, 'hic debet esse hoc quod Jordan scripsit', written at the foot of fo. 406v (the last and blank verso of a quire) is uncertain, but it is likely to have been a warning to the transcribers that at this point some additional material written by the scribe Jordan had to be inserted. Interesting though they are, these notes are irrelevant to the making of Domesday Book, if they are in a hand of much later date than Exon; they simply prove that, some time in the twelfth century, the manuscript was copied, wherever it was kept at the time, not necessarily for official purposes, but more probably for the private use of some religious establishment.

In Galbraith's view, although Exon Domesday and Little Domesday differed in one respect, the former being a draft and the latter a fair copy, they had at least one point in common: both had been written by scribes employed by the commissioners of the circuit concerned; local, provincial scribes, working in two separate offices, one for each of the two circuits.[2] If they really existed, these two offices, obviously staffed with a fair number of scribes, judging by the diversity of hands in both Exon and Little Domesday, would have been situated one somewhere in the south-western counties for Exon and the other somewhere in Essex, Norfolk or Suffolk for Little Domesday. But the precise location of the two offices has yet to be established. The fact that the manuscript of Exon Domesday is now in Exeter Cathedral and has been there for more than 300 years does not prove that it was there in the Middle Ages and still less that it was written there. Indeed Neil Ker's work on the beginnings of Salisbury Cathedral Library and on Exon itself has given us a tangible proof that at least one and possibly

---

[2] Galbraith (1961), 179.

two Salisbury scribes were engaged in writing parts of the manuscript.[3] It would be unwise, however, to speculate any further until Mrs Teresa Webber has completed her investigations into the connections between Exon Domesday and the Salisbury scriptorium. Suffice it to say that Osmund, royal chancellor until 1078, when he became bishop of Salisbury, would have been a fitting commissioner for the south-western circuit and his cathedral an ideal place for the writing of the circuit return, although no more central than Exeter. For Little Domesday we shall also await with keen interest the findings of two other young scholars, Mr Michael Gullick and Dr Alexander Rumble.[4]

It was Galbraith's opinion that, once they had been completed in the form of fair copies, the various circuit returns were sent to the royal treasury at Winchester. There the king's clerks proceeded to edit them, recasting and abbreviating whatever was necessary. The result of their work was Great Domesday, which was meant to cover the whole of England, although in the end it did not include East Anglia – the area covered by Little Domesday – apparently for no better reason than the untimely death of William the Conqueror, or the counties north of the Tees, which unaccountably seem to have been left out of the Survey altogether.

In spite of its unfinished state, Great Domesday was in Galbraith's eyes a remarkable achievement, perhaps the most outstanding feat of the whole Domesday operation. Although in *The Making of Domesday Book* Galbraith referred to the king's clerks [in the plural] at Winchester, he also expressed in the same book his conviction that Great Domesday bore 'the stamp of a single mind'. 'The script, the style, and the overall pattern in which the information is presented', he wrote, 'are constant throughout.' In other words, Great Domesday had been edited by one person only, who perhaps was also its scribe, 'a very senior official, and a trusted one'. The script of the volume, which in several passages he described as curial, had 'an old-fashioned air, more characteristic of a native than a foreign scribe'. 'It is quite possible', he added, 'that his name occurs in the book he wrote, though unlikely that we shall ever identify him'.[5] On this last point Galbraith had changed his mind by 1967: now he had a candidate to offer, Samson, chaplain of William the Conqueror and bishop of Worcester from 1096. He was the Winchester official who compiled Great Domesday and either wrote the volume himself or, more probably, left this side of the work to a scribe attached to him. Not only was Samson 'the man behind Domesday Book', but he was also 'the man behind the Survey' as a whole.[6]

The strongest argument in favour of Samson was based on Welldon Finn's discovery of two Somerset entries written in the typical hand and termin-

[3] N. R. Ker, 'The Beginnings of Salisbury Cathedral Library', *Medieval Learning and Literature: Essays presented to R. W. Hunt*, ed. J. J. G. Alexander and M. T. Gibson (Oxford, 1976), 35, 49; Ker, *Medieval Manuscripts in British Libraries*, ii (Oxford, 1977), 800–7, esp. 804.
[4] In addition to Dr Rumble's paper in the present volume, see Rumble (1985), 28–49.
[5] Galbraith (1961), 195, 203.
[6] V. H. Galbraith, 'Notes on the Career of Samson, Bishop of Worcester (1096–1112)', *EHR*, lxxxii (1967), 86–101.

ology of the scribe of Great Domesday on two previously blank pages of Exon Domesday.[7] One of these entries, concerning the manor of Templecombe, is an edited version of a longer entry written by one of Exon's original scribes; in this longer entry the name of Samson, the mesne tenant, is mistakenly placed first, and that of Odo, bishop of Bayeux, the tenant-in-chief, second (in an interlineation written in a hand different from that of the main body of the entry, but contemporary with it): 'Samson capellanus habet `de episcopo baiocensi´, etc. (Exon, fo. 467r). In his addition to Exon, the scribe of Great Domesday quite properly reversed the order and wrote: 'Episcopus Baiocensis tenet Come et Sanson de eo' (Exon, fo. 153v); he also condensed the text in his usual fashion. Whether or not one can draw from this the conclusion that Samson was the compiler and scribe of Great Domesday, one must at least agree with Galbraith that this compiler, whoever he was, did correct the text produced under the supervision of the circuit commissioners; he probably did so on the spot, that is to say wherever Exon was written.

The interest of the Templecombe entry does not stop here. If we compare the text added to Exon by the Great Domesday scribe with what he wrote in Great Domesday itself, we find that in the latter he gives the value of *Turnie*, which had been amalgamated with Templecombe, as 13*s* (GDB, fo. 87r), whereas in Exon he had valued it at 14*s* (fo. 153v), the figure also given in the longer entry due to one of Exon's original scribes (fo. 467r). Even the best scribes could under great stress make mistakes of this kind, and we know that the scribe of Great Domesday was no exception. Would he have done so, however, when working from his own beautifully written draft, which in fact does not look like a draft at all, but compares favourably with almost any page of Great Domesday? Perhaps after all he compiled Great Domesday not directly from Exon, but from an intermediary text, as Galbraith thought. What I find difficult to believe is that, after taking the trouble of adding to Exon in his own hand the Templecombe entry as well as another concerning the Somerset lands of Robert fitzGerold (fo. 436v), he would have returned the manuscript to the original scribes of Exon so that they might produce a tidier text for him. It seems more likely that he would have preferred to entrust this work to one of his own assistants, perhaps a pupil of his such as the scribe whose hand occurs in Exon, in a passage marred, as we shall see later, by a staggering although understandable misreading. What seems certain, at any rate, is that Samson ought to be crossed out from the list of possible writers of Great Domesday, since one would not expect a landholder to be inconsistent or make a mistake in the valuation of his own land.

There are other grounds on which Samson has to be rejected as the compiler and/or scribe of Great Domesday. Would a Norman like him have anglicised place-names, as Professor P. H. Sawyer has shown the scribe of

[7] R. Welldon Finn, 'The Evolution of Successive Versions of Domesday Book', *EHR*, lxvi (1951), 561–64.

Great Domesday to have done?[8] Would he have written such expressions as 'donec utlage fuit' (GDB, fo. 62v) or 'ii piscarize reddunt xl stiches anguillarum' (fo. 177r) or 'ad pascendos suos buzecarl.' (fo. 64v)? Other English words which occur in Great Domesday include 'huscarle' and variants (fos. 56r, 129r, 130r), and 'stalre' (fo. 139v). The value of this linguistic evidence, however, should not be exaggerated, since Great Domesday has a fair number of French words as well, for example a few 'arpenz' (fo. 74v: 'arpenz prati' and 'arpenz silvẹ') and many 'coscez' (e.g. fo. 75r; for Latin forms such as 'cotsetos' and variants in Exon, e.g. fo. 25r); we also find names of Normans in their French form, for example 'Willelmus Cievre' or 'Chievre' (fo. 110r; for 'Willelmus Capra' in Exon, fo. 399r) or 'Willelmus de Faleise' (fo. 100r; for 'Willelmus de Falesia' in Exon, fo. 366r). The compiler of the manuscript or its scribe or both obviously knew French and English. Perhaps one was English and the other French; at all events the scribe must have received his professional training in an English scriptorium and from an English master; otherwise he would not have used as consistently as he did the horned e, a feature typical of English native hands.[9]

Who then was the compiler of Great Domesday and who was its scribe? Before we examine the various possibilities opened to us of answering these questions, it might be useful to find out where the compiler and scribe might have worked. Although it is constantly repeated that the so-called circuit returns were sent to the king's treasury in Winchester, and that it was there that Great Domesday was written, the evidence for such statements seems to be lacking. The known fact that by the reign of William Rufus Domesday Book was kept in the royal treasury at Winchester does not prove that Great Domesday had been written there. It is certain, of course, that William the Conqueror already had a treasury, possibly his main or even his only treasury, in Winchester Castle; perhaps it was located in a tower designed to fill security needs rather than provide suitable facilities for a satisfactory scriptorium.[10] It may have been an adequate place for cutting tallies and storing valuables, but not necessarily for writing books such as Great Domesday. Why in any case should the book have been written in one single place like the treasury? Would it not have been more convenient for its compiler and scribe to move around from circuit to circuit and work in turn at each of the centres where the local returns had been put together? Such an arrangement would have made it easier for him to get a prompt answer to his queries, which we know to have been many. It would also explain why separate quires were used for individual counties and circuit returns without having to suppose that this division into independent booklets was forced

[8] P. H. Sawyer, 'The Place-Names of the Domesday Manuscripts', *Bull. John Rylands Library*, xxxviii (1956), 483–506.

[9] On the horned e see N. R. Ker, *Catalogue of Manuscripts Containing Anglo-Saxon* (Oxford, 1957), p. xxix. For its use by the scribe of Great Domesday, see Plate II. a.

[10] See T. F. Tout, *Chapters in the Administrative History of Mediaeval England*, i (Manchester, 1920), 75. For doubts expressed on the writing of Great Domesday in Winchester, see Finn, *Liber Exoniensis*, 150.

upon the scribe by the inevitably haphazard way in which the returns would have reached a static place of compilation such as Winchester.

Whether the scribe worked in Winchester or travelled from one circuit centre to the next, he is unlikely to have been a royal scribe. We cannot even be sure that William the Conqueror had at a given time more than one scribe whom he could call his own. The Northamptonshire geld roll refers to Osmund the king's *writere*, who is generally assumed to have been the same person as Osmund, royal chancellor from *c.* 1070 to 1078, in which year he was made bishop of Salisbury, relinquishing his royal office at the same time.[11] From this text it cannot be inferred that whenever the roll was composed, some time between 1070 and 1078 if the identification of Osmund is correct, the king had only one scribe at a time, but the evidence of the original diplomas and writs extant for the period *c.* 1080 to *c.* 1095 suggests that it was so under the Conqueror and for the major part of his successor's reign. For those fifteen years, covering the chancellorship of Maurice and Gerard as well as part of William Giffard's tenure of the same office, only five royal documents have been identified as the work of a royal scribe, and in each case the scribe is the same. Not only do these documents span a fairly long number of years, but they were also issued in a wide variety of forms for a representative selection of beneficiaries in England (north and south) and on the Continent (in Normandy and outside): a diploma of *c.* 1080 granted to the abbey of Cluny and confirming the foundation of the priory of St Pancras, Lewes, by William de Warenne and his wife Gundreda; a diploma dated 1085 and granting Steyning and Bury to the abbey of Fécamp; a writ of 1086 granting the tithe of Rutland to the abbey of Westminster; the foundation-charter of the see of Bath, a diploma dated 1091; and finally a writ of *c.* 1095 for the church of Durham.[12] That during this period of fifteen years the writer of the five documents just cited was the only scribe in the king's own service is virtually certain; the fact that he worked for two kings and under three successive chancellors is in my view significant. Only during the last five years of William Rufus's reign do we see the staff of the royal writing-office increased from one to two, an expansion which from that time onwards continued at a steady pace.[13] There is no sign that until the second half of the reign of Henry II there was any other royal secretariat than that which worked under the chancellor. Even as late as the 1170s and even in the Exchequer, as we know from the *Dialogus de Scaccario*, the only royal scribe who did not belong to the chancellor's staff was the treasurer's scribe, whose origins cannot possibly be traced back to the reign of William the Conqueror.[14]

It need hardly be stressed that a single royal scribe had to travel from place to place with his master, the chancellor, who in turn followed the king with the royal seal. From the latter part of 1086 until the Conqueror's death, a period of strenuous activity for the scribe of Great Domesday, the royal

[11] *Anglo-Saxon Charters*, ed. A. J. Robertson (Cambridge, 1956), 232, 482.
[12] Pierre Chaplais, *Essays in Medieval Diplomacy and Administration* (London, 1981), XVI. 94.
[13] T. A. M. Bishop, *Scriptores Regis* (Oxford, 1961), 30–3.
[14] *Dialogus*, 29.

scribe was, therefore, like the king, out of England and consequently unavailable for work on Domesday. His hand is in any case strikingly different from that of the scribe of Great Domesday; he probably was a Norman, whereas his alleged colleague of Domesday fame almost certainly was not.

If the scribe of Great Domesday was not attached to a royal department, he must have belonged to an ecclesiastical scriptorium and worked for the king in an incidental capacity only. The quality of his work and the importance of the task assigned to him suggest that he held a high position in the scriptorium in which he normally worked, perhaps the scriptorium of 'the man behind the Survey', the latter being probably an ecclesiastic of considerable eminence who at the same time enjoyed the Conqueror's complete confidence.

Although until now I have spoken loosely of *the* scribe of Great Domesday, it would be more accurate to refer to him as its main scribe. In an important article published recently Mr Michael Gullick has already pointed out, and he will demonstrate it at length elsewhere, that at least two scribes were involved in the writing of the manuscript: one was the main scribe – the man I am concerned with – and the other a corrector, whose contributions to the book generally consist of small additions and corrections, but also sometimes of longer passages.[15]

The hand of the main scribe is easily identifiable. One of its most distinctive features is the curious shape of one of the several types of suspension-sign which the scribe uses for *-us* after the letter *b*: not unlike the occasional *M* written sideways which occurs in some Northumbrian manuscripts in insular majuscule of the eighth century, the sign is best described as a *z* or arabic *3* with an upper tick slanting slightly upwards to the right of the vertical (Pl. III. d, *omnibus* and *consuetudinibus*). The scribe's letter *d* is sometimes half-uncial, with a vertical ascender, but he frequently uses the uncial, rounded form, the ascender being topped by a serif drawn at right angles (Pl. III. c and d for the former; e and f for the latter). In the main text the Roman numerals are normal, but in the lists of tenants at the beginning of each county, and also at the beginning of each section within the county, numerals containing more than two (and sometimes only two) successive *is* have the first *i* short, the second tall, resembling an *l*, the third short, and so on; in other words, short and tall *is* alternate, at least as a rule (Pl. III. e; but cf. III. f, *xxxiij*). The letters *f* and *r* often have a descender, sometimes with a slanting serif at the foot (Pls. III. c–g, IV. b); *s* also has a descender in *st* (Pl. III. e, *Execestre* and *Tauestoch*). The upper bar of *F* is almost vertical (Pl. IV. b, line 1, *PELIFORDE*). Finally the tironian *nota* for *et* resembles an arabic 7 with a high horizontal bar (Pl. IV. b, last three lines). The scribe's almost invariable use of the nota for *et* (as opposed to the ampersand, which he uses rarely in Great Domesday and frequently in his other works) and of the horned *e* entitles us to regard his hand as English, although it was strongly influenced in other ways by continental practice. It is likely

[15] Gullick and Thorn (1986), 78–80.

therefore that his scriptorium was an ancient native one, which was evolving under Norman influence.

In spite of its easily identifiable features, the hand of the main scribe of Great Domesday had not until recently been noticed elsewhere than on the two pages of Exon Domesday to which I have already referred (fos. 153v and 436v). Earlier this year, however, three further manuscripts containing the scribe's hand were discovered, two by Mr Michael Gullick and one by Mrs Teresa Webber. All three manuscripts come from ecclesiastical libraries and all three were undoubtedly written in an ecclesiastical scriptorium. Michael Gullick has already published a brief account of one of them, Oxford, Trinity College, MS 28.[16] The manuscript is made up of four parts written in three main hands: the first part (fos. 1r–80v), Bede's treatise *De tabernaculo*, is in one hand (Scribe A; Pl. I, b–d, extracts); the second part (fos. 80v–86r) consists of a treatise *De divinis nominibus*, interpolated into some manuscripts of the *Liber formularum* of Bishop Eucherius of Lyons to form Chapter I of this work; this second part and the third (fos. 86r–88r), the treatise *De ponderibus et mensuris* of Rabanus Maurus, attributed to Bede by some English scholars of the later Middle Ages, including the Franciscan compilers of the *Registrum Anglie*,[17] are in a second hand (Scribe B); the fourth and last part (fos. 89v–91r), a short sermon of just over three pages on the ten commandments and the ten plagues of Egypt, attributed to St Augustine, is the contribution made by the main scribe of Great Domesday to the manuscript (Pl. I. a, extract from fo. 90r).

One interesting feature of Trinity College, Oxford, MS 28, is that the unidentified scribe A, in the list of chapters of Books I and III of Bede's *De tabernaculo*, uses on three occasions short and tall *is* for Roman numerals: he writes *ili* for 3 on folio 1r, and *ili* and *illi* for 3 and 4 on folio 52v (Pl. I. b–c), a system similar to that adopted by the main scribe of Great Domesday (Pl. III. e). Scribe A also uses at least two of the *signes de renvoi* which occur in Great Domesday, the Greek letters psi (Trin. 28, fos. 12r and 24v; GDB, fos. 78v, 343r and 354v) and zeta with a slightly slanting bar through the middle of it (Pls. I. d and III. f–g). It may be more than a mere coincidence that in a Durham manuscript, the 'Carilef Bible', the same form of zeta (but without the slanting bar) is used as an alternative for *z*.[18] A possible connection between Trinity MS 28 and the Durham scriptorium is made more plausible by the striking similarity of Scribe A's hand to that of one of the scribes of another Durham manuscript, MS B IV. 24,[19] and by the obvious Durham interest in works written by Bede or attributed to him. A sixteenth-century inscription shows that at that time the book belonged to

---

[16] Ibid., 79.
[17] Oxford, Bodl. Lib., MS Tanner 165, f. 110r; M. R. James, *The Ancient Libraries of Canterbury and Dover* (Cambridge, 1903), 38, 499.
[18] *Durham Cathedral Manuscripts to the End of the Twelfth Century*, ed. R. A. B. Mynors (Oxford Univ. Press, 1939), Pl. 17, col. 2: *Booz* is written in the same line once with a *z* and once with a zeta.
[19] See, for example, fos. 81v, 82r.

St Swithun's, Winchester, which may have acquired it at the time of the Dissolution.

The second manuscript in which Michael Gullick discovered the hand of the main scribe of Great Domesday is British Library, MS Harley 12. Here again the scribe's contribution is the last item in the manuscript, a short and apparently uncommon life of St Catherine of Alexandria (fos. 141r–143v), of which there was a copy in Durham Cathedral Library in the twelfth century.[20]

My knowledge of the third manuscript, Hereford Cathedral Library, MS P.I. 10, I owe to the kindness of Mrs Teresa Webber, who identified the hand of the main scribe of Great Domesday in it while going through microfilms from Hereford in the Bodleian Library. In this manuscript the scribe wrote only the list of contents, eight lines altogether (Pl. II. a). The manuscript itself as in several hands, two of which use the same curious suspension-sign for -us as we found in Great Domesday (Pl. II. b–c).[21] Not only do the script and the decoration of the manuscript (Pl. II. d)[22] resemble those of Durham books, but the list of contents is in the same position, facing folio 1r, as it is in a manuscript of certain Durham origin, but of slightly late date, now Cambridge, Jesus College, MS Q.G. 16; in both the list is introduced by virtually identical words, 'In hoc codice continentur hęc' (Hereford MS) and 'In hoc uolumine continentur hec' (Jesus MS). It seems almost certain therefore that the Hereford manuscript was written in Durham and that the main scribe of Great Domesday, who wrote the list of contents, held a position of some importance in the Durham scriptorium.

Nine other manuscripts of the late eleventh or early twelfth century, all of certain, probable or possible Durham origin, have produced further examples of the same unusual suspension-sign for -us: three are still preserved in Durham Cathedral Library (MSS B II. 9, B IV. 13 and B IV. 14); one has been proved by Mrs Temple to have been written and decorated in Durham (Oxford, University College, MS 165);[23] another, Oxford, Bodleian Library, MS Bodley 783, resembles Durham manuscripts in script and decoration; the same is true of two other manuscripts in the same library, MS Bodley 691 and MS Lat. bib. d. 10, both acquired by Exeter Cathedral probably at the same time (c. 1100) as MS Bodley 717, part of which is in a hand which occurs in Durham Cathedral Library, MS B II. 18;[24] Cambridge, Corpus Christi College, MS 415 (O. 27), 'Tractatus Eboracenses', can be said because of its contents to be of northern origin; finally Cambridge, Trinity College, MS 722 (R. 5. 27), of unknown provenance, is a copy of Bede's Historia ecclesiastica. It seems that the special sign for -us was characteristic of

---

[20] Durham Cathedral, MS B IV. 24, fo. 2r: 'Vita sancte Katerine'.

[21] In this manuscript and in others, however, the sign is less cursive than it normally is in Great Domesday.

[22] Compare the posture of the animal in Plate II. d with that in *Durham Cathedral Manuscripts*, Pl. 34 (a).

[23] E. Temple, 'A Note on the University College Life of St Cuthbert', *Bodleian Library Record*, vol. ix, no. 6 (Jan. 1978), 320–2.

[24] See A. C. de la Mare, 'A probable Addition to the Bodleian's Holdings of Exeter Cathedral Manuscripts', *Bodleian Library Record*, vol. xi, no. 2 (May 1983), 79–88.

the Durham scriptorium, although it may have been adopted in due course by other northern scriptoria.

The evidence which has been produced above may be strong enough for connecting the main scribe of Great Domesday with the Durham scriptorium, but it does not explain why it was a northern scribe who had been entrusted with the writing of the final text of the Domesday Survey. I believe that the explanation is to be found in the famous passage of Exon Domesday which states that, at a meeting in Salisbury [possibly on 1 August 1086],[25] William the Conqueror ordered the bishop of Durham to write down *in brevibus* a grant to the bishop of Winchester of additions to the manor of Taunton which he, William the Conqueror, had just acknowledged. In Exon the statement occurs at the end of the section concerning the Somerset lands of Bishop Walkelin of Winchester (Pl. III. a–b); in Great Domesday the same statement is repeated *verbatim*, an unusual occurence, but in the middle of the section, not at the end (Pl. III. c). As Neil Ker pointed out, the whole section in Exon (fos. 173v–175v) is written in one good hand, without hardly any correction, a hand which according to him did not seem to occur elsewhere in Exon.[26] In fact, there is no doubt that the hand does not occur elsewhere in Exon. Ker also noted that the section did not seem to be in the right place, because it began on the verso of the last folio of the section dealing with the lands of the abbot of Glastonbury; according to the list of contents of the manuscript, the Somerset lands of the bishop of Winchester should have been placed between those of the bishop of Wells and those of the bishop of Exeter. It looked as if the misplaced section was a fair copy of an earlier version which had been discarded. The reason for the rewriting and change of order is plain enough: the earlier version lacked the mention of the additional grant acknowledged by the Conqueror at Salisbury, and there was no room for the addition to be made between the Wells and the Exeter sections. It is generally believed that it was because William of Saint-Calais, bishop of Durham, was one of the royal commissioners for the south-western circuit that he was ordered to write down the grant *in brevibus*, that is to say presumably in Exon. If that was the reason, however, we would have expected our fair copy to be in one of the hands found elsewhere in Exon, but it is not. The hand is very interesting indeed, sharing as it does several features with the hand of the main scribe of Great Domesday: this is true of the alternate use of short and tall *i*s in Roman numerals, except that in Exon this applied to the text, whereas in Great Domesday the system was restricted to the lists of tenants and to the headings of sections; this is true also of the use of the rounded *d* with a serif, and, above all, of the special suspension-sign for -*us* (Pl. III. a–b). The scribe must surely have been trained in Durham, possibly by the main scribe of Great Domesday, but at the time of the writing of Exon he had not reached the standard of his master, since in line 12 of fo. 174r he wrote the names of

---

[25] On the meeting of 1 August 1086, see Stenton, *English Feudalism* (1961), 112–14.
[26] Ker, *Medieval Manuscripts in British Libraries*, ii. 806.

two places as *bela* and *billa*, and five lines below as *hela* and *hilla*, the correct readings.

If it was not as a circuit commissioner that the bishop of Durham had the section rewritten by one of his own scribes, it could have been as a member of the second group of commissioners to which Robert of Hereford alludes, those who checked the work of the first group; as a stranger in a strange land he would have been very suitable for the post. But it may be that William of Saint-Calais acted in a still higher capacity, as 'the man behind the Survey', to copy the phrase of Galbraith once more. The same explanation might hold good for the two pages of Exon which are in the hand of the main scribe of Great Domesday (fos. 153v and 436v). In other words, the bishop of Durham, as the person ultimately responsible for the final version of Domesday Book, had ordered two of his scribes to make corrections to Exon, because he did not trust the local scribes. This hypothetical reconstruction becomes more plausible when we look at another famous writing connected with Domesday Book, the writ by which William the Conqueror reduced the hidage of the Westminster manor of Pyrford in the county of Surrey. The writ, dated 'post descriptionem totius Angliȩ', is witnessed by William, bishop of Durham, and Ivo Taillebois (Pl. IV. a).[27] The hand has not been identified, but it is consistent with what one would expect from a Durham scribe, for example the use of a long *s* in words with an *st* ligature. What is particularly interesting about the external features of the writ is that the wrapping-tie is placed above the tongue which bears the seal, not below as was usually done. This is a very rare practice indeed in English royal and non-royal documents of any date. Apart from William I's Pyrford writ, this sealing method has been noticed in only two other royal writs: the earlier of the two, issued by Henry I and granted – significantly – to the monks of Durham, is in an unidentified hand, probably that of a Durham scribe (Durham, D. & C., 2. 1. Reg. 10); the other, issued by Henry II in favour of Westminster Abbey, is also in an identified hand (W.A.M. XLI).[28] English episcopal documents are also rarely sealed in this way. The earliest of the few known exceptions is once again a Durham example, a vernacular writ issued in the name of Bishop Ranulf Flambard for the monks of Durham (Durham, D. & C., 2. 1. Pont. 9).[29] Later examples include documents in the names of Thomas or Thurstan, archbishop of York, Alexander II, bishop of Lincoln, and Theobald, archbishop of Canterbury.[30] All this evidence suggests that the Pyrford writ for Westminster Abbey was issued under the supervision of William of Saint-Calais and written by one of his scribes.

After the issue of the writ, the Great Domesday entry concerning Pyrford, which obviously had already been written, was corrected. The marginal note 'Modo geldat pro viij hidis' (Plate IV. b) was written by the main

---

[27] Bishop and Chaplais, Pl. XXIV, no. 26.
[28] *Regesta*, ii, no. 1604; Bishop, *Scriptores Regis*, 16 and Pl. VI (a).
[29] Ibid., 16 and ref.
[30] C. R. Cheney, *English Bishops' Chanceries, 1100–1250* (Manchester, 1950), 47–8.

scribe of the volume after the issue of the writ, not before.[31]

Thus the bishop of Durham was connected with the work on Domesday not only for Circuit II, which concerned the south-western counties, but also for Circuit I, which included Surrey. It does look as if he was indeed 'the man behind the Survey'. If he was, he could not have left England with the Conqueror in the latter part of 1086. Since the Pyrford writ is attested by him, it must have been issued before the king's departure for Normandy, in which case the section of Great Domesday for Surrey had been completed even earlier.

William of Saint-Calais was, of course, an ideal person to be put in charge of the whole Domesday operation south of the Tees, that is to say for all the counties where he could be expected to be impartial, and he had enough scribes to do the work required, scribes who could also be trusted to be without bias. But someone else had to deal with the lands of the bishop's own diocese, that is to say the county of Durham and whatever part of Northumberland was in the Conqueror's control, although he could act there as a circuit commissioner. Perhaps he did not have time before he was exiled in 1088. It is the general belief that the work on Great Domesday was interrupted by the death of William the Conqueror. Perhaps we ought to consider an alternative and hazard attributing the interruption to the exile of the bishop in 1088. William of Saint-Calais would no doubt have taken to France with him his favourite scribe, the main scribe of Great Domesday, a man who was irreplaceable for the completion of the work.

When the bishop was allowed to return three years later, with or without his scribe, it was too late. His connection with Domesday Book, however, was not completely at an end. Every writ of William Rufus which refers to Domesday Book is attested by the bishop either on his own or with someone else.[32] When we look at writs of Henry I with similar references to Domesday Book, we notice that they all are attested by Roger, bishop of Salisbury.[33] Roger probably acted then as justiciar, an officer who no doubt at the time was already in charge of the royal treasury above the treasurer, as he was in the reign of Henry II, and in that capacity had the official custody of Domesday Book. Perhaps similar powers without the title had been granted by Rufus to the bishop of Durham in 1091 or shortly afterwards.

After the death of Saint-Calais in 1096 we still find a hint of a connection between Domesday Book and Durham: in the section concerning the Bruce fee, which was added to Great Domesday some time after 1103,[34] there are two more examples of the curious suspension-sign for -us (Pl. III. h). Whether the connection had been perpetuated by Ranulf Flambard, William's successor as bishop of Durham, or by someone else cannot unfortunately be established.

---

[31] See Bishop and Chaplais, no. 26, where the opposite is argued. I alone am responsible for this error. See Galbraith (1961), 206–7.
[32] *Regesta*, i, no. 468; ii, 403 (no. 385b; see also no. 385c), 404 (no. 386a), 407–8 (no. 483a).
[33] Ibid., ii, nos. 976, 1000, 1500, 1515. See also no. 1488.
[34] Ibid., ii, no. 648. See also G. Fellows Jensen, 'The Domesday Book Account of the Bruce Fief', *English Place-Name Society, Journal* 2 (1969–70), 8–17.

The Domesday Manuscripts: Scribes and Scriptoria

Alexander R. Rumble

THE FACTUAL RECORD conveyed to us by the contemporary manuscript remains of William I's *descriptio* of 1086, Great Domesday Book (GDB), Little Domesday Book (LDB) and the Exeter Domesday in the *Liber Exoniensis* (Exon),[1] is of undoubted value to the historian and the geographer alike. The same manuscripts also constitute an important body of closely dated written work produced by a number of individual scribes which is worthy of close analysis by the palaeographer. The post-Conquest period to which they belong was one of conflict and compromise between Anglo-Saxon and Norman conventions not only in social and political fields but also in relation to scribal techniques and orthography. A number of styles of writing were taught and practised in England in the generation after 1066, some of them indistinguishable from those used in Normandy, others which were remnants of late Anglo-Saxon styles, and still others which represented varying degrees of Anglo-Norman intermarriage.[2] A palaeographical survey of the three surviving contemporary Domesday manuscripts reflects something of the mixed cultural background and training of the *scriptores* entrusted with the latter stages of the transcription of the Domesday record. Such a survey also confirms the qualities of the main scribe of GDB as both a writer and a page-designer, quite apart from his skill as an editor.

In a paper published last year I attempted to summarise the current state of our knowledge about the various codicological features of the three manuscripts under discussion.[3] In recent months, stimulated by the current

[1] Respectively, Public Record Office, Exchequer: Treasury of the Receipt, E 31/2 and 1; Exeter Cathedral Library, MS 3500. I am most grateful to Dr Daphne Gifford for the protracted loan of her volumes of the Ordnance Survey photo-zincograph for Essex, Norfolk and Suffolk. I have also benefited from correspondence and discussion about the Domesday scribes with Mr Michael Gullick and Mrs Caroline Thorn.

[2] For the variety of styles of script used in the second half of the eleventh century, see Ker, *English Manuscripts*, 22–32, and (for vernacular texts) N. R. Ker, *Catalogue of Manuscripts Containing Anglo-Saxon* (Oxford, 1957), xxv–xxxiii, lvi–lx; T. A. M. Bishop, *English Caroline Minuscule* (Oxford, 1971), xxiii–iv; 'Notes on Cambridge manuscripts: Parts I–III', *Transactions of the Cambridge Bibliographical Society*, i (1953), 432–41, ii (1955), 185–99; and Bishop and Chaplais, xvi–xix.

[3] Rumble (1985), 28–49.

novocentenary and associated with the publication of the new facsimile edition of GDB,[4] some further discoveries have been made about the scribal history of GDB and are still being investigated by their authors.[5] I shall refer briefly to such new facts as have already been published, but shall concentrate in the main on making a detailed analysis of the late eleventh-century hands in GDB and LDB and, after a very brief sidelong glance at Exon, try to place the writings in a broader palaeographical context.[6]

Working in reverse chronological order, back through the various stages of editing the Domesday record, we should begin with the colophon at the end of LDB (fo. 450r, lines 17–21; see below, Pl. V(b)), which reads:

ANNO MILLESIMO OCTOGESIMO SEXTO. AB INCARNATIONE DOMINI. VIGESIMO VERO REGNI WILLELMI FACTA EST ISTA DESCRIPTIO. NON SOLVM PER HOS TRES COMITATVS. SED ETIAM PER ALIOS

This was written in red ink in a mixture of rustic capital and uncial (**A**, **E**, **M**) majuscule forms with an occasional caroline minuscule letter interspersed (**a**, **e**, **i**, **s**, **t**). The same scribe (Scribe 7 in LDB; see below, Appendix) also added the rubricated running-title on the left-hand side of openings in LDB, that giving the county-name (Essex, Norfolk or Suffolk) relevant to the entries on the pages concerned. He also wrote most, and perhaps all, of the rubricated running-titles on the right-hand side of openings in LDB, those giving the name of the holder of the fief being described.[7] The colophon was probably written immediately after the completion of the county running-titles, very early in the reign of William Rufus, when it had been decided not to complete GDB but instead to cobble it, as far as it had then been written, together with LDB, the unabridged circuit-return for Essex and East Anglia.[8] A minimal amount of rubrication was added to LDB at that time in order to disguise as far as possible the rather different nature and appearance of the two volumes which were to make up the textual hybrid later known by the name of Domesday Book.[9] The scribe's reference in the colophon to the counties in LDB, whose names he had just finished writing as running-titles, as *HOS TRES COMITATVS* is to be seen as a direct contrast to those 'others' (*ALIOS*) included in GDB, the other volume in the set, rather than to those in other circuit-returns as has been suggested.[10] The date

---

[4] The facsimile, with accompanying translation, indices and maps, is currently in the course of publication by Alecto Historical Editions (1986–).

[5] Gullick and Thorn (1986), 78–80.

[6] The present study does not include the description of the fief of Robert de Brus added to GDB (fos. 332v–333r) in 1120 × 29. For additions of text made to GDB and LDB by official custodians in the early modern period, see Hallam (1986), 117, 122, 129 and Pl. 43.

[7] Sometimes these names are abbreviated down to their initial letter. On variations in the colour of the red ink used in LDB, see *Domesday Re-Bound*, 45–6.

[8] Galbraith (1961), 185, 205; Rumble (1985), 41, 47. For the nature of the circuit-returns, see Galbraith (1961), 29–35.

[9] The different sorts of rubrication in the Domesday manuscripts are summarised in Rumble (1985), 41.

[10] *Domesday Re-Bound*, 8.

(1086) given in the colophon is, however, that of the *DESCRIPTIO*, the Domesday Survey itself, not of the final completion of its record in 'mongrel form', which was probably soon after the unexpected death of William I on 9 September 1087.[11]

It is likely that the addition of the rubrication and colophon to LDB should be placed after the writing of some at least of the unrubricated entries in GDB. Such entries occur at the end of some counties and of some chapters within counties, and sometimes in the margin; they also include the whole of the list of *clamores* for Lincolnshire and most of that for Yorkshire.[12] The overwhelming majority of these entries, which appear to have been added as new information became available after GDB had been rubricated, were written by the main scribe of GDB (Scribe A). However, as has recently been observed by Michael Gullick, the penultimate entry in Berkshire (fo. 63v) is the work of another scribe.[13] This scribe (Scribe B) also acted as the 'checker' of the text in GDB and added a very few additional words or sentences *passim*.[14] His hand is rather similar to, and may be partly imitative of, that of Scribe A but has rather shorter ascenders in relation to minims and differs in particular in the abbreviation for -*bus* (b;), and in the making of the tironian nota for *et* (7) with a curved rather than a straight bar. Although the amount of text written by him is extremely minute in comparison to that by Scribe A, the presence of his hand in GDB is a significant new discovery in relation both to the criticism of the text and to the logistics of its inscription. It is worth noting that such a discovery has only been made possible now due to the making of the new facsimile edition which allows unfettered and convenient palaeographical study of GDB by those outside the Civil Service for the first time in 900 years.[15]

The addition of both full and semi-rubrication to GDB may have been effected as soon as the text of the counties in each separate circuit-volume, apart from LDB, had been edited into GDB, rather than in a single process. Some reference back to the circuit-volumes would have been needed for both the original numeration of the list of tenants in each county to be added

[11] For the description 'mongrel-form', see Galbraith (1961), 205. The statement, ibid., 184–5, that the word *descriptio* in the colophon refers to the text of LDB, rather than to the Survey itself, assumes that the colophon was written before GDB, which is unlikely.

[12] See, for example, GDB, fos. 63v (Berks.), 208v (Hunts.), 236v, 237r (Leics.), 250r, 250v (Staffs.), 278v (Derbs.), 288r, 289r, 291v (Notts.), 298v, 315r (Yorks.), 345r (Lincs.), 373v, 374r (Yorks. *clamores*), 375r–377v (Lincs. *clamores*). This list represents but a selection showing the various locations of these additional entries relative to their length and the amount of space available.

[13] The entry is illustrated in the plate on p. 52 of the *Exhibition Guide* (1986) to the Domesday 1086–1986 Exhibition at the Public Record Office. Its text is not complete in that the ploughland figure is lacking.

[14] Gullick and Thorn (1986), 79–80.

[15] See above, n. 4. The nineteenth-century facsimile edition, besides being not wholly accurate due to retouching and to the omission of marginalia, is inconvenient to use in the county volumes because of the lack of original foliation; *Domesday Book . . . Photo-Zincographed by Her Majesty's Command, at the Ordnance Survey Office, Southampton* (1861–3). On its production, see Hallam (1986), 154–7.

(even though it was in fact often not now strictly accurate)[16] and for the wording of the red ink titles to individual chapters. However, the total amount of such reference was greatly limited by the use of red-lining and red-flourishing added to words and letters already written in the ordinary ink of the text, rather than the use of full rubrication for these items.[17] All of the rubrication was probably the work of Scribe A. Its full effect is both to enliven the page and to make the text easier to use. The large red ink initials at the beginning of most counties in GDB were no doubt executed at the same time as the rubrication. These are plain in design, apart from those associated respectively with the archiepiscopal cities of Canterbury and York, which have attractive floreate terminals.[18]

Apart from the additions and corrections mentioned above, the primary text of GDB was written by a single scribe (Scribe A). Although varying in formality relative to its position within one of the county units of which GDB is composed,[19] the duct of the writing is fluent and the hand is distinctive.[20] Both vertical and curved strokes are cleanly executed with a firm regularity of stroke. The script employed for the main text, arranged in double column, is a form of caroline minuscule (*litera carolina minuscula*) adapted to the scribe's purpose by the frequent use of abbreviations and some occasional semi-cursive letter-forms. The initial letters to sentences and the whole of nearly all significant headings and names are written in a mixed majuscule script containing rustic capital, uncial and enlarged minuscule forms. Display capitals are used as paragraph-letters, marking the beginning of subdivisions of chapters.

In the minuscules, the ascenders of **b**, **h**, **k**, **l** and upright **d** are tall and very straight for most of their length; their tops are variously treated, being slightly clubbed, plain or ending in a serif to the left. At the bottom of the stem of **d** and **l**, as on the first minim of **h**, there is often a serif to the right; on **d** and **l** this curves upwards, on **h** it is usually horizontal. Minims in general either have horizontal feet or end in an upward curve to the right. The very straight descenders of **p** and **q** finish in various ways: they may taper or curve to the left, end in a serif to the right, or be finished by a transverse hairline.

Individual minuscule letter-forms characteristic of Scribe A are the following:

[16] Some minor modifications to the order and composition of chapters having been made during the course of editing the text of some counties into GDB, see Galbraith (1961), 33–4, and Rumble (1985), 37, 40.

[17] Red-lining is the practice of ruling a single red horizontal line through a word or words to highlight them. It is at least rare in medieval manuscripts and may even be confined to those associated with, or dependent upon, GDB.

[18] GDB, fos. 2r (Canterbury), 298r (York). Those associated with Dover (fo. 1r), Hertford (fo. 132r), Buckingham (fo. 143r) and Nottingham (fo. 280r) have simple panelled stems.

[19] The county units in GDB constitute textual 'booklets', not always coincident with the physical division of the volume into quires, see Rumble (1985), 29, 34–7.

[20] For the general significance of Scribe A's work, see Rumble (1985), 45–8; but on the number of scribes involved, cf. Gullick and Thorn (1986). For small samples of Scribe A's writing, see below, Pl. V(a); *Domesday Re-Bound*, Pls. III–IV; and Rumble (1985), Pl. 3.4.

d (upright) has a flat top to its bowl; **d** (round-backed) is sometimes completed by a transverse hairline on the ascender.

e has a slight horn to its left shoulder.

g has an open, scythe-shaped descender which emanates from the right-hand side of the head.

m often has its first two minims closer together than its second and third.

r descends below the line of writing to varying depths; its arm often links with the following letter in a word. The 2-shaped variety is very rare; it occurs after **q** in the abbreviations for *quarentina/e* 'furlong(s)' (fo. 87v, col. 2, lines 37–8; fo. 247v, col. 2, line 4) and in the *-orum* compendium.

t often has its back projecting very slightly above its bar.

ȩ (and **Ȩ**) has a simple, narrow, ovoid spur.

There is a ligature of **st** but *not* of **ct**.[21]

Of the majuscules, the following are noteworthy:

F has its top bar raised to an angle of 45°.

G is 6-shaped.

H (uncial) is usual; **H** (rustic) also occurs and sometimes has its cross-bar projecting through the left upright (fo. 87v, col. 2, lines 29, 35 *Huic*).

I is either long or stands on the line.

M is usually a tall, enlarged version of the minuscule form with a similar treatment of the space between the uprights, the third of which often has a foot turned to the right; **M** (uncial) also occurs, particularly in the abbreviation for *Manerium*.

N is often a tall, enlarged minuscule form with a foot turned to the right on its second upright; **N** (rustic) also occurs.

Q has its body suspended above the line with its tail hanging down; the body is sometimes formed by a 9-shaped curve (fo. 133r, col. 1, line 23, *Qua*).

T (rustic) and **T** (uncial) both occur.

There are ligatures of final **NS** and **NT** and of both initial and medial **TR**. The uprights of **H** (uncial and rustic), **I** (on the line), **L**, **P**, **R** and **T** (rustic) tend to be very straight until just before the bottom where there is a slight protrusion to the left, preceding the making of a horizontal foot to the right.

The display capitals are of some interest, particularly those of which there is more than one shape made (**A**, **D**, **E**, **G**, **H**, **I**, **M**, **S** and **W**). Baubles appear on terminals on **A** and **G** and on the bars of **E** and the arms of **S**. Horizontal approach strokes or transverse hairlines are often added. When there are several occurrences of the same paragraph-letter on a page there is a deliberate attempt to alternate or vary forms; this occurs most often with the letters **A** and **W**, and reflects Scribe A's attention to page-design.[22]

Most of the symbols and methods of abbreviation used by Scribe A are

[21] The avoidance of the **ct** ligature accorded with the best practice of the period, see N. R. Ker, 'The beginnings of Salisbury Cathedral Library' in *Medieval Learning and Literature: Essays presented to Richard William Hunt*, ed. J. Alexander and M. Gibson (Oxford, 1976), 23–49; reprinted in *Books, Collectors and Libraries: Studies in the Medieval Heritage*, ed. A. G. Watson (1985), 143–73, 147.

[22] For example, GDB, fos. 59v **A**; 61r, 192r **W**.

either the conventional ones of the period or are also found in other Domesday texts. A few forms would appear to be more personal to him however. These include the overline with an oblique hairline attached to each end, one rising, the other descending, whose shape was the result of writing at speed;[23] the very frequently used tironian nota for *et*, which has a straight horizontal bar and a long diagonal hairline descender sometimes overhanging the line below; the much rarer ampersand for *et*, which in the majuscule form ends in a rising line to the right;[24] and the abbreviation for -*bus* consisting of **b** followed by a long jagged diagonal descending line.

Punctuation is almost entirely by the simple point, both at the end of sentences or clauses and either side of sigla or roman numerals. The *punctus elevatus* occurs very occasionally, often preceding a sum of money in the value clause. The gallows-shaped *paragraphos* is sometimes, especially in the boroughs, used as an indication of a new entry, but in most of GDB is replaced by the paragraph-letters already mentioned above. The *paragraphos* also occurs at the end of a line before run-over of text from the line above or below. Various elaborate symbols are used as *signes-de-renvoi*.[25]

A well-formed Anglo-Saxon letter ash, in both minuscule and majuscule size, occurs in vernacular name-forms, but not thorn, eth or wynn.[26] The latter two letters at least seem to have been used in some of the returns preceding GDB, however, since **D** therein sometimes stands for majuscule eth and **P** is sometimes a misreading of wynn. Scribe A's more sympathetic treatment of vernacular place-name forms in GDB has been contrasted to the Normanisation or Latinisation of them in preceding stages of the record.[27] He seems to have translated many of them back into a more acceptable English form during the course of his editing. This would suggest that Scribe A was either a native Englishman or had lived in England from an early age. Certain features of his handwriting would support an English nationality and training: the addition to some minims of a horizontal foot (rather than a diagonal hairline in the Norman fashion); the use of an **e** with a horned shoulder; and its very long and straight vertical lines.[28]

Scribe A's writing in GDB tends to be most formal at the beginning of a county then to become more current (with a greater use of semi-cursive forms of **f**, **r**, **s** with descenders, and an increase in the length of the nota for *et*) as the end of the amount of parchment allotted to a particular county draws nearer. There seems to have been a deliberate attempt to limit the overall length of the

[23] The generic term 'overline' is used here to refer to the basic abbreviation-mark added above a letter to signify the omission of an unspecified letter or letters at that point in a word; it may be a short horizontal, or upward curving, bar, or a bar with accretions to its ends, sometimes giving it an angular **S**-shape.
[24] For example, GDB, fo. 298r, col. 1, lines 12–14. The minuscule form is not so unusual in shape and ends in a short downward stroke, ibid., lines 3–4, 7–8, etc.
[25] For example, GDB, fos. 1v, 4v, 19v, 120v and 121r, 128v, 200r, 274v, 277r, 352v.
[26] For both sizes of ash, see GDB, fo. 141r, col. 1, line 32, *Ælmæri*.
[27] See P. H. Sawyer, 'The place-names of the Domesday manuscripts', *Bulletin of the John Rylands Library*, xxxviii (1956), 483–506.
[28] For the first and third of these features, see Ker, *English Manuscripts*, 23; for the **e**, see Ker, *Catalogue*, xxix.

text of GDB by allotting only a fixed amount of parchment relative to the estimated size of the edited version of each county, and there was probably some reluctance to add extra leaves except in cases of large omissions of text (as in Surrey, Hampshire and Dorset).[29] The smaller size and greater currency of his writing in additional entries and interlineations on pages of GDB *passim* were also influenced by the amount of space available. It was this alternation between formal and more current modes of writing that led earlier commentators to believe that a number of scribes were responsible for its production.[30] This is a view less likely to be held if one thinks of GDB being written as a collection of separate county units of text rather than as a book copied from first to last page in an ordered sequence of work.[31] It is indeed probable that the order in which the counties in GDB were bound is not that in which they were written.[32] Apart from the differences in formality within counties, there are also differences in the ruling and the amount of general textual compression between counties, leading to theories as to their relative order of writing.[33] Although most of the text of counties previously in one circuit-volume may be said to have been edited into GDB before much of the text of counties previously in another such volume, it is doubtful whether there is any absolute order in which whole counties were written, since additions and corrections were no doubt made (by both Scribe A and Scribe B) to one county at intervals in the inscription of others.

The amount of care given to the embellishment of the paragraph-letters in GDB may indicate that, although written at some speed, the manuscript was not written in utmost haste. As there seem to be no guide-letters in the margins,[34] and the paragraph-letters are written in the ink of the text, it appears that the paragraph-letters were written *en passant*, rather than added later in gaps left for them. It is probable that the task of editing the circuit-returns into GDB was intended to proceed at a steady but dignified pace, once the circuit-returns (*ealle þa gewrita*)[35] had been shown to William I before his departure for Normandy in the late summer of 1086. Those concerned in the production of GDB were not to know that the king would die before the final record of the *descriptio* had been completed; they presumably merely intended to have it ready for his next visit to England. In assessing the pressure under which Scribe A worked we should be careful not to be too affected by the hindsight of our knowledge of William's death. As an

---

[29] GDB, fos. 33, 42, 76, 81. All, however, are considerably less than full size folios. The last three are parts of spoiled sheets turned sideways so that unaffected parchment might be utilised.
[30] W. de G. Birch, 'The materials for the re-editing of the Domesday Book', in *Domesday Studies*, ed. Dove, 486–515, 492; Galbraith (1942), 161–77, 164–5; R. Welldon Finn, 'The evolution of successive versions of Domesday Book', *EHR*, lxvi (1951), 561–4, 561. The suggestion that the Domesday text in GDB was the work of a single scribe seems first to have been put forward by A. J. Fairbank; see *Domesday Re-Bound*, 34.
[31] See Rumble (1985), 34–7.
[32] Ibid., 35; and Galbraith (1974), 54–5.
[33] Galbraith (1961), 203–4; Rumble (1985), 35–6. Cf. *Domesday Re-Bound*, 24–9, and Appendix II.
[34] I am grateful to Dr Helen Forde, of the Public Record Office, for information on this point.
[35] *The Peterborough Chronicle*, ed. Clark, 9, s.a. 1085.

editor, both manipulating and rewriting text, he cannot be expected to have worked as fast as someone merely making a fair copy from a text in near identical format. It has been suggested in the past that Scribe A was writing from dictation,[36] but the fluidity of duct of his writing and the apparent fewness of errors that could be the result of mishearing rather than of misreading tells against that.[37] It was no doubt because one man was both editing and writing the final Domesday text that it was thought necessary for another to check and correct it against the exemplars. This does not mean that the 'checker' (Scribe B) was in a superior position to Scribe A, however. It was after all on the latter that the greatest editorial responsibility seems to have been laid. The use of one main scribe in the work may be explained both by the desire for as much editorial consistency as was possible and also perhaps to add to the authority of the final record, since the addition of unauthorised material in a different hand could be easily detected.

In contrast to GDB, which is almost entirely an 'editor's manuscript', its companion volume has a somewhat different textual status. LDB seems to be a fair copy whose scribes put into a new sequence, according to county, the text taken from a collection of pre-existing feudal booklets for the eastern Domesday circuit, each of which was already largely in a desired internal format.[38] Its status as a fair copy, no doubt tidier in appearance than its exemplars but still not necessarily without textual error and still (to judge from the interlinear and marginal additions *passim*) capable of being slightly expanded, is reflected by the regularity of the make-up of its quires and the general fewness of blank folios in the volume,[39] showing that it was possible to estimate accurately in advance the amount of text to be copied in each feudal chapter. The regular length of some of the stints of copying by the various scribes (see below, Appendix) and of some of the insertions of previously omitted text are also suggestive of a standard page-length in an exemplar or exemplars.[40]

Since LDB does seem to have been a more or less straight copy, rather than an edition like GDB, its inscription was able to be divided between a number of copyists without the introduction of any major textual inconsistencies into the record. Apart from the writer of the colophon and running-titles, discussed above (Scribe 7), six scribes were involved to varying degrees in writing the single column of text in LDB (see below, Appendix). The script used by them all was *litera carolina minuscula*, but there are sufficient differences in letter-formation and usage of abbreviations to distinguish between their individual hands. The six text-scribes (numbered in the order of their first occurrence in LDB) need to be carefully differentiated before their individual

---

[36] F. H. Baring, 'The Exeter Domesday', *EHR*, xxvii (1912), 309–18, 311–12.

[37] For a number of personal-name forms in GDB and LDB which may be the result of misreading at some stage in the making of the Domesday record, see J. McN. Dodgson, 'Some Domesday personal names, mainly post-Conquest', *Nomina*, ix (1985), 41–51, 45–7.

[38] See Rumble (1985), 32–4, 37.

[39] Ibid., 33; cf. *Domesday Re-Bound*, Appendix I, B.

[40] For insertions of previously omitted text in LDB on fos. 181rv and 229r–230r, see Rumble (1985), 33.

contributions can be compared. Their writing may be distinguished as follows:

SCRIBE 1 wrote most of the Domesday text for Essex and parts of that for Norfolk and Suffolk, as well as making additions to the work of some of his fellows in the latter two counties.[41] On fo. 182rv his writing is well spaced in order to fill the second half of a supply bifolium (fos. 181–2); on fos. 209v–222r it is rather less formal than usual.

The letters **b**, **h**, **l** and upright **d** have rather high ascenders which are usually finished by the addition of serifs to the left. Minims are either completed by a short upward stroke to the right or are without serifs.

a is a neat caroline form.

d is more usually round-backed than upright; in the latter, the flat top to its bowl sometimes intersects the back (fo. 4r, line 1, *ad*).

e has an oblique hairline tongue which projects at the end of a word.

g has an open, hook-shaped, descender.

r is normally 2-shaped after **o**.

ę has a long, trailing spur.

There are ligatures of **ct** and **st**.

Most majuscule letters are usually forms of rustic capitals, but uncial **A**, **D**, **E**, **M**, and **T** occur; **H** is always in the uncial form. Some examples of **B**, **D**, **P**, **R**, and **S** are markedly tall and thin. The back of **B**, **D**, **E** (rustic), **F**, **H**, **K**, **L**, **P**, and **R** is sometimes bent to the left before the bottom, preceding a completing stroke which curves to the right. The middle bar of uncial **E** curves upwards. The first two legs of uncial **M** are sometimes closed into an oval.

A 7-shaped overline is common as an abbreviation-mark above consonants but occurs above all three letters in *.i.r.e.* The nota for *et* is found in a variety of sizes but usually with a curved bar. The ampersand appears to be reserved exclusively for the final syllable *-et* as in *ten&*; it is completed by a horizontal stroke to the left. The use of a ligature of **t** with a following long-**i** at the end of *p(ra)ti* is very frequent. *Hund* is consistently used as the abbreviation for *Hundret*, in contrast to most of his colleagues' preferred use of the initial letter alone, with abbreviation-mark.[42]

A subscript comma indicates a short insertion from above, while a colon or a cross are used as *signes-de-renvoi*.

SCRIBE 2 wrote large sections of the Domesday text for Norfolk and Suffolk.[43] He was also responsible for writing the list of tenants in Norfolk,

---

[41] For his main stints, see below, Appendix. For examples of his additions to the work of Scribe 2, see LDB, fos. 154r (line 2; see below), 318r (line 16), 326r (margin and line 15); to that of Scribe 3, see fo. 158v (margin and lines 2, 7, 10); to that of Scribe 5, see fos. 161v (line 17), 362v (margin and lines 18–22), 398r (lines 6, 15, 20). Several of the additions made by Scribe 1 supply information regarding the T.R.W. subtenant. See also below, nn. 44–5. For a photograph of his hand, see Pl. VI(a); also, *Domesday Re-Bound*, Pl. V, 1 and 2 (addition to fo. 154r, line 2).

[42] Scribe 5 also very occasionally used the longer form of abbreviation, see below.

[43] See below, Appendix. For an illustration of his hand, see Pl. VI(b); also, *Domesday Re-Bound*, Pls. V, 3 and 4 (except the latter part of line 2), and VI, 9.

part of that for Suffolk,[44] and three out of the four partial interim lists of tenants which occur in Essex and Suffolk.[45] The display majuscules which he used in these lists have contrasting thick and thin strokes and are sometimes embellished with baubles or simple floreation (fo. 9r, line 1, overline; fo. 109r, **N** of *NORFULC*); baubles or floreate terminals are also found on some letters **H** (for *Hundret*; fos. 109v, line 1; 118v, line 6; 128r, line 6) and an occasional bauble is also added to the *paragraphos* (fos. 140v, line 18; 281v, lines 1, 20). In Suffolk he began his stint in rather a small size of writing (fos. 281v–288v, 291r–295v) but later gradually increased it to a more readable size. Chapter 7 of Norfolk (fos. 153v–156r) is at the other extreme of size, being written rather larger than usual. Notches are often added to the ascenders of **b**, **h**, **k**, **l** and upright **d**, but sometimes these are just clubbed. There are diagonal hairline serifs on minims.

a is usually a simple triangular shape, but a caroline form sometimes occurs (fo. 291r, line 2, *rengestuna*).

d more often has an upright than a round back.

g has a sharp angle beneath the head and a descender which is often almost closed.

r; the 2-shaped variety after **o** is very rare except in the *-orum* compendium.

The ligatures of **ct** and **st** are both rather high; the latter was not consistently used on fo. 9r (line 4, *West monasterio*).

Examples of most of his non-display majuscule letters can be seen on fo. 304r. **B** and **R** are sometimes given a waist beneath the upper lobe. **F** has a very pronounced serif at the bottom of the stem. **S** has a flattened lower curve.

The nota for *et* (with a curved bar and a short vertical stroke) is much more frequent than the ampersand; the latter also occurs for final *-et* and is completed by a serif to the left on the upward diagonal. The French form *pors* occurs as the plural of *por* for *porcus* (fo. 115r, line 18).

In making an insertion of text on fo. 324r (line 7) he used a colon as a *signe-de-renvoi*. Many of the other insertions in his text are the work of Scribe 1, however.[46]

SCRIBE 3 wrote the main entry for the borough of Colchester and a small part of the *Invasiones* in Essex, and also just over five pages of Chapter 8 in Norfolk.[47] His hand is rather uneconomical of space, without much advantage to its legibility, and this may explain why he was not given too much of LDB to write. His writing has the roundness and large size associated with the work of English-trained, rather than Norman-trained, scribes of the

---

[44] LDB, fo. 281r, where the first three lines of the first column (including the county name) are the work of Scribe 2 and the remainder is the work of Scribe 1.
[45] Scribe 2 wrote those on LDB, fos. 9r, 17r and 372r; that on fo. 292r is the work of Scribe 1.
[46] For examples, see above, n. 41.
[47] See below, Appendix. For an illustration of his hand, see Pl. VI(c); also, *Domesday Re-Bound*, Pls. V, 3, and VI, 5.

period.[48] This general impression of Englishness is backed up by the frequent use of insular rather than caroline **h**, and the occurrence of horizontal feet on minims.

a is almost always a rounded, triangular form; a caroline form occurs on fo. 158v (line 16, *cár* and *ác*).

d in the round-backed form has an upward curl to its ascender.

g has an open descender, rather like a flat hook.

r is often, but not always, 2-shaped after **o**.

ę has a long, sharp spur.

The ligatures of **ct** and **st** are exceptionally wide.

A is almost triangular, with a notch at its apex.

E is usually a large form of the minuscule shape with a very pronounced upward-curling tongue (fo. 104r, lines 8–10, 12–14, *Et*), but an uncial form also appears (fo. 157r, line 16, *Et*).

F lacks the upper part of its stem, appearing like a figure 7 standing on the junction of two lines meeting at a right angle (fo. 105r, last line, *Filieman*; fo. 157r, hundred-heading, *ENSFORDA*).

U has a very wide space between the top of its two arms and is flat where it rests on the line.

W is formed by two overlapping letters **U**, as above.

Scribe 3 used a characteristic form of the overline which is set at an angle of 45° to the horizontal and ends in a downward serif. The nota for *et* is very frequent and has a long descender, often curving to the left; the ampersand also occurs for *(-)et* and is completed by an upward-curling line to the right (fo. 158v, lines 12–13, 18, 21). The semi-colon shape in the abbreviations for *-bus*, *-que* and *sed* has a long, sometimes curled, descender (fo. 107r, line 8, *quibus*, and line 16, *unaquaque*; fo. 158v, line 13, *sed*). The syllable *-que* also occurs as **q**: (fo. 107r, line 14, *unoquoque*). The insular abbreviation for *con-* appears (fo. 106v, line 2, *consuedinem*; fo. 104r, line 19, *consuetudinem*), but c̄ is also found (fo. 158v, line 20, *concedente*); the latter form is used for *cum*. A similar alternation between insular and non-insular forms also occurs with abbreviations for est (÷, ē and ė) and *uel* (ł and uł), and represents one particular area of potential conflict in a writing-office employing both English- and Norman-trained scribes after 1066.

SCRIBE 4 seems to have written a short insertion of text in Norfolk into a space left by Scribe 2 for its addition.[49] Part of the insertion is in an enlarged size of writing to fill up the space allotted. Although there are similarities here to the writing of Scribe 6 (particularly in the **S**-shaped overline and the spidery spur of **ę**), other features are consistently different from the work of that scribe (the **g** with a broken curve to its open descender; and the nota for *et*, which has its curved bar above the line and usually has a serif on its oblique descender). Since there are also differences to the work of Scribe 2,

---

[48] See Ker, *English Manuscripts*, 22–3; Bishop, *English Caroline Minuscule*, xxiii–iv.

[49] LDB, fo. 110v, line 7, *ad godric* and lines 8–10, *.i. soch(emannus)* to *In eadem* (inclusive). See Pl. VII(a).

who wrote the surrounding text, and to that of the other text-scribes in LDB, it is advisable to take the writing here to be the work of a different scribe, entrusted with the task of filling in the omitted information.

SCRIBE 5 wrote short stretches of the Domesday text for Norfolk and about half of that for Suffolk.[50] His writing contains some very fine oblique lines which contrast with the thicker vertical strokes. On fo. 427v he manages to make a very cramped but still legible insertion into a small amount of space. The ascenders of the letters in the first line of some pages are elongated into the upper margin. There is occasionally some crude penwork decoration to the initial letter of *HUNDRET* (fos. 159v, line 5; 197r, line 20), or to the *paragraphos* (fos. 159v, line 5; 163v, line 7).

The ascenders of **b**, **h**, **k**, **l** and upright **d** are clubbed and are sometimes notched. There are diagonal hairline serifs on the minims.

a usually has a hairline approach-stroke to the left of its apex, but is sometimes almost triangular in shape.

d (round-backed) often has a curl to the right at the top of its ascender.

e has a very distinctive downward serif to its hairline tongue (also found on **E**, **ę**, **Ę**, **Æ** and the ampersand).

g has a curved, often closed, descender and is sometimes 8-shaped (fo. 429v, line 2, *longo*).

r; the 2-shaped form seems in general to be avoided, except in the *-orum* compendium, but does occur on fo. 166r (line 13, *FEOR HOV*) after a majuscule **O**.

ę (cf. above, **e**) sometimes has a serif to the right at the bottom of its hairline spur (fo. 166r, line 4, *terrę*).

The ligature of **st** is always used, but that of **ct** is very infrequent (one occurs on fo. 389v, line 10, *Facta*).

E (cf. above, **e**) is an uncial form, with the middle bar at a rising slant.

M is usually an uncial form with its first two legs closed into an oval and the third leg in the form of a curved descender.

N is usually an enlarged form of the minuscule shape.

P has an elliptical bowl.

Ę has a similar tongue to **e**, above.

The ampersand for *et* is used more frequently than by the other scribes of LDB; it has a similar tongue to **e**, above, and is also used for *-et* in *ten&*. The nota also occurs, however; it has a curved bar and a serif to the right on its fairly short downstroke. The abbreviation for *sed* consists of **s** followed by the nota (fo. 199r, last line); that for *hoc* is **h** with a dot above the curved stroke (fo. 407r, line 6). The word *Hundret* is usually shortened to just the initial letter with an abbreviation-mark, but does also occur as *Hvnđ* (e.g. fo. 194rv; cf. above, Scribe 1).

Some multiple points are used after chapter-headings (Suffolk, Chs. 28, 32). The *paragraphos* is often given a very pronounced diagonal serif to the bottom of its stem. Insertions of text are sometimes indicated by a wavy

[50] See below, Appendix. For an illustration of his hand, see Pl. VII(b); also, *Domesday Re-Bound*, Pl. VI, 6.

vertical line preceding the words to be added (fos. 164r, line 17; 387v, line 6), while a cross is sometimes used as a *signe-de-renvoi* (fo. 376v, last line). A diacritic is occasionally added to the last vowel of the place-name *eli* (fos. 411r, line 2; 430r, last line).

SCRIBE 6 appears only in the Domesday text for Norfolk, where he wrote one short and one quite substantial stint.[51] His writing on fos. 229r–230v is compressed into many more lines per page than elsewhere in order to accommodate text previously omitted,[52] while on fos. 235r–242v it is in a rather more formal mode than usual.

The ascenders of **b**, **h**, **k**, **l** and upright **d** are sometimes notched. Minims are often finished by rather thick serifs rising at an angle to the right.

e has a rising hairline tongue, projecting at the end of a word.

g has a round head and a descender consisting of an open curve.

r; the 2-shaped form is normally used after **o**.

ę has a spidery spur.

There are ligatures of **ct** and **st**; in the latter, the bar of **t** does not always meet the back of **s**.

E (rustic) has a rising middle bar which transects the back of the letter; another variety, an enlargement of the minuscule form, occurs less frequently.

G has quite a tight curl to it but is not closed; it sometimes has a hairline descender (fo. 262r, line 12, *GRENEHOGA*).

Characteristic forms of the overline are both an **S**-shaped line and a line rising at 45° to the horizontal. The nota for *et* is very distinctive, with a wide, straight bar and an almost vertical descender. The ampersand is rarely used, but is completed by a short horizontal stroke to the left (fo. 235r, lines 2–5). A long **s** with an oblique line through its waist stands both for *solidi* 'shillings' (fo. 228v, line 1) and for *seruus* 'slave' (fo. 245v, lines 8, 12), being distinguishable only by the context. The form *.t.e.r.* instead of *.t.r.e.* is quite frequent, for *tempore Edwardi regis* rather than *tempore regis Edwardi*.

Insertion of text is sometimes indicated by a subscript comma (fo. 234v, lines 15, 23).

As may be seen from the above description of the hands of the text-scribes in LDB, there was quite a large degree of variation between them in the way that they formed letters and in the marks of abbreviation they employed. The pattern of variation in the orthography of certain Latinised vernacular words (such as in the terms *de geldo*/*gelto* or *ad socham*/*socam*) in different parts of LDB, as also in the way that vernacular name-forms are treated by the different scribes, are probably areas where a computer-generated concordance to the Latin text might be fruitfully employed, both to investigate scribal preferences and to assess the influence of earlier rescensions of the material.

---

[51] See below, Appendix. For an illustration of his hand, see Pl. VII(c); also, *Domesday Re-Bound*, Pl. VI, 7 and 8. Cf. following note.

[52] For a reduced illustration of fo. 229r, see Rumble (1985), Pl. 3.3.

The system of punctuation found in the text of LDB is so generally consistent that it is likely that it was that specified by the scribes' supervisor(s). The *paragraphos* is frequently used to indicate a new sub-section of text within a chapter or a hundred. Within entries, the most common mark is the simple point, with the *punctus elevatus* occurring only very occasionally to subdivide a clause. The *punctus versus* is used to indicate a major pause within a paragraph or at the end of a chapter or entry. Splitting of a compound word at a line-end is shown either by a single or a double (-/-) hyphen.[53]

Two among the six text-scribes of LDB (Scribes 1 and 2; see below, Appendix) probably enjoyed a status superior to that of their fellows. Both occur as text-scribes in all three counties, both were also involved in the drafting and finalising of the lists of tenants therein. Scribe 1, who wrote most of Essex, also acted as the corrector and as the inserter of additional material in the other two counties. Scribe 2 shared the writing of most of Norfolk with Scribe 6, and of most of Suffolk with Scribe 5; he also inscribed the details of the Suffolk lands currently in dispute between the bishop of Bayeux and Robert Malet's mother, on fo. 450r.

Scribe 5 appears in both Norfolk and Suffolk, Scribe 6 only in Norfolk. Of the remaining two scribes, Scribe 4 is only found filling in a lacuna of a few lines in Norfolk, on fo. 110v. Scribe 3 occurs at the end of Essex (in the *Invasiones* and in the main Colchester entry) and in the first part of Chapter 8 of Norfolk but, as suggested above, may have been discharged from the task because of the excessive space which his writing consumed.

In general, the inscription of LDB appears to have been well organised. There was a capacity to have written simultaneously major parts of the text of all three counties. One of the largest units of text in Norfolk, however, the fief of Roger Bigot (Ch. 9), was divided between four scribes working in turn through the exemplar(s).[54] A few of the other chapters in LDB were also shared, but the majority are the work of a single scribe, apart from the corrections and additions added by Scribe 1, *passim*. The organisation of the material was aided, at least in some places, by the drawing up of partial lists of tenants such as those which survive on fos. 9r, 17r, 292r and 372r, each of which gives the order of the fiefs set to begin during the quire just started. The full lists of tenants in each county of LDB seem to have been constructed only after the respective county text was written, and follow the same order as those texts.[55] Because such county lists stood at the beginning of the respective county texts in circuit-returns, such as LDB, each was apparently transcribed into GDB before the county text concerned was edited, thus explaining many of the discrepancies in GDB between these lists and those parts of county texts subsequently reordered by Scribe A.[56]

---

[53] The single hyphen at the line-end was apparently thought the better practice at this period, see Ker, 'Salisbury Cathedral Library', 148.

[54] LDB, fos. 173r–190v; Scribes 1, 2, 5 and 6 (see below, Appendix).

[55] See Finn, *The Eastern Counties*, 66–7; Rumble (1985), 40.

[56] Galbraith (1961), 32–4; cf. Rumble (1985), 40.

There is sometimes a connection between a change of scribe in LDB and the physical structure of the volume. Thus fos. 183r–190v, written by Scribe 6, constitute a complete quire, while fos. 109r–156r, written wholly by Scribe 2, apart from corrections, make up six quires.[57] Other stints of writing probably relate to lengths of previously omitted text (fos. 182rv, 289r–290v) or to pages of an exemplar (fos. 178v–179v, 279rv).

The working relationships between individual scribes and the physical nature of now lost exemplars can be studied now that the individual hands in LDB have been distinguished. Similar details would no doubt have been revealed had other manuscripts survived which were undoubtedly intended as direct sources for GDB. At present, LDB is the only such direct source generally acknowledged to survive, even though it was, in the event, never so used. Although the exact status of the Exeter Domesday, whether as a direct or an indirect source for GDB, is the subject of continuing investigation,[58] there is no doubt that Exon too would repay closer palaeographical analysis, and I am glad to know that further work upon it is already in train.[59] I have no time here for more than the briefest of comments on Exon.[60] Its scribes were partially described by Welldon Finn in 1959, who distinguished the work of two major and at least eleven minor scribes.[61] Neil Ker described their writing as 'many rather poor hands of Norman type', apart from a few exceptions, one of them being the record of the Somerset holdings of Winchester Cathedral on fos. 173v–175v. This group of entries he described as being 'in a good small hand' and perhaps, from its uniformity, constituting a fair copy written later than the rest of the Domesday text in Exon.[62] It may be significant that this Winchester section of text includes the well-known reference to the bishop of Durham, while at Salisbury, being ordered by the king to write *in breuibus* the king's concession of these Somerset lands to Bishop Walkelin.

In general there seems to be as much, if not more, interchange of hands in Exon as in LDB, although such interchange is more difficult to interpret because, in contrast to LDB which was designed as not more than three (county) units of text, Exon was designed as a large number of feudal booklets, each of which could be constructed and used as a separate unit.[63]

---

[57] LDB, fo. 156v is blank. For the collation of LDB, see *Domesday Re-Bound*, Appendix I, B; and Rumble (1985), 33.

[58] For a convenient summary of the literature and a renewed assertion that the Exeter Domesday was the direct source of GDB's description of the south-western counties, see *Domesday Book, 9: Devon*, ed. C. and F. Thorn (2 parts, Chichester, 1985), ii, Exon. Introduction. The topic cannot be said to have yet been exhausted, however; the logistical difficulties in using the raw Exon material, still arranged in feudal booklets, as the direct source for GDB, an edition arranged in county booklets, would have been great.

[59] By Mrs T. Webber in relation to her current research on Salisbury Cathedral manuscripts of the period.

[60] For further comments, see Rumble (1985), 42–3.

[61] R. Welldon Finn, 'The Exeter Domesday and its construction', *Bulletin of the John Rylands Library*, xli (1959), 360–87, 362–8.

[62] Ker, *Medieval Manuscripts*, ii. 806–7.

[63] See Rumble (1985), 29–32.

The present order of text in Exon is almost certainly not the order in which it was written; neither is its Domesday text now complete as a collection of material, since most of the booklets for Wiltshire and those for parts of Devon and Dorset have not survived. Close palaeographical study of the manuscript is also considerably hampered by the lack of a facsimile edition, particularly one with unbound quires.

The appearance of the hand of Scribe A of GDB in three entries in Exon, added on previously blank folios, has not yet been fully explained but the additions do seem to have been made after the formulae and abbreviations used in GDB had been settled (since the additions also use them).[64] Whether the Exon booklets were at the time at Winchester, or whether Scribe A was at the place of inscription of their fellow quires (perhaps, but not necessarily, Exeter) is not known; at any rate, both he and the booklets concerned were at one time in the same place.

Another scribe of Exon was shown by Ker to have also written in fourteen different manuscripts copied for Salisbury Cathedral library after 1075 and was regarded by Ker as probably having been trained in England and as perhaps being a professional scribe.[65] If so, he may not have been the only professional scribe to be employed in the writing of the Domesday manuscripts. Professional writers were employed for special commissions at St Albans and Exeter in the late eleventh century and at Abingdon and Norwich in the early twelfth;[66] they supplemented the sometimes inadequate writing resources of monastic and cathedral communities and probably built up a wide experience of the different textual requirements of their various patrons.

The existence of freelance professional scribes in late eleventh-century England is part of the rather complex palaeographical context within which the surviving Domesday manuscripts need to be viewed. The hands found in the few contemporary manuscripts whose place of origin (rather than of provenance) is known need not always have been representative of the style of writing actually *taught* at such a place.[67] Similar considerations probably apply to manuscripts produced at English monasteries immediately after the

---

[64] Exon, fos. 153v and 436v. See Welldon Finn, 'Successive versions', 561–4; also Rumble (1985), Pl. 3.5.

[65] Ker, 'Salisbury Cathedral Library', 142, 154–9, and Pls. 20, a, b.

[66] See, respectively, R. M. Thomson, *Manuscripts from St Albans Abbey, 1066–1235* (2 vols., Woodbridge, 1982), i. 13–14; Bishop, 'Cambridge manuscripts: Part III', 192–7; Ker, *English Manuscripts*, 11, and n. 1; and F. Barlow, *The English Church, 1066–1154* (1979), 241. For a probable instance of a professional scribe at Bury St Edmunds in the late eleventh century, see Ker, ibid., 11. The only scribe named in DB (i. 162a), William *scriba*, in the city of Gloucester, may have been in the service of Earl William of Hereford, see *Domesday Book, 15 : Gloucestershire*, ed. J. S. Moore (Chichester, 1982), note to G4.

[67] It is here assumed that local styles of writing the various scripts used in late eleventh-century England were regular enough to be perpetuated by teaching them to novice scribes. Little is known, however, about the actual process of learning to write at this period, cf. L. E. Boyle, *Medieval Latin Palaeography: A Bibliographical Introduction* (Toronto, 1984), nos. 1666–78; M. T. Clanchy, *From Memory to Written Record: England, 1066–1307* (1979), 97–103; and Barlow, *English Church*, 217–40.

importation of Norman monks into their communities after 1066,[68] as also to documents produced at royal and ecclesiastical administrative centres during William I's reign. It is probable that some scribes trained in the England of Edward the Confessor were still operating in 1086–7 (Scribe A of GDB and Scribe 3 of LDB, above, may have been such), side by side with scribes trained on the Continent, and with those trained in England since 1066. It is advisable to think of 'writing-centres' at this period in particular, rather than of scriptoria. The use of the term 'scriptorium' implies a rigidity of training and a sustained control of style and overall design only really possible in a closed monastic community, such as Wearmouth-Jarrow in the early eighth century,[69] or in the governmental offices and the episcopal chanceries of centuries after the twelfth.[70] In the years immediately after 1066 there was competition not only between Anglo-Saxon minuscule and caroline minuscule scripts but also between English and Norman varieties of the latter.[71] It is probable that some at least of the lost sources and working documents of the Domesday Survey were written in Anglo-Saxon minuscule, while others were written to varying degrees of competence in different styles of caroline minuscule.[72] Any of them could also have included text written in rustic capitals, sometimes mixed with forms from square capital or uncial scripts.

Something of the variety of hands occurring in caroline minuscule script in post-Conquest England is well illustrated by the apparently-autograph episcopal subscriptions to an original record of 1072 associated with the dispute over the primacy between the archbishops of York and Canterbury.[73] There is a marked contrast between the bold, rounded hand of Bishop Wulfstan of Worcester (1062–95), who had been educated at the English abbeys of Evesham and Peterborough,[74] and the smaller, more angular hands of his episcopal colleagues, Lanfranc of Canterbury, Walkelin of Winchester, Thomas of York, Remigius of Dorchester and Arfast of Thetford, all of whom had been trained on the Continent. (The subscription of the papal legate Hubert is in the diplomatic minuscule used in the papal *curia*.) The main text of the document is written in a diplomatic style of

---

[68] For this importation, see D. Knowles, *The Monastic Order in England: A History of its Development from the Times of St Dunstan to the Fourth Lateran Council, 943–1216* (Cambridge, 1940), 126–7; Barlow, *English Church*, 183–6.

[69] See M. B. Parkes, *The Scriptorium of Wearmouth-Jarrow* (Jarrow Lecture, 1982).

[70] See L. C. Hector, *The Handwriting of English Documents* (2nd edn., 1966), 64–8; C. R. Cheney, *English Bishops' Chanceries, 1100–1250* (Manchester, 1950), 55–6.

[71] As above, n. 2.

[72] Cf. the examples of misreadings given by Dodgson, 45–7.

[73] Canterbury, Dean and Chapter Muniments, Chartae Antiquae, A.2; *Regesta* i, no. 65. For a facsimile, see *Palaeographical Society*, iii (1873–83), Pl. 170; and for a modern edition, see *Councils & Synods with other Documents Relating to the English Church* I, AD 871–1204, ed. D. Whitelock, M. Brett and C. N. L. Brooke (2 parts, Oxford, 1981), ii, no. 91. On the subscriptions, see Bishop and Chaplais, n. 18 to Pl. XXIX.

[74] See *The Vita Wulfstani of William of Malmesbury*, ed. R. R. Darlington (Camden 3rd ser. xl, 1928), 4: *Primis elementis literarum apud Euesham; perfectiori mox apud Burch scientia teneras informauit medullas.*

caroline minuscule by a Norman scribe who also wrote a manuscript of Ambrose for Christ Church, Canterbury, in a more formal book-script.[75] His work is a reminder that, in most periods, but particularly in the early medieval one, we should not divorce the palaeography of documents from that of books, since a well-trained scribe could adapt his hand to the character of the particular text before him as required.

The variety of styles of caroline minuscule script which are to be found in the few surviving original writs issued in the name of William I and William II makes it unsound to use Galbraith's term 'curial' to describe the script written by Scribe A of GDB, since no such official style of script can be shown to have existed at that time in England, except in relation to the papal *curia* and its agents.[76] Each of the three scribes whom Bishop and Chaplais identified as members of the permanent staff of the Anglo-Norman chancery wrote quite different styles of script.[77] The term 'curial script' seems to be an anachronism here, due to the common practice among historians of looking back at the Domesday manuscripts from a twelfth-century viewpoint, rather than seeing them in strictly contemporary terms.

Both the few surviving original royal, episcopal and private documents and the relatively larger number of surviving manuscripts from the late eleventh century form a corpus of palaeographical material to which the hands found in the Domesday manuscripts may be compared. This process is not without difficulty, however, largely because the surviving manuscripts are unevenly distributed as to their provenance, the place of origin of many is not known, and the hands in most have yet to be adequately described.[78] The important recent discovery by Michael Gullick of the hand of Scribe A of GDB in Trinity College, Oxford, MS 28, a manuscript of the late eleventh century which has a later medieval *ex libris* inscription of Winchester Cathedral Priory,[79] is a hopeful indication that a thorough search of this rather amorphous group of material might yield clues, if not complete

[75] Cambridge University Library, MS Kk.1.23, fos. 67–134; see Bishop, 'Cambridge manuscripts: Part I', 436.

[76] Galbraith (1942), 164–5: ' . . . volume i . . . was written by the scribes of the royal curia, doubtless at Winchester'. Galbraith (1961), 31: 'The first volume is written in a single distinctive set hand; and, I think, a curial hand which has affinities however distant with the later official hands of the king's court'.

[77] Bishop and Chaplais, xvii–xix.

[78] Most of the relevant manuscripts are included, with a note of their provenance or origin if known, in H. Gneuss, 'A preliminary list of manuscripts written or owned in England up to 1100', *Anglo-Saxon England*, ix (1981), 1–60; the omission of both GDB and LDB from this list is remarkable, although Exon is included. According to Gneuss's list, the only really significant groups of surviving manuscripts from the period *c.* 1066–1100 whose provenance is known are those from, in descending order of size: Salisbury; Exeter; Christ Church, Canterbury; Durham; St Augustine's, Canterbury; Worcester; and Bury St Edmunds. There are, however, several manuscripts in the list whose provenance is not yet known and others whose date is given merely as 's.xi'.

[79] Scribe A of GDB wrote fos. 89v–91r of the MS, see Gullick and Thorn (1986), 79 and n. 10. For the later medieval provenance, see H. O. Coxe, *Catalogus Codicum MSS. qui in Collegiis Aulisque Oxoniensibus Hodie Adservantur* (2 vols., Oxford, 1852), ii, s.v. The text is *Sermo de decem praeceptis dei et totidem plagis Ægypti*, attributed to St Augustine.

answers, to the many riddles that still remain in the Domesday manuscripts. Examples of the work of the other scribes of GDB, LDB and Exon may yet still be found. Such examples, if discovered, will not necessarily prove that the related Domesday manuscript was written at a particular place, however, since some scribes at least were mobile in the period around 1086–7. The Domesday manuscripts may in any case have been written in *ad hoc* writing-centres set up for the convenience of the various circuit commissioners, rather than in established monastic or secular writing-centres.

Wherever the surviving Domesday manuscripts were written, their main importance to the palaeographer is as a corpus of dated hands which together reflect a coexistence of different styles of script in England in 1086–7. Amongst other things, they serve to remind us that some Englishmen at least seem to have been able to find employment within the Norman administration, although with varying degrees of success.

APPENDIX

The Interchange of Hands in Little Domesday Book[80]

Folio	Scribe	Text
1r–8v	1	ESSEX, List of Tenants; caps. 1–2.
[9r	2	partial List of Tenants.]
9v–16v	1	caps. 3–8.
[17r	2	partial List of Tenants.]
17v–99r (line 8)	1	caps. 9–90 (part).
99r (lines 8–15)	3	cap. 90 (part).
99v–103v	1	cap. 90 (part).
104r–107v	3	Colchester.
108rv	—	*blank.*
109r–110v (line 7)	2	NORFOLK, List of Tenants;
		cap. 1 (part).
110v (lines 7, 8–10)	4	cap. 1 (part).
110v (line 11)–156r	2	caps. 1 (part)–7.
156v	—	*blank.*
157r–159v (line 4)	3	cap. 8 (part).
159v (line 5)–172v	5	cap. 8 (part).
173r (lines 1–26)	1	cap. 9 (part).
173r (line 26)–176r (line 17)	2	cap. 9 (part).
176r (line 18)–176v (line 9)	5	cap. 9 (part).
176v (line 10)–178v (line 17)	2	cap. 9 (part).
178v (line 17)–179v (line 17)	5	cap. 9 (part).
179v (line 18)–181v	2	cap. 9 (part).
182rv	1	cap. 9 (part).
183r–190v	6	cap. 9 (part).
191r–193r (line 5)	1	cap. 10 (part).
193r (line 6)–208v	5	caps. 10 (part)–13.
209r–222r	1	caps. 14–19 (part).
222v–273v (line 6)	6	caps. 19 (part)–65.
273v (line 7)–279r (line 1)	1	cap. 66 (part).
279r (line 1)–279v (line 1)	2	cap. 66 (part).
279v (line 1)–280r	1	cap. 66 (part).
280v	—	*blank.*
281r	2, 1	SUFFOLK, List of Tenants.
281v–288v	2	cap. 1 (part).
289r–290r (line 1)	1	cap. 1 (part).

[80] The present list differs in several respects from the comments on the interchange of hands made by Finn, *Eastern Counties*, 68–70, and Finn (1961), 174–8. Cf. also *Domesday Re-Bound*, 44–5. The present Appendix includes all changes of text-scribe that I have noticed in LDB, apart from corrections and very short additions *passim* (mostly by Scribe 1). It excludes the running-titles (most, if not all, by Scribe 7).

Folio	Scribe		Text
290r (line 2)–290v	5		cap. 1 (part).
291r–292r (line 17)	2		cap. 2.
[292r (lines 18–19)	1		partial List of Tenants.]
292v–294v (line 9)	2		cap. 3 (part).
294v (lines 9–18)	1		cap. 3 (part).
294v (line 18)–297r (line 4)	2		cap. 3 (part).
297r (lines 4–11)	1		cap. 3 (part).
297r (line 12)–298v (line 4)	2		cap. 4 (part).
298v (lines 5–14)	1		cap. 4 (part).
298v (line 14)–354r (line 9)	2		caps. 4 (part)–9 (part).
354r (lines 10–11)	1		cap. 9 (part).
354r (line 12)–356r	2		caps. 10–13.
356v–372r (line 15)	5		cap. 14.
[372r (lines 16–19)	2		partial List of Tenants.]
372v– 378v (line 10)	5		caps. 15–16.
378v (lines 11–16)	1		cap. 17.
379r–388v (line 13)	5		caps. 18–21.
388v (lines 14–23)	1		cap. 22.
389r–449v	5		caps. 23–76.
450r (lines 1–16)	2		Malet/Bayeux dispute.
450r (lines 17–21)	7	COLOPHON.	
450v	—		blank.

Domesday Book and the Geographer

H. C. Darby

ANYONE WHO WORKS on Domesday Book soon comes to have two views about it.[1] On the one hand, he can have nothing but admiration for what may be the most remarkable statistical document in the history of Europe. It is not surprising that so many scholars have felt its fascination, and have discussed again and again what it says about economic, social and legal matters. It is also a great collection of geographical facts, and the geographer, as he turns over the folios, cannot but be excited at the vast array of information that passes before his eyes – information about population, and about arable, wood, meadow and other resources.

But there is another point of view. When this great wealth of data is examined more closely, one encounters many problems. Domesday Book calls itself merely a *descriptio*, but it is far from being a simple description and a straightforward document. It bristles with difficulties. What follows is a brief view of some of its frustrating aspects. While recognising the remarkable character of the Book, we must acknowledge that the evidence it presents to us is not without its limitations.

THE INCOMPLETE RECORD OF PLACE-NAMES

Any geographical study of Domesday Book must rest on the exact identification of place-names. Some 13,400 place-names are recorded, but about 3 per cent of these remain unidentified, and there are also other complications. Many large Domesday manors included a variety of components (berewicks, *membra* or *appendicii*), sometimes named, sometimes not. There is no way of telling whether the unnamed berewicks were at places described in other entries for a county. Thus in Shropshire, Ford (255b) had 14 such berewicks,

---

[1] Folio references to Great Domesday Book, Little Domesday and the Exeter Book are normally given in parentheses after a place-name. The context of the reference will make clear which book is meant.

and Worthen (255b) had 13. Altogether there were 135 unnamed berewicks in Shropshire. There are yet other entries that do not even tell us the number of dependencies attached to a manor, but merely refer to their existence. On fo. 65, unspecified numbers of such dependencies are entered for each of four Wiltshire manors – Corsham, Melksham, Netheravon and Rushall. Furthermore, even when there is no mention of dependencies, we may suspect their existence on many manors with substantial resources. It is very likely that, for example, the large Oxfordshire manor of Banbury (DB, i. 155a), with 40 ploughteams and a recorded population of 107, included the resources of Charlbury (a pre-Domesday name) and its hamlets. Sonning in Berkshire was another such manor (58a), so was Farnham in Surrey (31a).[2] Examples could be multiplied.

A further element of uncertainty arises from the fact that the folios often include a number of unnamed entries, and again we cannot tell whether these refer to places named elsewhere in the text. There were, for example, 16 such anonymous holdings in Berkshire, 26 in Surrey, and as many as 52 in Sussex.[3] Chance evidence for Herefordshire enables us to identify 14 of its 27 anonymous holdings; 4 of these were at places named elsewhere in the Domesday text, but the remaining 10 were not.[4] Other documents closely associated with Domesday Book (such as the Ely Inquisition and the *Excerpta* of St Augustine's Abbey) yield another 35 non-Domesday names, 26 of which can be connected with anonymous Domesday holdings.[5]

Documents of a slightly later date tell the same story. The evidence for Kent is striking. Here was the Weald with its countryside of hamlets. Three lists of places dating from about the year 1100 add over 150 place-names to the 347 recorded in the folios for Kent. The information about these small settlements (yet large enough to have churches) has been compressed under a more limited range of names in Domesday Book itself.[6] Then again, the Lindsey Survey (1115–18) adds 12 place-names to the 492 that appear in the Domesday description of Lindsey.[7] In the same way the Leicestershire Survey of 1129–30 (although not complete) adds 26 names to the 292 in the Domesday county.[8] To sum up: it is clear that the number of places named in Domesday Book was not the sum total of the separate units of settlement in England in 1086.

There is a further constraint on any study of settlement in 1086 in that Domesday place-names covered very different types of settlement, ranging from nucleated villages to dispersed hamlets and isolated farmsteads. We do not know, with any certainty, the relative distribution of these various types

[2] F. M. Stenton in *VCH Oxfordshire*, I (1939), 378, 393; M. Hollings in *VCH Oxfordshire*, X (1972), 135; J. H. Round in *VCH Berkshire*, I (1906), 301; Maitland, 13–14.
[3] *DB Gazetteer*, 17, 422, 433.
[4] V. H. Galbraith and J. Tait, *Herefordshire Domesday, 1160–1170*, passim.
[5] Darby (1979), 21–4.
[6] Ibid., 24–6.
[7] C. W. Foster and T. Longley, *The Lincolnshire Domesday and the Lindsey Survey* (Lincoln Record Society, 1924), xliv. 237–60.
[8] C. F. Slade, *The Leicestershire Survey* (Leicester, 1956).

in the eleventh century. The south-west peninsula, especially that part to the west of the River Parrett, is today very largely a land of dispersed settlements, and it was probably so in 1086. The Domesday place-names of Devonshire amount to 980, but the number of separate settlements in the county has been put at many times that total, by apportioning the details of Domesday manors among the isolated farmsteads of modern parishes.[9]

These limitations inherent in the evidence mean that maps of Domesday place-names enable us to gauge the intensity of settlement over the face of the country only in a general way. Certain broad features stand out – the barrenness of those uplands over, say, 800 ft above sea level, the emptiness of much of the Fenland and of the Breckland and other areas of light infertile soils. And, as we think of such areas, we must remember that the lack of Domesday names in the Weald, for example, does less than justice to its scattered pioneering communities.

THE INCONSISTENCIES OF THE CIRCUIT DOMESDAY BOOKS

The method of the making of the Survey is very relevant to our understanding of its contents. That method was geographical, and was based upon the ancient divisions of the realm, consisting in descending order of shires and then of hundreds or wapentakes and finally of vills. It is reasonable to suppose that the counties were grouped into circuits visited by different teams of commissioners. There is no proof of this, but it is suggested by differences in phraseology between groups of counties. There were probably seven circuits (Fig. 1) The older view was that the returns sworn at the courts of the hundreds were brought, by way of the shire courts, to the King's Treasury at Winchester where they were edited to produce the Book we know.[10]

This view was challenged in 1942 by Professor V. H. Galbraith of Oxford who produced a much more credible hypothesis. He believed that local summaries were made for groups of counties (that is for each circuit), and that it was these Circuit Domesday Books that were brought to Winchester for editing and assembly. One local summary, however (that for the three eastern counties) was never incorporated into Great Domesday Book, and it became known as Little Domesday Book. It so happened that the greater part of a draft of another circuit summary also survived, and this did get incorporated. It covers much of the south-western circuit, and is in the possession of Exeter Cathedral. Both these circuit summaries are far more detailed than Great Domesday Book. When one compares the Exeter Book with the final volume, one sees how the clerks made mistakes in copying, how they compressed their material and, above all, how much they omitted.

The differences between the seven Circuit Books were not only those of

---

[9] W. G. Hoskins, *Provincial England* (London, 1963), 15–52.
[10] V. H. Galbraith (1942), 161–77. Expanded in Galbraith (1961).

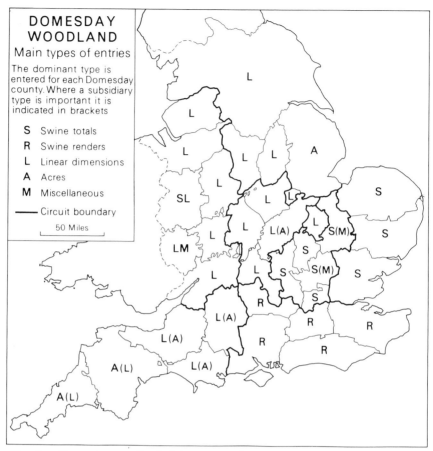

DOMESDAY WOODLAND
Main types of entries

The dominant type is entered for each Domesday county. Where a subsidiary type is important it is indicated in brackets

S Swine totals
R Swine renders
L Linear dimensions
A Acres
M Miscellaneous

—— Circuit boundary

50 Miles

Fig. 1. Domesday woodland: Main types of entries (by Domesday counties).

phraseology but often of substance, and this must be emphasised. Although the groups of commissioners followed the same general instructions, they did not always interpret their task in quite the same way. The result was differences in content, not only between the circuits, but between counties within a circuit, and sometimes between hundreds within a county. It seems as if behind the apparently monolithic character of Domesday Book lay, as Galbraith put it, 'a congeries of widely varying regions, each with its own age-long special customs and usages'.[11] Some day, perhaps, computer technology might be enlisted to explore the variation in the evidence presented to different hundred juries at an early stage of the Inquest.

A striking example of the way in which the returns differed is seen in the

[11] V. H. Galbraith (1974), 14.

treatment of wood.[12] One of the questions that was asked was *Quantum silvae*. How much wood? Broadly speaking the answers fell into one of five categories (Fig. 1). Sometimes they said that there was enough wood to support a given number of swine, for the swine fed upon acorns and beechmast. A variant of this was a statement not of total swine but of annual renders of swine in return for pannage. A third type of answer gave the length and breadth of wood in terms of leagues, furlongs and perches. A fourth variant gave the size of wood in acres, but we cannot assume that these were the equivalent of modern statute acres, or that they were constant from place to place. The fifth category of answers was a miscellanous one which included a variety of phrases, e.g. wood for fuel or for repairing houses. Normally each county was characterised by one type of entry with a few subsidiary entries in a different style.

The problem that results from this variety is clear. Apart from the difficulties presented by each type of entry there is an overwhelming obstacle. We cannot equate the different types, and so reduce them to a common denominator. It is true that when adjoining counties use the same notation we may assume that the relative distribution of woodland was more or less correct. But when we pass into areas with different notations we cannot be sure that our map conveys a correct visual picture. We may, of course, try to secure equivalence by making assumptions, but the result can only be subjective.

The type of wood entry differs, not only between circuits and between counties but sometimes also between hundreds. The normal formula for Norfolk was that of swine totals, but five of the eight vills with wood in Clackclose hundred made their returns in linear measurements. And in Lincolnshire the normal formula used acres, but some of the western wapentakes of the county returned their wood partly in linear measurements; the wood of Axholme hundred was returned entirely in this way. Or yet again, miscellaneous references to wood for fuel and for repairing houses occur for a group of twenty-nine vills in the western hundreds of Cambridge-shire in contrast to the swine entires used for the eastern hundreds of the county.[13]

Some hundreds, apparently, chose not to mention their wood or the scribe not to enter it. Thus no wood was entered for the six vills of Cottesloe hundred in the clay vale of Buckinghamshire. Even more striking is the absence of any mention of wood for the eight north-western hundreds of Berkshire. One of these was the hundred of Horner, set in the great bend of the Thames. In this hundred, several charters of the eleventh and twelfth centuries refer to the woods of Cumnor and Bagley, but there is no reference to wood in the Domesday entry for Cumnor nor is there any mention of Bagley Wood.[14]

---

[12] Darby (1979), 172–94.

[13] H. C. Darby, *The Domesday Geography of Eastern England* (Cambridge, 1971), 125 (Norfolk), 59 (Lincolnshire), 297–8 (Cambridgeshire).

[14] Darby (1979), 194; F. H. Baring, *Domesday tables for the counties of Surrey, Berkshire, Middlesex, Hertford, Buckingham and for the New Forest* (London, 1909), 133 (Bucks), 41 (Berks).

Fig. 2. Pasture in 1086: Frequency of record (by Domesday counties).

Other types of land utilisation also raise problems. This is certainly true of pasture (Fig. 2). In the north, none is mentioned for the counties of York and Nottingham, and only rarely does it appear for those of Derby and Lincoln. Likewise very little is recorded for the western circuit – none at all for the counties of Shrewsbury and Stafford and only infrequently for those of Chester, Gloucester, Hereford and Worcester. Or again, in the midland circuit it is difficult to see why pasture should be entered for nearly one half of the villages of Oxfordshire, but hardly ever for those of the counties of Northampton and Warwick, and never for that of Leicester. Only for the south-western circuit are pasture entries frequent.

Over the country as a whole, pasture was usually recorded in terms of acres or of linear dimensions. But for three adjoining counties, all in the same circuit, the usual formula was 'pasture for the cattle of the village' – for those of Cambridge, Hertford and Middlesex. Taking these three counties

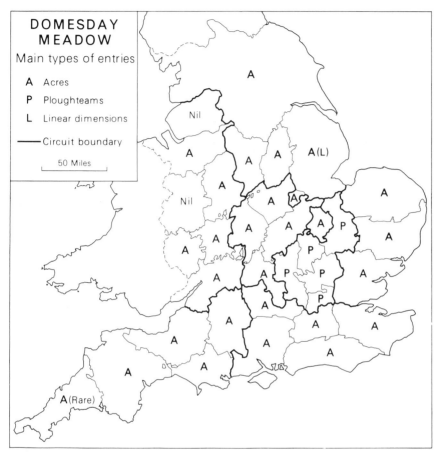

Fig. 3. Domesday meadow: Main types of entries (by Domesday counties).

In Lincolnshire, entries with linear dimensions form a very small proportion of the total number.

together, pasture was entered for some 63 per cent of their villages. The corresponding figure for the other two counties (those of Bedford and Buckingham) was below 3 per cent. Very little pasture was entered for the eastern circuit, but Essex was unusual in having a record not only of pasture but 'pasture for sheep' in 114 places (i.e. 26 per cent), mostly in a belt along the coastal marshes. Later evidence shows that, here, the making of cheese from the milk of ewes was an important activity.[15] To sum up: this irregular record makes it impossible to obtain any idea of the distribution of pasture over the kingdom as a whole.

Meadow, on the other hand, was more regularly recorded. It was usually measured in acres, and we are able to obtain a general idea of its distribution over most of the kingdom (Fig. 3). But even so there are problems. In the

[15] Darby (1974), 157–8; J. H. Round in *VCH Essex*, I (1903), 368–74.

first place we cannot assume that these acres were the equivalent of our modern statute acres, or that they were of uniform size throughout the country. The large amounts entered for the Lincolnshire villages are puzzling. It is difficult to see why they should be so large as compared with the amounts entered for, say, Norfolk and Suffolk. Can we suppose that the term 'meadow' was used in a more extended sense in Lincolnshire? Or might the explanation lie in a difference in size between the Lincolnshire and the East Anglian acre? There is yet another problem. The returns for one circuit did not follow the general style. For the five counties of the Bedford–Middlesex circuit the usual formula was 'meadow for n plough-teams' or 'for n oxen', that is the number of teams of eight oxen it was capable of feeding. These cannot be converted into acres with any certainty. Thirdly, and finally, why was no meadow entered for Shropshire, especially along the Severn lowlands?

Inconsistency and idiosyncracy also appear in the record of other items. We cannot believe that there were no markets in Dorset, in Essex, and in a dozen or so other counties. Or that there were no fisheries in the rivers of Leicestershire and Wiltshire, or no salt-pans off the coast of Somerset, or only one church in each of the adjoining counties of Leicester and Warwick. Nor can we believe that in the whole of England there were no more than 92 fishermen, or 64 smiths, or 10 iron-workers, or 6 millers, or a solitary carpenter. Or again, why should the mention of swineherds be limited to seven counties? And why should two-thirds of the total appear for Devonshire (370 out of 556)?[16] Are we to assume that these various categories of workers were entered by chance, and that elsewhere their respective fellow-workers were included in some general category such as villeins?

THE IMPERFECT COUNT OF POPULATION

Given the large body of material and the use of Roman numerals, it is not surprising that a count of population reveals many uncertainties. Comparison of the Domesday text with that of the Exeter Book shows many omissions and differences; so does comparison with the Cambridgeshire Inquisition.[17] Then again a number of entries are not specific. In Herefordshire, for example, there were unspecified numbers of men (*homines*) at Bromyard (DB, i. 182b). Hopley's Green (184b), Ledbury (182a) and Lyonshall (184b), and an unspecified number of bordars at Cradley (182a); while at Eastnor (182a) we hear of '2 bordars with certain others'. Similar examples could be given from other counties.

At times, the scribe was conscious of the imperfection of his work. An entry for Overton in Wiltshire (65b) leaves space for the number of villeins to be inserted, and in the margin the scribe wrote the letters 'rq' (*require*) in

---

[16] Darby (1979), 81–3.
[17] Darby (1979), 57–60.

red ink to remind himself to look into the matter, but if he did the answer was never entered in the Domesday text. No information at all appears for one of the two holdings at Woodchester in Gloucestershire (164a) because, so the entry runs, no one came to give an account of it to the king's commissioners, and no one was present at the making of the description (*De quo manerio nemo legatis regis reddidit rationem, nec aliquis venit ad hanc descriptionem*). Something similar happened at Hankham in Sussex (22) and at other places.

Another kind of imperfection can be seen in the entry for Avebury in Wiltshire (65b). It was assessed at 2 hides, was worth 40s a year, and had a church, but nowhere is there mention of those who worshipped there and of the land they tilled. This is not the only church without any record of a congregation. The entry does, however, mention a priest, which so many other entries for churches do not. We also hear of many monastic houses and cathedrals but only rarely of monks and canons. Thus Spalding in Lincolnshire is said to be a berewick of Crowland (351b), but of Crowland itself we are told nothing, neither of the settlement nor of its monks; and yet Crowland Abbey was large enough to hold property in Lincolnshire, Cambridgeshire and elsewhere. Moreover, associated with the greater abbeys there must have been servants and retainers, but only for the abbey of Bury St Edmunds in Suffolk are we given an account of those 'who daily wait upon the Saint, the abbot and the brethren' (DB, ii. 372a). Finally the households of the king and of the barons of the realm must have employed considerable numbers of people who went unrecorded. And to these must be added the garrisons of the castles built soon after the Conquest.

Other doubts arise, for example, from the uncertain record of rent-payers (*censores* or *censarii*).[18] Domesday Book enters a total of 160, distributed over six widely separated counties:

Yorkshire	55	Lincolnshire	14
Derbyshire	42	Dorset	11
Essex	36	Nottinghamshire	2

In Derbyshire, none of the forty-two *censores* are entered for the estates of Burton Abbey, but two early twelfth-century surveys show that the abbey did have *censores*, not only in Derbyshire but also in the adjoining county of Stafford for which none are recorded in Domesday Book. On thirteen of the abbey's manors in these two counties over one-third of the total recorded population were *censores* – that is within a generation or so after 1086. Some scholars have thought that they were omitted by the Domesday scribes. Others have believed that they were new settlers since 1086. Either hypothesis raises difficulties; and these are not lessened by what Stenton called the

---

[18] F. H. Baring, 'Domesday Book and the Burton Cartulary', *EHR*, xi (1896), 98–102; P. H. Sawyer, 'The wealth of England in the eleventh century', *TRHS*, 5th ser., xv (1965); J. F. R. Walmsley, 'The "censarii" of Burton Abbey and the Domesday population', *North Staffs. Jour. of Field Studies*, viii (1968), 73–80; P. Vinogradoff, *English society in the eleventh century* (Oxford, 1908), 462–3.

'capricious distribution' of *censores* which suggests that they may not have been consistently entered both over individual counties and over England as a whole.[19]

Apart from these uncertainties, and there are many of them, a more general question is raised by the enumeration of slaves. They numbered some 28,000, that is about 10 per cent of the recorded population. There has been argument about whether they were entered as individuals or as heads of households as for other categories of population.[20] One who considered what he called this 'difficult question' was Maitland, who said that we could not be sure that the enumeration of slaves was 'always governed by one consistent principle'. Such doubts affect any estimate of the importance of slavery in the realm as a whole, whether they amounted to 10 per cent of the working population or only some much smaller figure, such as 2½ per cent. It also affects any estimate of total population and any attempt to indicate its varying density over the face of the country.

The enumeration of slaves also raises another problem. Very few are entered for the counties of Derby, Nottingham and Lancaster, and none for those of Huntingdon, Lincoln, York and for *Roteland*. We might therefore conclude that slavery had ceased to exist in these latter counties were it not for the fact that a summary in the Ely Inquisition shows the presence of slaves on the four Huntingdonshire manors of the abbey.[21] They number just over 10 per cent of the recorded population of their manors, and this percentage is about the same as that for the slaves of the adjacent counties of Cambridge and Northampton. This immediately suggests the possibility of unrecorded slaves on the other fiefs of Huntingdonshire. That suspicion is strengthened by the fact that the 24 slaves recorded for Nottinghamshire are limited to 3 of the 30 or so fiefs in the county, and that of the 20 slaves recorded for Derbyshire, 13 are entered for a single fief out of 17 or so.[22] Might not the other fiefs of these two counties have had unrecorded slaves? Can we be sure that there were no slaves even in Lincolnshire and Yorkshire? It was Maitland who wrote: 'that there should have been never a *theów* in all Yorkshire and Lincolnshire is hardly credible, and yet we hear of no *servi* in these counties'.[23]

THE ENIGMATIC MEASUREMENTS

The linear measurements commonly used in the Domesday text are leagues, furlongs and, occasionally, perches. The length of each of these units is uncertain, and we cannot be sure of the relationship of the furlong to the

[19] F. M. Stenton in *VCH Derbyshire*, I (London, 1905), 314.
[20] Maitland, 17, 34; P. Vinogradoff, 463; Darby (1979), 73–4.
[21] ICC, 169; Darby, *Eastern England*, 330–1.
[22] F. M. Stenton in *VCH Nottinghamshire*, I (London, 1906), 243; F. M. Stenton in *VCH Derbyshire*, I (London, 1905), 314.
[23] F. W. Maitland, 34–5.

league. Moreover, in addition to this uncertainty, the significance of the formulae in which these dimensions appear is not clear, especially so in three contexts: (1) in the description of the wood of many counties; (2) in certain general formulae peculiar to Yorkshire and some other northern counties; (3) in the statement of assessment that is characteristic of East Anglia (Norfolk and Suffolk).

Measurement of wood in many counties

As we have seen, the woodland of many counties was measured by stating its length and breadth. But immediately we must ask: were these the extreme diameters of irregularly shaped areas or the mean diameters? Or were they intended to convey some other notion? It is impossible to tell; but we cannot assume that a definite geometrical figure was in the minds of those who supplied the information. Wood certainly did not grow in neat rectangular blocks. Some estimates, especially those for Shropshire, give only one dimension – *n leuuae silvae*. Comparison of the Exchequer entries with those of the Exeter text shows that, for the south-west at any rate, a single dimension was occasionally used when the length and breadth were the same, e.g. for West Stafford in Dorset (see below).

Whatever they imply it seems that sometimes these linear dimensions may have represented a total of separate tracts of wood. In the first place, the phrase *per loca*, which is found in a number of entries, implies a scattered distribution as at Bulcote (DB, i. 288b) in Nottinghamshire, where we read of wood 1 league by 8 furlongs. In the second place, a single set of measurements is often found in composite entries covering a number of widely separated places; thus the wood of Ashford and its twelve berewicks (272b) in Derbyshire is said to have been 2 leagues by 2. Even more striking examples appear in the abbreviated descriptions of some Lancashire hundreds; the wood of the fifteen manors of Newton hundred (269b) was 10 leagues long by 6 leagues and 2 furlongs broad. It is difficult to see by what arithmetic this total could have been reached. Similar problems are involved in linear entries for pasture and meadow.

The Exeter text sometimes gives separate quantities for components that are combined into single totals in Domesday Book itself. The amounts are usually in acres which involves only simple addition. But two entries in Dorset and one in Somerset are in linear dimensions. The relevant entries are underlined in the table on p. 112: the brackets in the West Stafford entries enclose information that is inferred (see above). Any hope that a comparison of the Exeter and Exchequer entries might provide a clue to the method of Domesday mensuration is soon dashed. It is at once apparent that the arithmetic behind the Domesday totals for linear measurements is very strange. Surely, at Frome, twice 8½ × 8½ furlongs of pasture do not make 17 × 17 furlongs (Fig. 4). Nor at West Stafford, do twice 8 × 8 furlongs of pasture make 16 × 16 furlongs. And at the three Somerset vills, it is impossible to reconcile the Exeter measurements of wood with the Domesday total, because one entry is in acres. From these unusual entries it is

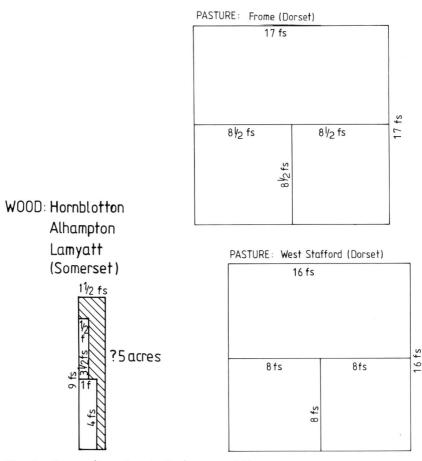

Fig. 4.   Linear dimensions in Exchequer and Exeter texts.

Frome (Dorset)
    Exchequer DB (81b): W. 9 acs; M. 20 acs; P. 17 fs × 17 fs
    Exeter DB (48b): (a) W. 4½ acs; M. 10 acs; P. 8½ fs × 8½ fs
                 (b) W. 4½ acs; M. 10 acs; P. 8½ fs × 8½ fs

Hornblotton, Alhampton, Lamyatt (Somerset)
    Exchequer DB (90b): W. 9 fs × 1½ fs; M. 55 acs; P. 20 acs
    Exeter DB (169b–70):
        Hornblotton: W. 4 fs × 1 f; M. 20 acs; P. (nil)
        Alhampton: W. 5 acs; M. 15 acs; P. (nil)
        Lamyatt: W. 3½ fs × ½ f; M. 20 acs; P. 20 acs

West Stafford (Dorset)
    Exchequer DB (83b): W. 8 acs; M. 24 acs; P. 16 fs (× 16 fs)
    Exeter DB (55b): (a) W. 4 acs; M. 12 acs; P. 8 fs (× 8 fs)
                 (b) W. 4 acs; M. 12 acs; P. 8 fs (× 8 fs)

difficult to see how the Domesday clerks dealt with the linear measurements that came their way. A simple diagram will emphasise the point (Fig. 4).

Linear measurements in Yorkshire, etc.

The Yorkshire folios are unusual in that linear dimensions frequently appear not only in connection with wood and sometimes with meadow but in a more general context.[24] Towards the end of many Yorkshire entries comes a statement that the whole manor (*Totum manerium*) or the whole (*Totum*) is so many leagues long and so many broad. Very occasionally the measurements refer not to 'the whole' but specifically to arable land (*terra arabilis*) to open land (*terra plana, campus*) or to moors (*morae*). These linear entries raise problems. Thus in the West Riding manor of Whiston with its sokeland at Handsworth (308), how did its woodland, 3 leagues by 1, fit into 'the whole manor', 2½ leagues by 2? Such entries are very numerous, and are far too frequent to be the result of chance error. Moreover, the dimensions sometimes cover a number of places geographically quite separate. Thus seven of the eight berewicks of the manor of Wakefield (299b) lay between 15 and 25 miles distant from the manor, and yet it seems clear that the phrase 'the whole, 6 leagues in length and 6 leagues in breadth' was intended to cover all nine vills.

In the rest of the northern circuit similar linear dimensions appear occasionally for Lincolnshire, e.g. on fos. 338a and 340a; they also occur in five entries for Derbyshire and in one for Nottinghamshire. There are, in addition, ten such entries for Cheshire in the western circuit. They occur nowhere else in Domesday Book. Very curiously, however, they are to be found in the Ely Inquisition, in entries for the four Huntingdonshire manors held by the abbot; and each statement is prefaced by the word *Totum*.[25] We may wonder whether they had appeared in the text of the circuit return but had been omitted from the Domesday text. But how they were calculated, and what they mean, we do not know.

Linear measurements in East Anglia

Linear measurements also appear in the folios for Norfolk and Suffolk, but they differ from those of Yorkshire in that they are associated with the method of geld assessment peculiar to these two counties.[26] This was based on the fiscal divisions of a hundred known as 'leets', and these in turn comprised villages. Each leet contributed so many pence to every 20s at

---

[24] H. C. Darby and I. S. Maxwell (eds.), *The Domesday Geography of Northern England* (Cambridge, 1977), 44–6, 125–8, 136, 200–2, 208.

[25] Darby, *Eastern England*, 46–7 (Lincolnshire); Darby and Maxwell, *Northern England*, 303–6 (Derbyshire); 245 (Nottinghamshire); 352–3 (Cheshire); Darby, *Eastern England*, 332–3 (Huntingdonshire); ICC, 166–7.

[26] C. Johnson in *VCH Norfolk*, II (1906), 5–6, 204–11; B. A. Lees in *VCH Suffolk*, I (1911), 361–4, 412–16; Darby, *Eastern England*, 119–22 (Norfolk), 175–7 (Suffolk); Finn, *The Eastern Counties*, 58–61.

which the hundred was assessed. There are variations in the formula, but the entry for Thorpland in Norfolk (DB, ii. 206a) may be taken as representative: 'This land is 1 league in length and 4 furlongs in breadth, and it renders 8*d* to the king's geld of 20*s*' (*Haec terra habet i leugam in longo et iiii quarentenas in lato et reddit viii d. in gelto regis de xx solidis.*]

A few entries record measurements in miles. Of ten such entries in Norfolk, eight come from South Greenhoe and two from Freebridge, two adjoining hundreds in the west. Here is another example of hundredal idiosyncrasy. Some entries are very detailed, but what do they mean? As measurement and geld are so closely linked in the text one might expect to find some correspondence between them. This is not so. They show no proportional relationship, neither between themselves, nor with the fiscal carucates that appear in the same entries. Much ingenuity over the years has failed to bring a solution.

THE MISSING LIVESTOCK

In its account of the making of the Survey under the year 1085, the Anglo-Saxon Chronicle says that not 'an ox nor a cow nor a pig' was left out. Great Domesday Book certainly mentions oxen in connection with ploughteams and pigs in connection with woodland, but it tells us practically nothing about such animals as cows, sheep, goats and horses, and includes only a few scattered references to such livestock.[27] There was, for example, a render of horses from Fulbourn (DB, i. 190a) in Cambridgeshire; there was a cattle farm (*vacaria*) at Denby (317a) near Cumberworth in the West Riding; there was a sheepfold (*ovile*) at Eynesbury (206b) in Huntingdonshire. One entry alone mentions shepherds (*berquaril*); there were ten at Patcham (26a) to the north of Brighton – a reminder that sheep-rearing must have been an important occupation on the South Downs. There is an entry in Great Domesday Book in which the fuller record of livestock seems to have survived from a Circuit Book (139a). It is an account of an unnamed holding of half a hide belonging to Humfrey (held from Eudo the Steward) in Hertfordshire. Here, we are told, were 68 *animalia* and 350 sheep and 150 pigs and 50 goats and 1 mare. It is difficult to see why this information should appear here except maybe by chance.

The two surviving Circuit Books, however, show what was omitted from Great Domesday Book. Little Domesday Book provides detail about the large demesne flocks on the light sandy soils of western Norfolk and Suffolk (Fig. 5). As many as 1029 sheep were entered for Mildenhall in Suffolk (DB, ii. 263a, 188b), and there were flocks of 750 and over at places nearby. The Cambridgeshire Inquisition and the Ely Inquisition extend the evidence into southern Cambridgeshire where there were 765 sheep at Weston Colville and 767 at West Wratting.[28] These and other flocks may

27 Darby (1979), 167–70.
28 ICC, 21–2, 23–4.

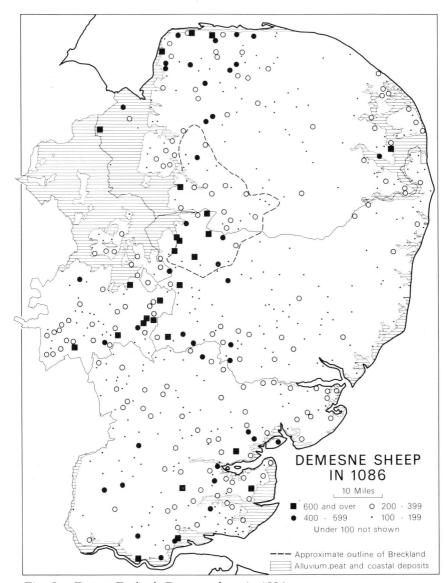

Fig. 5. Eastern England: Demesne sheep in 1086.

Note that vills with less than 100 demesne sheep are not plotted.

have grazed on the open chalk belt between Royston and Newmarket. Then again, on the siltlands of the northern Fenland as many as 2100 sheep were entered for West Walton (160a, 213a) and 515 for Terrington (206b, 251b). Among other large flocks in Norfolk were 600 sheep at Brancaster (215b)

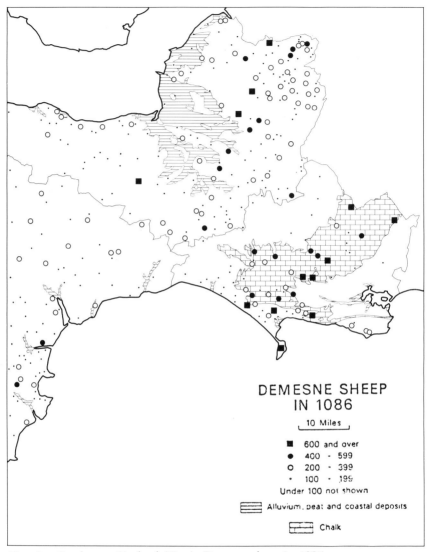

Fig. 6. South-west England (East): Demesne sheep in 1086.

Note that vills with less than 100 demesne sheep are not plotted.

and 660 at Heacham (163a) along the north coast, and 960 at Halvergate (128b) in Broadland. In the same way the Exeter Book records large flocks in the south-west, e.g. the Cranborne flock of 1037 (29a) and the Ashmore flock of 826 (20b). These, and other large flocks in Dorset, were most likely downland sheep (Fig. 6). Substantial flocks were also to be found in Somerset and, to a lesser extent, in Devon and Cornwall.

These references to large flocks of sheep show that arable was not the only type of farming in eleventh-century England. In the absence of similar information for the other circuits, our picture of the countryside of the time can only be incomplete. It has been argued that the relatively high annual values for the downland of Berkshire, and for the Chilterns, point not only to sheep but possibly to 'other non-arable resources such as dairy-cattle or pigs', and this may well be so.[29] High annual values are also to be found over the chalklands of Wiltshire and Hampshire.[30]

Non-Domesday evidence amply confirms such possibilities. An early twelfth-century survey of the English lands belonging to the Abbaye aux Dames at Caen shows that there was a flock of 1012 sheep at Avening, and another of 467 at Minchinhampton, both in the Cotswolds, which we can envisage as a district of sheepwalks. In the same way a Glastonbury Abbey survey from about the same period reveals flocks of 700 sheep at Idmiston, 1000 at Monkton Deverill, and 2500 at Damerham, all on the Wiltshire–Hampshire chalklands.[31] Such fragments of non-Domesday information provide some indication of what was lost when Great Domesday Book was made from the Circuit Books.

THE SCANTY INFORMATION FOR TOWNS

Whatever its uncertainties, the information for rural England is presented in an ordered manner, but when we turn to the towns all is different. The entries follow no pattern, and are as unsystematic as they are incomplete.[32] They range from long and involved statements about, say, legal matters, to what can only be described as incidental references. We are sometimes told of internal administrative divisions such as the 'wards' of Cambridge (DB, i. 189a) and of Stamford (336b), the 'quarters' of Huntingdon (103a), and the *scyrae* of York (298). We sometimes hear of town walls as at Chester (262b) and Oxford (154a). That the built-up area had expanded, in some towns at any rate, we may assume from references to houses outside the walls or outside the city as at Leicester (230b) and Canterbury (2a). But when all is said, it is impossible to form any certain idea, or sometimes any idea at all, of the size of a town.

It may come as a surprise that different lists of Domesday boroughs are not identical because they are based upon different criteria as to what was a borough, but it would seem that at least 112 places deserved the name. By far the largest must have been London, and we know something of its importance and of its trading connections with the continent. It is particularly unfortunate, therefore, that fo. 126, where London should have been described, is almost completely blank. There is also a great space on fo. 37

[29] P. H. Sawyer, 'Review of Domesday geographies of South-east and Northern England', *Econ. HR*, 2nd ser., xvi (1963), 155–7.
[30] Darby (1979), 224–7.
[31] R. Lennard, *Rural England, 1086–1135* (Oxford, 1959), 264.
[32] Darby (1979), 289–320.

where Winchester should have been described. An estimate might put the population of London at 10,000 and that of Winchester at, say, 5 to 6000. We might attempt other estimates, but each is little more than a guess. Places such as York, Lincoln and Norwich may have had 4 to 5000 inhabitants. Other county boroughs such as Leicester and Northampton may have had 2000 or a little more. At the lower end of the scale there were small boroughs with populations to be reckoned not in 1000s but in 100s. The total urban population for Domesday England may have reached 120,000, but we must emphasise the frailty of our evidence. These estimates may well be too low.

If we hope for any clear idea of what sustained these Domesday towns and boroughs we shall be disappointed, for their economic activities never come clearly into focus. Some, it is true, had a strong agricultural flavour. Thus Cambridge was a moderately substantial county town yet its burgesses had ploughteams; and we hear of other towns where burgesses worked on the land – at Huntingdon (203a) and York (298) for example. Only too often, the essentially urban activities remain indistinct. Of the sixty places with a record of markets only nineteen were boroughs. Or, again, it is true that the entry for Chester (262b) makes a vague reference to the coming and going of ships, but there is no reference to the trade of, say, Bristol or Exeter. Some coastal boroughs were centres of a sea-fishing industry – Yarmouth (DB, ii. 283a), Dunwich (312a) and Sandwich (DB, i. 3a) – but much is left to the imagination. In the west, the borough of Droitwich was unusual in being an industrial centre producing salt; on the basis of its Domesday record, it had under 1000 people, but there may well have been more.[33] In some towns, houses had been destroyed to make way for castles; other towns were centres of administration or had cathedrals or abbeys that needed to be maintained. What about their populations?

For only one place, Bury St Edmunds (DB, ii. 372a) in Suffolk, does something of the bustle of a town show through the Domesday text, and this was a place not specifically called a borough, although it has been included within the 112. It was already a substantial community in 1066, and the next twenty years were to see another 342 houses cover land which had been under the plough. We hear not of burgesses but of bakers, ale-brewers, tailors, shoe-makers, cooks, porters and the like who seemed to have been dependent on the abbey. It probably had a market and a mint although Domesday Book does not mention them. But in spite of the incompleteness of the information, the veil is lifted for a moment to show what, elsewhere in Domesday Book, has been hidden from our eyes.

DOMESDAY GEOGRAPHY

What are the redeeming features to be set against this catalogue of deficiency and frustration? The Domesday statistics for population raise many problems, but when all argument is over, we might end up with a total of

[33] H. C. Darby and I. B. Terrett (eds.), *The Domesday Geography of Midland England* (Cambridge, 1978), 263–4.

something under two million. This is not a precise figure and can only indicate an order of magnitude. Even to be able to do that for such a remote date is remarkable. What is more, we can obtain some general idea of the distribution of people over the realm. Then, too, the record of ploughteams provides a reasonable basis for reconstructing the distribution of arable land. When these two distributions are compared some fascinating conclusions emerge about the regional variety of agrarian England.[34]

Against the background of these two general distributions, we can perceive a number of local economies – dairying in the Vale of White Horse, cheese-making along the Essex coast, salt-making in Cheshire and Worcestershire with its network of trade over the country. To these we might add lead-working in the Pennines, and the making of wine in many places south of the latitude of Ely. Or again, with all its problems, a map of Domesday woodland leaves us in no doubt about the wooded nature of large tracts of the countryside. When such a map is discussed in connection with other evidence, it provides important clues to the history of settlement.

Instead of trying to add to this list, may I conclude with the words not of a geographer but of an economic historian who was also a Domesday scholar. It was in 1959 that Reginald Lennard wrote: 'In spite of these defects, Domesday Book tells us more about the human geography of the country in the eleventh century than will ever be known about the condition of any other part of the world at that early period.'[35]

[34] Darby (1979), 133–5.
[35] Lennard, *Rural England*, 4.

Domesday Book: Place-names and Personal Names

J. McN. Dodgson

THIS PAPER IS an outcome of my unlooked-for involvement, as acting general editor, in the Phillimore edition of Domesday Book, caused by the death in 1977 of Dr John Morris, my colleague at University College, London.[1]

The novocentenary observances in connection with the celebration of Domesday Book, which are the occasion of such publications as Elizabeth M. Hallam's *Domesday Book Through Nine Centuries*, London, 1986, and *Domesday Book, a Reassessment*, ed. Peter Sawyer, London, 1985; and of the activities reported for the National Committee for the 900th Anniversary of the Domesday Book in *Domesday, 900 years of England's Norman Heritage*, London, 1986; and of the Domesday Book Novocentenary Conference of the Royal Historical Society and the Institute of British Geographers at Winchester, July 1986; may fairly be said to have been inspired by that earlier conference, the octocentenary celebration, promoted by the Royal Historical Society in October 1886, whose proceedings were published in *Domesday Studies*, ed. P. E. Dove, 2 vols., London, 1888–91. It is doubtless to be expected that the historians alive in AD 2086 will wish to report their views of that momentous and portentous juncture, the Millennium of Domesday! In that millennial conference, we may confidently expect, they will report an onomastic bibliography of Domesday Book studies as much fuller, a state of knowledge of Domesday Book place-names and personal names as much more exact and satisfactory in 2086 than ours in 1986; as ours exceeds what was available a hundred years ago.

In 1886, in the world of onomatology contained in the bibliography, pp. xvii–xxxi, of Isaac Taylor's *Words and Places*, 2nd edn, London, 1865, the world of Grimm, Haigh and Kemble, and of Latham, Leo, Morris and Pott, and of the first edition (2 vols., Nordhausen, 1854–72) of E. Förstemann's *Altdeutsches Namenbuch*, there would have been little to report of onomastic studies in Domesday Book apart from *A General*

[1] It is complementary to, and an extension of, papers delivered to the XVth International Congress of Onomastic Sciences, Leipzig, 1984, and the XVIIth Conference of the Council for Name Studies in Great Britain and Ireland, Cambridge, 1985; the latter published as 'Some Domesday Personal-Names, Mainly Post-Conquest', *Nomina*, ix (1985), 41–51.

Introduction to Domesday Book, by H. Ellis (2 vols., London, 1833), and the important pioneer article 'Über das französische Sprachelement im Liber Censualis Wilhelms I von England' by F. Hildebrand, in *Zeitschrift für romanische Philologie*, 8 (1884), 321ff.

Here in 1986, had we room and leisure, there would be a good deal to report about the progress of English name-studies in general over the last hundred years.[2]

Noteworthy onomastic works particularly relevant to Domesday Book are not numerous,[3] but these few important items clearly point the way to that comprehensive study and careful interpretation of Domesday Book personal names and place-names which becomes practicable now that, in 1986, the Phillimore edition of Domesday Book and the Alecto facsimile edition are to hand. The apparatus is already available. The bibliography published in *Nomina*, ix, 49–51 (see n. 1 above), will serve pretty well, with four or five additions[4] for the investigation of the personal names of Domesday Book. For the work on the place-names of Domesday Book we would need to take up the numerous items of standard equipment common in current research on the place-names of England.[5] Already, the problems which need to be solved have been identified and understood, the potential value and application of the results have been discerned, and the direction of the work has been indicated, by Zachrisson, von Feilitzen and Sawyer (see n. 3).

The most immediately urgent problem which confronts us is the fact that Domesday Book abounds in garbled place-names and personal names; forms so distorted from that which we would have expected on the evidence of such earlier record of the names as exists, or of their subsequent

---

[2] The prolific bibliography in *Onoma*; *Namn och Bygd*; *Names*; *Nomina*; *Sydsvenska Ortnamnssällskapets Årsskrift*; the English Place-Name Society's *Journal* and the volumes of *The Survey of English Place-Names*, especially xxv–xxvi, *English Place-Name Elements Parts 1–2*, by A. H. Smith; *DEPN*.

[3] R. E. Zachrisson, *A Contribution to the Study of Anglo-Norman Influence on English Place-Names*, Lund, 1909; T. Forssner, *Continental-Germanic Personal-Names in England in Old and Middle English Times*, Uppsala, 1916; O. von Feilitzen, *The Pre-Conquest Personal-Names of Domesday Book*, Nomina Germanica, iii, Uppsala, 1937; G. Tengvik, *Old English By-Names*, Nomina Germanica, iv, Uppsala, 1938; P. H. Sawyer, 'The Place-Names of the Domesday Manuscripts', *Bulletin of the John Rylands Library*, xxxviii (1956), 483–506; Gillian Fellows-Jensen, 'The Domesday Book Account of the Bruce Fief', *JEPNS*, ii (1970), 8–17; *Domeday Gazetteer*.

[4] W. de G. Birch, *Index Saxonicus: an index to all the names of persons in Cartularium Saxonicum*, London, 1899; A. Longnon, *Les Noms de Lieu de la France*, Paris, 1920–9; H. Ström, *Old English Personal-Names in Bede's History, an Etymological-Phonological Investigation*, Lund Studies in English, 8, Lund, 1939; A. Dauzat and C. Rostaing, *Dictionnaire des Noms de Lieu de la France*, Paris, 1963; Veronica J. Smart, 'Moneyers of the Late Anglo-Saxon Coinage, 973–1016', *Commentationes de Nummis Saeculorum IX–XI in Suecia Repertis*, ii. 191–276, Kungl. vitterhets historie och antikvitets akademiens handlingar, Antikvariska serien 19, Stockholm, 1968.

[5] More particularly those which comprehend the important revisions of analysis and interpretation made in and marked by, or based upon, the work of J. Cameron, K. Cameron, R. Coates, B. Cox, J. McN. Dodgson, E. Ekwall, Gillian Fellows-Jensen, Max Förster, Margaret Gelling, K. H. Jackson, S. Karlström, M. T. Löfvenberg, O. Padel, O. Ritter, L. Rivet, K. I. Sandred, A. H. Smith, C. Smith and E. Tengstrand. Not all of this is yet as commonly understood as it should be.

development in Middle and Modern English, that the name-student would be justified in suspecting that the Domesday Book scribes may have been less interested in recording than in encoding the names of persons and places.

The circumstances which produce unexpected or unintelligible name-forms in Domesday Book are not far to seek. They arise from two causes. The first is mere history: between 1066 and 1086 there was a forceful political and cultural confrontation, juxtaposition and adjustment in English society – or, rather, among the inhabitants of England – between the indigenous landholding population which was, in general, of Anglo-Saxon extraction and of Anglo-Scandinavian and Welsh (and Cumbrian and Cornish); generally bearing personal names and using place-names which belonged to the Anglo-Saxon, Old Norse and Old Danish stock, or to the Welsh, Cornish or Irish; in general, speaking Old English and Anglo-Scandinavian, and the varieties of Old Welsh; their clerks generally used to reading and writing in varieties of the Insular Minuscules script as well as in the more modern Carolingian Minuscules – between that indigenous popu-lation and a new landholding aristocracy which was Norman or French or Breton or Flemish or whatever other breed or nationality of chivalrous but unscrupulous adventurer, desperate ne'er-do-well, or noble and dutiful vassal had been recruited to the Norman Duke's ominous enterprise of England – and ominous it was, indeed, for it set out under the mixed refulgences of Halley's Comet and a Papal Banner. God knows what He got for the comet; for the banner, the church of St Peter's Rome got Queen Edith's manor of Puriton in Somerset. This new society of immigrants and conquerors would be speaking all sorts of languages as well as the *lingua franca* in either the Norman or the Frankish varieties, and bearing names which were Franco-Danish, or French, or varieties of Continental Germanic, or Breton; their clerks generally used to reading and writing the Carolingian Minuscules script more familiar in continental practice.

The second cause of garbled name-forms in Domesday Book is the process of its compilation. As we are now advised[6] Domesday Book is a rapidly edited compilation, not finished in the time available, the result of abstracting and copying from written returns submitted first to regional and then to central offices, by circuit commissioners who ascertained the required particulars from the live and documentary sources and the reports, records and hearings of hundred and shire courts, relevant to their regions of survey.

So we have to allow for place-name and personal name spellings in Domesday Book which represent the mishearing, mispronunciation, mis-reading and miscopying of names at each stage of the process of transmission along the interfaces between different languages and different scripts, through the medium of good, bad and indifferent readers, writers, speakers, hearers and copyists; we have to allow for the acoustics of deafness and poor dentition; we have to allow for Francophone clerks taking down, dictating

---

[6] See Galbraith (1961); Galbraith (1974); P. H. Sawyer, 'Domesday Studies since 1886', in *Domesday*, 1–4.

of reading aloud to themselves as they work, these strange barbarian Anglo-Saxon names, and for continental-trained clerks not used to the old-fashioned Insular scripts they would find in some of the documentary records to which they would be referred for evidence, and from which they might be required to make extracts.

In *Domesday Book, a reassessment*[6] Peter Sawyer congratulates the English Place-Name Society's contribution to the equipment of the historian seeking to identify the place-names, and the places named, in Domesday Book and he salutes, as do we all, Olof von Feilitzen's *The Pre-Conquest Personal Names of Domesday Book*, Uppsala, 1937, and H. C. Darby's and G. R. Versey's *Domesday Gazetteer*, 1975, as important items of equipment for the more extensive and difficult analysis of Domesday Book nomenclature to which we are now, in 1986, ready to address ourselves.

Already, with no more than a knowledge of the onomastic equipment to hand, and of the usual historical grammars and dictionaries for the languages of north-west Europe in the eleventh century, and a fair acquaintance with the relevant kinds of medieval handwriting, it is possible to set about some of the more obvious of the strange effects of late Old English and Anglo-Norman French phonology, script and spelling which are attested in the Domesday Book names. Some characteristic specimens are exhibited in this paper which show that the Domesday Book names bear traces of mechanical miscopying as well as of orthographical representations of phonetic change.

For a paper in 1984[1] I drew up a provisional handlist of some thirty or forty typical palaeographical, literal, confusions due to miscopying and the clash of alternative alphabets. I take the liberty of appending it here, in its present, revised state.[7] It will soon be overtaken by further work, I have no doubt. But it will serve for the time being; the elucidation of the significance of the *form* of a Domesday Book name is as important as the elucidation of the significance of its meaning, and the elucidation of the significance of the form has to begin with the consideration of orthography as well as of morphology. One needs to know something of the history of the handwriting as well as of the history of the manuscript; the history of the languages and onomatology used as well as that of the things and persons named. There is much more interesting matter to be learned from the Domesday Book names than merely the names and identities of people and places.

The interaction of native and foreign characteristics may have as much to do with varieties in the documentation which the Domesday Book scribe was condensing, as with varieties of pronunciation and varieties of orthographic representation by the informants and compilers and editors of the Survey, or with any uncertainty on the part of the master scribe as to the identity of the place named or the correctness of the name used.

For example, in order to explain the spellings *GLOLE* and *CHENOLLE* (GDB, fo. 80r, 82r) for the name of Knowle, Dorset, we need to suppose Anglo-Norman phonetic modification of the late-Old English form *★cnol(l)e*,

---

[7] See Appendix.

the locative dative singular of Old English *cnoll* 'a small hill', which the later and the modern forms of the place-name lead us to suppose would be the basis of the Domesday Book forms. That modification would consist of the introduction of a glide vowel into the Old English consonant group *cn* /kn/, the voicing of the resultant /kən/ to /gən/, the assimilation of the nasal and liquid consonants /n/ and /l/ and the simplification of the resultant double consonant, /ll/.

The work of interpreting the vagaries of form in the Domesday Book names can be that complicated. More complicated is the next example. The spelling *SEIVETONE* (GDB, fo. 13r) for the name of Sevington, Kent, has to be compared with the spellings *Siuleldetune*, /sivleldətuːn/ and *Siuledtune*, /sivledtuːnə/ in Domesday Monachorum, which clearly indicate that the original place-name was Old English *Sigefledetune 'at Sigefled's estate' (from the Old English feminine personal name *Sigefled*; Ekwall in *DEPN* omits the comparison, and thus erroneously discerns the Old English feminine personal name *Saegifu*). The Domesday Book and the Domesday Monachorum spellings would seem to represent stages in a development – *siifledtone > *sifledtone > seifletone > *seiveltone > *seiventone – which involves the Anglo-Norman substitution of /sei-/ for Old English /sij-/ in the Old English personal name prototheme *Sige-*; the palatal quality of Old English g, /j/ or /i/; the assimilation of the consonants /d/ and /t/; the Old English voicing of /f/ > /v/ before and between vowels; the metathesis of /l/ in the middle syllable and the introduction of an unhistoric /l/ by inversion of the late Old English process of vocalising and eliding /l/ before consonants; the Anglo-Norman tendency to interchange or assimilate liquids and nasals /l/, /n/. The resultant form, *seiventone was, as it turned out, to be the basis of the Middle English development of the name of Sevington. It is hard to tell whether the Domesday Book spelling is the result of a pronunciation of the name (the loss of /n/ in the medial, quasi-inflectional syllables is a common feature in Old English Kentish compound place-names) or the result of an omission during writing or copying, of a contraction mark for the letter *n* in an abbreviated form of the name.

Badlesmere, Kent, is represented in Domesday Book by the Minuscules spelling *Bedenesmere* (GDB, fo. 12v) and the Capitals *BADELESMERE* (fo. 10r). The spellings *Baethdesmere*, *Badelesmere* in Domesday Monachorum indicate that there has been a scribal confusion between the minuscules letters *d* and 'eth' (ð) and between *d* and *el*, during a process of copying, and confirm that the original must have been an Old English place-name *Bæddeles-mere, based on an Old English masculine personal name *Bæddel. At Domesday Book fo. 10r when writing the place-name in Rustic Capitals, as heading to the main report on this manor of Badlesmere, the scribe uses the orthodox late Old English form as if he is following a return written by an Anglo-Saxon or, at least, a writer acquainted with Anglo-Saxon convention and Old English phonology. At Domesday Book fo. 12v, in a note about the tenure of an estate before 1066, the scribe writes a spelling in Minuscules, *Bedenes-*, produced by and representing a characteristic Anglo-Norman sound-substitution, the interchange of the liquids and nasals, /n/

and /l/ before the /m/ and the /r/ in the following syllable.

The Rustic Capitals spelling *AFETTVNE*, Kent (fo. 10v), spells the name of an unidentified place in Langport Hundred. The place and the name have not yet been located or registered elsewhere. But what name is to be sought? The analysis of the name recorded in Domesday Book indicates that the final element is Old English *tun*, but as it stands, the first element is unintelligible; nevertheless, if the Capitals here were the transcription of a misread Miniscules spelling *asettune*, in which the letter long -*s* represented Anglo-Norman /s/ for Old English /ʃ/ we might find the first element here to be Old English *æscett* 'an ash grove', a type of place-name element common in the south-eastern counties – this one is also the first element in the place-name Ashford, Kent, for instance; and we now need to look out for references, in medieval record, to a place called *Ashton* or *Asheton* or the like.

The spelling *ASMESLANT*, Kent (fo. 5r), for late Old English *almesland*, 'alms-land' (not a place-name), and the spelling *ESMETONE*, Kent (fo. 11v), for *elmetone*, now Elmton, are the result of a confusion between Miniscules *l* and long -*s*, in the text which was being transcribed into Capitals.

The Rustic Capitals spelling *FILLEICHA(M)*, Sussex (fo. 17r), represents a name of the place Sidlesham. The name *Sidelesham* is from Old English *Sidelesham* 'Sidel's village'; see *EPNS*, vi. 85, and *DEPN*. To explain the Domesday Book Capitals form, we may begin by supposing the Capital F transcribes a Miniscules *f* which was a mistake for a Miniscules long -*s*, and that the double Capital *L* represents a doubled consonant /l/ which would be the result of the assimilation of /d/ and /l/ in the consonant group /idlə/; but then we have no formula which allows us to derive, extract, or even wrest the putative form *silleic-* indicated by the Domesday spelling, from the Old English genitival-composition form *sideles-* recorded in Anglo-Saxon charters for this place-name. And unless we are to suppose that Domesday Book, here, is inexplicably inventive, we have then to suppose the place Sidlesham had alternative Old English names, the recorded *Sidelesham* and an hitherto unnoticed *Sid(e)lingham*, the one meaning 'Sidel's village', the other meaning 'village called after one Sidel', an alternation by no means unusual or unlikely in -*ing*-suffix English place-names. The Domesday Book spelling would then be explicable as a development from the form Old English *Sidlingham* by well-recorded late Old English and the Anglo-Norman modifications, i.e. the unvoicing and denasalisation of the consonant group in the -*ing* suffix, /ing/ > /ink/ > /ik/, perhaps aided by an omission of a suspension mark for the letter *n* in a spelling *-incham*; the inference of these features and the assimilation already proposed, enables the Domesday Book place-name form to be interpreted as a miscopy of a form which represented the Anglo-Norman phonetic modification of an alternative (otherwise unrecorded) name, Old English *Sid(e)lingham* > *Sill(e)i(n)cham*, for the place also alternatively named *Sidelesham* > *Sidlesham*. So, these nimble games are not without some value to the student of English place-names; were it not for this aberration in Domesday Book we might not have guessed that Sidlesham could have been, sometime, also called Sidlingham.

There is another obscured -ing-suffix place-name formation behind the Minuscules spelling *Warblitetone* Sussex (fo. 23v) for Warblington, Hants. The basis of the form appears to have been a late Old English ★*Warberincetune*, /inkə/, /ikə/, a reduction from the original Old English ★*Warburgingetune* 'at the estate called "At Warburging" (the place called after Warburg)'. From the putative ★*Warberincetune* the Anglo-Norman dissimilation of the liquid and nasal consonants /r/, /n/ and /l/, and the further reduction of the -ing-suffix, would phonetically modify the name to a form which could have been represented in Domesday Book as ★*Warb(e)linc(e)tone* or ★*Warb(e)li(n)c(e)tone*, i.e. as *Warblicetone* or *Warblīcetone*, either through phonetic loss of *n* or through scribal omission of a nunnation mark; which, by miscopying Minuscules *t* for *c*, would lead to *Warblitetone*.

The unusual spelling Rustic Capitals *ELSANGTONE* Dorset (fo. 80r) represents the place Ilsington, whose name must have been Old English ★*Ielfsigingtune*. This is an interesting name, in itself, for it appears to preserve a particular West Saxon dialect variant ★*Ielfsige*, of the Old English masculine personal name *Ælfsige*, analogous with the dialect variant ★*Ielfred* for *Ælfred* implied by the form of the place-name Ilfracombe, Devon. In order to reconcile the Domesday Book spelling with the tradition of the place-name Ilsington, Dorset, it would seem easier to suppose the Capitals transcribe a misreading in Minuscules of *a* for *ii* in a putative form ★*elsiingtone*, rather than to suppose that this Minuscules *a* represents a misreading of *u* in the rare alternative form, *-ung*, of the Old English suffix *-ing*.

The confusion of Minuscules *a* and *u* must have entered into the production of the alternative Domesday Book forms CAMERIC (fo. 78r), CVNELIZ (fo. 82r) for Kimmeridge, Dorset, which is derived in *EPNS*, lii. 84, and *DEPN*, from an Old English putative form ★*æt cyman rice* 'at the favourable stretch of ground'. We might have expected in Domesday Book a spelling resembling ★*cumeric*, so the Capital *A* in Domesday Book might represent the transcription of a misreading of Minuscules *u* and *a*. The Rustic Capitals spelling CVNELIZ preserves the expected letter *u* (for the sound /u/ or /ü/, /ui/, represented by the Old English letter *y*) but it represents more obviously the Anglo-Norman sound-substitutions /n/ for /m/, /l/ for /r/, and /ts/, written *z*, for Old English /tʃ/ written *c*. *Cuneliz* is a thoroughly Anglo-Norman version of the place-name of Kimmeridge whereas *Cameric* (which is also the spelling found in Exon, fo. 78) represents a more conservative English tradition.

These alternative spellings may well represent input to the Domesday Survey from different documentary sources, or even from different media, i.e. from dictation or transcription, one of which was more influenced by Norman-French pronunciation than the other.

For Duxford, Cambs., we find the spelling, in Minuscules, *Dodesuuorde* (fo. 194r) instead of the spelling *Dochesuuorde* we would have expected from the evidence of the pre-Conquest records of the name (*EPNS*, xix. 92). The Domesday Book spelling may be simply wrong, but it could be wrong in a complicated and interpretable way. The spelling *Dodes-* here could represent a mispronunciation /dodəs-/ due to a misspelling or misreading *dothes-, *doðes-, for the prototheme doches-.

The mistaking of c and t in Minuscules is a common confusion. The Minuscules spelling Hecteslei Cambs (fo. 196r) for Eltisley, a place-name derived from Old English *Heltes-lege 'at Helte's glade' can only be reconciled with the tradition of the place-name (see EPNS, xix. 158) if the spelling ct is taken to represent a miscopy of tt, that group representing a late Old English assimilation of the consonants /l/ and /t/; whence the Domesday Book spelling may record an otherwise unrecorded alternative development of the name, *Hetteslei, one which happened to be less productive than that which persisted in the evolution of the modern form.

The confusion of Minuscules d and cl is the most likely cause of the Rustic Capitals spelling CLONINCTVNE Sussex (fo. 17v) for Donnington, presumably through a transcription of a Minuscules form doninctune. This is a fairly simple solution. A little more complicated is that for the Rustic Capitals spelling DODEHAM Kent (fo. 10v) for Luddenham, /lΛdnəm/. If we suppose that the Domesday Book spelling is a transcript into Rustic Capitals of a Minuscules spelling *clodeham; that is, an unexceptionable Anglo-Norman representation – with /kl/ spelled cl substituted for Old English /χl/ spelled hl; the spelling o for Old English /u:/; and characteristic late Old English loss of medial inflexional n, /n/ – of the Old English basis, *Hludanham 'Hluda's manor', which is indicated by the development *(h)lud(d)e(n)ham which must lie behind the spelling Luddenham in Domesday Monachorum and the spellings Ludeham 1211, Lodenham 1242 (see DEPN and PNK, 287; KPN, 245). Here Domesday Book is presenting an Anglo-Norman modification of the Old English place-name whilst Domesday Monachorum maintains a more conservative, English, tradition.

The Minuscules spellings Biochest Sussex (fo. 22v) for Brockhurst, and Doddenhenc Essex (LDB, fo. 85r) for Doddinghurst, present different orthographic representations of the South-Eastern dialect form, herst, of the Old English place-name element hyrst 'a wooded hill'. The name of Brockhurst Sussex is derived by EPNS, vii. 331, from Old English *Brocc-herst 'Badger-hill'; in the Domesday Book spelling, Bio- probably stands for Bro written with a short-stemmed Minuscules r, and -hest probably stands, through confusion of Minuscules long r and s, for a spelling hert representing an Anglo-Norman pronunciation for herst with a characteristic Old French loss of /s/ in the consonant-group /rst/ remarked by both von Feilitzen, PNDB, cap. 112, and Zachrisson, ANInfl, 72 note.

The spelling Doddenhenc would appear to stand, through confusion of Minuscules n and r, and c and t, for this same Anglo–Norman modification, -hert for Old English -herst, in one of the alternative formations which can be inferred for the original of this place-name, i.e. Old English *Doddanherst or Old English *Dodding(e)herst, the former with the meaning 'Dodda's wooded hill', the latter 'the wooded hill called "Dodding(e)" (called after one Dodda)'.

The confusion of Minuscules n and r figures yet again in the evolution of the Rustic Capitals spellings LERTHAM (GDB, fo. 12r) and LERHAM (fo. 4v) for Lenham, Kent, where we might have expected *LEN(E)HAM. The Capitals spellings would appear to be the result of confusing Minuscules *n* for *r*; and of misreading a damaged or badly written Insular Minuscules *h* as a damaged or badly written runic letter 'thorn', *þ*. This would lead to a process *lenham > lerham > lerþam > lertham* which is entirely graphic, not phonetic.

The Anglo-Saxon runic letters were always troublesome to the post-Conquest clerks. The Rustic Capitals spelling *HERFELD* Somers (fo. 96r) for Heathfield, from Old English *hæþfeld*, for which we should have expected a Domesday Book spelling *hethfeld* must represent a transcription of Minuscules *herfeld*, a mistake for *heþfeld* through confusion of Minuscules long *r* and the runic letter 'thorn'. Confusion of the letters 'wynn' and 'thorn', which are the Old English runic letters for /w/ and /θ/, with the letters *þ* and *r* in Minuscules, causes misspellings.

An instance with an interesting consequence is the Minuscules spelling *Schildricheha(m)* Kent (fo. 1r). Both *Domesday Gazetteer*, 198, and *Phillimore DB: Kent*, note D 18, suppose this represents the same name and place as the Rustic Capitals spelling *CILDRESHA(M)* Kent (fo. 10r). Both forms have been derived as one name from a common original, Old English *Cildricesham*, /rikəs/, 'the manor of one *Cildric*'. However, there appears to be no sure evidence for the identity of the two places, or rather, the identity of the two names. The form *Cildresha(m)* (fo. 10r), also *Cyldresham* in Domesday Monachorum, probably represents another place-name, another place, i.e. Old English *Cildheresham* 'manor of one *Cildhere*'; perhaps this too was in Faversham Hundred, perhaps near to, and perhaps associated, in tradition and name, with the other, as if that other contained the Old English personal name *Cildric*, and as if this was a pair of names commemorating members of a family with a characteristic alliterative set of personal names.

But the name spelled *Schildricheha(m)* turns up in GDB, fo. 1r, in a list where one would not be surprised to find the name of Sheldwich, Kent (a place not named in Domesday Book, it has been supposed, although it is already recorded in an Anglo-Saxon charter, *BCS*, 243, as Old English *scildwic*; the name means 'an industrial settlement or trading estate or workplace, with a shelter'). It would be prudent to keep in mind, until further evidence comes to hand to confirm or confound the idea, the possibility that the *r* in this name represents a mistaken 'wynn' from a form *Schildwicheha(m)*, representing Old English *Scildwicheham* 'the manor at Sheldwich'.

The Rustic Capitals spelling *WERWELIE* (fo. 177r), instead of the expected *WERFELIE* for Warley, Worcs., Old English *weorfes-* or *weorfalege* 'cattle clearing', indicates that, in an original form, written in Minuscules, from which these Capitals were transcribed, the Minuscules *f* in *Werfelie* may have resembled a 'wynn', *þ*.

Different effects of the Old English letter 'wynn' are discernible in the Domesday Book spellings *PILESHAM* and *WILESHAM* (fos. 17v, 18r) instead of the expected *FILESHAM* for Filsham, Sussex, Middle English *Filesham*. These Capitals would appear to be transcriptions of Minuscules originals in which the badly drawn Minuscules *f* looked like *p* and 'wynn'. The alternation of *p* and 'wynn' is also discernible from the spellings *WADENEBERIE* Somerset (fo. 90r) for Panborough, and *PLATENOVT* Kent (fo. 12v) for Wadholt /wɔdout/.

The personal name spelling *Horrap* Essex (LDB, fo. 106r) remains a puzzle. In the context, it cannot be a place-name, so none of the speculative etymologies appropriate to toponymics would be appropriate; nor can we regard as anything more than a provisional, theoretic, speculation, the suggestion made in *Phillimore DB: Essex*, n. B 3a, that this may represent a misreading of a Minuscules spelling *⋆Hofwar* for the Old English personal name *Hofw(e)ard* (*PNDB*, 291) with a characteristic Anglo-Norman loss of final /d/ after /r/.

The same highly speculative quality is essential to the proposition that the Rustic Capitals spelling *PIRTOCHESWORDA* Somerset (Exon, fo. 79v) may represent a severely garbled version of a place-name spelling in Minuscules *⋆wistowesworð*, with 'wynn', Þ, for *w*, and *d* for *th*, and mis-readings of *þ* 'thorn' and *p* for 'wynn', and *ch* for *th*, thus *⋆Þistoþesþorð*, *⋆pirtothesword*; see *Phillimore DB: Somerset*, 364 n. 25. 33; 388.

There appears to have been a confusion of the diagraph *æ* 'aesc' with the ampersand *&* or its literal equivalent *et*, that is, *æ > & > et*, in order to produce the spelling *Etwelle* (GDB, fo. 13v) for (Temple) Ewell, Kent, derived from Old English *æwelle* 'river source, spring'. The interesting reciprocal was spotted by Alex Rumble and reported by Karl Inge Sandred in *Namn och Bygd*, lix (1971), 37–9: the letters *et* written as an ampersand and that transcribed as *æ* 'aesc' produced a garbled spelling of the place-name Old English *hiuet in hamstedi* 'the copse in the homestead' in a twelfth-century *Textus Roffensis* copy of the text of an eighth-century charter (*BCS*, 260; *ASC*, 37).

In one or two Domesday Book name spellings there is evidence of a confusion between Capital *B* and Capital *M*. The Minuscules form *Menetleam* Essex (LDB, fo. 40v) appears for *⋆Benetleam*, the accusative inflected form of the name for (Little) Bentley, Old English *⋆benetlea* 'at bent-grass glade'. This misspelling must be the result of a misreading of Capitals; it would not be easy to confuse Minuscules *b* and *m*. Similarly, it is the initial capitals that are involved in the spelling *Molebec* (GDB, fo. 56rv) for the surname of Hugo de *Bolebec* (fo. 56v). The significance of this substitution is, that the Capitals are unlikely to have been Rustics, but rather something more Lombardic, if shapes of B and M were to be susceptible of confusion. The documentation being processed into the Domesday Survey at these points might well have had a characteristic orthography, out of the ordinary run of documentary or business scripts.

An instance of misspelling which is the result of a phonetic characteristic is the Rustic Capitals spelling *BOLEBORDE* (fo. 118r) for Bulworthy, Devon (*EPNS*, ix. 390). The final element in this place-name is OE *worþe* locative of *worþ* 'private domain, enclosed estate'. The place-name is spelled *Bolehorda* (Exon, fo. 487v). Conversely, for another such place-name, Widworthy, Devon (*EPNS*, ix. 632), Exon, fo. 503r, reports *Vdeborda* alternative to

WIDEWORDE in Capitals, GDB, fo. 115v, *Wideworda* in Minuscules, Exon, fo. 410r. In these names and spellings the Minuscules *b* is a mistaken reading of a Minuscules *h* representing an Anglo-Norman phonetic hiatus (see *PNDB*, para. 145) resulting from the elision of the consonant and semi-vowel *w*, /w/, /u:/, when initial of a simplex name, or of the second element of a compound name (see *PNDB*, para. 55). This Anglo-Norman hiatus sign, the letter *h*, appears in the Domesday Book or Exon spellings for the other Devon place-names Ashmansworthy (*EPNS*, viii. 81; GDB, fo. 106r); Brexworthy (*EPNS*, viii. 133; GDB, fo. 118v), Broadwood Kelly (*EPNS*, viii. 136; GDB, fo. 106r); Cornwood (*EPNS*, vii. 268; GDB, fo. 105r); Farwood (*EPNS*, ix. 622; GDB, fo. 111v); Marwood (*EPNS*, viii. 50; GDB, fo. 115v); Wringworthy (*EPNS*, viii. 201; Exon, fo. 495r).

This is a matter of the historical phonology of the place-name forms in Domesday Book. Not all the misspellings are so organic. Some interesting results emerge from the simple confusion of letters in Rustic Capital forms. *HOILINGEBORDE* Kent (GDB, fo. 4v) instead of the more expected *Holingeborne* (fo. 4v) for Hollingbourne, may show the simple misreading of a Rustic Capital group *NE* as *DE* by the Domesday Book scribe, rather than the evidence of the unvoicing of the consonants /d/ and /n/ after /r/ (see *PNDB*, para. 78); but the Rustics *IL* spelling is very likely due to a misreading of Rustics *LL* in the same exemplar.

LITELFORDE Sussex (fo. 20v) for Itford (see *EPNS*, vii. 538, which probably gets it wrong), ought to have appeared as ⋆*IITESFORDE*, since the place-name represents Old English ⋆*igettesforde* (from Old English ⋆*iget(t)* 'yew grove'); probably the simplest way to explain the Domesday Book spelling is to suppose that a Minuscules long *s* and a Rustic Capitals initial *I*, in a spelling ⋆*Iitesforde*, were both misread as Minuscules *l* and the name misconstrued as OE ⋆*litelforde* by a scribe who had not heard it spoken by a native.

A similar name-formation and a comparable process seem likely to have produced the spelling *LVET* Sussex (fo. 19v, 20r). This form does not make sense, so far. It has been taken as a name for Lidham, Sussex (*Phillimore DB: Sussex*, n. 9. 106); but that name is more likely to be derived from Old English *hlyda* 'a bench; a hillside'. Prudently, *DEPN* and *EPNS*, vii. 509, do not mention it. *Domesday Gazetteer* reads the form '*Ivet*, unidentified'. This reading would give a credible representation of Old English ⋆*ifet* 'place growing with ivy'. The initial letter in this Rustic Capitals spelling in Domesday Book is ambiguous. Initial Capital *I* gives us an intelligible form; Capital *L* does not; there is a temptation to prefer the initial *I*.

The Rustic Capitals spelling *LOVINGETONE* Sussex (fo. 19r), *LOV-RINGETONE* Sussex (fo. 21r) instead of the expected ⋆*IOVINGE-*, for Jevington (*EPNS*, vii. 421), from Old English ⋆*Ge(o)fingetune* 'estate called "at *Geofing*" (place named after one Geofa)', show evidence of confusion with the name of Yeverington, Sussex, *Iovringetone* (fo. 20v) from Old English ⋆*Geofheringetune* 'estate called "at *Geofhering*" (place named after one Geofhere)'; but they also suggest erroneous transcriptions of forms written

131

in Minuscules but with initial Rustic Capital *I* which was misread as initial Minuscules *l*, thus setting up a process, *ιouinge- > louinge- > LOVINGE-*. Some name-forms can best be accounted for, if we suppose misreadings of Rustic Capitals ligatures *N* and *T* (𝐍𝐓) and *V* and *T* (𝐕). Such is *FAITVNE* Derbys. (fo. 275r), where we should have expected *FANTVNE*, for Fenton, Old English *fentune* (Old English *fenn* 'fen'; with Anglo-Norman sound substitution (/æn/ for /en/).

The spelling in Rustic Capitals, *WILRENONE* Wilts. (fo. 71r) represents an old name for Bathampton. It is not intelligible unless we suppose it is miscopying a Rustic Capitals spelling *WILRENTONE* containing the *NT* ligature and omitting the lid of the *T*. *Wilrentone* would represent Old English *Wilrunetune* 'at Wilruna's estate', from an Old English feminine personal name *Wilrune*.

The Rustic Capitals spelling *AENESTANEFELT* (fo. 248r) for Alston-field, Staffs., from Old English *Ælfstanesfeld*, shows the first Capitals *N* representing a Minuscules *n* which arises by minim confusion for Minuscules *u* representing the sound /v/ which is the result of vocalisation of the consonant /f/ in the Old English personal name *Alfstan* after a glide vowel has been introduced between the consonant groups /lf/ and /st/, hence a progression /ælfstan-/ > /ælvəstan-/ > /æːvəstanəs-/. These operations and indeed the subsequent elision of the genitive inflexion /s/ before the initial /f/ of the final element, are all features noted among Anglo-Norman character-istics by von Feilitzen; but we should be better advised to think of them as late Old English modifications, effects as open to English as to Anglo-Norman speakers.

Less complicated altogether is the task of accounting for the personal name form *Liuidi* Essex (LDB, fo. 105v), probably representing the Old Norse personal name *Lundi*. Here, it is a matter of counting the minims.

VNDEWICHE Somerset (GDB, fo. 89v) is shown by the corresponding report in Exon, fo. 186v, to represent a misreading of a Minuscules spelling *uudewiche*. The Old English original of the place-name was probably *wudewic* 'workplace or industrial estate at a wood'. The Minuscules minim letters *i, n, m, u* (the last interchangeable for *v*) generate numerous mistakes, especially in Minuscules forms.

The Rustic Capitals spelling *HAINTONE* Kent (fo. 13r) for Hampton, Old English *ham-tune*, probably represents a transcription of a Minuscules spelling *hamtone* with the Minuscules *m* misread as *in*. If we had only the Domesday Book form to rely upon, and lacked the rest of the spellings in the tradition of this place-name, we could not be sure that the first element was not Old English *hægen* 'a hedged enclosure' rather than Old English *hām*. This is a caution well worth noting.

Occasionally, a spelling indicates the process of the mistake in the supposed transcription from Minuscules to Capitals. The Rustic Capitals spelling *HERTENEL* corrected to *HERTEVEL* Sussex (fo. 21v) for Hart-field, late Old English *hertefeld*, offers evidence of scribal procedure. Apparently the scribe thought he saw the Minuscules letter *n* and transcribed Rustic Capitals *N*, but in fact he was looking at Minuscules *u* and ought to have put Rustic Capitals *V*. The correction and the mistake would be intelligible only if he were putting into Capitals an exemplar written in Minuscules.

The Minuscules spelling *Warthuil* (fo. 172r) for Wythall, Worcs. (*EPNS*, iv. 358), cannot be reconciled with the Middle English spelling *Wyhtehalle* 1283 nor with the presumed original, Old English ⋆*Wyht(e)hall* 'hall in a river-bend', unless we suppose either a distinct difference of names or no little distortion of the form. As to the first element, Old English *wyht* 'a river-bend', an Anglo-Norman spelling ⋆*wust* would be an orthodox representation of a late Old English form ⋆*wuht* due to the usual phonetic changes, sound substitutions and orthographic conventions (see *PNDB*, paras. 19–20 on Old English /y/ > /u/; para. 141 on Old English /ht/ > Anglo-Norman /st/). From such a putative spelling, ⋆*wust-*, a scribe's confusion of the Insular Minuscule letters *u* and *a*, and *s* and *r*, would produce the spelling *wart-* seen in Domesday Book. As to the second element, Old English *hall*, in order to explain the Domesday Book spelling *huil* we might suppose it was copying an original Minuscules spelling with a badly drawn first letter in the double *l*, which was read as *i*, and with an open *a* which was read as *u*; but it would seem just as likely that the Domesday Book spelling represents another final element altogether, e.g. Old English *hygel* 'small hill', and that the place-name Wythall, Old English ⋆*wyht-hall*, is in fact a different name from that recorded in Domesday Book, Old English ⋆*wyht-hygel*; although both may well have been used of the same locality, they would have referred to different features of it. Again, this is an informative and cautionary observation.

Sometimes the Anglo-Norman influence on the name-forms is very marked indeed, the distortions gross, and they present not only puzzles in Anglo-Norman but problems of English etymology as well.

The Rustic Capitals spellings *GOLLESBERGE* Kent (fo. 11r) and *WANESBERGE* (fo. 11v) have both been identified with Woodnesborough, Old English ⋆*Wodnes-berge*, ⋆*Wednes-berge* 'at the hill of the god, Woden'. It is at once obvious that, as they stand, these Domesday Book forms are unlikely to be simple and accurate representations of a unified Old English version of this place-name. *Gollesberge* would appear to represent the substitutions of Old French initial *gu-* /g/ or /gw/ for Old English *w-* /w/ (*PNDB*, para. 55), and of Anglo-Norman /l/ for /n/ in the group *odnes* /ɔdnəz/ > /ɔdləz/, and the assimilation of the resultant group /dl/ to the double consonant /ll/. So we can construct a sensible evolution of the rather heavily Frenchified form *gollesberge* < ⋆*godlesberge* < ⋆*wodles-* < ⋆*wodnesberge*. But as to the spelling *WANESBERGE* no confident projection can be made. It goes with the spelling *Wanneberga* in Domesday Monachorum – the loss of medial /s/ is not an unusual elision. But these spellings do not appear to represent the name 'Woodnesborough'. *Wanesberge, Wanneberga* may refer to the same hill or barrow, but it could be a different name: it is more likely to represent Old English ⋆*wænnes-beorg*, 'the hill of the mound' from Old English *wenn, wænn* 'a wen, a blister, a mound'; than some difficult-to-demonstrate modification of Old English *Wodnes-beorg*; nevertheless, if our inferences began with the common Old English variant of the god-name, *Weden-*, seen in the day-name Wednesday, we might evolve an explantory model *Wednes-* > **Wennes-* > *wænnes-* > *wan(n)e(s)-*. That would invite the observation that Domesday Monachorum and Domesday Book fo. 11v report a name-form which reflects an Old English vernacular dialect variant, whereas Domesday Book fo. 11r reports a French modification of a more regular Old English form.

The influence of the Old French initial /g-/, /gu-/ for Norman and English /w-/ is strongly if indirectly exerted in the development of the Rustic Capitals spelling *WENISTETONE* (fo. 74r) where we would have expected *CHENISTETONE, for Knighton, Wilts. (*EPNS*, xvi. 366. Old English *cnihta-tune 'the estate of the boys'). To account for the initial *W* we have to suppose that the initial /k/ in the syllable /kǝn-/ has become voiced, /gǝn-/, and that the result has been taken for an Old French form *guenistetone, and that, for this putative erroneous Old French initial /gu-/, the equivalent Anglo-Norman initial sound /w-/ has been substituted by a 'normalising', or 'Normanising', scribe who perhaps did not know or understand either the spurious place-name /wenistetonǝ/ he had 'restored' or the Norman mispronunciation /kǝnist ǝ tonǝ/ of the Old English name he had, by now, even deeper obscured. The modern place-name student feels deeply sympathic.

In *Nomina*, ix (1985), 47, in addition to discussing the Old French influence in the personal-name spelling *Gingomus* Norfolk (LDB, fo. 147r) for an Old French version *Guigoinus for Old German *Wigwin*; and the personal-by-name spellings *Cudhen* and *Gudhen* Essex (LDB, fos. 17v, 99r) for an hitherto unrecorded Old English word *wudu-henn to put alongside the better-known English by-name *Woodcock*; I drew attention to yet another, the most remarkable of the Domesday Book names which, like the series Woodnesborough – *Gollesberge*, show the Old French initial /g-/, /gu-/ rather than the Anglo-Norman /w-/, the remarkable surname of Willelmus *Goizenboded* Gloucs. (GDB, fo. 167v), *Phillimore DB: Gloucs.*, 34), Worcs. (fo. 177v) in which *-boded* looks like the past participle of Old English *bodian* 'to bode, to threaten, to foretell ominously'; the spelling *goi* could represent an Old French initial /gwi-/ for Old English initial /wi-/; and the letter *z* for /ts/ could be used to represent a Norman–French sound-substitution for Old English /tʃ/. Thus we may reconstruct from *Goizenboded* an Old English by-name *wiccanboded, past participle and adjective, 'foretold by a witch', or 'witch-cursed'.

The forms of the place-names and the personal names of Domesday Book are the result of a mixture of phonetic law and scribal accident. Whilst, generally, they represent the recognised and recognisable names of persons and places, they present us with numerous problems still to solve – despite the inspired improvisations to be found in the notes of the *Phillimore Domesday Book* volumes over which I have presided. The attempt at an elucidation of the puzzles, and even the onomastic experiments to that end which have, so far, achieved no acceptable result, bring out names which conceal surprising and illuminating evidence of the effect of those linguistic and scribal juxtapositions and confrontations which reflect the irrevocable social, cultural and political advances and disasters of the two dreadful decades in England which followed 1066.

APPENDIX

Curious and unexpected spellings of proper names in Domesday Book, due to confusion of one letter with another, listed under characteristic confusions. Unless otherwise marked, reference is to GDB.

1. l/s: ASMESLANT 5r, ESMETONE 11v.
2. s/f: Tosth 194v, cassa LDB 49v, Leffesse LDB 104v, Leffiuf LDB 105v, GRASTONE 172r, 74v, BEFORD 174v, AFETTVNE 10v, FILLEICHĀ 17r, pechefers 176r, CLISTONE 80r, CLISTVNE 176v.
3. si/f: FRICESCOTE 249r.
4. str/fer: ELSTRETVNE 278r.
5. a/cc: IACV̄BE 173r.
6. a/u: eudlac LDB 104r, CAMERIC 78r.
7. a/ii/u: ELSANGTONE 80r.
8. c/e: ARCLEI 9r.
9. c/r: Pirot(us) 197v, LDB 50v.
10. c/t: STREITVN 197v, BARCTVNE 274v, STOTTVNE 65v, STOTVNE 176v, Dodesuuorde 194r, Warblitetone 23v, Strami 74v, BOLTINTONE 68v, Scanburne LDB 55v, CHENET 246v, Hecteslei 196r, LAVERTESTOCHE 74r, WICHELESTOTE 73r.
11. d/cl: Medredive 2r, Adem LDB 70r, CLONINCTVNE 17v, DODEHAM 10v, LVNVREDELIE 177v.
12. el/d, tl/d: Bredege 180v, NEDESTEDE 8v, Ialelham LDB 419a.
13. d/ð: Esceprid 191v.
14. i/r: Biochest 22v.
15. nc/rt: Doddenhenc LDB 85r.
16. r/s, rc/se: HANCESE 250v, HASLESSE 19r, CLAVESHA 20r.
17. n/r: Hadreha 192r, LERHAM 4v, Wandrie 194r, BERMENTONE 73r, Dynechai LDB 320r.
18. r/þ: HERFELD 96r.
19. þ(w)/p/þ(th)/r: Schildricheham 1r, CILDRESHAM 10r.
20. æ/et/&: Etwelle 13v.
21. b/v/m, B/M: WERBLESTVNE 265v, BROCHESHALE 82v, WESTEWELLE 18v, PEVEMORE 177v, BROTEHAM 8v, Menetleam LDB 40v, Molebec 56rv.
22. B/R: DELBEBIE 276r.
23. L/h: HARDITONE 24r.
24a. b/h: Tichenballe 273r, BOLEBORDE 118r, Vdeborda Exon 503.
24b. þ/h: LERTHAM 12r.
25. H/bl: DuHel LDB 105r.
26. h/v: TORNVELE 74v.
27. I/L: LILEBERE 88r, LATVNE 89v, LODENWRDE 90v, Larpole 180r, HOILINGEBORDE 4v, LITELFORDE 20v, LVET 19v, 20r, LOV(R)INGETONE 19r, 21r.
28. N-T, V-T ligatures: FAITVNE 275r, WILRENONE 71r, NIVEMBRE 27r.
29. k/r: ARCLEI 9r, ERNOLE 96r.
30. f/p: CLIPTVNE 277v, SCEPTESBERIE 75r, Pleines 204v, Polcehard 60v, Hapra LDB 64r.

31. p/w/f: PILESHAM, WILESHAM 17v, 18r, WADENEBERIE 90r, PLATENOVT 12v, WERWELIE 177r.
32. nunnation errors, numerous.
33. cu/in: in Bertone 201v.
34. minim confusions: DOMNITONE 67v, Tumesteda LDB 40r, ÆNESTANEFELT 248r, Liuidi LDB 105r, VNDEWICHE 89v, NOIVN 96r, TELVVE 98r, HAINTONE 13r, NIWORDE 26r, HERTENEL 21v.
35. w/iv: WERSTE 20v.
36. lo/W: LODIVTONE 22r.
37. metanalyses: EILESFORD 173r, INGELINGEHAM 77v, INLANDE 80v.
38. i/j: CHEIESLAVE 70r.
39. Ic/k: Kkewortha LDB 357r.
40. L/E: EARLAFORDA LDB 400r.
41. R/K: Ranauaha LDB 403r.

The Domesday Manor[1]

J. J. N. Palmer

DOMESDAY SCHOLARS OF Maitland's generation were at one in recognising that his definition of the Domesday manor was both the most original and the least convincing feature of *Domesday Book and Beyond*. Tait, Round, Baring, Farrer,[2] and others all pointed to defects in the evidence for his argument that the 'manor is a house against which geld is charged'. With characteristic generosity, Maitland recognised the force of some of these points, observing in a letter to James Tait:

> I must confess that you have somewhat shaken one of my few beliefs in the matter of the *manerium*, namely that the term had *some* technical meaning. I can't give up that belief all at once, but may have to do so by and by.[3]

Further reflection served only to convince him, however, of the rightness of his case, and at one point he contemplated a reply to Tait's criticisms.[4] His unwillingness to accept defeat on this particular issue is scarcely surprising, for he viewed the development of the manor as central to much of the social and political history of the Anglo-Saxon age, the Domesday manor being the key to an understanding of much of that evolution. The question of the manor was '"pre-judicial" to all the great questions of early English history'.[5]

Despite the consensus against Maitland's thesis, his contemplated defence need not have been a forlorn attempt to retrieve something from the

[1] This paper is based upon research funded by the Economic and Social Research Council (ESRC), reference number B00232095. I have received considerable assistance from Mr Andrew Ayton, research assistant on the Hull Domesday project, in collecting the materials upon which the essay is based.
[2] James Tait, review of *Domesday Book and Beyond* in *EHR*, xii (1897), 768–77; J. H. Round, 'The Domesday Manor', *EHR*, xv (1900), 293–302; F. H. Baring, *Domesday Tables for the counties of Surrey, Berkshire, Middlesex, Hertford, Buckingham and Bedford and for the New Forest* (London, 1909), 79, 82, 94, 139–42, 177; W. Farrer, 'The Domesday Survey', *VCH Yorks.*, ii (1912), 143–5.
[3] *The Letters of Frederick William Maitland*, ed. Fifoot, 201.
[4] *Letters*, 264.
[5] Maitland, 357. Maitland was here speaking of the related question of the hide but the sentiment is appropriate. As he observed in his preface, his book was 'in some sort' an answer to Seebohm's theories of the manor.

wreckage of his theory, for there were and are compelling reasons for accepting that the term *manerium* had some precise – even technical – meaning, despite our difficulty in grasping what that meaning might be. In circuit six, for instance, thousands of holdings are meticulously classified as manors, berewicks or sokes, the exceptions being so few as to be certainly scribal errors. In Yorkshire, Nottinghamshire and Derbyshire, the relief paid by thanes varied according to the number of their manors.[6] In Norfolk, Suffolk and Essex in Little Domesday, and in the south-western counties in Exon and Great Domesday, the scribes were at pains to note in thousands of entries that a given holding was held *pro .. manerio*, to the extent of interlineating this phrase if they judged it to have been mistakenly omitted. Given the terseness of Domesday formulae in general, there would need to be compelling grounds for accepting that *pro .. manerio* was entirely redundant, and none have been suggested. Throughout Domesday, there are scores of individual entries, scattered throughout all circuits and most counties, which are intelligible only if the term *manerium* had specific connotation. What sense, otherwise, could be made of such entries as that for Chilfrome (Dors.), held for three manors but claimed by its tenant to be only two? Or to that for Startforth (Yorks.), where one tenant held two carucates and another four and 'one had a manor and the other did not'? Or to the occasional entries which note that a certain piece of land 'was in no manor', or had been but was no longer a manor, or was – or had been – 2, 4, 6 or 8 manors?[7] Or, finally, to such entries as that for Potton (Beds.), where it is carefully noted of a tiny holding of half a virgate: *Hanc terram tenuit comes Tosti in Potone suo Manerio*, the *manerium* of Potton being the subject of a separate and later entry?[8] In all these instances, amounting to many thousands of entries, the scribes of Domesday and related texts appear to be striving to distinguish manors from other types of holding. How could they have done so if *manerium* had no precise meaning for them? And why did they bother if such classification had no public, or at least royal, interest? Maitland was surely right to suspect that it had such an interest and that this interest was related to taxation, even if his own formulation of the relationship of geld and manor had discernible weaknesses.

The matter therefore deserves a fresh airing, the more so since recent work by T. Aston, Sally Harvey, Glanville Jones, Judith Green[9] and others has given renewed prominence to the geld and to the manor after a period in which both topics have tended to be relegated to the margins of Domesday concerns. In this paper, I shall concentrate attention on four of the five

---

[6] DB, i. 298b, 280b.

[7] Finn (1963), 45–51.

[8] DB, i. 217b *bis*.

[9] T. S. Aston, 'The Origins of the Manor in England, with a postscript', in *Social Relations and Ideas: Essays in Honour of R. H. Hilton*, ed. T. H. Aston, P. R. Coss, C. Dyer, J. Thirsk (Cambridge, 1983), 1–43; Harvey (1971), 753–73; Harvey (1980), 121–33; G. W. R. Jones, 'Multiple Estates and Early Settlement', in *English Medieval Settlement*, ed. P. H. Sawyer (London, 1979), 15–40; J. A. Green, 'The Last Century of the Danegeld in England', *EHR*, xcvi (1981), 241–58.

counties of circuit three, and upon Cambridgeshire and Bedfordshire in particular.[10] There are sound reasons other than space and my competence for these limitations. It was on this circuit, and upon Cambridgeshire most particularly, that Maitland, Tait and Round concentrated their attentions. The survival of the *Inquisitio Comitatus Cantabrigiensis* and the *Inquisitio Eliensis* allows us to check the data in Domesday, to winnow some scribal errors, and to confirm some doubtful readings.[11] Bedfordshire and Cambridgeshire contain highly manorialised vills alongside some of the least manorialised holdings in the country, providing difficult and varied material upon which to test any theory as to the meaning of the term *manerium*. Above all, circuit three is the only one of the seven circuits in which the scribe has made an explicit and determined effort to distinguish manorial and non-manorial holdings, thereby affording the most stringent of tests of any such theories. Although it is always necessary to heed Maitland's salutary warning that work on a single hundred or county is 'apt to engender theories which break down the moment they are carried outside the district in which they had their origin',[12] a circuit is perhaps a large enough, and Cambridgeshire a difficult enough, area in which to make a beginning.

II

One of the foundations of Maitland's theory was the argument that 'our record seems to assume that every holding either is a manor or forms part of a manor',[13] and one of the most damaging points made by his critics was that in circuit three in general, and in Cambridgeshire in particular, large numbers of holdings are apparently denied any manorial status or connection whatsoever. In this circuit, just over half the holdings – 873 out of 1655 – are described solely as *terra*; and although there is some exaggeration in Tait's claim that in Cambridgeshire 'the term employed for roughly nine out of every ten holdings is not *manerium* but *terra*', it is true that almost three-quarters of the holdings are so described.[14] This aspect of Maitland's thesis is quite definitely wrong, though the consequences for his definition of the manor are not as serious as would at first appear, for reasons which will be made clear in the latter part of this paper.

More serious is the further point made by Tait, and later elaborated by Round, that DB and ICC use the terms *terra* and *manerium* randomly or, as

---

[10] Hertfordshire is excluded because it has barely been touched by the rubricator so far as the marginal 'M' for manor is concerned. It is quite clear from the text of other counties that *one* of the functions of this rubrication was to correct errors in the manorial descriptions. In Hertfordshire, these are therefore significantly less reliable than in the remaining counties in circuit three.

[11] ICC.

[12] Maitland, 407.

[13] Maitland, 122.

[14] *EHR*, xii. 770. 319 of 450 holdings are described merely as *terra*.

Round preferred to phrase it, 'alternatively and quite indifferently'.[15] If this were the case, then it would be futile to pursue the search for a meaning any further, since the data in this circuit would be incapable of yielding a sensible answer. But Round's conclusion is suspect since it was reached by highly dubious methods. His approach was his customary one of collating DB and ICC, an exercise which yielded thirteen cases where the two documents disagreed as to the status of a holding.[16] Dismissing the cases of agreement as irrelevant, Round concluded:

> It is impossible to draw from this evidence any other conclusion than that *terra* and *manerium* were then used indifferently, whether we assign that use to the scribes or to those who made the original returns.[17]

Such confidence was quite unwarranted. In all, there are 289 cases where DB and ICC may be compared, the disagreements between them therefore representing about 5 per cent of the total, a figure which is not entirely out of the range of possible scribal error. However, there was a more fundamental flaw in Round's methodology. This assumed that Domesday and ICC had equal status and were independent views of the same body of material. Neither of these assumptions was valid, as Round was perfectly well aware. ICC is the product of an early stage in the Inquest, and the Domesday record for Cambridgeshire is based in part at least upon its findings. Unless there are compelling reasons for thinking otherwise, disagreements between the two are, in these circumstances, most naturally viewed as corrections made by the Domesday scribe to the materials before him. The only plausible argument to the contrary on this occasion is that the scribe's 'sense of Latinity', or his 'love of synonym and paraphrase',[18] led him to vary the language of his source from time to time, with random effects. But the effects are not, in fact, random. For although Round failed to point this out, there is only one case where the Domesday scribe has altered the *manerium* of ICC to *terra*.[19] In thirteen other cases he has altered the vague *terra* to the precise *manerium*.[20] In this situation, only a demonstration that *terra* and *manerium* were applied indiscriminately to holdings of every size and character could have rescued Round's thesis; but he did not even attempt to investigate the nature of the holdings to which the two terms were applied. It will be shown that there are, in fact, a number of objective tests which may be used to determine whether particular holdings are, or are not, manors. By these

---

[15] *EHR*, xv. 294.

[16] There are actually fifteen, for Round missed Abington and Ashley, both described as *terra* in ICC but as *manerium* in DB.

[17] *EHR*, xv. 294.

[18] Finn (1963), 49; J. H. Round, *Feudal England* (1895), 26.

[19] Dullingham. In a second instance, Wendy is described as both manor and land in ICC, the Domesday scribe following the latter, probably incorrectly: see Table 5.

[20] Abington, Ashley, Burrough Green, Carlton, Hildersham, Isleham, Quy, Rampton, Saxon Street, Stapleford, Stetchworth, Weston Colville and Wilbraham.

tests, the Domesday scribe rightly corrected his source in twelve instances,[21] a result which is inherently more plausible than Round's findings and one which provides some useful confirmation of the care taken by the scribe, the general accuracy of the Domesday record, and the importance of the distinction between manorial and non-manorial holdings to those conducting the Survey.

In circuit three, four rules governing manorial status may be deduced from that record. But before these are analysed, a preliminary difficulty must be faced. All four rules are evidenced by the preponderance of holdings which conform to them, usually in excess of 95 per cent of the relevant cases. The residue of exceptions are few enough to be considered scribal errors, the more so since in Cambridgeshire most can be shown to be such with the aid of ICC and IE. But it would be more satisfactory if suspicion of clerical error could be warranted by objective criteria other than statistical probability. Fortunately, some such criteria are available. In particular, two of the formulae employed by the scribe in this circuit appear to denote manorial status.

The first of these formulae is 'x holds y', a form used only of holdings which are entire vills or which are the largest holdings in their respective vills. The formula occurs 364 times in circuit three, in 22 per cent of the entries. It must occur thousands of times in the record as a whole and would thus provide an invaluable analytical tool if it proved to be a sure guide to manorial status.[22] It was a sure guide to such status in circuit three. In Cambridgeshire, for instance, there are 51 occurrences of the formula, 48 of which are used of holdings described as manors in their entries. Of the three exceptions, two – Shingay and Dullingham – are almost certainly scribal errors, Shingay because it is described as a manor elsewhere in the text of DB, and Dullingham because it is called a manor in ICC, this being one case where the testimony of ICC might reasonably be preferred to that of Domesday.[23] Both Shingay and Dullingham would also be accorded manorial status by one or more of the four rules to be examined below, as would Haddenham, the final exception. Converging lines of argument, happily supported by some textual evidence, confirm these cases to be errors, not exceptions. All 51 holdings described by the formula 'x holds y'

---

[21] The exceptions being Dullingham (n. 19) and Isleham, and the partial and uncertain case of Wendy.

[22] Other writers – notably Welldon Finn – have suspected that 'x holds y' denotes manorial status but have been confused by the fact that it is not applied to all manors, while some holdings described by the 'non-manorial' formula 'x holds z hides in y' clearly *are* manors. Both anomalies are easily explained. While all holdings described by 'x holds y' are manors, and all non-manorial holdings are described by 'x holds z hides in y', *manors in divided vills* were described by either formula. It is not clear why. In using the 'non-manorial' formula 'x holds z hides in y' for a manor in a divided vill, the scribe frequently showed an awareness of the apparent anomaly by adding *pro .. manerio* to the formula, to underline the manorial status of the holding (DB, i. 144bff., 151b–153a, 213aff). This, at least, was the usage in circuit three. A more detailed study might reveal some pattern to the manner in which manors in divided vills are treated.

[23] DB, i. 193a for Shingay, and above p. 142, n. 19, for Dullingham.

in Cambridgeshire are therefore manors or dependencies of such.

A similar result is obtained from Bedfordsire, Buckinghamshire and Middlesex, which together yield only eight apparent exceptions to the rule that 'x holds y' denotes manorial status. All eight exceptions are suspect on other grounds and are probably scribal errors.[24] There is thus not one case in circuit three where this formula is employed of a holding which is evidently not a manor, an impressive conclusion when it is recalled that more than half the holdings in this circuit are stigmatised as mere *terra* by the scribe.

The second formula which appears to indicate manorial status is *pro .. hidis se defendit*. Like 'x holds y', this formula implies that the holding concerned is an undivided vill, though it is not used exclusively of such vills, being occasionally applied to the largest holding in a divided vill. In Cambridgeshire, ICC allows us to see that the formula was originally employed there to describe the geld assessment of the entire vill and not the assessments of the individual manorial components of the vill, a feature which explains why it is normally applied to undivided vills in Domesday.[25]

In Cambridgeshire, 'answers for', or 'answered for', occurs 43 times in 39 different entries and in all but one case the holdings concerned are described as manors in the entries.[26] The single exception is Shingay. As already noted, Shingay is described as a manor elsewhere in the text of DB and is an apparent exception to several rules denoting manorial status. It is certainly a scribal error. Elsewhere in the circuit, the formula is used in a similar fashion. In all, it occurs 375 times, 272 in the four counties of Bedfordshire, Buckinghamshire, Cambridgeshire and Middlesex. In these four, there are just four further exceptions, all of which may be suspected of scribal error on

---

[24] The exceptions are Kinwick, Broom and Gladley in Beds., Oakley, Brook and Evershaw in Bucks., and Rug Moor and Tollington in Middlesex. All eight would be accorded manorial status by the operation of one or more of the four rules described below.

[25] Since the formula is not part of the manorial entries at all but is included in ICC to make a statement about the entire vill, its use very strongly implies that documents in the format of ICC – arranged hundred by hundred and vill by vill – lie behind the Domesday account of any county employing this formula. All the counties in circuits one and three employ it extensively (they account for more the 99 per cent of all occurrences of the formula in Domesday). If this conclusion is accepted, then Round's thesis about the making of Domesday is distinctly less shaky, and Galbraith's correspondingly less secure, than has been accepted. It is also worth noting that in six of the ten counties in circuits one and three the formula is also used in conjunction with geld reductions, such reductions being occasionally referred to in the other four counties (DB, i. 127a, 127b, 128b, 129b, 135a, 137a, 138a, 139a, 143a–b, 215b). Geld reductions may therefore have been a general, or at least common, phenomenon TRW, in which case one of the objectives of the Survey may have been to reaffirm the traditional assessments. In circuit three, the TRW assessments were discarded by the Domesday scribe, and we know that the TRE assessments were the ones generally retained. Is this a specific achievement which can be credited to the Domesday Inquest?

[26] The Domesday scribe sometimes abbreviated the *pro .. defendit* formula to '*Ibi x hidis*, a feature worth noting since this form appears in several counties where 'answers for' does not occur. Again, ICC allows us to see this very clearly in Cambridgeshire, where it is used in some thirty entries, all of them manors (e.g. Burwell, Wilbraham, Dullingham, Stetchworth, Burrough Green, West Wratting, etc.). It would be worth exploring the distribution of this formula in other circuits.

a number of different grounds.[27] *Se defendit* may therefore confidently be taken to denote manorial status.

Since the two formulae analysed above were normally applied to undivided vills, it will come as no surprise that the first rule determining manorial status in circuit three is that *undivided vills are manors* unless they are dependencies of other manors. Since almost 9500 vills in Domesday – approximately two-thirds of all Domesday vills – contained only a single holding, this one rule would be of great value if it proved to be of anything like general application. It therefore deserves careful consideration.

In Cambridgeshire, 48 out of 145 vills consisted of a single holding. Of these, 41 are described as manors, 4 as berewicks, and 3 as *terra*. Of these last 3, 1 is again Shingay, while the non-manorial status of another is explained by the record itself:

> Henny is an island in which there is half a hide of land. It does not give tax and never did before 1066.[28]

Neither a vill nor a geld unit, Henny's exceptional status is explained by either of these anomalies. As for the final exception to rule one – Haddenham – one must suspect scribal error, not merely because it fails to conform, nor even because one mistake in 48 is entirely possible, but because Haddenham is described by the manorial formula 'x holds y'.[29] For Cambridgeshire, therefore, rule one is well founded, though it should be remarked in passing that had we to depend upon the text of ICC, the rule is unlikely to have been deduced, since nine of Domesday's undivided vills were there designated *terra*, too high a proportion to be taken as scribal errors (though they were such in ICC).[30] All were corrected by the Domesday scribe. He, at least, could recognise a manor when he saw one, perhaps by virtue of the rule just described.

For Bedfordshire, Buckinghamshire and Middlesex, the results of applying this rule are almost as clear-cut as for Cambridgeshire. In these three counties there are 237 undivided vills, of which 223 are described as manors in their respective entries. The 14 exceptions are probably due to scribal error of one sort or another. Three of the properties, for instance, are of a single virgate, which suggests that they have either been wrongly named or that other entries for these 'vills' have been omitted from the record:[31] a one-virgate vill does not make much administrative sense.[32] Of the remaining

---

[27] They are Kinwick and Broom in Beds., Oakley in Bucks. and Rug Moor in Middlesex. All four also employ the 'x holds y' formula (see n. 24) and all would be accorded manorial status by at least one of the rules discussed below.

[28] DB, i. 192a.

[29] DB, i. 192a.

[30] Abington, Ashley, Burrough Green, Hildersham, Rampton, Saxon Street, Shingay, Stapleford and Wilbraham.

[31] ICC reveals that DB omits four entries in Cambridgeshire, and this will have happened in other counties. In addition, anonymous entries add to the number of 'missing' entries which might complete the manorial details of a vill. *Domesday Gazeteer*, 10, 25, 31, 192 and 261 lists 38 anonymous holdings for circuit three.

[32] Shirdon and Sudbury in Beds., and Southcote in Bucks.

11 cases, Broom (Beds.) is probably incorrectly described as it is a late, marginal addition to the text; while in the case of Oakley (Bucks.), the scribe may have been distracted from his proper business by the interest of the entry he was abstracting: it is the entry which concerns lessons in gold embroidery for the sheriff's daughter. Both vills are substantial holdings of 5 or more hides, and both are described by the manorial formula 'x holds y', which is true also of seven more of these entries. All these were probably scribal errors.[33] Only Stanestaple and Stoke Newington in Middlesex remain as exceptions to the rule, less than 1 per cent of the total.[34]

While rule one applied throughout the circuit, and may possibly apply throughout the country, the second rule determining manorial status applied with full force only in Cambridgeshire, though it had marked effect in both Bedfordshire and Middlesex. The second rule is that *no vill may contain more than one manor*. This is a very curious rule, and it is astonishing that it has escaped notice in a county so thoroughly analysed as Cambridgeshire has been. It helps to explain the paucity of manors in the county.

Of the existence of the rule there can be no doubt. There are 96 manors in Cambridgeshire, of which 42 have been accounted for as undivided vills, leaving 54 distributed among the remaining 103 vills. At first sight, 7 vills contain more than a single manor, too high a proportion to be ascribed to clerical error. But five of these seven cases are misleading. ICC is particularly valuable here since it reveals that there were two villages of Abington, Wilbraham and Wood Ditton, each containing one manor apiece.[35] ICC also states that the smaller of two holdings in Isleham said to be a manor in DB is actually mere *terra*.[36] The formula used in Domesday – 'x holds z hides in y' – does not controvert this; and since it fits the pattern of the remaining evidence, it may be accepted as a second case where ICC is right, and Domesday wrong, in its classification. Finally, one of the two manors assigned to Soham is a duplicate entry,[37] leaving Cottenham and Whittlesey as the sole exceptions to rule two. Two cases out of 96 might plausibly be accounted scribal errors. In the case of Whittlesey, moreover, it is easy to see how error may have arisen since the larger holding, which would normally have been designated the manor for the vill, was in the soke of the lord of the smaller holding.[38] As for Cottenham, Domesday hints that there may have been two Cottenhams, each containing one manor.[39]

---

[33] Broom, Kinwick and Gladley in Beds.; Bradenham, Brook, Evershaw and Oakley in Bucks.; Rug Moor and Tollington in Middlesex. Several employ the 'answers for', as well as the 'x holds y' formula.

[34] One might suspect here that the other holdings in these vills have been accidently omitted from the record.

[35] ICC, 10–11, 15, 31, 35, 60–1.

[36] ICC, 8; DB, i. 199b.

[37] DB, i. 189b.

[38] DB, i. 191b, 192b. The smaller holding has the 'x holds y', the larger the 'x holds z hides in y' formula.

[39] DB, i. 201b refers to 'eadem Coteham', perhaps implying an *alia* Cottenham. The total assessment – 26 hides – could well include 2 vills.

This curious rule had some force in Bedfordshire and Middlesex too. In Middlesex, 51 of the 62 vills contained one manor. In 38 of these, manor and vill were identical; in 11, the vills contained a single manor alongside non-manorial holdings; and in 2, there were more than one manor in the vill. The two exceptions were the enormous vills of Fulham and Stepney. They appear to be quite certain exceptions for the texts are insistent on the manorial status of more than one holding in each, and all aspects of the text, including the formulae, support this status. In Bedfordshire, too, scribal error does not seem the most likely explanation of the apparent exceptions to rule two. Here, 118 vills contained a manor, 107 of them a single manor, and 11 more than one manor. The proportions between these figures are such that there can be no doubt that rule two had considerable force in Bedford-shire. Equally, however, it was not enforced with the rigour detected in Cambridgeshire, the 11 exceptions being too numerous to be ascribed to error, though one or two of them probably were mistakes. Finally, in this as in almost every other respect, Buckinghamshire presents a sharp contrast to the remaining counties in the circuit, with 41 vills containing more than one manor. In Buckinghamshire, with its higher proportion of undivided vills, its considerably fewer fragmented vills, and its absence of large numbers of sokemen, there was no need for the strict manorial discipline enforced in the counties to the north-east, and rule two therefore had little currency within its borders.

The third rule may be promptly disposed of since it requires little in the way of demonstration. *In divided vills, the manor will be the largest holding.* The exceptions to this rule are remarkably few. The unusual case of Whittlesey has already been mentioned. The only instance noted in Bedfordshire is similar in essentials, since the two holdings concerned were both held by the same man, making clerical confusion only too likely.[40] In Buckinghamshire, there are two cases involving Great and Little Marlow which have every appearance of scribal error. But overall, it is clear that size, or more accurately the size of the geld liability, had a determining rôle in deciding manorial status. As much energy has been consumed in the past in the search for an absolute standard by which properties might be judged to be manorial or otherwise, it should be added that it was not the absolute size of the geld assessment which mattered but its proportion to that of other holdings within the vill.

Before stating the fourth and final rule which determined manorial status in this circuit, a brief overview of the non-manorial vills is necessary in order to grasp the need for, and the nature of the arrangements produced by the operation of this rule. Much can be summarised in a few statistics (Table 1). In Buckinghamshire and Middlesex, non-manorial vills – that is, vills without any manor in them at all – were a negligible feature. In Hertford-shire they were important, though not as important as these figures suggest, for reasons given above. But in Bedfordshire, and above all in Cambridge-shire, they were a major feature of the landscape, the dominant one in many

---

[40] Podington: DB, i. 215b, 216a.

TABLE 1: VILLS CONTAINING NO MANOR IN CIRCUIT 3

County	% of vills	% of holdings
Cambs	31.5	44.4
Beds	13.8	23.6
Herts	12.2	23.7
Bucks	2.8	4.4
Middx	1.6	4.0

parts of those counties. Their social and tenurial characteristics were sharply etched by Maitland, in his fine analysis of Wetherley hundred. After first remarking that in this part of Cambridgeshire 'we may easily find a village which taken as a whole has been utterly free from seignoral domination', Maitland continued:[41]

> Now if by a 'manor' we mean what our historical economists usually mean when they use the term, we must protest that before the Norman Conquest there were very few manors in the Wetherley hundred. In no one case was the whole of a village coincident with a manor, with a lords' estate. The king had considerable manors in Comberton and Haslingfield . . . But . . . in Barton, Grantchester, Shepreth, Orwell, Wratworth, Whitwell and Arrington, we see nothing manorial, unless we hold ourselves free to use that term of a little tenement which to all appearances might easily be cultivated by the labour of one household, at all events with occasional help supplied by a few cottagers. . . .

As a piece of social analysis, the few pages devoted by Maitland to Wetherley hundred have not since been improved upon. But Maitland did fail to notice one crucial detail: that King William's contemporaries were more or less of the same opinion as the 'historical economists' of his own day in their judgement of what was and what was not manorial. They were, if anything, severer judges of what should constitute a manor. For where Maitland could name up to 8 of the 54 holdings in the 12 vills of Wetherley as potential manors, King William's commissioners could find only 3.

How, in these circumstances, were matters pertaining to the geld and to other public burdens managed? In areas 'utterly free from seignoral domination', how was leadership at the local level organised and institutionalised? It was to meet such situations that rule four must have been devised, the rule being that *where a vill contains no manor, it is subordinated to a manor in an adjacent vill.* The vills were then grouped to produce manorial blocks.

A normally manorialised hundred will provide a useful contrast to hundreds such as Wetherley. Staploe, the first hundred described in ICC, provides such a normal example (Table 2).

There are 10 vills and 10 manors in the hundred, every vill containing just 1 manor. Half the vills are single-manor vills and undivided, 2 others containing just 2 holdings. The geld arrangements illustrate clearly the

---

[41] Maitland, 129.

TABLE 2: STAPLOE HUNDRED

Status	Vill	Hides	Holdings
M	Kennett	3.5	1
M	Badlingham	3.5	1
M	Chippenham	10.0	1
M	Snailwell	5.0	1
M	Exning	15.0	2
M	Burwell	15.0	5
M	Soham	11.5	4
M	Fordham	10.0	4
M	Iselham	10.0	4
M	Wicken	7.0	1

5-hide principle, though it is not uniformly present. All the holdings designated manors are substantial properties, the average for the hundred being over 7 hides. All had demesne teams, peasant teams, a dependent peasantry (in considerable numbers), and all were held by magnates both TRE and TRW, 8 of the 10 manors being held by the king, the church, or Edeva the Fair TRE, the remaining 2 by royal thanes. All would have satisfied the most stringent criteria of 'our historical economists' as to their manorial status.

These remarks apply with equal force – in some cases with greater force – to the adjacent hundreds of Cheveley, Staine, Radfield, Flendish, Witchford and Wisbech. With the exception of Chilford hundred in the extreme south-east, the entire eastern half of Cambridgeshire is thereby accounted for. Although these hundreds accounted for just over a quarter of the hidage and just over a third of the vills of the county, they contained no less than 52 per cent of the manors and 69 per cent of the undivided vills. Eastern Cambridgeshire was as highly manorialised as most parts of old Wessex. The manorial structure here was entirely capable of supporting the public burdens laid upon the hundred.

Not so in Wetherley hundred, where there were only 3 manors among the 54 holdings and 12 vills. In this hundred, therefore, all 54 holdings and 12 vills were subordinated to the three manorial centres, as this table illustrates (Table 3).

It must be emphasised that this arrangement has not been achieved by juggling with figures to produce neat arithmetical results. The neat arithmetical results are the work of the Anglo-Saxon or Anglo-Norman administration. The order of the vills here is that of ICC and DB;[42] the three blocks of 20, 40 and 20 hides are distinct geographical areas; the three manors are the only holdings identified as manorial by either Domesday or ICC; and all three conform to the criteria of manorial status of 'our historical economists'. Finally, the three manors were held respectively by the king,

---

[42] As reconstructed by C. Hart, *The Hidation of Cambridgeshire* (Dept of English Local History Occasional Papers, no. 6, Leicester, 1974), 46–67, which I have found invaluable for this purpose and for several other aspects of the work on Cambridgeshire.

TABLE 3: WETHERLEY HUNDRED

Status	Vill	Hides	Holdings
M	Comberton	6	5
	Barton	7	3
	Grantchester	7	6
	SUB-TOTAL	20	
M	Haslingfield	20	7
	Harlton	5	2
	Barrington	10	5
	Shepreth	5	5
	SUB-TOTAL	40	
	Orwell	4	8
	Wratworth	4	5
	Whitwell	4	4
	Wimpole	4	2
M	Arrington	4	2
	SUB-TOTAL	20	

the king, and Earl Roger. Despite the paucity of manors in Wetherley hundred, the public burdens were in responsible hands.

In selecting Wetherley hundred to illustrate rule four I have not 'studiously sought a rare case', as Maitland elegantly described this academic ploy.[43] All the hundreds in western Cambridgeshire reveal this same pattern; not all, it is true, with the same harmonious proportions and elegant simplicity, but still with the essential structures visible. Three further examples will reveal some of the variations. Chesterton hundred offers a particularly neat arrangement because the hundred comprises three detached areas. Two of these consisted of 30 hides apiece, and each contained just one manor:

TABLE 4: CHESTERTON HUNDRED

Status	Vill	Hides	Holdings
M	Cottenham	26	5
	Westwick	4	2
	SUB-TOTAL	30	
M	Histon	30	4
	SUB-TOTAL	30	
	Dry Drayton	20	5
M	Childerley	10	3
	SUB-TOTAL	30	
M	Chesterton	30	1
	SUB-TOTAL	30	

[43] Maitland, 134.

The third detached area contained 60 hides but these clearly divide into a northern group of 30 hides and a southern group, also of 30 hides, each containing a single manor.

Armingford, in the extreme south-west of the county, is interesting in a quite different manner. The western part of the hundred contained 6 vills and 22 holdings subordinated to one manor, an arrangement balanced by an eastern block of 4 vills and 22 holdings, also subordinated to one manor. Separating the two was an island of the strictest manorial propriety, where every vill contained just one manor, and every manor was properly manorial:

TABLE 5: ARMINGFORD HUNDRED

Status	Vill	Hides	Holdings
M	Steeple Morden	10	3
	Tadlow	5	3
	Guilden Morden	5	4
	Clopton	5	2
	East Hatley	5	3
	Croydon	10	7
	SUB-TOTAL	40	
M	Wendy	5	2
M	Shingay	5	1
M	Litlington	5	2
M	Abington Piggotts	5	6
	SUB-TOTAL	20	
M	Bassingbourn	10	3
	Whaddon	10	8
	Meldreth	10	6
	Melbourn	10	5
	SUB-TOTAL	40	

Finally, the puzzling case of Whittlesford hundred. The arrangement here is quite as neat as the other examples; the units again correspond to geographical realities, forming definable and self-contained areas:

TABLE 6: WHITTLESFORD HUNDRED

Status	Vill	Hides	Holdings
M	Whittlesford	12	3
	Sawston	8	3
	SUB-TOTAL	20	
M	Hinxton	20	4
M	Ickleton	20	2
	Duxford	20	5
	SUB-TOTAL	40	

But in other respects, Whittlesford forms a distinct contrast to Wetherley. There is in this hundred nothing like the extreme fragmentation of holdings found in Wetherley; and the two vills without manors – Sawston and Duxford – each contain one substantial holding with distinct manorial characteristics. Both, it is true, were somewhat more fragmented TRE and TRW but not, one would have thought, to the extent of losing viable manorial status, though Sawston approached this. A clerical error in the case of the holding of Count Eustace in Duxford might reasonably be suspected here.

It will be apparent from all this that circuit three presents the sharpest of possible contrasts to that other circuit in which the Domesday scribe meticulously rubricated the manorial status of all holdings, circuit six. Of this circuit, Stenton could write: 'it is substantially correct to say that every parcel of land in this district is understood to form part of some manor', adding that 'there is no example . . . of the employment of the neutral *terra* in contradistinction to *manerium* and *soca*'.[44] In circuit three, however, the scribe has officiously striven to make just that distinction, using the term *terra* with anything but neutrality. But the very sharpness of the contrast between the two circuits suggests that the term *manerium* was used with deliberation. Local variations there undoubtedly were, but they were variations upon a common theme, adapting a common terminology to differing social and tenurial realities.

This last point is worth emphasis because failure to take account of the social and tenurial context of the geld arrangements was arguably the one serious weakness in Maitland's thesis. This context largely explains the differences between circuits three and six on the one hand, and differences within circuit three on the other. Rule two had little effect in Buckinghamshire because the social structure there was quite dissimilar to that of Cambridgeshire, where the rule had maximum application. Within Cambridgeshire, Wetherley hundred had only three manors among 54 holdings and 12 vills because it was a hundred dominated by tiny holdings, held for the most part by groups of sokemen TRE. Cheveley, by contrast, with 7 vills and only 8 holdings, had a manor in every vill, all held by substantial men TRE and TRW. Although the block-structuring of lordless vills found in Wetherley and much of western Cambridgeshire reveals at one level 'the make-believe of ancient finance',[45] this same feature was nevertheless an expression of the social and tenurial realities of the day and should be viewed as a successful adaptation of the geld system to those realities.

For the geld was at the root of all the rules deduced for circuit three. Undivided vills were manors, which means in effect geld centres. In fragmented vills containing a manor, the manor is the holding with the largest geld liability, the geld centre in the vill. Vills with no manor at all were subordinated to a manor in a neighbouring vill. In all this, as in the

---

[44] F. M. Stenton, *Types of Manorial Structure in the northern Danelaw* (Oxford Studies in Social and Legal History, ii, 1910), 4, and note.
[45] Maitland, 473.

peculiar Cambridge rule that no vill may contain more than one manor, manorial status was determined in relation to the geld, taking account of the social and tenurial structures of the area. Maitland's fundamental perception therefore remains valid: 'About details we may be wrong, but that this term (*manerium*) has a technical meaning which is connected with the levy of the danegeld we can not doubt'.[46] If we were to reformulate Maitland's famous aphorism, we might perhaps replace 'a house against which geld is charged' with 'a house at which geld is collected'.[47]

---

[46] Maitland, 128.

[47] This definition, and all of the rules deduced for circuit three, would exclude virtually all sokemen and petty landowners from responsibility for the geld, leaving responsibility in the hands of the holders of officially designated 'manors'. James Campbell's paper in this volume has some interesting things to say about the reeves mentioned in the Geld rolls in connection with the collection of gelds. These reeves are referred to as the officials of the greater landowners in the area covered by the Geld rolls. They were presumably the agents operating from officially recognised manorial centres. Petty landowners are unlikely to have employed such officials. See below, 205–7.

Domesday Book: Estate Structures in the West Midlands

JOHN D. HAMSHERE

SINCE THE 1950s the geography of Domesday England has been available to us in the pages of Professor Darby's magisterial studies.[1] A series of brilliantly executed maps have allowed us to trace the spatial patterns of the population, ploughteams, meadow, woodland and other Domesday resources both at a county and a national level. We have been able to assess the impact of the environmental conditions of soil, topography and water supply on those re-created spatial patterns of King William's England. There is, however, another, less well-studied, geography within Domesday Book: the geography of landholding. It is this tenurial geography, as Lennard has called it,[2] comprised of the complex geographical patterns of landholding, and the impact it had upon the related Domesday Book statistics that forms the subject of this paper. The area selected for study is the three west midland counties of Warwickshire, Worcestershire and Gloucestershire.

The study of individual estates and their component manors have for many years been the subject of Domesday research. Few attempts, however, have been made to put together these findings on a regional basis such that it would be possible to ascertain any impact that ownership might have had on the areal variation of the statistics contained in Domesday Book. Analysis upon these lines was suggested by Professor Kosminsky's study of the Hundred Rolls of 1279.[3] Kosminsky found that the proportion of demesne arable and the social structure of the population appeared to co-vary with the size of manor. Considerable differences thus existed between what Kosminsky defined as large, medium and small manors.[4] It was suggested that these differences were as apparent in Domesday Book as they were in 1279. Although Kosminsky did not directly associate the size of manors and their internal structures with different types of ownership, he did recognise the distinctive characteristics of ecclesiastically held manors, a high proportion of which were very large. The theme of the rôle of demesne agriculture within Domesday Book estates has been further developed by Dr Sally

---

[1] H. C. Darby, *The Domesday Geography of England* (7 vols., Cambridge, 1952–77).
[2] Lennard, *Rural England* (1959).
[3] E. A. Kosminsky, *Studies in the Agrarian History of England in the 13th Century* (Oxford, 1956).
[4] Kosminsky, 96.

Harvey. In a recent study, Dr Harvey utilised the ratio of demesne plough-teams to peasant ploughteams as an index of the extent of demesne agriculture on a number of Domesday Book estates. She concluded that demesne agriculture was, by and large, more important on smaller estates and, by comparison with their values, more profitable to their holders.[5] In a similar vein, my own analysis of the estate of the church of Worcester[6] was able to demonstrate that its component parts – the demesnes of the bishop and of the monks and the holdings of the subtenants – were not only different in terms of areal size but also in terms of the allocation of their ploughteams and the social structure of their dependent peasantry. Evidence accumulated from these and many other estate studies,[7] suggests that estate ownership and the complex patterns of landholding within estates could be an important factor in explaining the spatial variation of many of the phenomena that are recorded in Domesday Book.

Although Domesday Book is, of course, organised by major landholders, formidable difficulties exist in establishing the geography of landholding and in assigning the relevant statistics to the areas so identified. Domesday Book does not describe the areal extent of each of its entries and this geographical pattern has to be painstakingly reconstructed, utilising ancient ecclesiastical parish and township boundaries. Whilst this method appears successful, in that few entries remain unidentified, it still has to be viewed as an approximation, and the maps produced here should be seen in that light. Furthermore, the complex nature of feudal relationships, expressed through the process of subinfeudation of landholdings, gives many Domesday Book manors a very contorted structure, within which there can be considerable confusion of terminology. To illustrate this, Fig. 1 has been prepared, in order to display the complexities of landholding within west midland Domesday manors. A manor could either be held in demesne, that is in the hands of the tenant-in-chief, or it could be subinfeudated, that is sublet, usually on payment of some form of feudal rent. On many occasions a single manor could contain both elements, being partly retained in demesne and partly sublet. In certain instances the subinfeudated portion formed, to all intents and purposes, a sub-manor within the main manorial structure. The term 'demesne' is thus employed in this sense to differentiate between lands held directly by the tenant-in-chief and those that have been sublet. A further complication in the second tier of Fig. 1 is produced by the practice of many tenants-in-chief of 'farming' (or renting) their manors for an agreed annual return. Lennard has suggested that this practice was likely to be more common than Domesday Book apparently reveals.[8] In the west midlands

[5] S. P. J. Harvey, 'The extent and profitability of demesne agriculture in England in the late eleventh century', in T. H. Aston, P. R. Cross, C. Dyer and J. Thirsk (eds.), *Social Relations and Ideas* (Cambridge, 1983), 45–72.

[6] J. D. Hamshere, 'The Structure and exploitation of the Domesday Book estate of the church of Worcester', *Landscape History*, 7 (1985), 41–52.

[7] For example, F. R. H. Du Boulay, *The Lordship of Canterbury* (1966); E. Miller, *The Abbey and Bishopric of Ely* (Cambridge, 1951); C. E. Dyer, *Lords and Peasants in a Changing Society* (Cambridge, 1980).

[8] Lennard, 105–41.

the 'farming' out of such manors finds no mention save on royal estates, although it would be unwise to assume that all tenants-in-chief retained an equal interest in the direct cultivation of their demesne manors. Clearly subtenants stood in a different relationship to the tenant-in-chief than did the holders of these 'farms', although both would have acted as the immediate lord of the dependent peasantry. Some subtenants appear to have acted as tenants-in-chief by further subletting lands on which they themselves were only subtenants.

The third tier of Fig. 1 reveals a second use of the term demesne. In this case, the term is used in the sense of the lord's home farm, that is the manorial lands that were devoted to agricultural production for the lord. Throughout Domesday Book the lands of both the greatest tenant-in-chief and the most minor subtenant are almost invariably divided between the home farm (demesne) and the lands of the peasantry (*terra villanorum*). The only indication of the relative size of those two elements is given by the ploughteams ascribed to each.

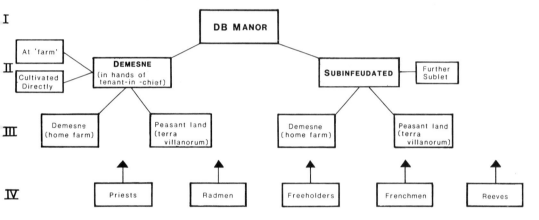

Fig. 1. Manorial structure in Domesday Book: West Midlands.

The fourth tier of the diagram shows a range of small landholding elements that are ascribed both hidage and ploughteams in the west midlands. It is often unclear from Domesday Book whether these landholders held their land within the demesne or peasant land, or whether they formed a separate landholding element within the manor.

The Domesday Book manors of the west midlands thus exhibit a complex and diverse structure. Some manors, notably large ecclesiastical ones, exhibit most of the features on Fig. 1, whilst other, often small, manors held by a subtenant, exhibit an apparently simple structure with only a division between demesne and peasant lands. From this complex structure it is possible to identify four major landholding groups which have been further employed for analysis of the Domesday Book statistics. These are the royal demesnes, the ecclesiastical demesnes, the demesnes of lay tenants-in-chief and the lands of the subtenants. The first task is to ascertain whether or not these groupings exhibit different profiles within the Domesday Book statistics. In order to achieve this, the laborious task of sorting the Domesday Book entries between tenant and subtenant has to be undertaken. This task was made much easier by the employment of a micro-computer which not only enables greater flexibility in manipulating Domesday Book data but also allows simple statistical analysis to be undertaken.

ESTATE GROUPS IN THE WEST MIDLANDS

In order to identify any differences between the four estate groups, thirteen categories of Domesday Book data have been selected for study. They include the number of landholdings, as expressed by the number of Domesday Book entries, and aspects of the hidage, population, plough-teams, value and meadowland. Each of these are widely recorded throughout the three counties. It would, for instance, have served little purpose to include ploughlands as they are only recorded for one of the three counties. As a preliminary study, each data category has been expressed as a percentage of the west midland total, by estate. Thus in Table 1, royal demesne comprised 15 per cent of all hidage in the three counties, ecclesiastical demesne 26 per cent and so on. The final column expresses the mean percentage of all thirteen categories of data for each estate. This facilitates comparison of each data category by estate. Hence royal demesnes have an average of 16 per cent of the thirteen categories, of which villeins, plough-teams, peasant ploughteams and 1086 value are significantly above that mean, whilst slaves, demesne ploughteams, meadow and 1066 value are below it. Ecclesiastical demesnes, averaging a quarter of all data categories, display less variation, but have miscellaneous population, peasant plough-teams and meadowland above that mean, and slaves, bordars and demesne teams set below it. Lay demesnes, with 28 per cent of the overall resources, have higher proportions of villeins, slaves and 1066 values, whilst their ploughteams are more equally allocated between the demesne and the peasantry. The subtenants, possessing the largest average percentage of the resources shown (31 per cent), have greater proportions of bordars, slaves and demesne ploughteams, whilst, like lay demesnes, their share of the overall value declined markedly between 1066 and 1086.

Clearly the four estate groups display marked differences in their share of different categories of Domesday Book data. Some of these distinctions, particularly those concerning demesne ploughteams, are reminiscent of those that Kosminsky associated with manorial size.[9] If Kosminsky's three manorial categories are translated into hides from the acreage figures he gives, at the notional rate of 120 acres to the hide, then large manors would be the equivalent of 8.3 hides and over, medium manors 4.2–8.2 hides, and small manors under 4.2 hides. If ploughteams were to be employed as a

[9] Kosminsky, 87–101.

TABLE 1: PERCENTAGES OF SELECTED DOMESDAY BOOK STATISTICS BY ESTATE

Estate	DB Holdings	Hides	Popu-lation	Villeins	Bordars	Slaves	Other Popu-lation	Plough-teams	Demesne Plough-teams	Plough-teams of Men	1066 Value (£)	1086 Value (£)	Meadow (Acres)	Mean X
Royal Demesne	7	15	18	19	18	14	18	19	13	21	9	25	10	16
Ecclesiastical Demesne	16	26	24	26	21	22	28	27	22	29	26	25	30	25
Lay Demesne	28	28	29	30	27	32	32	27	27	27	32	24	21	28
Subtenants	49	31	29	25	34	32	22	27	38	23	33	26	39	31
Total	100	100	100	100	100	100	100	100	100	100	100	100	100	100

TABLE 2: MEAN SIZE OF DOMESDAY BOOK
LANDHOLDINGS BY ESTATE

Estate	DB Holdings (Nos.)	Hides (Mean)	Population (Mean)	Ploughteams (Mean)	1086 Value £ (Mean)
Royal Demesne	72	9.9	47.5	20.4	15.3
Ecclesiastical Demesne	168	7.5	27.4	12.6	6.4
Lay Demesne	295	4.6	18.8	7.3	3.6
Subtenants	517	2.9	10.9	4.9	2.2
Total	1052	4.6	18.3	7.5	4.1

more sensitive index, at the rate of 100 acres to each team, as suggested by Professor Darby,[10] then the equivalent figures would be 10, 5 and under 5 teams. On Table 2, which shows the mean size of Domesday Book land-holdings by estate group, royal demesnes fit Kosminsky's classification of large manors in terms of both hidage and ploughteams, whilst ecclesiastical demesnes fit this classification on ploughteams but not on hidage, suggesting, perhaps, the equivalent of a mixture of large and medium-sized manors. The lay demesnes appear as the equivalent of medium-sized manors on both criteria and the subtenants' holdings that of small manors.

These figures must be regarded as notional, particularly as the distinction between the manor as an administrative area as opposed to the actual operating agrarian units, that has been made by Professor Kosminsky,[11] is even more pronounced when considering Domesday Book entries. Royal and ecclesiastical demesnes have a considerable number of composite Domesday Book entries in which the returns of many townships' areas have been aggregated together. By contrast, the subtenancies most frequently deal with holdings that comprise but a single township and on occasions only a part of a township.

Even taking into account these *caveats* it is clear that sufficient differences exist in these aggregated Domesday Book statistics to reward closer inspection of the tenurial geography of the estate groups. To this end each estate group will be considered in turn, utilising the actual Domesday Book figures rather than percentages, and, as a further guide to regional variation, subdividing these statistics between their constituent counties.

ROYAL DEMESNE

The distribution of royal demesne is shown in Fig. 2. The immediate impression is one of extensive contiguous blocks of territory often centred on large federated manors that had previously been held by King Edward. Thus Berkeley and Tewkesbury in Gloucestershire, Bromsgrove and Kidderminster in Worcestershire and Stoneleigh in Warwickshire form the

[10] Darby (1977), 131.
[11] Kosminsky, 75–6.

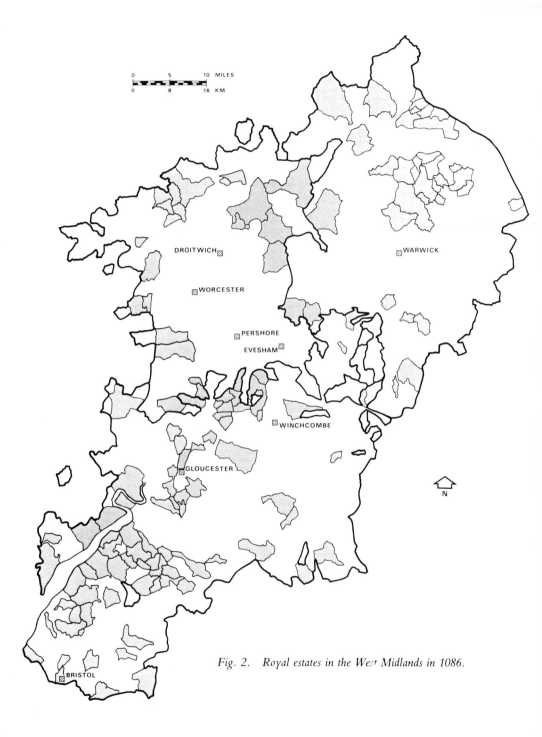

DROITWICH

WARWICK

WORCESTER

PERSHORE
EVESHAM

WINCHCOMBE

GLOUCESTER

N

Fig. 2.   Royal estates in the West Midlands in 1086.

BRISTOL

0   5   10 MILES

0   8   16 KM

centres of extensive possessions. Around these core-areas have been added manors that were not in Edward's possession in 1066. Apart from the addition of Harold Godwinson's manors other notable acquisitions were drawn from the estate of Brictric and his thegns and Bishop Odo in Gloucestershire, Countess Godiva in Warwickshire and Earl Edwin in both Warwickshire and Worcestershire. Generally these additions complemented the Edwardian possessions, although the process of agglomeration had not been an uninterrupted one. In Gloucestershire many large federated manors had been dismembered at some stage, possibly during the stewardship of William FitzOsbern. There are signs, however, that some attempt had been made to re-create something of their previous structure in that the lands of Tewkesbury church are surveyed as part of the royal possessions in 1086, perhaps in an attempt to bring together the disparate manor of Tewkesbury.

Royal demesne is largely absent from many areas long associated with the richness of their agricultural produce, such as the Vale of Evesham, the Feldon area of Warwickshire and the north-eastern Cotswolds. Comparisons with the distribution of class 1 and 2 agricultural soils, as defined by the Ministry of Agriculture,[12] however, does suggest that the royal demesnes did have a wide access to high yielding arable land. This is found at its greatest extent on the Gloucestershire royal demesnes, at Berkeley and Thornbury in the Vale of Berkeley, at Bitton on the Bristol Avon and in the Thames Valley at Down Ampney and Fairford. In Worcestershire such soils were restricted on royal demesnes to the Bromsgrove series, found most extensively in the manor of Tardebigge, whilst in Warwickshire the upper Liassic soils of the manor of Brailes and the terrace deposits of the Avon Valley at Kenilworth and Bidford form the most important concentrations. In such large blocks of territory it is clear that environmental conditions must have varied enormously and it is unfortunate that the aggregated statistics of Domesday Book generally do not allow us to investigate the internal variation between the multiplicity of agrarian units that went to make up these large federated manors.

Table 3 demonstrates the considerable wealth of the royal demesne, totalling over 700 hides, with a recorded population in excess of 3400 persons and clothed with nearly 1500 ploughteams. In 1086 it contributed over £1100 to the revenue, a figure that would have to be inflated in real terms due to the practice of assaying and weighing the cash returns. Overall, the royal demesnes exhibit a statistical profile that might be expected from estates that were largely geared to maximising cash revenue for the Crown. Villeins at 50 per cent of the recorded population are relatively over-represented compared with the average for all three counties, just as slaves are under-represented (15 per cent compared with 19.3 per cent). The proportion of ploughteams in demesne, at 19 per cent, is the lowest of all four estate groups, whilst the average return of £1.5 per hide is the highest in the west midlands and exactly double that yielded from the estates of the

---

[12] Ministry of Agriculture, *Agricultural Land Classification of England and Wales* (1974).

subtenants. Much of this conforms to Kosminsky's findings for large manors in the thirteenth century,[13] where he suggested peasant rents were a more important feature than service leading to a diminution of the proportional contribution of the demesne arable. Indeed this would recommend itself as a sensible *modus operandi* for those individuals involved in operating the royal demesnes in the eleventh century. Faced with the very heavy cash returns expected of them, what Hoyt has called the rack-renting of the Conqueror,[14] they would have opted to raise the revenue directly in the form of rents, rather than through the more indirect method of exacting demesne service and then marketing the produce. This receives some support from the extensive nature of the units of royal desmesne which would have caused severe logistic problems in organising service from a widely scattered peasantry. Secondly, the peasantry on royal demesne were well equipped with their own ploughteams, with an average of 2.9 persons to each peasant team, a resource that could readily be exploited by some form of rent.

Whilst these general trends in the data underpin all royal demesnes in the west midlands, Table 3 does offer evidence of some variation between the three counties, most notably in the higher proportion of bordars in Worcestershire, of villeins in Warwickshire and of slaves in Gloucestershire. These three features are common to most of the estate groupings and clearly reflect a regional or county element within the population statistics. Northern and western Worcestershire, in general, is characterised by high proportions of bordars within its population structure, a feature that has been associated with the extensive woodlands found in that area.[15] This correlation, however, is not absolute on royal demesnes, for only at Bromsgrove and Kidderminster is there a coincidence between extensive woodland and bordars; the well-wooded manors of Hanley Castle and Feckenham not being marked by high proportions of bordars. Indeed, on the Worcestershire royal demesnes, the incidence of bordars within the population would seem to coincide more with a manorial structure in which there was a central administrative settlement, organised by a reeve and beadle, surrounded by a widely scattered group of berewicks, possibly occupied by the bordars.[16] Despite this high proportion of bordars, the dependent peasantry were exceptionally well equipped with their own ploughteams, averaging 1 peasant team to every 2.2 of the recorded population.

The Warwickshire royal demesnes were only slightly larger in total area than their Worcestershire counterparts, yet were occupied by a much bigger recorded population, heavily dominated by villeins. A feature of the whole of Warwickshire is the high proportion of villeins within its population, but this is particularly accentuated on the three large royal demesnes of Kineton

[13] Kosminsky, 273–8.
[14] R. S. Hoyt, *The Royal demesne in English Constitutional History, 1066–1272* (Ithaca, 1950), 78.
[15] J. D. Hamshere, 'A computer-assisted study of Domesday Worcestershire', in T. R. Slater and P. J. Jarvis (eds.), *Field and Forest: an historical geography of Warwickshire and Worcestershire* (Norwich, 1982), 112–13.
[16] DB, i. 172a.

and Wellesbourne, Brailes and Stoneleigh. A further concentration of villeins is apparent on the six manors surrounding Coventry, that had belonged to Godiva in 1066, but were in royal possession in 1086. All together these manors account for 77 per cent of all villeins on royal demesne in Warwickshire. The higher status of the peasantry was not reflected in their ploughteam possession, for there was only one peasant team to every four recorded population on the Warwickshire demesnes. In addition, the revenue derived from Warwickshire is considerably underestimated on Table 3, for no value is given for those manors William inherited directly from Edward. Instead the preamble to the Warwickshire folios lists a further £193 that was raised from these manors.[17] This has the effect of virtually doubling the value shown in Table 3 and putting the return to the Crown at £3 per hide of the demesne. It must be remembered that this figure does include the pleas of the county and the returns of the borough of Warwick. Even so, such high revenues suggest that the Warwickshire villeins would be required to yield far more for their smaller holdings than the lower status Worcestershire bordars.

The greater part of the royal demesne lay in Gloucestershire, accounting for 70 per cent of the hidage, 63 per cent of the ploughteams and 73 per cent of the revenue derived by the Crown from the three counties. Perhaps the outstanding feature of the Gloucestershire demesnes is the higher proportion of slaves in the population, although at 22 per cent this is still below average for that county as a whole. Closer inspection of the Domesday Book returns reveals a confused and confusing pattern. Not only are many entries composite ones, with single sets of statistics covering vast territories, but also the format in which they are given is very different from that used on royal demesne in the other two counties. The context in which many of the statistics are placed is that of 1066, particularly on those Edwardian manors that had formally paid the farm of one night. The format used on these manors is to give the hidage and demesne ploughteams TRE followed by the other manorial statistics. Almost as a footnote we are informed of the additions that had been made by the sheriff or reeve, making any calculation of the 1086 population very problematic. In certain instances, notably on the huge federated manor of Berkeley, the statistics for the outlying members, amounting to a recorded population of 567 persons, seems only to be given for TRE. The population returns are thus very difficult to disentangle and the figures given in Table 3 must be treated with some caution. It may well be that we are seeing, in part at least, a pre-Conquest situation in which slavery was an important element in the production of the farm of one night. Certainly the twenty years following the Conquest had witnessed many changes on the Gloucestershire royal demesnes, particularly in the commutation to money of all but one of the farms of one night,[18] and the considerable raising of revenues elsewhere on the estate. This may well have

[17] DB, i. 238a.

[18] P. H. Stafford, 'The Farm of One Night and the organization of King Edward's Estates in Domesday', *Economic History Review*, 33 (1980), 491–502.

TABLE 3: ROYAL DEMESNE IN THE WEST MIDLANDS

County	Holdings	Hides	Popu-lation	Villeins	Bordars/Cottars	Slaves	Other Popu-lation	Plough-teams	Demesne Plough-teams	Peasant Plough-teams	1066 Value (£)	1086 Value (£)	Meadow (Acres)
Worcestershire	12	103.75	503	180	239	42	42	258.5	31.5	227	102	143.8	0
Warwickshire	19	109.25	915	578	268	44	25	283.5	55	228.5	83	149.5	600
Gloucestershire	41	503.62	2004	948	463	443	150	924.25	186.25	738	96.75	809.7	144
Total	72	716.62	3422	1706	970	529	217	1466.25	272.75	1193.5	281.75	1103	744

POPULATION AND PLOUGHTEAMS: PERCENTAGES BY COUNTY

County	Villeins	Bordars/Cottars	Slaves	Other Population	Total	Demesne Ploughteams	Peasant Ploughteams	Total
Worcestershire	36	48	8	8	100	12	88	100
Warwickshire	63	29	5	3	100	19	81	100
Gloucestershire	48	23	22	7	100	20	80	100
All Three Counties	50	28	16	6	100	19	81	100

had the effect of reducing the proportion of slaves within the population. In the seven entries where Domesday Book informs of 'added' resources, only 5 slaves are mentioned amongst a total of 44 persons.[19] Also, at Barton Regis, where figures are given for 1066 and when Roger acquired the manor, it is the slaves and coliberts which show the greatest level of reduction.[20] Similarly, at Tewkesbury, in the head of the manor, the 50 slaves and 16 bordars of 1066 are recorded as 22 slaves and 13 burgesses in 1086.[21] There are, thus, some indications that slavery might well be over-estimated in Table 3 and that the royal demesnes in Gloucestershire were becoming more like those in Warwickshire and Worcestershire as vehicles for the raising of revenue.

Responsibility for collecting revenue and overseeing the demesnes was also apportioned differently between the three counties. In Worcestershire, the sheriff, Urse d'Abitot, seems to have been responsible for all demesnes save those that had been transferred to the 'farm' of Herefordshire by William FitzOsbern. In Warwickshire, responsibility was shared between the sheriff and two others,[22] whilst in Gloucestershire a considerable number of individuals appear to have participated in what Round termed 'the game of speculation of farming the King's manors'.[23] Despite these and other differences between the counties, the same underlying principles seem to apply to all royal demesnes in the west midlands. Generally they are characterised by a large areal extent, high proportions of villeins, very high revenues, low proportions of slaves and ploughteams in demesne and a dependent peasantry that was well equipped with their own ploughteams. In many respects this profile complies with Kosminsky's findings for large manors in the thirteenth century. If Kosminsky's conclusions regarding the balance between peasant rents and services on such manors can be extended back to the eleventh century,[24] then it is possible that the low level of service requirements associated with the privileges of ancient demesne[25] might well have its origins in the economic organisation of the immediate post-Conquest royal demesne.

ECCLESIASTICAL DEMESNES

With 37 per cent of the total west midlands hidage, the church appears amongst the most important landholding groups in the region. Fig. 3 shows their estates to have been concentrated in southern Worcestershire centring

---

[19] In total these amounted to 9 villeins, 30 bordars and 5 slaves.
[20] DB, i. 163a; TRE: 22 villeins, 25 bordars, 9 slaves, 18 coliberts; when acquired: 17 villeins, 24 bordars, 4 slaves, 13 coliberts.
[21] DB, i. 163a, 163b.
[22] Nicholas, Geoffrey de la Guerche.
[23] J. H. Round, *VCH Hampshire*, 1, 414.
[24] Kosminsky, 192.
[25] P. Vinogradoff, *Villainage in England* (Oxford, 1892), 89–126.

Fig. 3. *Ecclesiastical estates in the West Midlands in 1086.*

Church of Worcester
Church of Westminster
Church of Evesham
Archbishop Thomas of York
Others

on the confluence of the Avon and Severn Valleys. Further important holdings were found in the Cotswolds and in north-western and southern Gloucestershire, giving access to the high yielding soils of the terraces of major river valleys as well as the prized sheep pastures of the Cotswolds. The church estates were shared by twenty-seven institutions and bishops of which seven were actually located within the region. Not surprisingly, this latter group represented the major landholders, amongst which the church of Worcester was pre-eminent. Fig. 3, however, considerably overestimates the amount of land held in demesne by the church, for some 29 per cent of the 1768 hides recorded were subinfeudated. This is particularly prominent at the very core of the church estates in southern Worcestershire, where 38 per cent of the hidage was subinfeudated in 1086.

The complex structure of church estates can best be illustrated by reference to the largest and best documented estate, that of the church of Worcester. This estate covered some 317 square miles, 72 per cent of which was located in the county of Worcestershire. Fig. 4 refers to the 23 manors in that county, of which 11 were held by the bishop and 12 by the monastic community. The bishops' manors were the most heavily subinfeudated with only two manors retained entirely in demesne. In addition the bishop allocated some detached portions of his Cotswold manors to the support of the monastery. In all, 53 pieces of land in 13 manors were subinfeudated to 19 subtenants who, in turn, further sublet 13 of the holdings. The variability of manorial structure across the estate was thus considerable. Some manors, most typically those held by the priory, were held entirely in demesne whilst others, notably those held by the bishop, expressed all of the tenurial complexities shown in Fig. 4. Detailed analysis of the demesne element of this church's estate[26] has revealed distinctions between the holdings of the bishop and those of the monastery. The bishop's demesnes generally comprised larger units with a lower proportion of both demesne teams and slaves. The dependent peasantry were better equipped with their own teams on the bishop's demesnes and the bishop had much better access to income derived from woodland, town houses, mills, salt works and jurisdictions. This allowed the bishop to act as a powerful feudal magnate, subinfuedating sizeable parts of his estate and diminishing the relative importance of his demesne arable whilst advancing the cash revenues from his possessions. The monastery, on the other hand, had smaller holdings with more limited resources, and placed greater emphasis on demesne arable and slave labour in order to feed their community, possibly through the operation of a series of food rents.

Unfortunately Domesday Book does not allow a similar breakdown of the statistics pertaining to other ecclesiastical bodies in the west midlands. There are, however, hints that this duality of purpose does underpin the statistics shown in Table 4. As compared to royal demesnes, ecclesiastical demesnes display a slightly stronger demesne component amongst their

---

[26] J. D. Hamshere, 'The structure and exploitation of the Domesday Book estate of the church of Worcester', *Landscape History*, 7 (1985), 41–52.

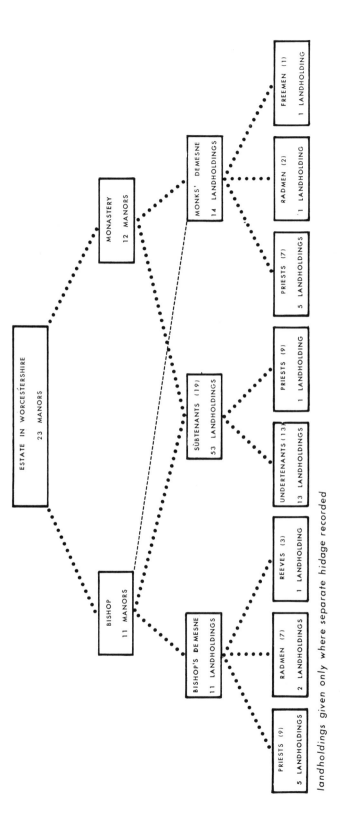

ESTATE IN WORCESTERSHIRE
23 MANORS

BISHOP
11 MANORS

MONASTERY
12 MANORS

BISHOP'S DEMESNE
11 LANDHOLDINGS

SUBTENANTS (19)
53 LANDHOLDINGS

MONKS' DEMESNE
14 LANDHOLDINGS

PRIESTS (9)
5 LANDHOLDINGS

RADMEN (7)
2 LANDHOLDINGS

REEVES (3)
1 LANDHOLDING

UNDERTENANTS (13)
13 LANDHOLDINGS

PRIESTS (9)
1 LANDHOLDING

PRIESTS (7)
5 LANDHOLDINGS

RADMEN (2)
1 LANDHOLDING

FREEMEN (1)
1 LANDHOLDING

landholdings given only where separate hidage recorded

Fig. 4. Structure of the church of Worcester's estate in Domesday Book (1086).

TABLE 4: ECCLESIASTICAL DEMESNE IN THE WEST MIDLANDS

County	Holdings	Hides	Population	Villeins	Bordars	Slaves	Other Population	Plough-teams	Demesne Plough-teams	Peasant Plough-teams	1066 Value (£)	1086 Value (£)	Meadow (Acres)
Worcestershire	65	493.1	1908	832	578	289	209	844	175.5	668.5	337	389.13	989
Warwickshire	28	141.25	643	400	157	81	5	253.5	45.5	208	106	161.6	620
Gloucestershire	75	624	2053	1062	419	461	111	1017	240.5	776.5	370	524.2	653.4
Total	168	1258.35	4604	2294	1154	831	325	2114.5	461.5	1653	813	1074.93	2262.4

POPULATION AND PLOUGHTEAMS: PERCENTAGES BY COUNTY

	Villeins	Bordars	Slaves	Others	Total	Demesne Ploughteams	Peasant Ploughteams	Total
Worcestershire	44	30	15	11	100	21	79	100
Warwickshire	62	24	13	1	100	18	82	100
Gloucestershire	51	20	23	6	100	24	76	100
All Three Counties	50	25	18	7	100	22	78	100

ploughteams in all three counties and slaves are a more significant element within the population. It is notable that ecclesiastical demesnes have a total of 461 demesne teams compared to only 272 on their royal equivalents. Interestingly, slaves are more strongly correlated with demesne teams, with a coefficient of .78,[27] than on any other estate grouping, suggesting that their rôle on ecclesiastical demesnes was largely concerned with ploughing. Even so, the population is structured much more towards higher status peasantry, well equipped with their own ploughteams. In part this may reflect the operations of church magnates, such as the bishop of Worcester, who possibly utilised his demesnes for raising revenue to sustain ambitious building programmes. On the other hand, the possibility of extensive service requirements from the peasantry, long associated with church estates, could have had the effect of increasing the demesne component over and above that suggested by the division of their ploughteams. This may well have been a significant feature on those Cotswold demesnes where livestock would have undoubtedly been an important, but unrecorded, element within their agrarian economy. Either way, it is inconceivable that the relative wealth of the dependent peasantry would not have been exploited in some way or another.

Whilst it is impossible to identify any internal division of the demesnes on most west midland ecclesiastical estates, Domesday Book does distinguish five estates as being held by a bishop or archbishop rather than by a church.[28] Not only were these particular estates more heavily subinfeudated, the bishop of Coutances, for instance, subinfeudating the entirety of his west midlands holdings, but also those manors retained in demesne tended to be larger than those of the eight leading abbey and priory estates. The bishopric demesnes averaged 11 hides and 18 ploughteams as against 6.8 hides and 9.8 ploughteams of the abbey and priory demesnes. Similarly, the proportions of both demesne teams and slaves tended to be higher on the latter than on the former.

Despite these differences and those expressed on a county basis, there remains some degree of coincidence between these findings and those of Kosminsky for the thirteenth century. Kosminsky characterised ecclesiastical estates as having some 20 per cent of their manors defined as large.[29] Generally he felt that ecclesiastical manors conformed most to the traditional image of the serf-cultivated manor with an integration of demesne and villein land, although the latter tended to considerably outweigh the former. In this respect he argued that the rôle of peasant rents had been under-estimated by comparison with service, a situation that might well equally apply to the evidence cited here from Domesday Book.

---

[27] A correlation coefficient (r) measures the degree of association between two variables. Its values range from ±1.0 to 0.0. A value of ±1.0 indicates that all points lie on a straight line; a value of −1.0 indicates a negative relationship.
[28] The estates of the archbishop of York, the bishop of Worcester, the bishop of Hereford, the bishop of Exeter and the bishop of Coutances.
[29] Kosminsky, 109–16.

DEMESNES OF LAY TENANTS–IN–CHIEF

Ninety-nine lay tenants-in-chief collectively held over 2000 hides of land in the west midlands in 1086. Widespread subinfeudation of their estates had the effect of reducing the demesne holdings by 38 per cent of this total. In fact the mean size of each tenant-in-chief's total demesne holdings was only 13.6 hides, although this figure is affected by a sizeable number of land-holders, such as the king's thegns in Gloucestershire, who had very small estates often comprising only 1 or 2 hides. Even so, the largest estate in lay hands, that of the count of Meulan in Warwickshire, had only 97 hides of demesne, which is the equivalent of the modest demesne of Winchcombe Abbey, one of the smaller ecclesiastical demesnes. Thus, only four tenants-in-chief had more than 50 hides of demesne, as most of the major landholders subinfeudated the greater part of their estates. The incidence of subinfeuda-tion was not even. Warwickshire had the greatest hidage in lay possession, but 51 per cent of this was subinfeudated, whilst in Gloucestershire only 22 per cent of the lay possessions were similarly sublet. This had the effect of producing the greatest extent of lay demesne holdings in Gloucestershire rather than in Warwickshire.

Inevitably, the distribution of lay demesnes had to fit around the pattern already created by royal and ecclesiastical estates, producing some degree of fragmentation. The incidence of subinfeudation, however, increased this fragmentation so that no lay tenant-in-chief held a block of territory equivalent to either the royal or ecclesiastical estates. None the less, it is noticeable that the vast majority of lay tenants-in-chief retained demesne in only one county, their landholdings, if they had any, in the other two counties being subinfeudated. Generally the distribution of lay demesne is very fragmented and they are found widely scattered throughout the region. Only in Worcestershire is there a concentration of lay demesne, which is due entirely to the vast church possessions that dominated the south, restricting lay demesnes to the least populated north and western areas of the county.

The summary figures in Table 2 revealed that the mean size of lay demesne amounted to only 4.6 hides making them equivalent to Kosminsky's classification of medium-sized manors. This smaller size finds reflection in the lower means for both population and ploughteams shown in Table 5. In addition, lay demesnes are distinguishable from both royal and ecclesiastical demesnes in the greater proportion of ploughteams in demesne and the greater percentage of slaves within the population. Overall, slaves achieve a significant correlation with demesne teams although the coefficient is slightly lower than that for many ecclesiastical demesnes. The dependent peasantry were more poorly equipped with their own ploughteams, there being one peasant team to every 3.6 recorded population. These figures are consistent with the impression of modest landholders possessed of small estates upon which they were largely dependent for the upkeep of their immediate household. Lay demesne holders had less peasant wealth to exploit and they had less access to other forms of income than their royal and ecclesiastical

172

TABLE 5: DEMESNES OF LAY TENANTS-IN-CHIEF

County	Holdings	Hides	Population	Villeins	Bordars	Slaves	Other Population	Ploughteams	Demesne Ploughteams	Peasant Ploughteams	1066 Value (£)	1086 Value (£)	Meadow (Acres)
Worcestershire	32	94.75	562	175	235	69	83	254	36	218	107.55	97.85	60
Warwickshire	98	489.575	2193	1286	496	335	76	667	168	499	338.25	456.8	1165
Gloucestershire	165	761.79	2785	1202	708	780	95	1238.5	357	881.5	545.05	511.55	432
Total	295	1346.115	5540	2663	1439	1184	254	2159.5	561	1598.5	990.85	1066.2	1657

POPULATION AND PLOUGHTEAMS: PERCENTAGES BY COUNTY

County	Villeins	Bordars	Slaves	Others	Total	Demesne Ploughteams	Peasant Ploughteams	Total
Worcestershire	31	42	12	15	100	14	86	100
Warwickshire	59	23	15	3	100	25	75	100
Gloucestershire	43	25	28	4	100	29	71	100
All Three Counties	48	26	21	5	100	26	74	100

counterparts, having on average far less mills, town houses, salt workings, woodland and meadow. In these circumstances it is not surprising that the demesne and its produce formed a more significant part of the return from these smaller lay estates.

Table 5 does reveal some county variation from this norm. Some aspects of this variation, for instance the higher proportions of villeins in Warwickshire and slaves in Gloucestershire, have been encountered on other estates. The small number of lay demesnes located in Worcestershire, however, do stand out as being very different from lay demesnes in the other two counties. In Worcestershire not only is the average size of lay demesne much smaller, at only 2.9 hides, but also slaves form a relatively low percentage of the population. Similarly, only 14 per cent of the ploughteams are assigned to the demesne, whilst the peasantry are relatively well equipped with teams. Values display a decline between 1066 and 1086, whilst hidage is relatively low compared with other resources and underploughing is frequently recorded.[30] It is possible that landlords in this area of low returns opted for a rent income, or that livestock, in the form of pig farming, may have formed an important but unrecorded element in these well-wooded districts.

Whilst some variation is apparent both between counties and between a handful of individual demesnes of lay tenants-in-chief,[31] there is a general degree of consistency within the statistical profiles that marks these demesnes as being different in both structure and purpose from those on royal or ecclesiastical estates.

HOLDINGS OF THE SUBTENANTS

Of all the landholding groups it is the subtenants that have received least attention from Domesday Book scholars. Yet both nationally, where it is estimated that some 6000 subtenants held land,[32] and locally in the west midlands, they formed a major landholding group. Reasons for this lack of attention are not hard to find. Subtenants form a very heterogeneous group, both illusive in their identification and often possessing small amounts of land. Due to the tenurial complexities of Domesday Book landholding they could vary in status from amongst the most powerful in the land down to the holder of a mere virgate or two. Yet collectively they held a very

---

[30] In Worcestershire, ploughlands are not recorded in DB, but the formula *carucae possient esse* is employed. The vast majority of these entries are located in the north and west of the county on lay held estates.

[31] There is some evidence to suggest that three individuals operated their demesnes in a different manner from other lay tenants-in-chief. These are the demesnes of William of Eu in Gloucestershire, Robert Dispenser in Gloucestershire and Worcestershire and Osbern Fitz-Richard in Worcestershire and Warwickshire. All three demesnes demonstrate a remarkably low percentage of ploughteams in demesne, suggesting perhaps a greater reliance on rent income than demesne produce.

[32] Darby (1977), 89.

considerable amount of land and they, more than any other landholding group, were placed at the interface between the new Norman aristocracy and the old Anglo-Scandinavian peasantry. As a group, they were far more likely to have been resident on their small possessions and to have numbered amongst their ranks survivors of the pre-Conquest landholding groups.

In the west midlands the subtenants' holdings comprised 31 per cent of the total hidage with a mean of under 3 hides per holding. These landholdings were thus the smallest found on any estate grouping and form the equivalent of Kosminsky's definition of small manors. There are many ways in which the subtenants' holdings could be analysed both areally and in terms of the individuals involved. Initially, I have chosen to categorise subtenancies by the type of tenant-in-chief to whom they owed their feudal dues. Hence, in Fig. 5, the distribution of subtenancies is plotted, distinguishing between the subtenants of royal, ecclesiastical and lay tenants-in-chief. In all, 517 holdings are involved of which 60 per cent were lay, 29 per cent ecclesiastical and 11 per cent royal.

The subtenancies are located on the map, within their dependent manors, but, as a high proportion of them formed only a fraction of the manorial area, the boundaries shown cannot be taken as a guide to the extent of the subtenants' land. None the less, the overall distribution displayed does not suggest that subtenancies were necessarily restricted to the poorer soils. They are well represented in the plain of Worcester, in the Feldon area of Warwickshire and in the Cotswolds. Admittedly, subtenancies are largely absent from the fertile Vale of Evesham and the Vale of Gloucester, but they are equally scarce in those well-wooded and rather empty areas west of the Severn and in northern Worcestershire and Warwickshire. Detailed analysis of the subtenants' holdings on the estate of the church of Worcester[33] has, however, been able to demonstrate that where the demesne of tenants-in-chief shared the same manor as the subtenants' holdings, it was the demesne that occupied the better class 1 and 2 soils. Most subtenancies were located on class 3 agricultural land, which tends, today, to be the heavier claylands with moderate limitations on their arable usage. Under medieval conditions these soils were extensively pressed into arable service as is attested by the ridge and furrow that still marches across so much of the west midlands. The distribution of the three classes of subtenancies shown on Fig. 5, of course, complies with the location of the three major estate groupings, that is, most ecclesiastical subtenancies are found in Worcestershire, the lay subtenancies predominating in Warwickshire, whilst Gloucestershire has a more mixed pattern, but contains a high proportion of all royal subtenancies.

From Table 6 it can be seen that, overall, the subtenants commanded very impressive resources, amounting to over 5600 dependent peasantry, 2135 ploughteams and more acreage of meadowland than any other estate group. In addition to their smaller mean size, there are substantial differences between the subtenancies and the other estate groups already considered. On the subtenancies, the dependent peasantry were generally ascribed a more

---

[33] J. D. Hamshere, 48–9.

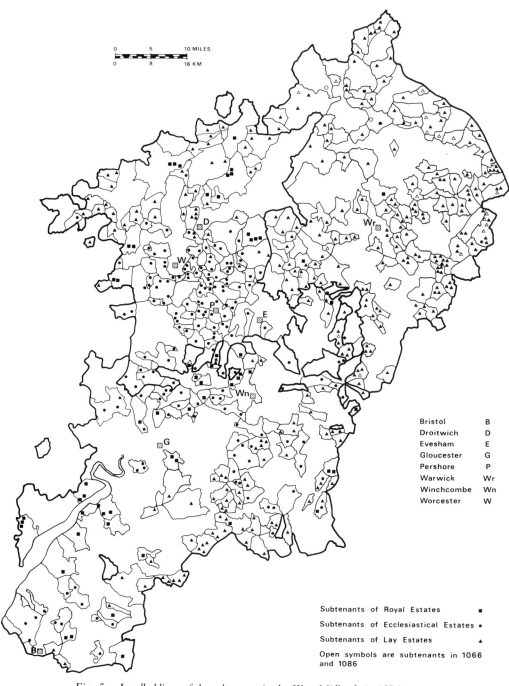

Bristol   B
Droitwich   D
Evesham   E
Gloucester   G
Pershore   P
Warwick   Wr
Winchcombe   Wn
Worcester   W

Subtenants of Royal Estates   ■
Subtenants of Ecclesiastical Estates ●
Subtenants of Lay Estates   ▲
Open symbols are subtenants in 1066
and 1086

Fig. 5.   *Landholdings of the subtenants in the West Midlands in 1086.*

servile status, with lower proportions of villeins and increased proportions of slaves within the population. The peasantry were also less well equipped with their own ploughteams with only one team to over four of the recorded population. At the same time a far higher percentage of ploughteams (36 per cent) were in the demesne, although it is notable that slaves were less well correlated with demesne teams than they were on other estate groups. Demesne arable as judged by the division of ploughteams, was thus proportionally at its largest on the subtenancies, although slaves do not appear as closely linked with demesne arable as elsewhere, suggesting slaves fulfilled a wider rôle than that of ploughmen. Overall, the statistical profile is that which would be expected from small-scale landholdings with predominantly resident landlords, who were dependent upon limited resources for the sustenance of their immediate households.

Although these general trends are apparent throughout the subtenant's holdings, there is some variation between the three groups identified on Table 6. The royal subtenants fall into two distinct groups in terms of their holdings. Firstly, there is a group typified by the subtenants of large royal manors in Worcestershire. These tended to hold very small pieces of land averaging under one hide each, either in return for some service, such as that of forester, or because they had been enfeoffed by the sheriff or Earl William FitzOsbern. These holdings average a population of only three and, as is common on very small landholdings, the demesne teams achieve almost parity with those of the peasantry.[34] Secondly, there is a larger group of subtenants on the royal manors of Warwickshire and Gloucestershire, who held much more substantial holdings. Some, such as Roger of Berkeley, held manors in return for supervision of royal demesnes, whilst others were the recipients of gifts from Queen Matilda.[35] A few manors appear to have been leased before the Conquest and these had been placed out of the revenue. The largest group, however, appear as subtenants of manors that had formerly belonged to the thegns of Brictric. As with most subtenants, these individuals are identified only by a single personal name and their holdings ascribed a value rather than a render. Clearly these subtenants were of a different status from the more powerful figures involved in the speculative venture of 'farming' royal demesne, just as their landholdings were also different. The subtenancies averaged around 4 hides, with a recorded population of 10 and just over 5 ploughteams per holding. By the standard of subtenancies these were larger then average, but still demonstrate similar features of high proportions of slaves and demesne ploughteams. Equally, they display a further difference from royal demesnes in that their values declined between 1066 and 1086.

Subtenants on ecclesiastical estates also possessed more substantial holdings, averaging 3.4 hides. Some 70 per cent of these holdings were in Worcestershire, where most were established on the estates of the churches

---

[34] J. D. Hamshere, 50–1.
[35] DB, i. 163a, 163b, 164a.

TABLE 6: LANDHOLDINGS OF THE SUBTENANTS

	Holdings	Hides	Popu-lation	Villeins	Bordars	Slaves	Others	Plough-teams	Demesne Plough-teams	Peasant Plough-teams	1066 Value (£)	1086 Value (£)	Meadow (Acres)
Royal Subtenants	57	160.4	461	187	121	111	42	228	79	149	109.65	107	87
Ecclesiastical Subtenants	149	509.8	1647	586	510	406	145	675.25	283.5	391.75	240.35	306.9	868.1
Lay Subtenants	311	821.4	3538	1488	1219	641	190	1231.75	415	816.75	678.82	710.1	2001.5
Total	517	1491.6	5646	2261	1850	1158	377	2135	777.5	1357.5	1028.82	1124	2956.6

POPULATION AND PLOUGHTEAMS: PERCENTAGES

	Villeins	Bordars	Slaves	Others	Total	Demesne Ploughteams	Peasant Ploughteams	Total
Royal Subtenants	41	26	24	9	100	35	65	100
Ecclesiastical Subtenants	36	31	24	9	100	42	58	100
Lay Subtenants	42	35	18	5	100	34	66	100
Total Subtenants	40	33	21	6	100	36	64	100

of Worcester, Pershore and Westminster.[36] The vast majority of these subtenants represent the successors of pre-Conquest lease holders and their landholdings had been subinfeudated for some considerable time. With their larger size in terms of hidage, population and ploughteams, it is no surprise that these subtenancies proved attractive to Normans of some substance and standing. Hence major tenants-in-chief, such as Roger de Lacy, appear amongst the subtenants, as do all the local sheriffs. Particularly prominent amongst this latter group was Urse d'Abitot, sheriff of Worcester, who used the opportunity offered by ecclesiastical subtenancies to amass an estate of some 200 hides. The value placed upon these subtenancies can be gauged from the fact that Urse chose to subinfeudate all but one of the manors he held as tenant-in-chief, but retained in demesne close upon 70 per cent of the land he held as a subtenant. Further subinfeudation by the subtenants on ecclesiastical estates is not uncommon; Roger de Lacy, for instance, further sublet three of his five subtenancies in Worcestershire. As it was only the larger landholders that further sublet their subtenancies, the overall effect was to produce a situation in which the vast majority of subtenants actually holding land were men of very modest means, no doubt reliant upon their single, or at best very few, landholdings for their immediate support. Hence slaves form high proportions of the population, averaging 24 per cent, but reaching 32 per cent in Gloucestershire, and demesne ploughteams form 42 per cent of the total plough strength. Another feature of ecclesiastical subtenancies is the consistent rise in values that occurred between 1066 and 1086.

Of all the subtenancies, it is those subtenants of lay tenants-in-chief which form the largest group, having 311 landholdings, mainly located in Warwick- shire. The average size of the lay subtenants' holdings appears significantly smaller at 2.6 hides than those located on royal or ecclesiastical estates. It is noticeable, however, that the average recorded population was very similar to the holdings of ecclesiastical subtenants, although the number of plough- teams per holding was less. The values on lay subtenancies show a slight rise between 1066 and 1086, but this is almost entirely generated by the county of Warwickshire, as lay subtenancies in the other two counties display a decline in value between the two dates. Whilst the general profile of the Domesday Book statistics of the lay subtenancies is similar to that of all subtenants, some variation is apparent amongst the lay subtenancies within Gloucestershire. In this county, slaves form 40 per cent of the recorded population, the highest figure recorded for any estate group in the west midlands. Similarly, the percentage of ploughteams in demesne (46.5 per cent) is also the highest recorded. These figures, however, only represent an accentuation of trends already noted on subtenancies in general.

The main difference, apart from size, between the lay subtenancies and their royal and ecclesiastical counterparts appears to be in the individual landholders themselves. Very few lay subtenants can be identified as tenants-

---

[36] The Westminster estates in the west midlands were created by the Confessor from the possessions of Pershore Abbey.

in-chief in their own right. The vast majority are merely identified in Domesday Book by a single personal name and it has usually been assumed that they represent the personal followers of the tenant-in-chief upon whose estate they were located. In this respect it is interesting to note that 16 subtenancies are recorded as having been held by the same person in both 1066 and 1086. Of these, 14 were lay subtenants[37] and their holdings are mostly found along the north-eastern county boundary of Warwickshire. Added to this is a sizeable number of 1086 lay subtenants, particularly in Warwickshire, who appear to possess Old English name forms. Of course, great caution has to be expressed about any assumption of nationality from personal names, but it seems more than coincidental that these name forms should appear so frequently in a county that already records 16 instances of the survival of pre-Conquest landholders. In this respect it is instructive to compare the incidence of such names on the two largest and heavily subfeudated lay estates in Warwickshire, these being the estates of the count of Meulan and Thorkell of Warwick. Of the 44 subtenancies on the count's estate, 14 were held by subtenants with Old English name forms, forming 32 per cent of the subtenancies on that estate. Thorkell of Warwick was himself a very rare English survivor as a major tenant-in-chief and on his estate 29 of the 64 subtenancies (45 per cent) had holders with Old English names. Comparison of the Domesday Book statistics relating to, firstly, the Old English name group and, secondly, to other subtenants on these two estates does produce some interesting variations. Generally the Old English group have slightly smaller holdings, expressed in terms of hidage or ploughlands, and on Thorkell's estate they tend to retain a higher proportion of ploughteams in demesne. The most striking difference, however, is in terms of value change between 1066 and 1086. On the count of Meulan's estate the holdings of the Old English group show a decline in value over the period as against a rise in average value of £1.8 to £2.2 amongst other subtenants. On Thorkell's estate both groups of subtenancies display a rise in value but amongst the Old English group it is only from an average of £1.2 to £1.4, as against £1.4 to £2.0 amongst the other subtenants.

Clearly such results, based on personal names, have to be treated with some caution, but they do suggest that sufficient differences exist to reward a wider analysis, particularly in the light of recent suggestions made by Professor Sawyer[38] concerning the basis upon which lay estates were granted in the post-Conquest period.

CONCLUSION

In the introduction to this paper the stated intention was to employ the framework of the tenurial geography of the west midlands as a basis for the analysis of Domesday Book statistics. By this means it has been possible to

[37] The other two subtenants holding in both 1066 and 1086 are found on ecclesiastical estates.
[38] P. H. Sawyer, '1066–1086: A tenurial revolution?', in *Domesday reassessment*, 71–85.

demonstrate that significant statistical differences can be observed between estates that undoubtedly affect the spatial variation of Domesday Book phenomena. Most notable amongst these differences were: the variation in the area of the units within which the Domesday Book data were recorded; the allocation of ploughteams between the demesne and the peasantry; the social structure of the recorded population; the level of ploughteam provision amongst the dependent peasantry; and, finally, the amount of financial return as expressed by the Domesday Book valuations. Each estate group thus had a distinctive statistical profile, much of which could be explained by the purposes to which the particular estate's resources were likely to have been put. For instance, the necessity of raising large cash revenues on royal demesnes produced a statistical profile that contrasted with that found on ecclesiastical demesnes, where there seems to have been a greater degree of balance between cash revenue and the production of foodstuffs from the demesne. Similarly, the lay tenants-in-chief and the subtenants both had more limited resources and produced statistical profiles that suggested a proportionally greater emphasis was put upon demesne arable production. It was discovered, however, that some internal variation within each of the estate groups was evident, and that some of this variation appeared specific to individual counties. Hence, in Worcestershire, high proportions of bordars, well equipped with ploughteams, appeared throughout most of the estate groups. In Warwickshire it was villeins, less well equipped with ploughteams, that dominated the population structure, whilst in Gloucestershire it was the coincidence of slavery and higher proportions of demesne teams that was most notable. Such variation between counties is unlikely to be explained by what Round has called the Domesday commissioners' 'love of diversity'[39] and must express real distinctions within the environmental conditions and socio-economic organisation of the counties that was to some extent independent of their tenurial geography.

In this respect, the analysis of Domesday Book through its tenurial geography can be seen as complementary to the *Domesday Geography* of Professor Darby. Both approaches reveal different aspects of the spatial variation of the data, although neither can afford, on its own, a complete assessment. The different distributional aspects revealed by the two approaches should be viewed side by side, the one aiding the interpretation of the other, rather than being seen as alternative explanations of the same spatial variations. In reality, environmental conditions and the geography of landholding were inextricably bound together within the eleventh-century agrarian structures that characterised the west midland landscape.

One important element that is revealed by the study of Domesday Book tenurial geography is the influence on the statistical profiles of the areal size of the units within which the data were recorded. Comparison was made with Professor Kosminsky's study of the Hundred Rolls and many similarities were noted with his findings, despite the many changes that occurred in the intervening two centuries. In Domesday Book, the areal size of

[39] Round, *Feudal England*, 83.

recording unit does co-vary with the type of estate, in a descending order from the royal demesne through to the holdings of the subtenants. It must be stressed, however, that these units of landholding, that Domesday Book is based upon, do not represent the actual units of agrarian organisation of the period. At one end of the scale the royal demesnes often cover a multiplicity of agrarian operations whilst, at the other end, we cannot be certain to what extent the subtenancies form merely a fragment of some larger organisation. This clearly has important implications for the study of economic and social organisation from Domesday Book, none more so than in the large-scale statistical analyses that are now beginning to be undertaken.[40] As has been discovered by social scientists working on modern census material, variation in the geographical size of the recording units has profound implications for the analysis of spatially organised data, particularly in the application of multivariate statistical techniques.[41] Generally social scientists have found it necessary to structure their data in such a way that these variations are minimised. In the case of Domesday Book, one way to achieve this would be to employ tenurial geography to structure the data into estate groups, in which the areal size of the units are roughly equivalent. In this manner it may be possible in the future to exploit the machine readable texts now in preparation at the universities of Hull and California, Santa Barbara,[42] in order to gain further insight into the complex relationships that exist within the statistics of Domesday Book.

[40] J. McDonald and G. D. Snooks, 'Were the tax assessments of Domesday England artificial? The case of Essex', *Economic History Review*, 38 (1985), 352–72, and J. McDonald and G. D. Snooks, *Domesday Economy: A new approach to Anglo-Norman History* (Oxford, 1986).

[41] I. S. Evans, 'Bivariate and multivariate analysis: relationships between census variables', in D. Rhind (ed.), *A Census Users Handbook* (London, 1983), 199–242.

[42] J. Palmer, 'Domesday Book and the Computer', in *Domesday reassessment*, 164–74.

The Portrayal of Land Settlement in Domesday Book

GLANVILLE R. J. JONES

IN A CONTEMPORARY account, Robert Losinga, bishop of Hereford, who may have been present when the project for the Domesday Inquest was discussed, reported on the Survey that was undertaken. Thus: 'in the twentieth year of his reign by order of William, King of the English, there was made a survey of the whole of England, that is to say, of the land of the several provinces of England, and of the possessions of each and all of the magnates. This was done in respect of ploughlands and habitations (*in agris eorum, in mansionibus*), of men both bond and free, both those who dwelt in cottages, and those who had their homes and shares in the fields (*tam in tugaria tantum habitantibus, quam in domos et agris possidentibus*); and in respect of ploughs and horses and other animals; and in respect of the services and payments due from all men in the whole land. Other investigators followed the first, and men were sent into provinces which they did not know, and where they themselves were unknown, in order that they might be given the opportunity of checking the first survey and, if necessary, of denouncing its authors as guilty to the king. And the land was vexed with much violence arising from the collection of the royal taxes'.[1] Besides emphasising the thorough and comprehensive nature of the Survey, Robert Losinga stressed the attention given to the possessions of the magnates. In so doing he accorded priority to two features, ploughlands and habitations, thereby implying that the siting of settlement was linked to the disposition of arable land. If, following such a Survey, the findings had been fully recorded, a remarkable portrayal of land settlement in the late eleventh century would be available to us. The purpose of this review is to consider to what extent the findings of the Inquest, in the form in which they were recorded in Domesday Book, match the claimed thoroughness of the Survey.

As presented in summary form in Great Domesday Book, and in slightly less summary form in Little Domesday Book, the record of the Survey is neither as complete nor as thorough as Robert Losinga's account would lead us to expect. The Inquest, a survey alike of fiefs and manors, their resources

[1] W. H. Stevenson, 'A Contemporary Description of the Domesday Survey', *EHR*, xxii (1907), 72–84; *EHD*, ii. 912.

and their fiscal obligations,[2] used as its local territorial framework the vill, a tract of land containing besides habitations, arable land, as well as pasture, meadow and, sometimes, woodland. Thus, when Domesday Book mentions the name of a place, as Maitland observed, 'we regard the name as the name of a vill; it may or may not be also the name of a manor. Speaking very generally we may say that the place so named will, in after times, be known as a vill and in our own day will be a civil parish'.[3] Accordingly, Domesday Book, as a record of territorial units, is only indirectly a record of settlements. The details of men and resources were usually recorded in a similar fashion alike for those vills with a dispersed settlement pattern and for those which contained but one nucleated village. Especially was this the case where standard formulae were used so that the Domesday record provides only an imprecise guide to the form of settlements.

Domesday Book is likewise an inadequate guide to the distribution of settlements in England and Wales during the late eleventh century, despite its naming of well over 13,000 places. Of these, 13,278 were in England and, less precisely given the inadequacies of the record, about 140 in Wales, but, although 97 per cent of these have been identified and located, many gaps remain.[4] Some are due to the exclusion of large areas from the purview of the Survey. The northern counties of Durham, Northumberland and the greater part of Cumberland and Westmorland were not surveyed, and the record for a large part of modern Lancashire was incomplete. North Wales, corresponding roughly to the modern Gwynedd, was dismissed in a few lines as being 'held by Robert of Rhuddlan from the king at farm for £40, except the land which the king gave him in fee, and except the lands of the bishopric (i.e. of Bangor)'.[5] The land which King William gave Robert in fee comprised Rhos and Rhufoniog, in the north-western part of modern Clwyd; and for these two hundreds Domesday Book merely records that 'there are 12 leagues of land in length and 4 leagues in width. There is land for 20 ploughs only. It is valued at £12. All the other land is in woods and moors and cannot be ploughed'.[6]

Yet, even for the areas surveyed in full there are indications from other, earlier or near-contemporary, sources that the total number of vills must have been much greater than the number of named places, and that some Domesday names covered more than one settlement already in being by 1086. As Professor Darby has indicated, a number of these came to be represented in later times by two or more adjoining places distinguished by such appellations as Much or Little.[7] Moreover, if some manors coincided with vills, and others with subdivisions of vills, yet many manors were composite entities embracing several vills. Frequently the components of these composite manors, whether vills or dependencies, described as *appendicii*, *berewichae*, *membrae*, *pertinentes* or *terrae*, were not named. Where the occupants of villages, hamlets or farms paid tax or rendered dues through a manorial centre, the presence of these component settlements

[2] Harvey (1975), 182–9.
[3] Maitland, 12.
[4] Darby (1977), 38–9.

[5] DB, i. 269a.
[6] DB, i. 269a.
[7] Darby (1977), 19–20.

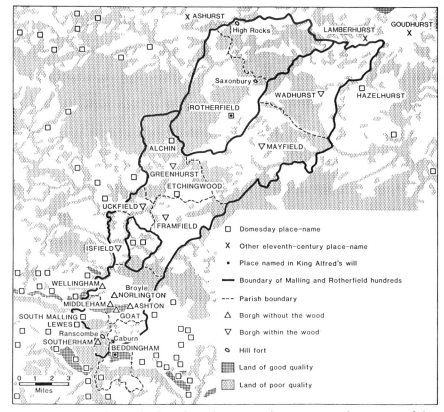

Fig. 1. Domesday and other eleventh-century place-names in the vicinity of the manor of South Malling, Sussex.

might not be indicated at all. Thus for many named manors with large totals for men, ploughteams, mills and churches, or where a large adjoining area appears to be ignored in the Domesday record, we may strongly suspect the existence of a multiplicity of vills and dependencies.

Such was the manor of South Malling held in 1086 by the archbishop of Canterbury (Fig. 1). Although represented by but one main entry in Domesday Book, this huge manor was then taxed for 75 hides and in the whole estate there was land for 50 ploughs. On the demesne there were 5 ploughs and in the whole manor 219 villeins and 35 bordars had 73 ploughs and 43 crofts. There were no less than 5 mills which yielded £4 10s and 2,000 eels. Within the manor as a whole there were 195 acres of meadow. There was also woodland so extensive that a pig-rent of no less than 300 swine was paid for the pannage it supplied; and the pastures were broad enough to yield 38s 6d as well as 355 swine for pasturage. Within the manor, moreover, there were 5 unnamed subtenancies including, among the most substantial, that of the canons of St Michael at South Malling proper, where there was 1 plough in demesne, and 6 villeins together with 16 bordars had 2 ploughs.[8]

The South Malling estate, which had belonged to the archbishop of Canterbury from the early ninth century, extended from the fertile lowlands near South Malling proper far into the upland interior; for the 'archbishop's boundary' indicated in a charter of 1018 as flanking 'the copse of Hazelhurst in the well-known forest of the Weald', coincided with the north-eastern boundary of both the manor and the hundred of Malling.[9] In the interior, 'within the wood' where by 1273 there were six *borghs* or territorial tithings each embracing a large number of hamlets, some permanent settlement had already been effected by 1086; hence the single recorded virgate held of the manor of South Malling at Alchin (Fig. 1). To the north-east was the Rotherfield estate, with its *caput* at Rotherfield, named as a royal residence in King Alfred's will. Not surprisingly, therefore, it was well settled in 1086 when there were 4 ploughs in demesne and 14 villeins with 6 bordars had 14 ploughs. To the east of the South Malling estate, Hazelhurst likewise was quite substantially settled by 1086 for its lands were worked by 11 ploughs, and its 10 villeins and 2 cottagers were already served by a church.[10] Further to the north, beyond the limits of the South Malling estate, the Weald was far from being occupied only seasonally for the exploitation of pasture and pannage; for, as Professor Eila Campbell has shown, Goudhurst, although not named in Domesday Book, was listed among other churches in the Domesday Monachorum as making payments to Christ Church, Canterbury; and since the lists date from about the year 1100 a settlement at Goudhurst must have been in existence by 1086. So too churches at Ashurst and Lamberhurst were listed in the Textus Roffensis which is ascribed to the decade 1140–50, and therefore settlements were probably in being there as well some sixty or so years earlier.[11] Given the presence of such settlements it is highly likely that similar Wealden settlements, albeit not provided with churches, existed within the far-flung boundary of the South Malling estate by 1086. Clearly, therefore, in a composite manor, such as South Malling, Domesday Book is a very imperfect guide to settlement.

Where vills were recorded separately a much better impression of the distribution of settlement and resources, notably those of arable land, is given by Domesday Book. This is true even in the relatively poor Breckland where by 1086 most, if not all, territory was embraced within vills and many of these were already provided with a church. Such was the case with the radial group of vills converging on Rymer Point where water supplies could be obtained from a large mere and where heathland pasture was also available (Fig. 2). Within their respective hundreds vills were already grouped into leets for the payment of geld, as for example were Great

[8] DB, i. 16a–b.
[9] G. R. J. Jones, 'Multiple Estates and Early Settlement', in *Medieval Settlement*, ed. P. H. Sawyer (1976), 26–35.
[10] DB, i. 19a.
[11] E. M. J. Campbell, 'Kent', in *The Domesday Geography of South-East England*, eds. H. C. Darby and E. M. J. Campbell (Cambridge, 1962), 495–500.

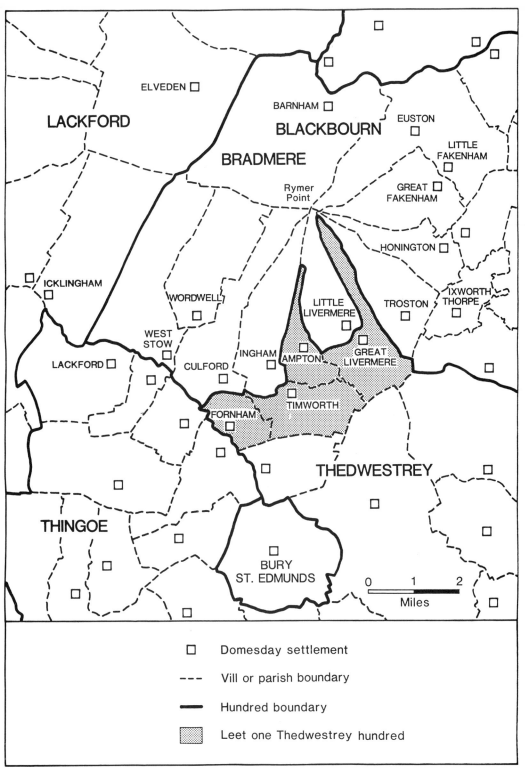

Fig. 2. *The pattern of Domesday settlement in the vicinity of the Breckland of Suffolk.*

Livermere, Ampton, Timworth and Fornham (St Genevieve) in leet one of the hundred of Thedwestre. From the recording of these Breckland vills, and certainly those converging on Rymer Point, we may infer a functional land division with water meadows on outer river frontages, and, near the overlooking settlements, arable land backing on to drier pastures in the interior. Thus, at West Stow, recorded in Domesday Book as being approximately 10 furlongs in length and 5 in width, there were 2 carucates of land. Here 6 ploughs were at work in 1086 and there were 2 acres of meadow. For their lands, which they held in soke from the abbot of Bury St Edmunds, the 21 freemen of West Stow owed customs and performed service at Lackford. The church, with 12 acres of free land in alms, was said to lie in another hundred, probably Lackford. It stood where it still stands in the south-eastern corner of the vill of West Stow, and here at least by the eleventh century there must have been a cluster of settlement; but reference in the Domesday record to a freeman, with half a carucate of land, hints at the existence further to the west of one outlying homestead.[12]

At Troston, recorded as being 10 furlongs in length and 5 in width, 24 freemen held 2½ carucates of land from the abbot of Bury St Edmunds. Here, as Domesday Book reports, 'always' there were 5 ploughs at work. Valued at 26s in 1066 it was worth 30s in 1086; but within this valuation, and valued relatively highly at 20s, was the 1 carucate of land held by one Frodo, on which there were 12 freemen with 2 ploughs. In addition, Domesday Book reports that 'others hold there' but tantalisingly these 'others' were not specified.[13] Nevertheless, the substantial accuracy of what is specified in the Domesday record can be demonstrated from the Kalendar of Abbot Samson. By the date of the Kalendar, 1186 × 1191, the land held from the abbot was deemed to amount to 1 carucate and this contained 120 ware acres, that is acres which, as Professor Ralph Davis has demonstrated, defended themselves and were thus rated for some hundredal exaction.[14] In agrarian reality, however, there were in Troston, according to the Kalendar, '9 equal lands, called in English shifts, of which 5 belong to the lord abbot and are of 1 carucate of socage land which is in the vill (ix paria terre que anglice dicuntur sifte quarum v^{que} pertinent ad dominum abbatem et sunt de 1 carucata que est in villa de socagio). There remained 4 shifts which were recorded in the twelfth century and these we may be reasonably certain were the lands of the 'others' said in Domesday Book to hold there. Each of the abbot's 5 shifts was recorded in the Kalendar as containing 60 acres, giving a total of 300 acres. In 1086, apart from the land held by 'others' there were 2½ carucates of land at Troston; if, as is highly likely, there were 120 acres in each carucate,[15] then in the 2½ carucates there were 300 acres. Since in 1086, as in 1066,

---

[12] DB, ii. 364a.   [13] DB, ii. 366b.

[14] The Kalendar of Abbot Samson of Bury St Edmunds and Related Documents, ed. R. H. C. Davis (Camden 3rd ser., lxxxiv, 1954), xi–xxxviii, 43–4.

[15] That these were components of carucates each of 120 statute acres is implied by the dimensions recorded for 1 carucate of land in Kingsland in East Suffolk; this carucate was said to be 4 furlongs in length and 3 in width, so that if the furlong was based on statute rods the carucate would have contained 120 acres each of 4840 square yards.

there were 5 ploughs at work, the shifts were evidently real carucates or ploughlands; and, as in later centuries, certain portions of each shift were set aside every year for crops and, in alternate years, as fallow, subject to right of fold. Confirmation is provided by an extent of *c.* 1286 which records that the arable land in Troston amounted to 543 acres, in other words almost exactly the total area of 9 equal shifts of 60 acres; and that the abbot of Bury St Edmunds had 290½ acres of arable land and 20 acres of heath which his *gersum* sokemen held from him with their messuages.[16]

Where it was especially necessary to define rights over territory the testimony of Domesday Book, although brief, is very precise. Thus, for example, in relation to the extensive composite manor of Ripon, Domesday Book records that within this wider area was St Wilfrid's League. Unlike the numerous berewicks and sokelands of Ripon this league apparently did not pay geld. Within the league, where there could be 10 ploughs, the archbishop of York had 2 ploughs in 1086 while his 8 villeins and 10 bordars had 6 ploughs; but 'of this land' also the canons were said to have 10 bovates. The short Domesday account of Ripon proper then concludes with the phrase 'the whole one league around the church'.[17] That this dimension was accurate can be demonstrated from the testimony produced in a suit of 1228 between the archbishop and the canons which included, *inter alia*, a charter allegedly granted by Athelstan.[18] This exempted the church and chapter from payment of geld and granted the right of sanctuary, in the words of a late rhyming version, 'on ilke syde ye Kyrke amyle'.[19] According to the evidence presented in 1228 the area within which the right of sanctuary obtained was delimited by Athelstan's eight crosses. But, of the surviving crosses near Ripon, only one bears Athelstan's name and this at a site over two miles to the north-east of Ripon minster. In Edward I's day, however, it was complained that bailiffs, no doubt to the prejudice of the crown, had added half a league by moving this stone from its original site to the north-east.[20] The late-surviving Athelstan's cross must therefore have been 1½ leagues from the minster. Accordingly it is possible to demonstrate that the length of the league at Ripon was about 1⅓ statute miles. Appropriately, it is at a distance of between 1 mile and 1¼ miles from the minster that the outer boundary of the vill of Ripon meets the old roads radiating from Ripon proper. The one exception is in the west where, to accommodate this radius, the neighbouring vill of Bishopton would have to be included. Yet, this exception does not detract from the accuracy of the Domesday description, for an earlier survey of the archbishop's lands of *c.* 1030 records 'At Ripon first the space of 1 mile on each side and Bishopton is within that, 2 hides'.[21]

[16] *A Suffolk Hundred in the Year 1283*, ed. E. Powell (Cambridge, 1910), 37–9; K. J. Allison, 'The Sheep-Corn Husbandry of Norfolk in the Sixteenth and Seventeenth Centuries', *Agricultural History Review*, v (1957), 12–30.   [17] DB, i. 303b, 380a.
[18] *Memorials of Ripon*, ed. J. T. Fowler (Surtees soc., lxxiv, 1881), 51–63.
[19] *Early Yorkshire Charters*, ed. W. Farrer (3 vols., 1914–16), i. 107–8.
[20] *Rotuli Hundredorum*, i (1812), 124.
[21] *The York Gospels*, fo. 157v (Dean and Chapter Library, York).

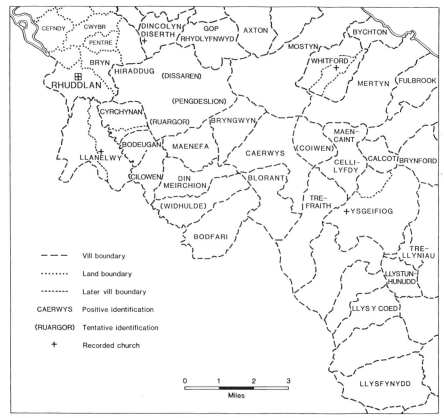

Fig. 3.   Rhuddlan and some of the Domesday berewicks of Englefield in North-east Wales.

At the extreme western limit of the area surveyed in any detail was the manor of Rhuddlan shared by Earl Hugh of Chester and Robert of Rhuddlan. Because of its peripheral location in the border hundred of Ati's Cross it had not been hidated, and had never paid geld.[22] Nevertheless it was portrayed in Domesday Book as a settled territory (Fig. 3). Thus most of the vills recorded for this area in the Lay Subsidy Roll of 1291–2 were already in being in 1086 as vills, berewicks or lands (*terrae*).[23] At Rhuddlan proper was a new borough with 18 burgesses, as well as a castle and church. Immediately adjacent was the vill of Bryn with its lands (*terrae*) or berewicks as at Cefndy, Pentre or Cwybr. Here altogether there was land for 6 ploughs which were there in demesne with 13 slaves; and there was also a mill. Among Earl Hugh's berewicks in the adjoining Englefield were 'Mertyn, Calcot and a third part of Whitford' in which there was a church and land for 1 plough

---

[22] DB, i. 269a.
[23] Public Record Office, E 179/242/52.

which a priest with 6 villeins had there; and there was also woodland half a league long but a mere 20 perches wide. Whitford was one vill or berewick which Earl Hugh and Robert shared. Thus among Robert's berewicks were 'Whitford and Bychton' where there was land for 1 plough which was there with 2 villeins and 12 male and female slaves; and there was a fishery as well as woodland half a league long but 40 perches wide. Evidently the tripartite division of Whitford, recorded in 1291–2, had already been effected; but Earl Hugh's third in Whitford Lan (Whitford Church), in the middle division of the vill, was narrower than Robert's portion in Whitford Garn (Whitford Cairn) to the north-west. The woodland recorded with such precision lay probably in Whitford, for Earl Hugh's woodland, although of the same length as that of Robert, was only half as wide.

Despite this preoccupation with detail there was, however, no mention of the already well-established church at Llanelwy in the entry for Robert's berewicks of 'Caerwys, Llanelwy and Cyrchynan' because it yielded no revenue to him. The 3 berewicks were recorded together as having land for 1 plough which was there with 1 slave and 6 bordars. Although the neighbouring vills of Llanelwy and Cyrchynan were over 3 miles distant from Caerwys the arable in the 1 ploughland was probably shared between the 3 berewicks; for at a later date Llanelwy, Cyrchynan and part of Caerwys were components of the church estate of Llanelwy.[24] Altogether in Englefield Earl Hugh had a total of land for 8 ploughs shared between 21 berewicks and his third part of Whitford; and Robert had a total of land for 15 ploughs shared between 32 berewicks and his third of Whitford. Even if, as is likely, the ploughlands thus recorded were composed of the large acres of 10,240 square yards later recorded for Englefield, the areas shared between berewicks were small.[25] It may be suspected, therefore, that the ploughlands in the berewicks of Englefield represent not the total cultivated area but only fractional shares of clanland holdings in widely separated sharelands which had been forfeited to Earl Hugh and Robert of Rhuddlan. If so, in these berewicks habitations would have been disposed as they were in a later period, in girdle patterns on the outer edges of arable sharelands.[26]

Nor was such cultivation recent for further south in the hundred of Ati's Cross was the manor of Bistre, held by Earl Hugh's men. As Domesday Book records, Bistre in the time of King Edward was a manor of Earl Edwin's but it had not been hidated and had never paid geld. It was then waste and was likewise waste when Earl Hugh received it. Yet, there and in its 12 berewicks, was land for 7 ploughs and in 1086 there were 6¾ ploughs at work. Domesday Book also provides the additional information that king Gruffudd (ap Llywelyn of Gwynedd) had 1 manor at Bistre and had 1 plough in demesne whereas his men had 6 ploughs; and that when the King (i.e.

[24] PRO, SC 6 1143/22; 23.
[25] National Library of Wales, SA/MB/22, fos. 6v–19r.
[26] G. R. J. Jones, 'The Ornaments of a Kindred in Medieval Gwynedd', *Studia Celtica*, xviii–xix (1983–4), 135–46; *idem*, 'Forms and Patterns of Medieval Settlement in Welsh Wales', in *Medieval Villages*, ed. D. Hooke (Oxford University Committee for Archaeology, Monograph No. 5, 1985), 155–7, 162–4.

Gruffudd) came there 'every plough rendered him 200 loaves (*hesthas*) and a vat (*cuvam*) full of beer and a vessel (*ruscam*) of butter'.[27] Thus, despite the wasted condition of Bistre and its berewicks alike in 1066 and when Earl Hugh received it, probably in 1070–1, the number of ploughlands recorded for 1086 matched exactly the number of ploughs in the time of King Gruffudd, that is before his death in 1063. Moreover the Domesday record makes it explicit that the food rent contributed to the Welsh king was assessed, even before 1063, in terms of the area of land tilled by these ploughs.

For the southern border district of Archenfield Domesday Book reveals the Welsh foundations of territorial organisation. Thus it records a Mainaure, that is a *maenor* or Welsh estate 'in the border (*in fine*) of Archenfield'.[28] A marginal annotation in the twelfth-century transcript of Domesday Book for Herefordshire identifies Mainaure with Birches, that is the vill of Much Birch or, more probably, both Much Birch and the adjoining vill of Little Birch (Fig. 4).[29] In 1086 it was held from Roger de Lacy by the son of the Costelin who had held it in 1066, and for the 4 ploughs there he rendered 10*s* and 6 sesters of honey, a characteristic Welsh due. But, in addition, Roger had there 1 Welshman who rendered 5*s* and 1 sester of honey. Comprising at most only two vills Mainaure by 1086 was a mere remnant of a wider *maenor* fissioned by the alienation of its other components. Thus under the rubric 'Wormelow Hundred' Domesday Book records a Westwood and reveals that 'the head (*caput*) of this manor' which had been held by King Edward was held in 1086 by St Peter's of Gloucester. In Westwood there were 6 hides, one of which was said in Domesday Book to have 'Welsh custom and the others English'.[30]

Westwood, however, was a composite rather than a unitary manor. An early twelfth-century list of tenants reveals that only 2 of the 6 hides were held by St Peter's.[31] These were in the Villa Asmacun which was equated with Westwood in the twelfth-century transcript; and therefore they lay in the vill literally below Aconbury hill fort, in other words in Much Dewchurch (Dewi's church) which was later a manor of St Peter's. Here in 1086 there was said to be 1 plough in demesne although, curiously, 2 ploughmen and 2 bordars were present. Nevertheless, no ploughlands were recorded.

The part of the manor of Westwood which, according to Domesday Book, Roger de Lacy held in 1086 and Odo from him, comprised 2 hides at Wormeton Tirel, as the twelfth-century and other records reveal.[32] There in 1086 were 2 ploughs in demesne and 2 ploughmen with 2 slaves. In addition there were 9 bordars with 2 ploughs, and 1 Frenchman with 2 bordars had 2 ploughs. Again no ploughlands were recorded.

The part of the manor of Westwood held in 1086 by Ralph de Saucey was, as the later sources reveal, at Wormeton Saucey. There, however, according

[27] DB, i. 269a.
[28] DB, i. 181a.
[29] *Herefordshire Domesday*, 20, 88.
[30] DB, i. 181a.
[31] *Herefordshire Domesday*, 78, 127.
[32] *Herefordshire Domesday*, 78; Hereford & Worcester Record Office, AD2/II 94; 100; 102; 115.

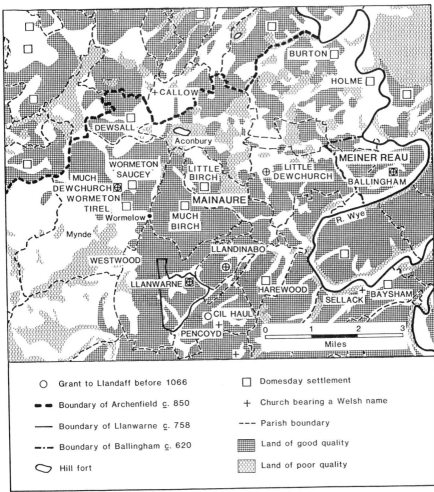

Fig. 4. Territorial organisation in northern Archenfield, Herefordshire, in 1086.

to Domesday Book, Ralph had land for 2 ploughs (*terram ad ii carucas*) and there was 1 plough with 2 ploughmen, but there was also 1 Welshman with half a plough who rendered 1 sester of honey. Appropriately, according to the twelfth-century list of tenants, Ralph de Saucey had there '1 English hide and the other Welsh'. Moreover the twelfth-century transcript records that at Wormeton Saucey there was land for 3 ploughs (*terram ad iii carucas*) rather than for 2 ploughs as stated in Domesday Book.[33] Since the Welsh hide was tilled in 1086 by half a ploughteam, presumably half a notional team of 8 oxen, it was probably smaller than the English hide and could be equated with land for 1 plough. On the other hand, given the presence on the

[33] DB, i. 181a; *Herefordshire Domesday*, 21.

English hide of 2 ploughmen it appears that this could be equated with land for 2 ploughs; and here the formula land for 2 ploughs appears to refer not to potential arable land but rather to the fact that there were actually 2 ploughs at work tilling the soil of 1 English hide. The Welsh hide, as later sources reveal, was in the Mynde (*la Montayne*) in the infertile upland to the south of Much Dewchurch, whereas the English hide was on the richer lowland to the north (Fig. 4).[34]

Yet a further component of Westwood, where there was 1 hide, was held by Ralph de Tosny in 1086 and by William and Ilbert from him. This component, as the twelfth-century transcript reveals, was at Dewsall (Dewi's well). There in demesne were 2 ploughs and 1 slave while 4 bordars had 2 ploughs. In addition, St Mary's of Lyre (in Normandy) then held the church of this manor (i.e. Westwood) with a priest and land for 1 plough.

At Llanwarne, also in Westwood, there was, according to Domesday Book, a church and 3 ploughs but the land of this church did not pay geld.[35] It belonged, however, to Holme, the large and productive manor of the canons of Hereford. This latter, in 1086, was flanked on the north by Burton, another large and productive manor belonging to the canons of Hereford. To the south Holme was adjoined by a manor, not named in Domesday Book but identified in the twelfth-century transcript as Ballingham; and in the same source Ballingham was equated with Meiner Reau, a name probably referring to the former inclusion, within a *maenor fro* (lowland estate), of Ballingham where 4 freemen in 1086 owed characteristically Welsh dues.[36] A late medieval entry in the twelfth-century transcript indicates there was a 'manor of Wormelow in Archenfield', named after the hundredal moot which was recorded in Domesday Book as being at Wormelow. It was thus designated probably because of the alienation of the 6 hides of Westwood, for in 1373 it was described as a manor without buildings or demesne lands and consisting only of rents of assize and the pleas and perquisites of court.[37] After the entry 'manor of Wormelow' in the transcript were recorded numerous components of Archenfield, including Meiner Reau, Mainaure and Westwood. It appears, therefore, that earlier there had been one wider *maenor* in northern Archenfield. For the upland *maenor* the court was probably at Much Dewchurch, the Villa Asmacun below Aconbury hill fort, and the royal *caput* of Westwood in 1066; but the principal church was at Llanwarne hence the tithes it later received from the Minster Farm at Much Birch. For the lowland *maenor* adjoining the Wye, the *caput* was probably at Burton (the settlement belonging to the fort), until it was severed from Archenfield, for the king still had the woodland of this manor in his demesne in 1086; but the major church was at Holme to which Llanwarne was still subsidiary in 1086.[38]

[34] *Historia et Cartularium Monasterii Gloucestriae*, ed. W. H. Hart (Rolls ser., xxxiii, 1863–7), ii. 224; PRO, C 133/91/1.

[35] DB, i. 181b; *Historia Glouc.*, i. 123.

[36] DB, i. 181a; *Herefordshire Domesday*, 19.

[37] *Calendar of Inquisitions Post Mortem*, xiii (1954), 196.

[38] DB, i. 181b.

From this wider *maenor* lands had been granted for the support of churches very long before 1066. Among these were 2½ *unciae* of land around the religious settlement (*podum*) at Ballingham, which were granted *c.* 620.[39] Within the bounds specified in its perambulation the 2½ *unciae*, which lay within the great bend of the River Wye, contained some 1285 statute acres, so that each *uncia* would have amounted to about 515 statute acres (Fig. 4). Another grant was that made to Hennlennic (the old subsidiary church) that is Lannguern (Llanwarne) *c.* 758. This was for an *ager* (land) of 3 *modii*, an area defined in the grant as a quarter of an *uncia*.[40] The perambulation indicated that the *ager* lay between the River Gamber, an old ditch, and a way which can be none other than the Roman road leading towards Wormelow. Here, however, the area delimited amounted to 530 statute acres, or about 1 *uncia*. Thus the land of 3 *modii* granted *c.* 758 consisted, not of a specific area marked by bounds but of a fractional share of a larger expanse, as is implied by its definition as a quarter of an *uncia*; and this lay probably in open-field to the south of the pre–existing church of Llanwarne. It is likely that these 3 *modii* corresponded to the 3 ploughs at Llanwarne said in Domesday Book to be free from payment of geld. If so, a measure can be obtained of the area tilled by 3 ploughs at Llanwarne for in one text of Welsh law the land of a *modius* was said to contain 300 acres for arable, pasture and fuel wood, plus 12 acres for buildings.[41] The land of a *modius* was a quarter of a wider area from which was contributed to the king a food rent consisting of loaves, cheeses, a vessel (*ryschen*) of butter and a cask of beer containing 4 *modii*; and this render in its make-up, although not its scale, closely resembled that recorded in Domesday Book as being made from each plough in Bistre before 1063. The acre of a *modius*, like that of its equivalent the shareland, was very small, so that 312 acres would have ranged in statute measure between 33 and 70 acres, with the smaller area being characteristic of the fertile lowlands, as at Ballingham and Llanwarne.[42]

Besides portraying the tenurial complexity of Westwood, and the location of arable lands, Domesday Book gives some impression of the disposition of settlement. It indicates that apart from Much Dewchurch there were in the main part of Westwood at least three other clusters of settlement at Dewsall, Wormeton Tirel and Wormeton Saucey. In these, besides the subtenants, were ploughmen, resident servants who presumably had their own habitations. Otherwise, apart from the slaves at Wormeton Tirel, the occupants of these four hamlets, each of which had its own demesne, were bordars, who recall the bordars living 'around the hall' in Tewkesbury.[43]

---

[39] *The Text of the Book of Llan Dav*, eds. J. G. Evans and J. Rhys (Oxford, 1893), 164–5.

[40] ibid., 81; W. Davies, *The Llandaff Charters* (Aberystwyth, 1979), 104–5, 116.

[41] *The Latin Texts of the Welsh Laws*, ed. H. Emanuel (Cardiff, 1961), 135–7.

[42] Holdings of this order of magnitude are recorded in Domesday Book for areas in western Herefordshire with Welsh associations. A holding of 57 acres formed part of the manor of Gruffudd, son of King Maredudd at Lower Lye. In the castlery of Ewyas Lacy there was a holding of 32 acres for which honey was rendered.

[43] DB, i. 163a.

For the manor of Helstone in Cornwall first impressions of the Domesday record suggest a very different estate structure and settlement form. The single entry for Helstone records that the manor, held by the count of Mortain in 1086, although assessed for 2 hides paid geld for only 1 hide. At Helstone there was land for 15 ploughs. In demesne there were 4 ploughs with 18 slaves, on land assessed for 1 hide, and on the remaining land, assessed for 1 hide, there were 20 villeins and 15 bordars with 8 ploughs. There were also 10 acres of woodland, and pasture, 3 leagues in length and 2 in width.[44] Helstone, however, was far from being a unitary settlement with one village in the midst of its fields. The arable land was far more extensive than is implied by the assessment for 2 hides and more in keeping with the new assessment that there was land for 15 ploughs; for the hide here consisted of 12 geld-acres each containing 64 acres,[45] and thus resembled the *uncia* of Archenfield with 12 *modii* of roughly the same statute acreage. Like Much Dewchurch, Helstone (the old court *ton*) was the *caput* of an estate which embraced a number of outlying settlements. A survey of 1337 reveals that of the 19 free conventionary messuages and the 74 villein messuages then in the manor, almost all were in clusters of 2 or more habitations (Fig. 5). It was no mere chance that Helstone, the largest cluster with 2 free messuages and 10 villein messuages, should have borne the name of the manor. As at Helstone there was a common green at the larger of the hamlets, but at every settlement there was arable land in Cornish acres which ranged in size from 26 English acres (31 statute acres) to 66 English acres (78 statute acres).[46] Between 1086 and 1337 there had occurred at least a doubling of the arable area. Nevertheless there need be little doubt that the main features of the settlement had already been established by 1086. In particular the hamlets of Helstone, Fentonadle, Michaelstow, Treveighan, Tregreenwell, Trewalder, Tremagenna and Trevia, where villeins by descent (*nativi de stipite*) were present in 1337, would probably have been occupied already in 1086 by the slaves and bordars of the manor.

The existence of this kind of settlement pattern is sometimes indicated by statements supplementing the standard formulae of the Domesday record. Such was the case in Leeds. The main part of the Domesday entry gives the impression that Leeds, held by Ilbert de Lacy in 1086, was a large unitary settlement, a sizeable village with its church and mill, and occupied by 4 sokemen, 27 villeins and 4 bordars who between them had 14 ploughs. But Domesday Book also provides the additional information that 'Before 1066, 7 thegns held (it) as 7 manors'.[47] If we may judge from later evidence, some of these manors at least were centred in separate hamlets. There is no

[44] DB, i. 121b; iv. 237a.

[45] L. F. Salzmann, 'Domesday Survey', in *VCH Cornwall*, viii (1924), 47–52. These were probably acres each of 5760 square yards.

[46] *The Caption of Seisin of the Duchy of Cornwall (1337)*, ed. P. L. Hull (Devon and Cornwall Record Soc., new series, xvii, 1971), lix–lxviii. 12–24; PRO, E 142/41; E 306/2. M. W. Beresford, 'Dispersed and Group Settlement in Medieval Cornwall', *Agricultural History Review*, xii (1964), 12–27.

[47] DB, i. 315a; 379a.

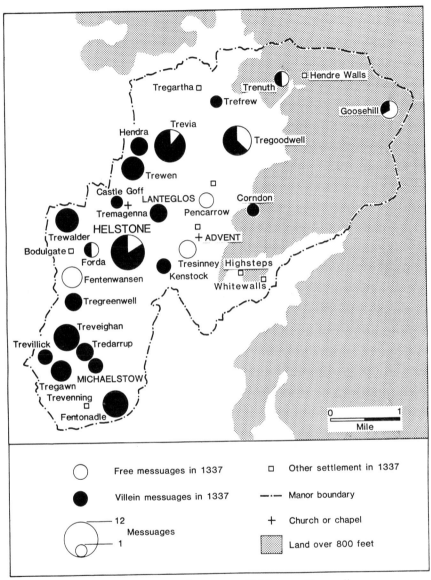

Fig. 5. Medieval settlements in the manor of Helstone, Cornwall.

reason to suppose that the church of 1086 was other than the church of the eighth century on the site that it later occupied in the manor of Kirkgate. Nor was the mill likely to have been new in 1086 so that there was already a second cluster of settlement in its vicinity near the *caput* of Leeds manor, some half a mile west of the church. Three furlongs to the north was yet the third manor of North Hall, while in an outlier nearly two miles to the south-west was the sub-manor of Cad Beeston.[48]

For some districts Domesday Book provides only a listing of vills and their assessments, as for example in Craven in the Yorkshire dales. Conistone is recorded as a manor, but otherwise we are informed only that Arnketill had '3 carucates for geld', and that 'Ketill has (it)'.[49] Yet when Conistone is viewed in its setting this limited record provides a substantial amount of information about the stage attained in the history of settlement. At Conistone in Kettlewelldale the only area potentially suitable for tillage was confined to a very narrow and sloping zone between the lowest of the limestone scars on the valley side and the meadows on the valley floor. This amounted to a mere 213 statute acres and the whole of this area had been terraced into lynchets.[50] As the Domesday assessment of 3 carucates indicates, most, if not all, of the terraced area had been brought under the plough by 1086. At best, therefore, the average carucate in Conistone could not have contained more than about 70 statute acres. Given these constraints on arable farming here it is probable that the small settlement at Conistone was already by 1086 confined to a small area and nucleated around its green.

Where two or more manors, or components of manors are recorded within one vill in 1086, as well as in 1066, a more precise insight into the form of settlement can sometimes be attained. This was the kind of situation which obtained within the vill of Wales in south Yorkshire, where the count of Mortain had 1 manor of 1 carucate for geld but where, in addition, there were 3½ carucates for geld which belonged to the soke of Roger de Busli's composite manor of Laughton-en-le-Morthen.[51] In subsequent centuries a clear distinction continued to be drawn in documentation about the two units (Fig. 6).[52] The count of Mortain's manor came to be known as the manor of Wales in the parish of Treeton. Even in 1066 its precursor had been held by the Morcar who also held a manor of 2 carucates in the vill of Treeton; and in 1086 the Richard who held the manor of 1 carucate in Wales from the count of Mortain also held the manor of 2 carucates in Treeton from the count. Hence the incorporation of the small manor of Wales in the parish of Treeton.

Domesday Book too indicates that the relative assessments for geld of the count of Mortain's manor in Wales and of Roger de Busli's soke in Wales were in the proportion of 1:3½, and appropriately, as was recorded in 1662,

---

[48] *Documents Relating to the Manor and Borough of Leeds, 1066–1400*, ed. J. le Patourel (Thoresby soc., xlv, 1956), 10–42, 83–103; *The Manor and Borough of Leeds, 1425–1662: An Edition of Documents*, ed. J. W. Kirby (Thoresby soc., lvii, 1983), xxiii–xxvi. 16; G. R. J. Jones, 'To the Building of Kirkstall Abbey', in *Leeds and its Region*, eds. M. W. Beresford and G. R. J. Jones (British Association for the Advancement of Science, Leeds, 1967), 121–30.

[49] DB, i. 331b.

[50] A. Raistrick and S. E. Chapman, 'The Lynchet Groups of Upper Wharfedale, Yorkshire', *Antiquity*, iii (1929), 174–81.

[51] DB, i. 308a, 319a, 379a.

[52] *Early Yorkshire Charters*, vi. 58, 209–11; vi. 338–9; *Taxatio Ecclesiastica*, 304; *Valor Ecclesiasticus* (6 vols., 1810–34), ii. 125; Yorkshire Archaeological Society, DD5, fos. 4–12, 14–15; University of York, Borthwick Institute of Historical Research, CCP/Lau 9: Lau 1, 109, 777; Dean and Chapter Library, York, Register of Leases, 1801–15, WL 381.

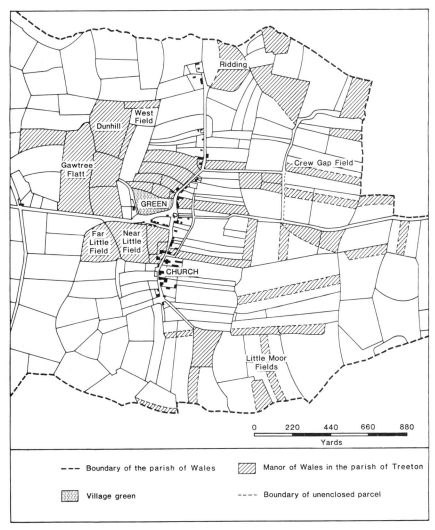

Fig. 6.   The form of medieval settlement in the vill of Wales, Yorkshire.

the rectory of Treeton, some four miles distant, received the tithes of 'about a third part of Wales and Wales Wood'.[53] It is, therefore, significant that, even in 1838, the frontages of the messuages and crofts in the village of Wales which formed part of the parish of Wales were about 3½ times longer than the frontages of messuages and crofts which formed part of the Manor

[53] Borthwick Institute, Terriers Ter. F (Doncaster) D, Treeton; Wales. The main part of the vill of Wales, which came to form the parish of Wales, was earlier in the parish of Laughton-en-le-Morthen.

199

of Wales in the parish of Treeton.[54] Although the number of parcels of land within the Manor of Wales had probably been increased with the enclosure of the common pastures, and their layout modified with the consolidation of open-field selions into compact blocks, it is unlikely that the disposition of the messuages and crofts along the village street would have changed. Already before 1086, therefore, Wales was probably an elongated village which extended to the north and south of the village green.

The example of the village of Wales highlights one of the major problems associated with the portrayal of land settlement in Domesday Book. Rarely, if ever, is there in the Domesday account of a manor or vill sufficient topographic detail to give more than an impression of the form of settlement. Nevertheless, the positive information provided by Domesday Book, when it can be tested against other near contemporary evidence, is usually correct and reliable. Particularly is this the case where Domesday Book deviates from its standard formulae or adds brief explanatory phrases; for it is quite unlikely that meaningless information would have been assembled in this summary record of an inquest itself meant to be thorough and comprehensive. Yet even for those manors or vills where the record in Domesday Book departs from its standard form, and thus gives some impression of the form of settlement, the Domesday evidence, if it is to yield its full potential, must be supplemented by later evidence. When this is done, given enough supplementary information, the deviant features are usually found to have existed and to be explicable.

On the other hand the portrayal of the disposition of arable land is much more detailed and complete, save in composite manors. This portrayal thus seems to provide a better pointer both to the broad pattern and to the scale of settlement. The record of ploughlands probably represented a new fiscal assessment;[55] but it was an assessment which, as most of the examples considered in this review suggest, was based on an attempt to record the area normally tilled within field hides or field carucates in terms of the common denominator of a ploughland of 120 statute acres. Hence, in areas where small hides or carucates persisted there were marked discrepancies between geld hides or carucates and ploughlands; or, where ploughlands were not systematically recorded, between geld hides or carucates and ploughs, even when beneficial hidation was not involved. In areas where already the field hide or carucate approximated to 120 statute acres, if only because small hides or carucates were estimated in large customary acres, discrepancies are much less in evidence. Where ploughlands are concerned, Domesday Book presents the results of an attempt, in part successful, to record the actual amount of arable land held by all sorts and conditions of men. To that degree it provides a literal *pied-à-terre* for the portrayal of the nature and scale of land settlement achieved by the late twelfth century.

---

[54] PRO, IR 29/43/414; IR 30/43/414.
[55] Harvey (1985), 86–103.

Some Agents and Agencies of the Late Anglo-Saxon State

JAMES CAMPBELL

THE ORGANISATION AND the economy of a state are largely reflected in and determined by its organisation for war. So, in considering the nature of the English state in the mid-eleventh century, one may turn, in search of helpful stimulus, to such a masterly survey of the relations between societies, economies and warfare as Professor William H. McNeill's *The Pursuit of Power*. There we read of the 'overwhelmingly rural' world of the eleventh century, to which 'market behaviour' was deeply alien; and of how the military systems characteristic of such worlds were transformed during the later Middle Ages by the 'commercialisation of organised violence' as mercenary troops came increasingly into use in Italy and elsewhere.[1] One may be touched, as not infrequently, by the faithfulness with which a modern historian can stick to his cherished old stereotypes of the Middle Ages. But the best advice to give to those who hold such views as Professor McNeill's is: that they should tell them to the *lithsmen*. The study of Domesday makes nonsense of such stereotypes. Any defensible interpretation of the English state at that time has to take account of the circulation of a great deal of coin,[2] and of much 'commercialisation', not least of military service.

No source does more to show how far this was so than the annals of the Chronicle relating to the reign of Harthacnut, 1040–2. E.g. 'King Harold died . . . And in his time 16 ships were paid for at eight marks to each rowlock, just as had been done in king Cnut's time'.[3] Harthacnut's advisers 'decreed that 62 ships should be paid for at eight marks to each rowlock'.[4] 'In this year the army-tax was paid, namely 21,099 pounds, and later 11,048 pounds were paid for 32 ships'.[5] 'And in this year Hardacnut had all

---

[1] W. H. McNeill, *The Pursuit of Power. Technology, Armed Force and Society since AD 1000* (Oxford, 1983), 63, 69–79.
[2] The most recent estimates are those of D. M. Metcalf, 'Continuity and change in English monetary history', *British Numismatic Journal*, 1 (1980), 20–49, li (1981), 52–90.
[3] D. Whitelock, D. C. Douglas and S. I. Tucker, *The Anglo-Saxon Chronicle. A Revised Translation* (2nd edn., 1965), 105 (E version, *s.a.* 1039, *recte* 1040).
[4] Loc. cit.
[5] Ibid., 106 (E version, *s.a.* 1040, *recte* 1041).

Worcestershire ravaged for the sake of his two housecarls. The people had then killed them within the town in the minster'.[6] The Worcester chronicler 'Florence' gives more details here.[7] He indicates that the sending of housecarls to Worcestershire was part of a more extensive exercise: the king sent his housecarls through all the provinces to collect the *tributum* which he had imposed. The killing of the housecarls at Worcester in May was punished in November. The king sent several earls ('Florence' says there were five and names others) and 'almost all his housecarls'. Their orders were to kill *omnes viros*, if they could; to plunder and burn the city; and to ravage the *provincia*. The *cives* and *provinciales* made a stout resistance and were allowed to come to terms. But the *inimici* as 'Florence' revealingly calls them, ravaged for four days, and burned the city on the fifth. Then they went home with their booty, *et regis statim quievit ira*.

These passages are important. First, they bear on the problem, crucial for the understanding of the history of the English state, of the acceptability of the very high figures for danegeld and heregeld stated in the Chronicle. Between 981 and 1018 these total £240,500. The highest levy reported, that of 1018, was £82,500.[8] If what the Chronicle says is accepted, then Cnut raised more money in that one year than did any of his successors as rulers of England in any one year for many generations.[9] The round figures of the relevant annals up to, and including, that for 1018, by their very roundness inspire mistrust, and, as Corbett long ago suggested, look as if they may reflect not so much the annalist's knowledge of a total sum raised as his multiplying up the rate he knew to have been levied per hide, by what he believed to be the total of hides.[10] But, once one comes to the annals for Harthacnut's reign the figures turn, convincingly, odd. It may not be beyond human ingenuity to find explanation for the figures £21,099 and £11,848 other than that they derive from accounts, written accounts. But common sense does seem to suggest that, more likely than not, they do so derive. If so, they tend to validate the orders of magnitude indicated by the annals relating to earlier years.

Dr Lawson, in a paper which calls on many sources to demonstrate the heavy reality of danegeld/heregeld in early eleventh century England, has drawn important deductions from another, most significant, element in the *Chronicle*'s account of the reign of Harthacnut: not only does it give numbers of ships, it also, by saying 'eight marks to each rowlock' almost certainly

---

[6] Ibid., 106 (C version, *s.a.* 1041).

[7] *Monumenta Historica Britannica*, ed. H. Petrie, i (1868), 600. Florence's annals, as we have them, were composed much later. But the details which this annal provides on names and dates and its relating to Worcester, speak strongly for its reliability.

[8] M. K. Lawson, 'The collection of Danegeld and Heregeld in the reigns of Aethelred II and Cnut', *EHR*, cix (1984), 721, 736–7.

[9] Of course, allowance has to be made for inflation; and the determination of the quantity of silver involved is fraught with difficulties, e.g. an increase in the amount levied in terms of £ of account did not necessarily indicate an increase in the physical weight of silver levied, Pamela Nightingale, 'The ora, the mark and the mancus: weight standards in eleventh-century England', *Numismatic Chronicle*, cxliii (1983), 248–57; clxiv (1984), 234–48, esp. 242.

[10] W. J. Corbett, 'The Tribal Hidage', *TRHS*, new ser., xiv (1900), 220.

indicates the annual rate of pay for their crews. If, as is probable, the ship's companies each consisted of eighty oarsmen paid at eight marks and a steersman paid at twelve marks, then the annual cost of one ship was 652 marks.[11] Such data make it possible to work out the likely cost of fleets; and this information further strengthens the case for the general plausibility of the Chronicle's geld figures.

The annals for 1040 and 1041 bring into focus two features of the English state. It was, at least for periods, oppressively taxed for the maintenance of standing forces. Standing forces could be used to enforce the payment of tax; and in that sense were part of the apparatus of government though we cannot tell to what extent they were regularly used in this way.[12]

In referring to the housecarls (Chronicle, *hus carla*, 'Florence', *huscarlae*) used by Harthacnut to collect and enforce tax as 'standing forces' I imply some disagreement with a recent, and weighty, article by Mr Nicholas Hooper.[13] He argues that the long-accepted views of L. M. Larson on the housecarls rest too much on late Scandinavian sources. Some of the important questions he discusses, for example that of whether the housecarls constituted a 'law-bound guild' are no more than indirectly relevant to my present purpose. The question of whether there was a standing paid force, of the kind the housecarls have long been believed to have constituted, is directly relevant. I would suggest that the absolute distinction which he draws between a 'standing army' and stipendiary members of the royal household (which he agrees housecarls, or some housecarls, to have been) could mislead.[14] Here we should think of Mr Prestwich's fine article on 'The military household of the Norman kings'.[15] In this he shows that these kings maintained a military household not too unlike that of Edward I, that it included men of varied status, some or all of whom were paid annually. The military household was variously used in varying circumstances: sometimes to provide a field force, sometimes as garrisons, sometimes as a nucleus for larger armies. It was recognised by contemporaries as an institution. Such institutions, or forces, existed elsewhere, and, probably, long before. Suger indicates the likely importance of the *domestici milites* of Louis VI.[16] Besides Asser's account of Alfred's paid *ministri* and *bellatores*, must be set in the Carolingian world the paid troops, sometimes household troops, whose

---

[11] Lawson, 'The collection of Danegeld . . .', esp. 721–3, 737–8. It is not easy to determine what a 'mark' was at this time. Dr Lawson, 722 n. 3, assumes that it was 10s 8d., while allowing for the possibility that it was 13s 4d. Dr Nightingale, 'The ora, the mark and the mancus . . .' (1984) 286, argues for 16s.

[12] N. Hooper, 'The housecarls in England in the eleventh century' (*Anglo-Norman Studies*, vii. 1984), 175, points out that the circumstances of 1041 were abnormal in that Harthacanut had just entered England as an invader. It is true that there is no other known instance of the use of troops to enforce tax. But the sheer weight of the gelds (Lawson, 'The collection of Danegeld . . .', *passim*) strengthens the case for believing that armed force may not infrequently have been the sanction.

[13] Hooper, 'The housecarls . . .'.

[14] Ibid., 170–1.

[15] *EHR*, cvi (1981), 1–35.

[16] *Suger. Vie de Louis VI Le Gros*, ed. and trans. H. Waquet (Paris, repr. 1964) 78, 90.

importance has been brought out by Dr Reuter.[17] I would suggest that 'housecarl' often means something like *domesticus miles* and that a later parallel to two housecarls riding out to collect the geld from Worcester is four household knights, riding out to murder Becket. To call such a body, never to be numbered in more than hundreds, a 'standing army' may well be to strain a point. To deny it some of the functions of a standing army may be to miss a point.

One of these functions may have been the enforcement of taxation.[18] It is this which adds to the neuralgic interest of the question of how much, and how permanently, Edward gave away when he dropped the heregeld in 1051: for in abandoning the geld he may have reduced his means of enforcing its reintroduction.[19] It would be possible to be more categorical about these matters if the rôle of the crews of the standing fleet, the *lithsmen*, were better understood. These certainly did, until 1049/50, comprise a standing force of some size. The Danish kings had kept such a fleet; Edward the Confessor had fourteen ships in 1049, when he paid off five; the C annalist's statement that in 1050 he paid off all his *lithsmen* probably indicates the paying off of the remaining five. The abandonment of the standing fleet was very probably connected with the dropping of the heregeld.[20] It is obviously important to know whether the *lithsmen* could be employed on land

---

[17] *Asser's Life of King Alfred*, ed. W. H. Stevenson (Oxford, repr. 1959), 86; cf. Hooper, 'The housecarls . . .', 170; T. Reuter, 'Plunder and tribute in the Carolingian empire', *TRHS*, 5th ser. (1985), 75–94, esp. 82–3).

[18] Another may have been garrison duty. The Domesday reference to fifteen acres at Wallingford 'where the housecarls used to live' (DB, i. 56a) has often been cited in this connection. Mr Hooper is right in saying that it is hard to know 'precisely' ('The housecarls . . ., 171) what this reference means, but that it is to a garrison has always seemed a fair guess. Wallingford may have been exceeded in importance as a fortress only by Winchester and London. It is alone with Winchester in being allocated a hidage as high as 2400 in the Burghal Hidage. Its fortifications enclosed a hundred acres. Their continuing importance is indicated by their later being faced with stone (C. A. Ralegh Radford, 'Late pre–Conquest boroughs and their defences', *Medieval Archaeology*, xiv (1970), 92–4). A curious indication of its ninth-century importance is that the Alfredian translation of Orosius locates one of Caesar's battles there (*The Old English Orosius*, ed. Janet Bately (Old English Text Society, suppl. ser. 6, 1980, 126). (I owe this reference to an anonymous London University examination candidate.) The *Chronicle's* annal for 1006 shows that to an Anglo-Saxon mind Wallingford lay in precisely the area which seemed the heart of the kingdom (Whitelock, Douglas and Tucker, *s.a.*). That the Conqueror crossed the Thames there may be less to be explained by the weakness of the fortress, than by whatever accounted for the high favour in which Wigod *oppidanorum Wallingfordensium dominus* (and a kinsman of Edward the Confessor) was later held by William (Freeman, *Norman Conquest*, iv (2nd edn, 1876), 728–31). J. Tait, *The Medieval English Borough* (Manchester, 1936), 148, suggests that the evidence of Domesday and of the Pipe Rolls indicates that Wallingford had a 'special relationship' with the Crown, e.g. the Pipe Rolls indicate that it was never farmed by the sheriff and there is no indication of payment of the earl's third penny at Wallingford.

[19] The question of whether geld was reintroduced before 1066 seems unanswerable; for discussion see F. Barlow, *Edward the Confessor* (1970), 155–6.

[20] Lawson, 'The collection of Danegeld . . .', 721–2; Hooper, 'The housecarls . . .', 170; C. Warren Hollister, *Anglo-Saxon Military Institutions on the Eve of the Norman Conquest* (Oxford, 1962), 16–19.

as well as on sea; but the question remains one for speculative argument.[21] Whether or not that was so, they must have been important. The crews of fourteen ships probably totalled 1120 (apart from their steersmen); the likely annual pay of each man was something over £4, perhaps something over £6.[22] This is big money; using a very rough rule of thumb, about the annual value of 5 hides of land. If the fleet was based on London then the *lithsmen* of London who helped to determine the succession to the throne in 1036 (and perhaps on other earlier and later occasions) may have been its crews.[23] And what we know of their pay suggests their high status. Collectively they received an annual sum about equal to the regular annual income of the Crown (exclusive of geld).[24] Their individual incomes would have put them among the tiny proportion of the population which was really well off; with an annual income as high as that of the more prosperous kind of post-Conquest *miles*, much higher than that of the ordinary *miles*.

› There can be little doubt that the England which William conquered was, or at least until very recently had been, a state in which a high proportion of the income of the inhabitants was taken away; and moved up, through the hands of agents, perhaps of a series of agents, to the king. ¶Then it moved down again as the king spent it, in ways which may have much affected the balance of wealth within society. (Though much of the expenditure of the Anglo-Danish kings went overseas.) This state probably was (or, again, it is tedious, but necessary, to say: 'or had, fairly recently, been') a highly stressed one in which there was a relationship between the power to enforce tax and the use of tax to maintain standing forces. It must have been in important ways highly centralised; one in which the connections between the central authority and the localities mattered very much and one in which the number of men, below the level of sheriff, who were in some sense agents of government, was very large.

The ultimate link in the chain which led from the king to a village was the village reeve. 'Reeve' (*gerefa*, *praepositus*, usually in Domesday) is a pretty general sort of word, used for administrative agents at very different levels of importance. However, the articles of inquiry preserved in the *Inquisitio Eliensis* indicate something not too unclear, and by no means unimportant, about one kind of reeve, viz. that it could be assumed (no doubt as no more than a rough generalisation) that there was a reeve in every village and that

---

[21] It is not certain that the term has necessarily to indicate a sailor at all. G. W. N. Garmonsway translates the term as 'household troops, troops', *The Anglo-Saxon Chronicle translated with an Introduction*, 274. Professor Hollister (*Anglo-Saxon Military Institutions*, 16) says the term seems to mean 'warrior' in the Norse literature (though he gives no examples) and he draws attention to one *Chronicle* passage (*Two of the Anglo-Saxon Chronicles Parallel*, ed. J. Earle and C. Plummer (2 vols., Oxford 1892–9), i. 197) where *lith* seems to mean 'troops' or 'household troops', Whitelock, Douglas and Tucker, 144, Garmonsway, 197. Barlow, *Edward the Confessor*, 172, is against the identification of lithsmen and housecarls.

[22] See above, pp. 202–3.

[23] May MacKisack, 'London and the succession to the Crown during the Middle Ages', *Studies in Medieval History Presented to F. M. Powicke*, ed. R. W. Hunt, W. A. Pantin, R. W. Southern (Oxford, 1948), 76–8.

[24] Barlow, *Edward the Confessor*, 153.

he could be regarded as having a kind of public responsibility: '. . . inquisitio . . . per sacramentum . . . presbiteri, praepositi, vi. villanorum uniusque villae'.[25] The significance of this, as of so much else about Domesday, was best brought out by Reginald Lennard.[26] He drew attention to the *tungerefa* who appears in the laws of Ethelred, and to the passage in the *Leges Henrici Primi* which says that the priest, the reeve, and four of the better villagers are to attend the shire-court as substitutes for the lord or his steward when these last are absent. No shirker of difficulties, Lennard raised several. Who is this reeve? Is he simply the lord's reeve with public obligations imposed on him? Who would be 'the reeve' in the *Inquisitio Eliensis* sense when, as often, more than one lord held land in a given village? We can only conclude, with him, that there are unplumbable ambiguities here, which may worry us more than they did contemporaries.

But we should also observe that village reeves were regarded as having a kind of responsibility to the king as well as to their lords. The significance of this is much increased if, as in particular certain entries in the Geld Rolls strongly suggest, geld was collected not via the lord of an estate, but directly from his reeves. This is indicated by references to reeves 'retaining' geld. In Wiltshire, e.g. in Warminster Hundred the reeve of St Stephen of Fontenay 'retains' the geld from two hides; in Heytesbury Hundred the reeve of Osbern Gifford that from half a hide; in Thornhill Hundred he of the abbot of Glastonbury from three and a half hides.[27] If the king's agents could, as it were, short-circuit landowners and descend on their reeves, one can see how geld-collection could have been the more efficacious for it (though it is not easy to see whether such direct dealings with reeves were normal or not). One may also glimpse something of a spirit of government such that the question of what such and such a place owed to the king mattered as or more directly than that of what such and such a great man owed; and even, not impossibly, have some inkling of why Domesday is so much concerned with bringing together a territorial and a tenurial approach.

Men whom one might call 'village reeves' (though that could hardly be a very uniform category and must cover a multitude of various grades of sinner) are not recorded in anything remotely like a methodical comprehensive way in Domesday, except, to some extent, in the western circuit, and, in particular, in Herefordshire Domesday. Ten reeves are mentioned in Herefordshire TRE; thirty-four *nunc*.[28] All of the 1066 10 were on royal estates: 8 on the great Leominster complex, whose 16 component members were served by 8 reeves, 8 beadles and 8 radknights. Of those mentioned for

[25] W. Stubbs, *Select Charters* (9th edn, corrected 1951), 101.

[26] Lennard, *Rural England*, 271–6. The presence of the reeve as an essential representative of a village or manor is important, of course, in the later history of the sheriff's tourn and of the general eyre.

[27] *VCH Wiltshire*, ii. 188–9 (prepositus sancti Stephani de Funteneio retinuit geldum de ii hidis); the reeves of two other ecclesiastics are mentioned as 'retaining' geld from a total of nine hides, ibid., 190, 206. A royal reeve could also 'retain' geld, ibid., p. 179.

[28] DB, i. 179b (2), 180a; 179b (2), 180a (3), 180b (4), 181b, 182a (2), 182b (2), 183a (3), 184a (3), 184b (5), 186b, 187a (2).

1086 10 were on royal lands, 5 on those of the see, 8 on those of Hugh de Lacy and the remainder on those of various secular lords. It would be agreeable, indeed helpful, if we could regard such indications, or at least those for 1086, as having some kind of claim to comprehensiveness; in the sense that, though there must have been many other reeves, those recorded had something conspicuously reeveish about them, were nearer to being full-time than part-time reeves, or something like that. But there is no means of knowing this, and the incidental mention of a reeve at Frome, not listed like the other reeves among the tenants, but mentioned incidentally as the holder of a mill, stands in the way of even so tentative a conclusion.[29]

The Herefordshire data on reeves are nonetheless useful. Lennard drew out their significance. The Herefordshire entries (and some from other shires) show the reeve 'associated with the plough-owning peasants', never among the lower orders of the village.[30] His landholding varies: a virgate, half a hide, a whole hide.[31] Some, as one would expect, had their opportunities. There is a reference in the entry for Marden to forty acres 'which king Edward's reeve leased to a relative of his'.[32] At Eardisland (*Lene*) we have an indication of a reeve handling considerable sums of money. TRE, when the *domina* (this would have been Morcar's wife) came to the manor, the custom was for the reeve to give her eighteen *ora* of pence 'ut esset ipsa laeta animo'; and ten shillings to the steward and other officers.[33]

Many of the most enlightening Domesday entries relating to reeves mention them in relation to their misdeeds.[34] Particularly interesting is such an item as that which comes in the account of Westminster Abbey's estate at Battersea. It says that the *prefectus villae* has taken a hide from the Westminster manor and put it into Chertsey (*misit in Chertsey*); and the abbot of Chertsey now holds it.[35] It is not possible to be certain as to exactly what is indicated here; but it is worth noticing that if 'village' reeves were responsible for collecting geld, then the close connection between the payment of geld and the establishment of title (a connection probably very important for the understanding of Domesday) may have enabled such reeves to manipulate title.[36]

There were a variety of agents of government between village/manor reeves and sheriffs. For example, there are hundred or wapentake reeves, mentioned in the laws of Ethelred II and appearing on occasion in

[29] DB, i. 182a.
[30] Lennard, *Rural England*, 272–3.
[31] DB, i. 180a, 182a, 182b. There is a problem as to the nature of 'reeveland'. References are collected by Ellis (1833), i. 231. The most important modern suggestions are those of R. R. Darlington, *VCH Wiltshire*, ii. 62, 82–3.
[32] DB, i. 179b.
[33] DB, i. 179b.
[34] References in Domesday to reeves and, in particular to their misdeeds are collected by Freeman, *Norman Conquest*, v (1876), 811–18. See also Ellis (1833), i. 245.
[35] DB, i. 32b.
[36] Lawson, 'The collection of Danegeld . . .', 723–4, 729, 732. Cf. DB, i. 30b relating to two hides and a virgate at Etwell, Surrey, which had been *subtractae* and *prepositi accomodaverunt eas suis amicis*.

Domesday.[37] Perhaps the fullest details relating to such a reeve in Domesday are those provided in relation to the activities of the reeve of West Derby Hundred.[38] West Derby lay between Ribble and Mersey. This is one of the areas where in the middle ages serjeants of the peace performed functions which elsewhere were performed by the frankpledge system. When Stewart Brown wrote an admirable monograph on them he did not realise how likely it was that the origins of the office lay in the remote Celtic past.[39] The reeve of West Derby Hundred in Domesday was probably what would later have been called a serjeant of the peace or hundred serjeant. One would hardly be able to work out from Domesday the importance of the office, let alone its antiquity. Even more important than hundred and wapentake reeves could have been the reeves of ridings, to whom the *Leges Edwardi Confessoris* allocate an important rôle in the Danelaw, presumably in Yorkshire and Lincolnshire.[40] They do not appear in Domesday. Indeed, so far as I know they appear only in the *Leges Edwardi Confessoris*; but it is hard to believe they were invented by the author of this work. We should again be warned against the supposition that Domesday gives anything like a complete picture of the administrative scene.

What it does bring home is the force of the commonplace observation that in most societies administrative function and profit go hand in hand. Not improbably, most of the best businesses in eleventh-century England were those which involved the management of some part of the royal revenues. For example, among the *praepositi* subordinated to sheriffs (and it is an interesting, if inscrutable, question how numerous such subordinates were) were those who farmed royal manors. Lennard showed that sheriffs, at least sometimes, farmed out to *praepositi* what they themselves farmed from the king.[41] They were, as he put it, the farmers of farms. Another class of functionary, with its rewards and opportunities, the geld collectors, shows up, in particular, in the Geld Rolls. In Devon each collector seems to have been allowed to retain the tax on one hide. In Dorset one collector is mentioned as having retained so large a sum as £40 which he should have handed over.[42]

Questions about the business of administration, about administration as a

[37] W. A. Morris, *The Medieval English Sheriff to 1300* (Manchester, 1927), 25; Ellis (1833), i. 22, 188.
[38] DB, i. 262b.
[39] R. Stewart Brown, *The Serjeants of the Peace in Medieval England and Wales* (Manchester, 1936), G. W. S. Barrow, *The Kingdom of the Scots* (1973), 1–30. esp. 26–7.
[40] H. R. Loyn, *The Governance of Anglo-Saxon England* (1984), 145. Professor Loyn regards the description of riding reeves in the *Leges Edwardi Confessoris* as 'probably a reflection of twelfth century conditions' but there seems no reason why the institution should not have been considerably older.
[41] Lennard, *Rural England*, 146–50, cf. Morris, *Medieval Sheriff*, 28, 34. An obscure, but plainly important, passage in Domesday for Wiltshire seems to relate to the sheriff as a farmer of farms: 'habet (sc. the sheriff) etiam quater xx libras valentiis inter Reveland et quod inde habet. Quando prepositis firma deficit, necesse est Edwardo (the sheriff) restaurare de suo', I am not certain what the first sentence means, but the implication of the second seems to be that when lesser reeves' farms fell short the sheriff had to make up a deficit, *VCH Wiltshire*, ii. 62, 135.
[42] *VCH Wiltshire*, ii. 170; Finn, *Liber Exoniensis*, 101–3.

business, have a particular interest when applied to towns. There has been no survey of what Domesday tells us about this area of constitutional economic history since Tait's; and he was not, strictly speaking, an economic historian.[43] But the interest to the economic historian of what he teased out is not small. He made a good case for concluding that town reeves, or reeves in towns, were not always (and probably not normally) subordinated to the sheriff. He showed that some of them enjoyed positions of considerable authority and, one may deduce, emolument.[44] At Hereford the reeve had a third of the proceeds of the sale of burgess tenements; apparently farmed the whole of the issues of the town, paying their respective shares to king and earl.[45]

What Domesday tells about Huntingdon is particularly worth notice. It seems to say, Tait showed, that someone (presumably some Huntingdon burgess) farmed the variable revenues for both king and earl on a contract the terms of which were adjustable.[46] At the end of the Huntingdonshire section of Domesday, in the account by the jurors of outstanding cases, we learn how close, how brisk, was the relationship between this minor provincial centre and the court. The abbot of Thorney had mortgaged (invadiavit) the church of St Mary and its land to some, or the, burgesses (burgensibus). Then Domesday darkly says (or the jurors darkly said) 'however' (autem) King Edward gave the church to two of his priests. They sold it to his chamberlain, Hugh. Hugh sold it to two priests of Huntingdon. They have King Edward's sigillum for it. Now Eustace has it 'sine liberatore et sine breve et sine saisitore'.[47] As so often in Domesday a richly evocative packet of information, preserved by chance, almost at random, is a key to the understanding of, or anyway, not unreasonable guesses about, the late Anglo-Saxon state. The obscure statement about the farm: 'Preter haec habebat rex xx libras et comes x libras de firma burgi aut plus aut minus sicut poterat collocare partem suam' comes to life and Tait's interpretation of it (see above) makes good sense when put into the context of what the jurors tell us about St Mary's church, where they enable us to catch a sight of the wheeling and dealing between the priests and chamberlains of the king, and men who were on the make, even in Huntingdon.

It is a question of how important townsmen were in administration other than in the towns and as moneyers. It could be that in England, and elsewhere in Europe, administration was in part in the hands of something like a patriciate, to be understood as part of a social scene in which being a moneyer, being a merchant and being say a royal chamberlain (perhaps being a royal priest) could be closely related avocations. Suggestive here is Dr Nightingale's account of the Deorman family.[48] She strengthens the case

---

[43] Tait, Medieval English Borough, 143–4.
[44] Ibid., 147.
[45] Ibid. 101, 143.
[46] Ibid. 144–5; DB, i. 203a.
[47] DB, i. 208a.
[48] P. Nightingale, 'Some London moneyers and reflections on the organisation of English mints in the eleventh century', Numismatic Chronicle, cxlii (1982), 35–50.

for identifying the Deorman of London whom Domesday shows holding half a hide in Islington with the Deorman to whom an early writ of William the Conqueror restored land and with the Deorman holding fairly extensive lands in Hertfordshire and Essex. She shows not only that it is likely that all three references are to the same man, but also that he is probably to be identified with a London moneyer who struck coins before the Conquest, who was not improbably related to a series of moneyers with the same name who had struck coins in London since the time of Ethelred II. The family remained important in the twelfth century, producing not only moneyers but, for example, a canon of St Paul's, an alderman of London and a *justiciarius*. That the Domesday Deorman is described as a king's thegn makes it not unlikely, though not certain, that he had some administrative function. His kind of man and his kind of family may have been very important in the organisation of the state.

Here it is of some interest to observe that among the considerable number of Englishmen who were important in the administration of England after the Conquest a noticeable proportion were on occasion named as *de* some town. Among the English sheriffs whose interest has been brought out by Dr Green should not improbably be included Edward 'of Salisbury'.[49] In Norfolk Aelfwine 'of Thetford' was a *praepositus* of some kind in Norfolk, with considerable property till it was forfeited some time after the Conquest.[50] In Suffolk we hear of the misdeeds of another reeve called Aelfwig 'of Colchester'.[51] In Bedfordshire we read that Ordwig 'of Bedford' had misappropriated land.[52] It is noticeable that the three most conspicuous Anglo-Saxon survivors after 1070 (Edgar the Atheling set on one side) were Wigod 'of Wallingford', Coleswein 'of Lincoln' and Thurkill 'of Warwick' (though we do not know of the last two of these that they held administrative office – they could have done).[53] Again the possibility of a nexus between commerce and administration occurs.[54]

A high proportion of administration must have been part-time, performed as an incident of tenure. Here a crucial question is that of the origins of what was known to lawyers of the thirteenth century and later as service by serjeanty.[55] Thirteenth-century surveys record numerous serjeanty tenures relating very often to minor services in the royal household and to hunting, but also to administrative and military functions. The possible relationship between these tenures and those of the *ministri, servientes, taini*, etc., listed at

[49] Judith Green, 'The sheriffs of William the Conqueror', *Anglo-Norman Studies*, v (1983), 129–45, *VCH Wiltshire*, ii. 99.
[50] Freeman, *Norman Conquest*, v (1876). 815–16.
[51] Ibid., 813.
[52] Ibid., 812–13.
[53] For Wigod see above, p. 204 n. 18 and Harmer, *Anglo-Saxon Writs*, 577; for Coleswein, J. W. F. Hill, *Medieval Lincoln* (Cambridge, 1948), 48–9: for Thurkill, Green, 'Sheriffs . . .', 130 n. 7, 131 (the above may include sheriffs named after shire towns, J. H. Round, *Feudal England* (1895), 168).
[54] A turn of phrase of Professor Barlow's comes to mind here. 'Reeves and other speculators', *Edward the Confessor*, 144.
[55] J. H. Round, *The King's Serjeants and Officers of State* (1911), E. G. Kimball, *Serjeanty Tenure in Medieval England* (New Haven and London, 1936).

the end of some county surveys in Domesday has not gone unnoticed. Dr M. C. Hill, in her work on the *King's Messengers* puts the problems admirably. She drew attention to serjeanty services described in thirteenth-century surveys and to the distribution of royal writs, etc., in particular to a Wiltshire tenancy by the service of carrying the king's writs in that shire and one in Leicestershire by that of carrying the king's writs all over England for forty days. She observes that these services are likely to have been old when first recorded and relating to a system, or what could well have been a system, which was superseded in the thirteenth century.[56] She raises important questions about serjeanties as they appear, almost certainly in their decline, in the Book of Fees, etc., and repeats a question raised by Le Patourel: 'Could they have had the same significance in the organisation of the king's civil and domestic service as knight service had in the organisation of the feudal army?'.[57] Serjeanties do not seem to be much regarded by students of the English state; they can seem, at best, a fascinating backwater. But, it could be that the serjeanties, as they come to light, or twilight, in the thirteenth century are the semi-fossilised remnants of important parts of the Anlgo-Saxon governmental system.

Consider, for example, what the late R. R. Darlington said in the course of his investigation of Domesday for Wiltshire. 'When the Wiltshire sections of the lists of serjants of 1198, 1236 and 1250 are examined it is found that in a remarkable number of instances the land held by serjeanty, when its location is given, and the place is among those which occur in Domesday lies in a village where one or more thegns or *ministri* held land. Though no connection can be established between the thirteenth-century holder and the individual who occurs in Domesday, it may be inferred that the estate was held by serjeanty in the eleventh century and that some *taini* were English serjeants'.[58] Or again, take the observation by William Hudson, in regard to the Norwich herring pie render. The city of Norwich, in the middle ages, and until 1816, made an annual render of twenty-five herring pies to the King. It is not known how old the service was. 'However, some 30 acres of land in East Carleton, a village about four miles from Norwich were burdened with the obligation that their owner should carry the pies to the King, and Domesday Book under the *demesnes of the King's men* does show a similar extent of land there apparently charged with some personal service'.[59]

An example of thirteenth-century carrying services with more serious governmental implications than the transportation of herring pies, and which may have Anglo-Saxon origins are those to which Dr Hill and Dr

[56] M. C. Hill, *The King's Messengers 1199–1377* (1961), 8–10.
[57] Ibid., 10; for Le Patourel see *EHR*, liii (1938), 694–6. For suggestions on royal messenger services at an even earlier date, L. M. Larson, *The King's Household in England before the Conquest* (Madison, 1904), 176–7.
[58] *VCH Wiltshire*, vii. 77–8. The possibility of thirteenth-century serjeanties having pre-Conquest origins had not, of course, escaped Round, *The King's Serjeants*, 14–16, 18–20, 270. It is however only on rare occasions that continuity can be demonstrated, even from 1086. Thus Darlington's observations of the implications of the general pattern of such tenures in Wiltshire has special value.
[59] W. Hudson and J. C. Tingey, *The Records of the City of Norwich* (2 vols., 1906, 1910), ii. 13.

Kimball have drawn attention in regard to the royal manor of Marden, Herefordshire.[60] In the thirteenth century tenants there owed the services of carrying the king's treasure to London, of summoning certain lords and of distraining for the king's debts. It is suggested that the three radknights who held there TRE may have performed the same functions; and that the whole country may have been covered by a network of such services.

The question of what Domesday means by thegns is important here. Round suggested that the chief distinction between *taini* and *servientes* in Domesday was that by the former were intended men who performed the same kind of functions as the latter but were of English birth or of English domicile before 1066.[61] Darlington extended this suggestion when he wrote: 'It seems not unlikely that all the men entered as thegns were in the royal service and that all Englishmen who held estates of the king in 1086 had survived because they were already or had become royal servants'.[62] These suggestions both help to bring out the relationship between thegnage and serjeanty and stress the functional aspect of thegnage. 'Thegn' is not a word which can be reduced to one meaning. But it seems that the ministerial element in thegnage (and, after all, the commonest Anglo-Latin word for thegn is *minister*) was central to the use of the word in Domesday. It looks as if a Domesday thegn was often someone who held land in return for the performance of a service, not infrequently a service at court.[63]

This fits with the well-known early eleventh-century account of how a ceorl might thrive to thegnright. We are told that what the upwardly mobile ceorl had to get was not only 5 hides of land but 'a seat and a special office in the king's hall'.[64] Compare one of Darlington's instances. In the thirteenth century land at Winterbourne Gunner and Laverstock was held by the serjeanty of serving as usher in the king's hall. In Domesday a thegn called Saric held a little estate in each of these two places. Darlington's suggestion that there was real continuity between Saric's tenure and what is recorded in the thirteenth century looks much more likely than not.[65]

In the account in the tract on status of the tenure of a thegn considerable stress is laid on the importance of communication. A thegn (sc. king's thegn) is one who 'served the king and rode in his household band on his missions'.

---

[60] Hill, *King's Messengers*, 9; Kimball, *Serjeanty Tenure*, 99–100.

[61] *King's Serjeants*, 12–14.

[62] *VCH Wiltshire*, ii. 76. I am obliged to Dr C. Harfield for having allowed me to see his useful paper on 'The thegns of the Conqueror' after I had given the present paper.

[63] Round, *King's Serjeants*, 14–16 emphasised the extent to which thegns, or some thegns, continued to have ministerial functions (in opposition to Maitland). Cf. Barlow, *Edward the Confessor*, 148. 'Without this class of noble servants, endowed with land and commended to the king, England could not have been governed.'

[64] *EHD*, i (1979), 468.

[65] *VCH Wiltshire*, ii. 77; cf. 77–8 for other instances. An interesting possible link between late Anglo-Saxon arrangements and those which appear in thirteenth-century lists has to do with feeding the poor. Compare Athelstan's ordinance: 'make known to all my reeves that you shall always provide a destitute Englishman with food, if you have such a one, or can find one' (*Laws of the Earliest English Kings*, ed. F. L. Attenborough, Cambridge, 1922, 126–7) with the service later performed by the Russel family of feeding two paupers daily, for the benefit of the king's soul (Kimball, *Serjeanty Tenure*, 117).

(Dr Whitelock's translation. She says that the word used in this passage *radstefn* is unique and 'probably refers to important errands undertaken by a mounted messenger'.[66] Beside this put a well-known passage in the Domesday account of Torksey; one which, though it cannot be proved to relate to the circumstances of Edward the Confessor's reign, may well do so. It says that when the *legati regis* come the burgesses are to escort them and their ships to York and the sheriff is to provide victuals for them and their sailors.[67] *Legati* is generally translated 'messengers'[68] but *legatus* in the language of Domesday can mean something grander than that: the Domesday commissioners were *legati*.[69] One is reminded of Freeman's (not always sufficiently regarded) observations on the late Anglo-Saxon state when he speaks of 'commissioners . . . sent in the king's name', who 'answer exactly to the *missi* of the Carolingian Emperors and Kings'; ('it is of little consequence whether we look on their employment as actually suggested by the employment of the *missi* or whether we hold that Germany and England were both capable of independently inventing so obvious a way of doing business').[70] He quotes the *Judicia Civitatis Lundoniae*: 'When Aelflah Stybb and Brihtnoth the son of Odda attended the assembly at the request of the king',[71] and a number of documents which show the presence of agents of the king at local trials, for example a Herefordshire hearing of Cnut's reign, where not only were the bishop, the earl and other great men present, but also 'Tofi the Proud came there on the king's business'.[72] Such examples do not *prove* more than that on occasion Anglo-Saxon kings sent agents to the provinces to attend hearings in which the king was interested, and, doubtless to make the royal will known; but they could be related to the extensive use of royal emissaries to the provinces.[73] Communication with the king's court was necessarily two-way. The status that says that one of the qualifications which would enable a lesser thegn to represent his lord in certain legal affairs was to 'have thrice gone on his errand to the king'.[74]

At other levels and in other contexts the maintenance of communications must have been of great importance. A great eleventh-century estate was a constellation of settlements, many of them small, scattered over hundreds of square miles, and each at the end of a long, muddy track. The control and exploitation of such rural empires was probably not something which could be left to the peasants and the village reeves with an annual collection of dues.

---

[66] *EHD*, i (1979), 468.
[67] DB, i. 337a.
[68] E.g. *The Lincolnshire Domesday and the Lindsey Survey*, trans. and ed. C. W. Foster and T. Longley (Lincoln Record Society, 1914), xxxv and 11.
[69] *legatio* may, however, be used to indicate a message-carrying service in the account of Archenfield (DB, i. 179).
[70] Freeman, *Norman Conquest*, v (1876), 445–8.
[71] *Laws of the Earliest English Kings*, ed. Attenborough, 166, 167.
[72] *Anglo-Saxon Charters*, ed. Robertson, no. LXXVIII.
[73] Much light will be cast on such matters when Mr Patrick Wormald's researches on Anglo-Saxon and Anglo-Norman lawsuits are completed.
[74] *EHD*, i (1979), 468.

As with a king and his shires, so with a lord and his vills; he must have needed men to ride to and fro, e.g. radmen, radknights.[75]

The problem of estimating the density and frequency of written communication comes in many forms. A particularly important one is that of how often writs were sent. The frequency with which Domesday mentions the king's 'writ and seal' or his *mandatum* suggests that this frequency was considerable. On this Freeman put forward another important hypothesis. It seemed to him that the Domesday evidence could suggest that no tenure of land was secure unless the hundred and/or shire had either seen a relevant royal writ, or transfer had been made on the instructions of someone sent by the king, called by such terms as *famulus regis, legatus regis, liberator regis.*[76] He suggested that all Englishmen who were allowed to retain, or regain, their lands after 1066 had to have them confirmed by one or the other means, at a price.[77]

It is true that many, perhaps a disproportionate number, of the Domesday references to the king's writs have to do with lands held or claimed by Englishmen. For example, two of the three tenants in Bedfordshire who produced the king's writ and seal as evidence for their tenure were English.[78] The third instance, that of the canons of St Paul's in relation to their estate at Caddington is not without interest. The larger part of this estate lay in Hertfordshire; but Hertfordshire Domesday says nothing about the production of documentary evidence in relation to this estate. Round's conclusion was 'that in this as in so many other matters the silence of Domesday is not evidence and that in all such cases proof was called for and produced'.[79] It is a truism that far more royal documents were issued than survive. Perhaps many of the writs which are lost were used to confirm the tenure of small men rather than that of large, for whom a visit by a *famulus, liberator, legatus* to the shire-court may have been more appropriate. For example, Berkshire Domesday records a claim to a very small holding by Godric. A man called Aluricus said he had seen a *breve regis* which gave the land to Godric's wife, for the service of looking after some of the king's dogs. But, says Domesday: 'no one in the hundred has seen this writ, except Aluric'.[80] The implication is apparently that there was no such writ; but also that there was a context in which small men might have writs which were considered at hundredal level. The Domesday evidence for the extensive use of writs relates largely to the years after the Conquest; but granted the absence of evidence for anything corresponding in pre-Conquest Normandy, it is not unreasonable to regard

[75] The presence of 8 radknights beside the 8 reeves and the 8 beadles in the account of Leominster (with its 16 members) TRE, DB, i. 180a is an indication that radknights had, or could have, administrative functions.

[76] *Norman Conquest*, v (1876), 787–98, cf. ibid., iii (1875), 730, v, 24.

[77] Ibid., 796–8. Note the reference in Domesday for Suffolk to a period 'quando redimebant Anglici terras suas', DB, ii. 360b. Cf. *Anglo-Saxon Chronicle* (E), *s.a.* 1087 (*recte* 1086).

[78] DB, i, 218a (2).

[79] J. H. Round, *VCH Bedfordshire*, i. 206. Domesday references to the production of documentary evidence of title before the commissioners are collected by Ellis (1833), i. 331.

[80] DB, i. 57b. For examples of tenure by the service of feeding hounds, Ellis (1833), i. 40n.

what happened in this regard under William as deriving from what happened under Edward.[81]

The density of communication and the extent of written record mattered at levels of relationship other than and below that of the king and the shires. Domesday casts the occasional gleam of light on the use of written record in minor administration. I am thinking in particular of an entry in Hertfordshire Domesday relating to half a hide of land held by a man called Humphrey. TRE it had been held by Leofsi, *praepositus regis Edwardi*, Odo of Bayeux had taken it from him and given it to Eudo.[82] When Humphrey had acquired it he got with it 68 cattle, 350 sheep, 150 pigs, 50 goats, 1 mare, 13s. 4d. *de censu regis* and cloths and vessels worth 20s.

Various things seem odd. How can so many livestock have been kept on half a hide? That we are told that there is land for only two ploughs indicates that this cannot be an example of extensive beneficial hidation. There is something equally odd about the mere recording of livestock numbers, this being Great Domesday. And why give them not for the present but for the occasion in the past when the present holder acquired the land? I suggest that what we have here is information drawn from a document describing what Eudo handed over to Humphrey; that Eudo and Humphrey were, like their predecessor Leofsi, reeves (though Domesday does not say this of them); that the sum of money *de censu regis* was a balance handed over from one reeve to another; and that the numerous livestock were beasts taken in distraint, herded, rather than pastured, on this rather small property. These suggestions are hypothetical and the statement that the land has been *occupata . . . super regem* is not explained by my suggestions; but it is in any case hard to escape the conclusion that a document of a kind which does not otherwise survive lies behind this entry. Documents of many kinds may have been used in royal and loyal administration, and for quite some time. For example, if clause 3 of VI Athelstan does not prove that keeping of written accounts for the thief-hunting association was intended, it nevertheless makes it seem by no means unlikely.[83] If an eleventh-century site were to produce documents on the scale of a *Vindolanda* or a Novgorod, it would not be so very surprising.[84]

A conclusion can be expressed in reflections on two relationships, that between the administration and the economy and that between the central authority and the provinces. The nature of the English state, and above all of its fiscal system, ensure that to separate the study of administration from that of society and the economy is even more than usually misleading. England was run in such a way that a fairly high proportion of the population was involved in administrative activity (on behalf of the king or of some other lord) in more than a purely passive sense. For example, some 5 per cent of the recorded population of the Leominster estate TRE were reeves, beadles or

---

[81] Writs were used to give the king's peace as well as to grant land, e.g. DB, i. 82b, 252 b, 292 b, 336 b; similarly a *legatus* could give the king's peace as well as grant land, DB, i. 262b.
[82] DB, i. 139b.
[83] *Laws of the Earliest English Kings*, ed. Attenborough, 158–9.
[84] M. W. Thompson, *Novgorod the Great* (1967), 55–63.

radmen.[85] In some societies and circumstances administrative involvement has been a burden. The guarantee that the reeves, using the term in the general sense in which it was used by some contemporaries, of late Anglo-Saxon and early Anglo-Norman England, were not decurions is the extent and manner to which they were denounced. Wulfstan lamented the rapacity of reeves. Homilies of the late tenth and early eleventh century describe the *gerefa* as a man to be dreaded.[86] When in his letter of 1027 (in the Latin version which is all we have) he instructs his *vicecomites* and *praepositi* that they were not to employ *vis injusta*, one can be sure that that is what they were using.[87] We get a glimpse of the seigneurial reeve much later in the century when Eadmer, in explaining Anselm's visits to his rural manors, says: 'if he had not been present in his manors to hear their (sc. his men's) complaints, his reeves would have oppressed them in many ways (as often happened) until, as the oppression got worse and worse, they were utterly destroyed'.[88] Instances of reeveish oppression are not lacking in Domesday and something of the spirit in which reeves were regarded comes through in a passage in Domesday for Hampshire relating to a dispute between Hugh de Port and Picot. Of Hugh it says 'de hoc suum testimonium adduxit de melioribus et antiquis hominibus totius comitatus et hundred' while 'Picot contra duxit testimonium de villanis et vili plebe et de praepositis'.[89]

Office brought the opportunity for enrichment; in a country so wealthy as eleventh-century England there must have been many such opportunities. A, perhaps the, principal means of advance in that society was very likely through performing administrative functions. The most remunerative service must have been that of the Crown. Its very wealth would have seen to that. Professor Barlow suggested that the explanation for the twelfth-century shire farms being 'so much smaller than Domesday would give us to expect' is that more than half the notional income of the Crown was consumed by administration and collection: 'Edward could not have bargained with his reeves for as much as half the amount due to him'.[90] Another, and a more convincing, explanation for the discrepancy to which he refers has now been found.[91] This hardly diminishes the general weight of his suggestion that the one important effect of the power and wealth of the Old English kings was the enrichment of their agents. Not only is it possible that the way in which the geld was expended had a major effect on the balance of society; the opportunities afforded to those involved in its collection may have been similarly significant. Important questions arise about the nature of the connection between towns and administration; how far townsmen acted as

---

[85] DB, i. 180a.
[86] Instances are collected by Morris, *Medieval Sheriff*, 15–16.
[87] *The Laws of the Kings of England from Edmund I to Henry I*, ed. A. J. Robertson (Cambridge, 1925), 150–1.
[88] *The Life of St Anselm Archbishop of Canterbury by Eadmer*, ed. R. W. Southern (corrected edn, Oxford, 1972), 71.
[89] DB, i. 45b.
[90] Barlow, *Edward the Confessor*, 153.
[91] J. Green, 'William Rufus, Henry I and the royal demesne', *History*, lxiv (1979), 337–52.

royal agents; how far involvement in the royal fiscal system was the means to accumulate capital. The Normans' capacity to run and exploit England must have owed a very great deal to the availability of numerous English agents of government in the shires, men such as Domesday allows us sometimes to see doing well out of the Conquest. In its account of the property of one (possibly) English administrator in the Conqueror's service, Edward of Salisbury, a Domesday commissioner or clerk for once permitted himself a value judgement; it was *à propos* of Edward's house at Wilcot: *domus obtima*.[92] It puts one in mind of Chaucer's reeve, a different kind of reeve, but similarly comfortable. 'With grene trees yshadwed was his place.'[93]

A major element in English government and not least in linking the centre and the provinces was the royal household. That this has not received all the attention it deserves may be seen from the extent to which Larson's book has not been superseded. His is a very good book, but it was published in 1904. Much that he suggested is worth more attention than it has received. For example, his use of late Scandinavian evidence, though it may be regarded with justifiable reserve, sets doors ajar which otherwise might remain completely closed. True, the *Lex Castrensis* is a twelfth-century compilation which may well tell us nothing for certain about the eleventh. But there is something suggestive about, for example, its emphasis on the maintenance of a strict order of precedence among the housecarls when they sat at table (demotion in that order being regarded as a sign of disgrace), when this is set beside the order of precedence so well observed by Dr Keynes in the witness lists to Ethelred the Unready's charters.[94] Or again Larson's suggestion that some elements in royal household organisation in medieval Norway and princely household organisation in medieval Wales are to be explained by a common origin in Anglo-Saxon England is not unreasonable.[95] Perhaps he was sometimes wrong but he raised questions about the heart of the Anglo-Saxon state which remain at best incompletely unanswered.

Larson did not consider the possibilities and problems associated with serjeanty tenures as they appear in the thirteenth-century surveys. Indeed, I think no one has faced them head on. Much learning has been devoted to them: Round and Kimball (and Blount is not altogether to be forgotten) provided the basis of our knowledge. Hill and Darlington have illuminated some of these tenures from different viewpoints. Still, most historians concerned with the English state in the eleventh and twelfth centuries seem to regard them as of no more than marginal, perhaps simply antiquarian, interest. But the possibility that in so regarding them we are blinkered deserves consideration. That these services in considerable measure were, when they come to light, semi-fossilised remnants of the eleventh-century governmental system is harder to demonstrate, but does seem very likely. Not the

---

[92] DB, i. 92a. He had a 'new church' there too and a 'good vineyard'.
[93] *Complete Works*, ed. W. W. Skeat (Oxford, 1894), i. 18, line 605 (609)
[94] Larson, *The King's Household*, 159; S. Keynes, *The Diplomas of King Aethelred 'the Unready' 978–1016* (Cambridge, 1980). The appended Tables illustrate the extent to which an order of precedence was maintained.
[95] Larson, *The King's Household*, 196–8.

least interesting thing about them is the link they demonstrate, at least in some areas, between landholders and the court, expressed in the performance of household services (perhaps originally on a rota basis?); though there is no means of telling how far such services were, or had by 1066 become, more formal than substantial.

Crucial questions in regard to the relationship between king and provinces relate to the density and frequency of communication. We know that writs, for one purpose and another, and emissaries, for one purpose and another, went out from the court. 'How often?' and 'For what purposes?' are harder questions to answer. Domesday seems to show that by 1086 the use of writs to make or confirm grants of land, not infrequently to quite lowly people, and to give the king's peace was fairly common, perhaps very common. In the case of *legati* and the like, our evidence is very fragmentary, and to the extent that derives from Domesday and is not specifically related to the time of King Edward, it is not easy to know how far it can be applied to the period before 1086; but we probably ought to think of the late Anglo-Saxon period as one in which men from the court frequently ride out to the shires and men from the shires frequently rode in to court.

'Probably', 'perhaps', 'there are indications that': such are the leitmotifs of this speculative paper. It is selective and incomplete, not least in saying nothing about, not even asking questions about, the major agents of the state. I will conclude by asking one or two such questions. Edward the Confessor had quite an administrative machine. Who actually ran it? A reasonable, if unprovable, guess is Stigand. A plausible explanation (though not the only possible one, of course) for his extraordinary success as a pluralist, his wealth, his control over ecclesiastical patronage and the number of men he had commended to him is that he was Edward the Confessor's Roger of Salisbury.[96] A second question. Did earls pay geld? Domesday indicates that they and their tenants, did. This should be put beside something else which marks them off from men who could appear their counterparts overseas; they did not issue charters. Both things are indications of the sovereignty which the Saxon kings had established in England and which the Normans nearly lost.

---

[96] Barlow, *The English Church 1000–1066*, 77–81. Barlow observes the possibility that Stigand may have come from 'Norse trading stock' (p. 78 n. 1); cf. 210 above.

The Greater Domesday Tenants-in-Chief

C. Warren Hollister

IT IS A deeply appreciated honour to have been invited to discuss the greater Domesday tenants-in-chief at this historic conference – an honour and also a formidable challenge. So many distinguished scholars of the past and present have devoted their attention to 'those wise and eloquent men,' as Orderic Vitalis described them, 'who through long years dwelt in King William's court, observed his deeds and all the great doings there, knew his deepest and most secret counsels, and were endowed by him with riches that raised them above the station to which they were born.'[1] A great many pages could have been devoted to these men, Orderic says, and indeed a great many have. In returning to the topic of the greater Domesday tenants-in-chief on this ninth centenary of Domesday Book, I find myself astride the shoulders of such giants as John Horace Round, William J. Corbett, Sir Frank Stenton, David Douglas, Reginald Lennard, John Le Patourel, and J. C. Holt – and even thus upraised I am by no means confident that I can see farther than they.

It was W. J. Corbett who in 1926 first subdivided William the Conqueror's lay tenants-in-chief into categories based on the value attributed to their Domesday estates.[2] In this present paper I will follow Corbett's scheme of categorising the Domesday aristocracy into Classes A through E in descending order of wealth, and will attempt, through prosopographical analysis, to answer certain questions about its upper echelon: To what degree did the distribution of wealth among the greatest men and families of Domesday England reflect the distribution of wealth and power in Normandy at the time of the Conquest? To what extent was a Domesday landholder's wealth apt to be based on ties of kinship or long-standing friendship with the Norman ducal house? To what extent were the kinship bonds linking the duke and his greater magnates simply a Norman myth reflected in chimerical genealogies provided by Robert of Torigny in the mid-twelfth century? And, related to that question, did the Conqueror's upper aristocracy consist primarily of old or newly risen families?

---

[1] Orderic, ii. 190.
[2] William John Corbett, 'The Development of the Duchy of Normandy and the Norman Conquest of England', *Cambridge Medieval History*, 5 (Cambridge, 1926, reprinted 1968), 505–13.

I shall begin with Corbett's list of Class A magnates, with Domesday lands valued at between £750 and £3240 a year (Appendix A). I use round figures because the estate values of the greater landholders are impossible to determine with precision. To begin with, Domesday leaves portions of England, most notably far northern England, unsurveyed. Moreover, the meaning and significance of the Domesday value figures have themselves been much debated.[3] And it must always be kept clearly in mind that Corbett's lettered categories are constructs of the twentieth century, not the eleventh. Nevertheless, the magnates in Corbett's Class A – eleven as I count them – whose collective lands, valued at over £15,000, represented nearly half the total land value of all lay tenants-in-chief – can safely be regarded for the purposes of this analysis as an aristocratic upper crust. Apart from the king himself, they were the foremost beneficiaries of the greatest upheaval that the English ruling classes have ever known.

The Class A magnates are listed in Appendix A. At the top of the list are four men of surpassing wealth: Odo bishop of Bayeux and earl of Kent (about £3240); Roger of Montgomery, earl of Shropshire (about £2100); Robert, count of Mortain and earl of Cornwall (about £1975); and William fitz Osbern, earl of Hereford until his death in Flanders in 1071 (about £1750).[4] These great men, who also figure among the most frequent attestors of King William's charters, are followed by William of Warenne (about £1140); Count Alan of Brittany,[5] Eustace count of Boulogne, Hugh *vicomte* of Avranches and earl of Chester, Richard fitz Gilbert of Clare, Geoffrey of Mowbray bishop of Coutances (we are now down to about £788), and the bottom man on Corbett's Class A list, Geoffrey de Mandeville, the value of whose lands – about £740 as I calculate it – actually drops him into the £100 limbo between the floor of Corbett's Class A (£750) and the ceiling of his Class B (£650); but why be fussy?

The Domesday aristocracy, as Professor Holt has aptly observed, constituted 'a very fluid society'.[6] It was, indeed, so extremely fluid that the fitz Osbern earls of Hereford and Odo bishop of Bayeux – who are normally included among its greatest members – had fallen some years before the survey of 1086. Odo would return from captivity on William the Conqueror's death in 1087, only to forfeit his vast Domesday lands in 1088 and be banished from England forever. The traditionally accepted Class A list is thus not a TRW list but a 'when received' list, based on the wealth of the

---

[3] See, for example, Darby (1977), 208–59; Harvey (1985), 86–103; G. D. Snooks and J. D. McDonald, 'The Determinants of Manorial Income in Domesday England: Evidence from Essex', *Journal of Economic History*, 45 (1985), 541–56.

[4] Corbett included William fitz Osbern on his Class A list but omitted the king's half-brothers, Odo of Bayeux and Robert of Mortain, regarding them instead as members of the royal family. In regarding Odo and Robert as Class A magnates, I am following the example of Le Patourel, *The Norman Empire*, 32, 308, 335–6, and Lennard, *Rural England, 1086–1135*, 25–6 and 26, n. 1.

[5] Corbett omits Alan of Brittany; but see J. F. A. Mason, 'The Honour of Richmond in 1086', *EHR*, 78 (1963), 1–28.

[6] J. C. Holt, 'Feudal Society and the Family in Early Medieval England: I. The Revolution of 1066', *TRHS*, 5th series, 32 (1982), 208.

Conqueror's greatest magnates in England at whatever moment between 1066 and 1086 it reached its maximum.

Class A families continued to teeter and topple during the two decades between Domesday and Tinchebray: in 1095 the curtain fell on Robert earl of Northumbria, Geoffrey of Coutances's nephew and heir. Henry I seized the earldom of Cornwall in 1104 when Robert of Mortain's son and heir, William, opted for Duke Robert Curthose, and two years later, at Tinchebray, Henry I seized and imprisoned William of Mortain himself. Roger of Montgomery's heir, Robert of Bellême – that intriguingly evil genius – lost the Montgomery earldom of Shropshire in 1102 and his own freedom a decade thereafter. And other Class A lineages had some very close calls: the Clares in 1095, the Warennes in 1101–3, Eustace of Boulogne after 1088, the Mandevilles after 1101. In short, the massive disruption of England's aristocracy that began in 1066 was followed by a series of after-shocks for almost half a century. Thereafter, inheritances became distinctly more secure through the remainder of the High Middle Ages.[7]

In this paper, however, I intend to trace the Domesday aristocracy backwards rather than forwards, and I shall begin by comparing the magnates in the Corbett Class A group with William's wealthiest magnates in Normandy on the eve of the Conquest to see to what extent the two groups match. It will doubtless be objected that without a Norman Domesday Book aristocratic wealth cannot be measured. But there are other means of gauging wealth in Normandy – less precise certainly, yet not to be despised.

I propose that the members of the Norman upper aristocracy of 1066 are identified by name in a well-known and often maligned list appended to the Bodleian manuscript of the *Brevis Relatio* enumerating the ships contributed to the Conqueror's invasion fleet by fourteen of his magnates and prelates, plus the duke's own flagship, the *Mora*, contributed by the Duchess Matilda.[8] This list, in the form we now have it, postdates the Conquest by some years.[9] It has been badly garbled by its modern editors: the largest contributor on it, who provided 120 ships, was mistranscribed by Silas Taylor in the seventeenth century as Robert of Mortemer.[10] In the nineteenth century J. A. Giles emended the name to Roger of Mortemer,[11] presumably on the grounds that Roger of Mortemer was a well-known Conquest magnate whereas Robert of

---

[7] RaGena DeAragon, 'The Growth of Secure Inheritance in Anglo-Norman England', *Journal of Medieval History*, 8 (1982), 381–91.

[8] Oxford, MS. Bodl. Lib. E Museo 93 fol. 8v (p. 16), printed in Silas Taylor, *The History of Gavel-kind with the Etymology Thereof* (London, 1663), 209–10; and *Scriptores Rerum Gestarum Willelmi Conquestoris*, ed. J. A. Giles (Caxton Society, 1845, reprinted 1967), 21–2.

[9] The list describes Hugh of Avranches as 'postea comite de Cestria' and Remigius almoner of Fécamp as 'postea episcopo Lincoliensi'. Hugh became earl of Chester in 1071 or soon thereafter (*Complete Peerage*, 164); Remigius became bishop of Dorchester *c.* 1067 and transferred his see to Lincoln *c.* 1072: John LeNeve, *Fasti Ecclesiae Anglicanae, 1066–1300*, III, *Lincoln*, compiled by Diana E. Greenway (London, 1977), 1.

[10] Taylor, *Gavel-kind*, 209.

[11] *Scriptores*, 22.

Mortemer was not. Had Giles consulted the Bodleian manuscript, of which Dr Elisabeth Van Houts very kindly provided me a photocopy and transcription, he would have discovered that the name in question is – without the slightest ambiguity – Robert of Mortain, the Conqueror's half-brother and the third wealthiest Anglo-Norman magnate in Domesday Book.

Although the list purports to account for a total of 1000 ships, the ships ascribed to the fourteen named contributors (excluding Matilda's *Mora*) actually total 776 – suggesting either that some names had been dropped in the process of copying an earlier list – or earlier lists – or else that the compiler was extraordinarily bad at addition. That the list is incomplete is made clear in the document itself: following the name of the last of the fourteen contributors is the statement, 'Besides these ships, which altogether added up to a thousand, the duke received many other ships from various of his men, each in accordance with his means (*secundum possibilitatem*).' Nevertheless, as I shall argue, there is reason to suppose that the men credited with providing the most ships constituted a Norman aristocratic upper-crust. The fourteen names occur in the manuscript in no apparent order. When one rearranges them in descending order of the number of ships contributed, as I have done in Appendix B, a fascinating symmetry emerges. The three largest contributors – Robert of Mortain, Odo of Bayeux and William count of Évreux – provide 120, 100 and 80 ships respectively – a total of 300 ships. The next five men – William fitz Osbern, Hugh of Avranches, Robert count of Eu, Roger of Montgomery and Roger of Beaumont – contribute exactly 60 ships each, making a second group of 300, or a total of 600 ships thus far. The list concludes with four more laymen – Hugh of Montfort-sur-Risle, Fulk of Aunou, Gerald *dapifer* (the Roumare paterfamilias), and Walter Giffard – owing between 50 and 30 ships each (for a total of 160 ships); then Nicholas abbot of St-Ouen with 15 ships and Remigius almoner of Fécamp and future bishop of Lincoln with 1 ship. Apart from Remigius, whose inclusion seems idiosyncratic, the list appears to disclose a hierarchy of contributors, each in proportion to his possessions, with an élite group of three men providing more than 60 ships each, five great men providing exactly 60, four laymen providing fewer than 60, and two well-connected churchmen tagging along behind.

In analysing the list, I will exclude Remigius from consideration and will also bear in mind that others among the lesser contributors may in fact have blended with some of the unidentified providers of additional ships whom the document mentions. A further complication is that four of the fourteen named contributors of ships are reported to have provided fixed numbers of knights as well: Nicholas abbot of St-Ouen, for example, provided 15 ships and 100 knights; Hugh of Montfort, 50 ships and 60 knights. For the purposes of this analysis, the difficulty can only be resolved by disregarding the information on knight contributions on the grounds that the list does not provide it on a systematic basis. When one rearranges the list as I have done in descending order of ships contributed, it immediately becomes evident that none of the eight great men contributing 60 or more ships are credited with providing any knights whatever. Rather than supposing that men of the stature of Robert count of Mortain or William fitz Osbern brought no knights to Hastings, it seems preferable to conclude that the information is simply missing from the list for some reason or other – perhaps because it went without saying that anyone contributing 60 or more ships to Duke William's fleet would have brought his share of knights.

On the whole, the list is very plausible. Of its 11 laymen, 9 – including all 7 contributing 60 or more ships – are major ducal officials: 3 counts, 3 *vicomtes*, and a steward who was also titled 'count of the palace'.[12] The one abbot on the list, Nicholas of St-Ouen, was Duke William's first cousin and the most frequent abbatial attestor of his pre-Conquest *acta*; the one Norman bishop on it is the Conqueror's half-brother. The list is consistent with Orderic's testimony that 'both clergy and laity devoted their time and money to building [ships]' in preparation for the 1066 crossing,[13] and with William of Malmesbury's statement, echoed by the author of the *Brevis Relatio*, that the duke, at the council of Lillebonne, obtained commitments from his great men to provide ships for the campaign 'in proportion to the extent of their possessions'.[14] It is my contention, therefore, that the 8 men on the ship list contributing 60 ships or more constitute a Norman aristocratic élite comparable to the 11 Class A magnates of Domesday Book.

This contention receives powerful corroboration in William of Poitiers' *Gesta Guillelmum*. Writing about this same council of Lillebonne, William of Poitiers singles out seven Norman lay lords as 'outstanding', 'shining like luminaries and ornaments', and equal in wisdom to the entire Senate of republican Rome.[15] These seven names correlate most remarkably with the eight men atop the ship list (Appendix B). One of the eight, Odo bishop of Bayeux, is absent from William of Poitiers' list because William is naming only laymen (he praises Odo lavishly elsewhere).[16] The remaining seven atop the ship list match William of Poitiers' magnificent seven family for family and, with one exception, man for man. If we emend the ship list by substituting Richard count of Évreux for his son William (who fought at Hastings in the place of his aged father and inherited the county in 1067),[17] the two lists become identical. One might almost suppose that William of Poitiers was writing with some such ship list at hand.

The list is further corroborated by the fact that all seven laymen, or their

[12] David Bates, *Normandy before 1066* (London, 1982), 155.

[13] Orderic, 144; cf. William of Poitiers, ed. Foreville, 150; and the legend on the Bayeux Tapestry, Pls. 34 and 35: 'Hic Willelm Dux iussit naves edificare'; see further *Le roman de rou de Wace*, ed. A. J. Holden (3 vols., Paris, 1970–3), ii. 114.

[14] William of Malmesbury, *Gesta Regum Anglorum*, ed. William Stubbs (2 vols., Rolls Series, 1887–9), ii. 299; *Brevis Relatio*, in Giles, *Scriptores*, 5: '. . . praecepit ut quam citius possent omnes barones Normanniae unusquisque secundum suam possibilitatem naves praepararent. . . .' Note the similar language at the end of the ship list itself: 'Extra has naves quae computatae simul m. efficiunt, habuit dux a quibusdam suis hominibus secundum possibilitatem unius cuiusque multas alias naves.'

[15] William of Poitiers, 148.

[16] Ibid., 134–6, 240–2.

[17] Ibid., 194–6 and 196 n. 1.

immediate antecedents, had founded or refounded Benedictine abbeys in Normandy during the years between *c*. 1030, when the earliest non-ducal foundations commence, and the mid-1070s when William of Poitiers was writing.[18] The founding of a full-scale Benedictine abbey was at once fashionable, pious and extremely expensive; families of less than formidable wealth had to settle for priories. A recent paper by my doctoral student Cassandra Potts, published in *Études normandes*,[19] discusses some nineteen non-ducal abbeys founded in this period, by some twelve aristocratic families (Appendix C). Among these twelve families are those of all seven leading laymen identified in William of Poitiers and the ship list. Collectively, the seven ship list families were responsible for thirteen of the nineteen abbeys – more than two-thirds of the total.[20] These seven families included four of the five Norman lineages known to have founded more than one abbey, and independent evidence demonstrates that the heirs of the fifth multiple founder, Goscelin *vicomte* of Rouen – whose two foundations date from *c*. 1030–40 – had fallen on hard times by 1066.[21] Another abbey-founding family, the Taissons, can be shown to have suffered a similar decline.[22] If, therefore, we exclude these two declining families and their abbeys from our investigation of the upper aristocracy in 1066, it results that the seven lay lineages at the top of the ship list founded over 80 per cent of the remaining

[18] On the Norman non-ducal foundations in general see Bates, *Normandy*, 115–16, 218–25. On the date of William of Poitiers' *Gesta Guillelmi* see Foreville in William of Poitiers, xvii–xx (suggesting 1073–4) and R. H. C. Davis, 'William of Poitiers and his History of William the Conqueror', in *The Writing of History in the Middle Ages: Essays Presented to Richard William Southern*, ed. R. H. C. Davis and J. M. Wallace-Hadrill (Oxford, 1981), 71–100 (suggesting, more probably, *c*. 1077).

[19] Cassandra Potts, 'Les ducs normands et leurs nobles: la patronage monastique avant la conquête de l'Angleterre', *Études normandes*, iii (1986), 29–37. My Appendix C is derived from an earlier and fuller version of this paper with a valuable appendix that will remain unpublished for the time being.

[20] The total of 19 is approximate because of the difficulty in determining the dates of many of the foundations. The most valuable sources are J.-M. Besse, *Abbayes et prieurés de l'ancienne France* (Paris, 1914); *La Normandie bénédictine au temps de Guillaume le Conquerant (XI siècle)*, ed. Gabriel-Ursin Langé (Lille, 1967); and Robert of Torigny, 'De immutatione ordinis monachorum. De abbatibus et abbatiis normannorum et aedificatoribus earum', in *Chronique de Robert de Torigni*, ed. Léopold Delisle (2 vols., Rouen, 1872–3), ii. 184–206.

[21] Goscelin and his wife Emmeline founded La Trinité-du-Mont, Rouen, *c*. 1030, and St-Amand, Rouen, *c*. 1030–40: Besse, *Abbayes*, 62–3. In 1047 Goscelin's son-in-law Godfrey was deprived of some of his lands by William count of Arques, and Godfrey's son William did not retain the *vicomté*: Bates, *Normandy*, 104 and n. 42; *Complete Peerage*, x. 48.

[22] Ralph Taisson (who founded Fontenay *c*. 1050) and his son and namesake attested ducal *acta* frequently: *Recueil des actes des ducs de Normandie (911–1066)*, ed. Marie Fauroux (Caen, Mémoires de la Société des Antiquaires de Normandie, vol. 36, 1961), *passim*; Ralph II attests the ducal charter issued at the dedication of La Trinité, Caen, on 18 June, 1066 (Fauroux, no. 231), but the name does not occur in the witness lists of any act of King William I calendared in *Regesta*, i. By the time of the Conquest the Taisson estates, originally substantial, had become fragmented by division between sons and grants to vassals: Lucien Musset, 'L'aristocratie normande au xie siècle', in *La noblesse au moyen age, xie–xve siècles: Essais à la mémoire de Robert Boutruche*, ed. Philippe Contamine (Paris, 1976), 81–2.

aristocratic abbeys. These families were clearly dominant among those whom Orderic Vitalis describes as vying with each other in the founding of religious houses 'as befitted their rank'.[23]

The dominance of the families atop the ship list remains evident, more than a century later, in the Norman *infeudationes militum* of 1172.[24] This survey of Henry II's provides data, not always complete, on the military quotas to the duke and the total enfeoffments of some 185 lay and ecclesiastical honours. I have no intention of reviving Haskins's views on the antiquity of knights' quotas.[25] But since many Conquest honours survived more or less intact through the twelfth century, even when passing from one family to another, their military quotas and enfeoffments recorded in 1172 would seem to have some bearing on their wealth in 1066. It is not of course an exact relationship. As families rose and fell, honours might grow or crumble. Enfeoffment policies and quota assessments might well have been idiosyncratic at times. Worst of all, the survey of 1172 concludes with a list of 23 landholders, including representatives of some very celebrated families, who, most deplorably, neglected to provide any information at all.

Bearing these problems in mind, it is reassuring to discover that when one rearranges the names on the 1172 inquest in descending order of quotas and enfeoffments (Appendix D) one finds at the top the count of Mortain, whose enfeoffment total cannot be determined but whose quota of 29⅔ knights is by far the highest reported in the survey,[26] and the bishop of Bayeux, whose 120 knights' fees are the most numerous of those reported and whose quota

---

[23] Orderic, ii. 10. Of the abbey-founding families prominent in 1066 who are absent from the ship list, the Tosnys and Giroie were immigrant families (below, p. 238), the Grandmesnils are of indeterminate origin and may or may not be an ancient aristocratic family, and the family of Ivry seems to have risen through the butlership of the ducal household only to decline into mediocrity in the decades following the Conquest: see Appendix C and n. 2. The tradition that Roger of Mortemer transformed St-Victor-en-Caux from a priory to an abbey in 1074 rests on a forged charter: *Regesta*, ii. 392, no. 77.

[24] The survey survives in two manuscripts commonly referred to as Registers A and B: see in general Jacques Boussard, 'L'enquête de 1172 sur les services de chevalier en Normandie', *Recueil de travaux offerts à M. Clovis Brunel* (2 vols., Paris, 1955), i. 193–208. Register A is printed in *Recueil des historiens des Gaules et de la France*, ed. M. Bouquet and others (24 vols., Paris, 1738–1904), xxiii. 693–9; Register B is printed in *The Red Book of the Exchequer*, ed. Hubert Hall (3 vols., Rolls Series, 1896), ii. 624–46. The information is very conveniently presented and annotated in a standardised format in Appendix I of Thomas K. Keefe, *Feudal Assessments and the Political Community under Henry II and His Sons* (Berkeley, 1983), 141–53, to which the reader is referred for all future references.

[25] See, most recently, Marjorie Chibnall, 'Military Service in Normandy before 1066', *Anglo-Norman Studies*, v. 1982 (1983), 65–77; and Emily Zack Tabuteau, 'Definitions of Feudal Military Obligations in Eleventh-Century Normandy', in *On the Laws and Customs of England: Essays in Honor of Samuel E. Thorne*, ed. Morris S. Arnold, Thomas A. Green, Sally A. Scully and Stephen D. White (Chapel Hill, 1981), 18–59.

[26] The next highest quotas reported in the Inquest are 20 each for the bishops of Bayeux and Lisieux. The Beaumont quota of 25 in Appendix D was derived by combining the actual 1172 quotas of the count of Meulan (15) and Henry of Neubourg (10), both of whose honours belonged to Roger of Beaumont in 1066.

of 20 knights is exceeded only by that of the count of Mortain.[27] In short, the county and bishopric that head the ship list also appear to head the Inquest of 1172. The successors of four of the remaining six men atop the ship list – the count of Alençon (succeeding Roger of Montgomery),[28] the earl of Chester, the earl of Leicester (succeeding William fitz Osbern), and the count of Meulan and lord of Neubourg (succeeding Roger of Beaumont) – are among the most heavily enfeoffed on the 1172 survey, ranging from the earl of Chester's 52 knights up to the count of Alençon's 111. The two remaining ship list families – the counts of Évreux and Eu – are listed as non-reporters in 1172, but independent evidence suggests that the count of Évreux had enfeoffed some 58 knights.[29] If this evidence can be accepted, then six of the eight top ship list honours were among the ten honours known to have enfeoffed 50 or more knights in 1172 (with the enfeoffments of the counts of Eu and Mortain remaining undiscoverable). Moreover, two more families lower down on the ship list – the Giffards and Montforts – are also reported to have enfeoffed more than 50 knights in 1172. Thus, ship-list families account for some 80 per cent of the Norman honours owing 50 or more knights in 1172.[30] The aristocracy of 1066 was fluid, to be sure, but the configurations of its estates proved remarkably durable.

Let me now compare the eight men atop the ship list with the nine Normans among the Domesday Class A group – i.e. excluding Count Alan of Brittany and Eustace count of Boulogne. The comparison discloses continuity at the very top – the Domesday top four are among the top eight on the ship list, and Hugh of Avranches is in both groups, too. Three of the ship list's top eight – the counts of Eu and Évreux and Roger of Beaumont – are missing from the top Domesday group, but the absence of at least one of these families, the counts of Eu, requires little explanation: Robert count of Eu was Domesday lord of the rape of Hastings, and Domesday Book reports that he and his son and heir William – always listed separately and never in the same

[27] The Bayeux Inquest of 1133 reports the same episcopal quota of 20 knights but only 100 fees: *RHF*, xxiii. 699; cf. C. Warren Hollister, *The Military Organization of Norman England* (Oxford, 1965), 77–8. The Bayeux Inquest was undertaken during a vacancy in the bishopric; two bishops, Richard son of Samson bishop of Worcester and before him Turold of Envermeu, had ruled Bayeux since Bishop Odo's death, and under their leadership the wealth of the bishopric declined sharply: S. E. Gleason, *An Ecclesiastical Barony of the Middle Ages: The Bishopric of Bayeux, 1066–1204* (Cambridge, Mass., 1936), 17–25. The quota and enfeoffments of 1133 must surely, then, reflect the immense wealth of the bishopric in Odo's time rather than any subsequent enrichment.

[28] *L'art de vérifier les dates*, 18 vols. (Paris, 1818), xiii. 148–55.

[29] Keefe, *Feudal Assessments*, 152, 242 n. 68.

[30] Similarly, of the total number of knights on honours with 50 or more fees in 1172, *c.* 82.5 per cent were on ship list honours. If one excludes from consideration the Tancarvilles, who can be shown to have acquired much of their wealth after 1066 (Appendix D, n. 4), the figure rises to 93 per cent. On the one remaining non-ship-list family in this category, the Tosnys, see Appendix E, n. 2. Appendix D is a list of twelve holdings with at least 50 fees or with ducal quotas of at lest 20: nine of the twelve can be traced back to men on the ship list; the remaining three are the d'Tancarvilles, the Tosnys and the bishopric of Lisieux (on which see Appendix D, n. 3).

shire – held lands worth collectively £690, a value that joins the Mandevilles' in the gap between Corbett's Classes A and B. The Domesday commissioners may possibly have been recording a moment in the process whereby the comital lands in England were passing from father to son. Whatever the case, the estates would have coalesced when Count Robert died and William succeeded *c.* 1090–1. (The fact that the young man's days were numbered is beside the point.)[31] I doubt that the family felt itself short-changed in the Conquest settlement.

The poor Domesday showings of the counts of Évreux and the Beaumonts are much more puzzling. The Domesday estates of the count of Évreux, £42 in Berkshire and Oxfordshire, seem a miserable pittance for a Norman count and ducal kinsman whose son fought at Hastings. The same is true of Roger of Beaumont, an extremely frequent attestor of Duke William's charters and by all indications one of the very wealthiest Normans of his generation. His son Robert – future count of Meulan – fought bravely at Hastings.[32] Yet Roger, with Domesday lands worth about £72, is in the depths of Class E, and Robert count of Meulan, with lands worth £255, is low Class C. Considered as one, the two honours, father's and son's, are still Class C. Even without Domesday statistics, contemporaries could see that something was amiss. William of Malmesbury, in explaining the paucity of Roger of Beaumont's English estates, reported that the Conqueror had often invited Roger to come to England and receive whatever possessions he chose, but that Roger replied that he was content with his inheritance and would not covet or seize foreign possessions that did not belong to him.[33] Malmesbury was writing some six decades after the Norman Conquest, and Roger of Beaumont's alleged remark seems a suspiciously tactless reply to the conqueror of England. But the probability that Roger's poor showing in Domesday Book was a consequence of his own choice rather than King William's stinginess is suggested by the great frequency with which Roger attested the Conqueror's acts after the Conquest as well as before, and his aversion to England is reflected by the fact that he attested no post-Conquest royal acts known to have issued from there.[34]

The explanation may well be that generational changes among both the Beaumonts and the counts of Évreux were occurring at precisely the wrong time. William of Poitiers says explicitly that by 1066 Roger of Beaumont's fighting days were over and that his son Robert, who fought at Hastings, was a *tiro* – newly knighted.[35] Richard count of Évreux must have been quite elderly too. He would have been well into his maturity when he succeeded his aged father as count of Évreux in 1037, and, like Roger of Beaumont, he

---

[31] William of Eu, accused of treason against King William Rufus during the rebellion-conspiracy of 1095, was blinded and castrated the following year: Anglo-Saxon Chronicle, s.a. 1096.

[32] William of Poitiers, 192, 260.

[33] *Gesta Regum*, ii. 482–3.

[34] *Regesta*, i. nos. 25a, 69, 72, 73, 75 (executed by Bishop Odo, signed by King William), 76, 92a, 105, 116, 117, 118, 119, 123, 125, 146a, 150, 168, 170, 172, 173.

[35] William of Poitiers, 192, 260.

sent a young son, William, to represent the family at Hastings.[36] We cannot be certain of William of Évreux's age, but he and his Beaumont companion at Hastings both died natural deaths in 1118, fifty-two years after the Conquest. Both were probably teenagers in 1066, and although Robert of Beaumont rose to the modest respectability of a Class C Domesday magnate, it seems reasonable to suppose that during the bloody and hazardous years just following the Conquest, King William was not prepared to entrust a great frontier earldom or a Sussex rape to a boy.[37]

Conversely, four Domesday Class A magnates – William of Warenne, Richard fitz Gilbert of Clare, Geoffrey of Mowbray bishop of Coutances, and Geoffrey de Mandeville – are absent from the ship list. Representatives of three of these four families – William of Warenne, Richard fitz Gilbert, and Roger of Mowbray (brother of Bishop Geoffrey) – turn up on a list of 'outstanding' magnates of 1066 in Orderic, a list which itself is a slightly edited and much expanded version of William Poitiers' list, which Orderic clearly used as his model (Appendix E).[38] Orderic's list should not be lightly dismissed, but it is by no means a contemporary judgement as is William of Poitiers', and it seems a bit contaminated by the rise of post-Conquest family fortunes and the wisdom of hindsight.

All four Class A magnates whom Orderic has added to William of Poitiers' list seem to have been, at best, magnates of the second rank in 1066. Gilbert count of Brionne, Richard fitz Gilbert's father, was clearly a formidable figure in the Norman aristocracy of his time, but his murder *c.* 1040 amidst the anarchic conditions accompanying Duke William's minority forced Richard and his younger brother Baldwin (future sheriff of Devon) to take refuge for a time in Flanders; when they returned Duke William divided portions of their father's estates between them, but he kept Brionne as a ducal castlery and seems to have put Roger of Beaumont in charge of it.[39] The duke did not restore the comital title to Richard, whose frequent attestations of the Conqueror's charters as 'Richard son of Count Gilbert' seem almost a reproach. The family remained fairly prominent in Normandy – Richard fitz Gilbert's Norman heir, Roger of Bienfaite, could subsequently play a rôle of some importance in Henry I's victory at Brémule (1119) – but Roger is earlier

---

[36] Ibid., 194–6; Count Richard issued a charter in favour of Jumièges in 1038: Fauroux, no. 92; he succeeded to Évreux on the death in 1037 of his father, Robert archbishop of Rouen, who died in his old age after having held his office for 48 years; Richard was the eldest of his three sons: Orderic, iii. 84.

[37] One must also bear in mind that Roger of Beaumont's marriage to Adeline, sister and heiress of Hugh II count of Meulan, promised to extend the Beaumont fortunes south-eastward into the French Vexin and to provide their son Robert with a comital title; by 1081 Robert was attesting as count of Meulan. William of Évreux had the further disadvantage of being noticeably dull-witted; Orderic reports (vi. 148) that his county of Évreux was run by his wife, the Countess Helwise.

[38] Orderic, ii. 140; Le Patourel, *Norman Empire*, 335–8.

[39] Richard received Orbec and Bienfaite; Baldwin received Meules and Le Sap: Orderic, iv. 206–8; Robert of Torigny, in *Gesta Normannorum Ducum*, ed. Jean Marx (Rouen, 1914), 288; cf. David C. Douglas, 'The Earliest Norman Counts', *EHR*, lxi (1946), 133–5; the brothers were back in Normandy by 1053: Fauroux, no. 130.

described as trying unsuccessfully to improve his lot by joining the German imperial court.[40] The family reascended to the uppermost level only in England.

Similarly, William of Warenne was a man on the rise. The younger son of a lesser magnate, Rodolf, with lands near Rouen and in the Pays de Caux,[41] William fought bravely for the duke at the battle of Mortemer (1054) and was rewarded with the castlery of that name, forfeited by Roger of Mortemer (the phantom of the ship list), and with substantial estates in its neighbourhood and elsewhere. But not until he had been granted vast estates in Sussex did he undertake to found a great Benedictine house – the Cluniac priory of Lewes. And a meticulous study of William of Warenne's Norman estates led Lewis C. Loyd to conclude that they were insufficient in extent to place him and his heirs among the greatest of the Norman lords. 'It was to their English lands,' Loyd writes, 'that their power and importance were due.'[42]

The same seems true of the Mowbrays. Roger of Mowbray was a lord in the Cotentin said to be a kinsman of its *vicomte*, Nigel of St-Sauveur. Roger's Norman estates, forfeited by his son Robert earl of Northumberland in 1095 and regranted to Nigel of Aubigny, are recorded in 1172 as owing the relatively modest quota of 5 knights, from a similarly modest enfeoffment total of about 11⅖.[43] Geoffrey bishop of Coutances evidently owed his enrichment to his intimate friendship and devoted administrative service to the Conqueror: his 34 attestations of King William's charters are exceeded only by Roger of Montgomery's 40.[44]

There remains Geoffrey de Mandeville, whose grandson and namesake would be the first earl of Essex, but whom Orderic doesn't trouble to include in his enlarged list. Unlike the other Domesday Class A magnates, he is virtually invisible in the sources of pre-Conquest Normandy. If he is the *Gofredus de Magna Villa* who attested a pre-Conquest grant by William fitz Osbern to St-Amand, Rouen, and then placed the grant upon the abbey's altar in William fitz Osbern's behalf,[45] he might then be supposed to have owed his subsequent rise to having a powerful friend at the ducal court. But the identification is uncertain and there is little else to suggest such a

[40] Orderic, vi. 168, 234–8.

[41] The modest extent of Rodolf's lands, most of which passed to William of Warenne's elder brother Rodolf II, is suggested by the fact that the honour was reported in the Inquest of 1172 to have had only 12¼ fees and a quota of 3: Lewis C. Loyd, 'The Origin of the Family of Warenne', *Yorkshire Archaeological Journal*, xxxi (1933), 104–6; Keefe, *Feudal Assessments*, 146 (Robert of Esneval).

[42] Loyd, 'Origin of Warenne', 111, from an analysis on 110–11; the family was among those listed as not reporting in the Inquest of 1172.

[43] Keefe, *Feudal Assessments*, 148 (Nigel of Mowbray); *Complete Peerage*, ix. 368, 372; Le Patourel, 'Geoffrey of Montbray,' 133; Lewis C. Loyd, *The Origins of some Anglo-Norman Families*, ed. C. T. Clay and David C. Douglas (Leeds, Harleian Society, 1951), 71; *Gallia Christiana*, xi. 'Instrumenta', col. 222.

[44] C. Warren Hollister, 'Magnates and "Curiales" in Early Norman England', *Viator*, viii (1977), 64–5, 75 Table D, a list of the most frequent attestors of the Conqueror's *acta* as calendared in *Regesta*, i.

[45] Fauroux, no. 182 (c. 1042–66): 'Gofredus de Magna Villa, qui super altare Sancti Amandi, ex parte Willelmi Osberni filii, donum posuit.'

friendship. John Le Patourel observed that Geoffrey's origins and relationships are 'certainly obscure',[46] and they are likely to remain so.

The Normans in the Domesday Class A group thus include five families from the Norman upper aristocracy of 1066 (six if one includes the count of Eu), three more from the middle aristocracy – Clare, Warenne, Mowbray – of whom the powerfully connected Clares had recently suffered a decline – and that mysterious stranger, Geoffrey de Mandeville. Although these figures are not particularly surprising, it is interesting to observe that the greater Domesday tenants-in-chief were not simply the Norman power structure of 1066 transferred to England. There are some intriguing omissions and additions.

I turn finally to the question of whether the Conquest aristocracy consisted primarily of new or old families. Was it, as David Douglas and Lucien Musset taught us, a newly risen group of ducal favourites and kinsmen only two or three generations old?[47] Or is David Bates correct in his recent and challenging argument that our inability to trace most Norman lineages back past the early eleventh century is best explained not by the emergence of new families but by the transformation of old families from collateral kin groups, using personal names or patronymics, into lineages with *caputs*, toponymics, a shift toward primogeniture, and a consequent interest in genealogies.[48] The elegance of this thesis as proposed in Bates's distinguished book, *Normandy before 1066*, is that it accounts for the apparent newness of the Norman aristocracy simply by positing a phenomenon which Gerd Tellenbach and his pupils, followed by other scholars, have shown to have been occurring among the aristocracies of other French principalities in the tenth or eleventh centuries.[49] A potential weakness, as some reviewers have pointed out,[50] is that it has not been tested prosopographically. As Bates observes, the old aristocracy alleged to have been superseded by the Conqueror's families is largely undiscoverable.[51] But the origins of William the Conqueror's upper aristocracy can in many instances be reconstructed with some confidence, and I will now address myself to this task with respect to the eight great men at the top of the ship list.

It can be demonstrated first of all, from unambiguous evidence, that at least five of the eight were kinsmen of the duke – his two half-brothers of

---

[46] Le Patourel, *Norman Empire*, 337.

[47] Douglas (1964), 83–104; Musset, 'L'aristocratie normande', 71–96.

[48] Bates, *Normandy*, 34–6, 133–4; echoed in Marjorie Chibnall, *Anglo-Norman England, 1066–1166* (Oxford, 1986), 162.

[49] Gerd Tellenbach, 'Zur Erforschung des hochmittelalterlichen Adels (9.–12. Jahrhundert)', in *XIIᵉ Congrès Internationale des Sciences Historiques* (Vienna, 1965), i. 318–36; Karl Schmid, 'The Structure of the Nobility in the Earlier Middle Ages', in *The Medieval Nobility: Studies on the Ruling Classes of France and Germany from the Sixth to the Twelfth Century*, ed. Timothy Reuter (Amsterdam, 1978), 37–59; Georges Duby, *The Chivalrous Society* (London, 1977), 59–80, 94–111, 134–57.

[50] Most skilfully by Emily Zack Tabuteau in *Speculum*, lix (1984), 612–14, in the course of an otherwise very favourable review of Bates's book.

[51] Bates, *Normandy*, 134; for a likely exception, Heugon, see below, 240.

Bayeux and Mortain, the counts of Évreux and Eu whose direct descent in the male line from Duke Richard I has left clearly visible traces in contemporary narrative and record sources, and the steward William fitz Osbern, whose descent from Arfast, brother of the Duchess Gunnor, traced by Robert of Torigny in the mid-twelfth century, can be confirmed at every step.[52] William fitz Osbern was further connected to the ducal house through his mother Emma, daughter of Duke Richard I's half-brother, Count Rodulf, lord of Ivry. The great honours of Breteuil and Pacy, with their 98½ knights' fees in 1172, have been traced by David Bates – in an article expertly emending David Douglas – from Count Rodulf to his son Hugh bishop of Bayeux and, at Hugh's death in 1049, through his sister Emma to her son, William fitz Osbern. It was only then that William founded his two abbeys of Lyre and Cormeilles, endowing them with some of his newly acquired riches.[53]

One can very probably add a sixth ducal kinsman to the list of eight. Robert of Torigny traces the Montgomery family back through Roger of Montgomery's father Hugh, to Hugh's wife Josceline, whose mother, Wevia, was a sister of Duchess Gunnor, wife of Duke Richard I.[54] Robert of Torigny adds that Roger's immense holdings in various regions of Normandy came to him as a consequence of his mother being Gunnor's niece.[55] Contemporary record evidence assures us that Robert of Torigny erred in identifying Roger's father as Hugh; it was Roger, as Robert of Torigny himself informs us in another of his works.[56] But the notion that Roger II of Montgomery's mother was a niece of Gunnor receives what seems to me impressive corroboration in a letter of Ivo bishop of Chartres to King Henry I c. 1113 containing a genealogy intended to prevent the marriage of a noble couple already betrothed: the powerful frontier lord Hugh of Châteauneuf and an unnamed bastard daughter of Henry I. Ivo traces Hugh's lineage to his mother Mabel, Mabel's father Roger II of Montgomery, Roger's mother

[52] *Gesta Normannorum Ducum*, 287, 328; cf. Douglas, 'Earliest Norman Counts', 132–3, 135–40; 'The Ancestors of William fitz Osbern', *EHR* lix (1944): 62–79. Osbern the Steward, a frequent attestor of Duke Robert I's *acta*, sometimes attested as 'Osbern son of Arfast': Fauroux, nos. 49, 65; the kinship tie was well known to Orderic: *Gesta Normannorum Ducum*, 156; Orderic, ii. 140: 'Willelmus Osberni filius ducis cognatus et dapifer'. Similarly, the kinship between the Conqueror and the counts of Eu was known to the author of the Anglo-Saxon Chronicle, s.a. 1096, where William of Eu is described as 'the king's kinsman.'
[53] Douglas, 'Ancestors of William fitz Osbern', 68–79; corrected by David Bates, 'Notes sur l'aristocratie Normande, 1.-Hugues évêque de Bayeux (1011 env–1049)', *Annales de Normandie*, xiii (1973), 7–21; *La Normandie bénédictine*, 306–7; August Le Prévost, *Mémoires et notes pour servir à l'histoire du département de l'Eure* (3 vols., Évreux, 1862–72), i. 414–15; Orderic, ii. 282.
[54] *Gesta Normannorum Ducum*, 321; cf. 328–9.
[55] Ibid.: 'Ipse autem Rogerius natus est ex quadam neptium Gunnoris comitissae, scilicet ex Joscelina, filia Weviae; unde et ipse ingentes possessiones habuit in diversis regionibus Normanniae.'
[56] 'De Immutatione', 199: 'Rogerius de Monte Gommerici, filius Rogerii vicecomitis Oximensis, in honorum sancti Martini duo monasteria aedificavit. . . .' Cf. Fauroux, nos. 69 and 94. Roger II of Montgomery had a brother named Hugh: ibid., no. 74; and Roger II's son, Hugh of Montgomery, inherited his earldom of Shrewsbury.

Josceline, and Josceline's mother, a sister of Duchess Gunnor.[57] According to Ivo, this sister's name was Seufria, not Wevia as Robert of Torigny names her.[58] If Bishop Ivo can be trusted then Robert of Torigny, despite getting two names wrong, rightly connected Roger II of Montgomery to the ducal family, and in the correct degree. And Ivo, although a rather late source, gains credibility from the fact that the betrothed couple, whose wedding would have sealed an urgently needed political alliance, did not marry. Ivo took the matter very seriously: 'What we are saying,' he wrote to King Henry, 'we do not base on conjecture, because we have between our hands a written genealogy which noble men issuing from the same family have compiled, and who are prepared to demonstrate (computare) this genealogy before ecclesiastical judges and to prove it in accordance with the law.'[59] Perhaps Ivo was misled by the growth of a legitimising family legend, but if so, it was, on this occasion, a singularly inconvenient, self-defeating legend. Indeed, I rather suspect that most Conquest families would have been disinclined to invent legends of kinship with the Gunnorai that would have impeded actual intermarriage with the ducal house. In the case at hand, the combination of Robert of Torigny's testimony and Ivo of Chartres' prohibition make it distinctly more probable that the Mongomerys did in fact descend from a sister of Gunnor than that they did not. The anthropological concept of legitimising myths has proven to be an extremely valuable intellectual tool; it is also so extraordinarily fashionable at present that we would probably be well advised to be a bit wary of overusing it. The Montgomery evidence suggests that Robert of Torigny's genealogies are not aristocratic family myths but are simply rather sloppy.

But whether the Montgomerys' descent from Gunnor's sister is fact or myth, the enrichment of the family to which Robert of Torigny alludes is fully verified by contemporary records. They show how major centres of Montgomery power, including the sites of the Montgomery abbeys of Troarn and Almenèsches, had originally been ducal demesne lands granted out by Richard I or Richard II to the older abbeys of Bernay, Jumièges, and Fécamp.[60] Troarn and Almenèsches were in Fécamp's possession as late as 1025 but drifted into Montgomery hands before c. 1050, in time for Roger II

---

[57] *Patrologia Latina*, 162, cols. 265–6 (ep. 261); cf. Georges Duby, *Medieval Marriage: Two Models from Twelfth-Century France*, tr. Elborg Forster (Baltimore, 1978), 26–8; for the date, C. Warren Hollister, 'War and Diplomacy in the Anglo-Norman World: The Reign of Henry I', *Anglo-Norman Studies*, vi. 1983 (1984), 83.

[58] Robert of Torigny does mention Gunnor's sister Seufria (*Gesta Normannorum Ducum*, 323) but makes her out to be a forester's wife of whom Duke Richard I was enamoured and who protected her virtue by substituting Gunnor in Richard's bed: on this folk-tale motif –the 'bed trick' – see Eleanor Searle, 'Fact and Pattern in Heroic History: Dudo of Saint-Quentin', *Viator*, xv (1984), 133–5.

[59] *Patrologia Latina*, 162, cols. 265–6; about a decade later Hugh of Châteauneuf married a sister of Waleran of Meulan and joined him in rebellion against Henry I: Orderic, vi. 332.

[60] Torigny, 'De Immutatione', 194; R. N. Sauvage, *L'abbaye de Saint-Martin de Troarn* . . . (Caen, 1911), 18–20; Lucien Musset, 'Les premiers temps de l'abbaye d'Almenèsches des origines au xiiᵉ siècle', in *L'abbaye d'Almenèsches-Argentan et Sainte Opportune. Sa vie et son culte*, ed. Yves Chaussy (Paris, 1970), 19–24.

of Montgomery to found his abbeys and, perhaps surprisingly, to appoint a monk of Fécamp as the first abbot of Troarn.[61] Roger II then added enormously to his already considerable fortune by marrying Mabel, heiress of the great Bellême holdings around Sées, where Roger founded his third abbey, and across Normandy's southern frontier.[62] Without suggesting that the Montgomerys emerged from the dust, it seems reasonable to regard them as newly risen members of the upper aristocracy.

Robert of Torigny asserts that the Beaumonts too spring from a sister of Gunnor, Duvelina, who married Roger of Beaumont's grandfather, Turold of Pont Audemer, and gave birth to Roger's father Humphrey of Vieilles.[63] In this instance Robert of Torigny's testimony cannot be checked against independent and earlier evidence as it could, fortuitously, in the case of the Montgomerys. Nevertheless, as prior of Bec, Robert would have known the Beaumont family better than any other. The Beaumonts had been generous benefactors of Bec, and their stronghold at Brionne was only four miles from the abbey, over which the Beaumont lord, Waleran of Meulan, asserted some sort of advocacy in Robert of Torigny's time.[64] Roger of Beaumont's father, Humphrey of Vieilles, is plainly visible as a regular attestor of Duke Richard II's charters,[65] and we have at least Orderic Vitalis's corroboration that Humphrey's father was indeed named Turold[66] – although the toponymic 'of Pont Audemer' is doubtless an anachronism on Robert's part.

Again, it could be argued that the Gunnor connection was the product of twelfth-century Beaumont myth-making. But Waleran count of Meulan was in fact the great-grandson of the Capetian King Henry I and took some pride in tracing his ancestry back to Charlemagne. It is therefore difficult to imagine a motive at this late date for inventing a relationship with a sister of Gunnor, whom Robert of Torigny reported – on the testimony of old men – to have been the sister-in-law of an obscure forester.[67] Robert and his old men were clearly in error on this matter: Dudo and, following him, William of Jumièges both place Gunnor in a Danish family of the highest nobility,[68] and there is much to be said for Eleanor Searle's suggestion that Richard I's marriage to Gunnor, and the marriages of Richard's followers to Gunnor's sisters and nieces, constituted a web of alliance woven between the older

---

[61] Fauroux, no. 34; Torigny, 'De Immutatione', 200.

[62] See Kathleen Thompson, 'Family and Influence to the South of Normandy in the Eleventh Century: The Lordship of Bellême', *Journal of Medieval History*, xi (1985), 222–4.

[63] *Gesta Normannorum Ducum*, 324. The name Dunelina, a variant of Duvelina, occurs subsequently in the Beaumont family: David Crouch, *The Beaumont Twins* (Cambridge, 1986), 117.

[64] *CDF*, no. 373; Crouch, *Beaumont Twins*, 204–5; cf. Douglas, *Domesday Monachorum*, 65, where, for similar reasons, Douglas accords special respect to Robert of Torigny's knowledge of the neighbouring Montfort family, six miles down the Risle from Bec.

[65] Fauroux, nos. 29, 30, 32, 50, 55.

[66] Orderic, ii. 12; iv. 206; Fauroux, no. 118, refers back to a 'Turoldus comitisse Gunnoris camerarius', but there are far too many Turolds in the ducal *acta* to permit an identification.

[67] *Gesta Normannorum Ducum*, 323; above, n. 58; Crouch, *Beaumont Twins*, 10–12, 211–12.

[68] *Gesta Normannorum Ducum*, 68; Dudo of St-Quentin, *De Moribus et Actis Primorum Normanniae Ducum*, ed. Jules Lair (Caen, 1865), 289; above, no. 58.

settlers around Rouen and a group of Danish newcomers.[69] Their motive for intermarriage seems considerably clearer than the motive for great twelfth-century Norman families fabricating Gunnor connections at a time when Gunnor herself was plunging in status from a chieftain's daughter to a social nobody. In the light of Robert of Torigny's demonstrable carelessness with regard to genealogical detail,[70] the Beaumont descent from a sister of Gunnor certainly cannot be accepted unreservedly. But neither should it be dismissed out of hand. It is a distinct possibility.

That the Beaumonts were a newly enriched family like the Montgomerys there can be no serious doubt. Almost every major centre of later Beaumont power – Beaumont itself with neighbouring Vieilles, Pont-Audemer, Vatteville with the adjacent forest of Brotonne, and the castlery of Brionne – had belonged in the early eleventh century either to the dukes or their close kinspeople. Beaumont, Vieilles and their surroundings had originally been ducal demesne lands and had constituted part of the endowment of Bernay Abbey; Brionne was in the possession of the duke's kinsman Gilbert of Brionne until his death c. 1040 and was afterwards a ducal castle.[71] Pont-Audemer belonged to Duke Richard II in 1025 but had passed to Humphrey of Vieilles by about 1035 or 1040.[72] Vatteville and the forest of Brotonne can first be found in the possession of Duke Richard I's kinsman, Hugh bishop of Bayeux, who probably received them from his father Count Rodulf.[73] Afterwards these properties turn up in the hands of Duke Richard II's son, William count of Arques.[74] They passed into Roger of Beaumont's possession only after William of Arques' rebellion and dispossession in 1052–3. If the Beaumonts possessed vast landed wealth in Normandy before

---

[69] Searle, 'Dudo', 135–6.

[70] See G. H. White, 'The Sisters and Nieces of Gunnor, Duchess of Normandy', *Genealogist*, new ser. xxxvii (1920), i. 57–65, 128–32.

[71] Beaumont, Beaumontel and Vieilles are among the places given to the Duchess Judith by her husband, Duke Richard II (Fauroux, no. 11, AD 996–1008); by 1025 they were among the lands with which Judith endowed Bernay Abbey (Fauroux, no. 35). Robert of Torigny ('De Immutatione', 194) reports that Humphrey of Vieilles obtained Beaumont and Ouche from Ralph *custos* of Bernay, a monk of Fécamp who was administering Bernay in lieu of a prior, and who was evidently a kinsman of Humphrey's: Ralph became abbot of Mont-St-Michel in 1048 and was known in the records of that house as Ralph of Beaumont: *Gallia Christiana*, xi. 515; Le Prévost, *Eure*, i. 202; Neithard Bulst, 'La réforme monastique en Normandie: étude prosopographique sur la diffusion et l'implantation de la réforme de Guillaume de Dijon', in *Les mutations socio–culturelles au tournant des xie–xiie siècles: Études Anselmiennes (ive session)* (Paris, 1984), 320. Following the death of Gilbert count of Brionne, Roger of Beaumont, presumably acting as ducal castellan, granted the abbey of Bec the tithe of the forest of Brionne: Fauroux, 33, no. 16; cf. Orderic, iv. 204–8.

[72] In 1025 Richard II granted Fécamp a fishery on the Risle at Pont-Audemer (Fauroux, no. 34), but sometime between 1035 and c. 1040 Duke William gave six villeins to the abbey in exchange for the fishery at Pont-Audemer 'videlicet, in commutatione Rogerio filio Hunfredi' (who attests the act: Fauroux, no. 94).

[73] Fauroux, no. 36 (1025); Bates, 'L'aristocratie normande', 10–12; the evidence suggests that Count Rodulf had himself been immensely enriched from ducal demesne lands: Douglas, 'Ancestors of William fitz Osbern', 69–72, 74–7; *William the Conqueror*, 89–90.

[74] Ferdinand Lot, *Études critiques sur l'abbaye de Saint-Wandrille* (Paris, 1913), 56–7 (no. 15), AD 1032–47; cf. Fauroux, no. 234; Crouch, *Beaumont Twins*, 189–90.

these acquisitions, it is difficult to imagine where it might have been or what became of it.

It is not always clear whether the enrichments of the Beaumonts, Montgomerys and other rising families resulted primarily from ducal generosity or from sheer thievery made possible by anarchic times. Doubtless both factors played their part. But the greatest winners tended also to be the duke's kinsmen, staunchest supporters and most frequent charter attestors – men like Osbern the steward and his son William, Roger of Montgomery, Roger of Beaumont, the counts of Brionne, Évreux and Eu, and William count of Arques, who attested ducal *acta* regularly before his rebellion and fall. Roger of Beaumont's attestations of Duke William's pre-Conquest *acta* are exceeded only by those of William fitz Osbern and Roger of Montgomery. If Robert of Torigny was correct in stating that Roger of Beaumont was a ducal kinsman, as all of the others certainly or probably were, it would not be at all surprising.

It has been the policy of most princes in all ages – including most emphatically the Norman ducal house – to enrich their kinsmen. Thus, as William of Jumièges informs us, Duke William as a youth had granted the wealthy *vicomté* of Le Talou as a benefice to his uncle, William, who thereby became count of Arques.[75] Similarly Duke William granted what appear to have been the greatest Norman lay and ecclesiastical lordships to his two half-brothers, who were themselves of extremely mediocre birth. Their mother Herleve was later said by Orderic to have been the daughter of a mortician named Fulbert, who ascended into the modest respectability of a ducal chamberlainship – presumably through his daughter's influence – and nothing whatever is known about the background of their father, Herluin.[76] He attested as *vicomte* of Conteville, but only once, in a ducal act of 1059–66,[77] three decades or more after his marriage to Herleve. And since his attestation constitutes our earliest evidence of the existence of a *vicomté* of Conteville, one can reasonably suppose that the *vicomté* had been tailor-made for Herluin by Duke William, or possibly his father. Herluin collaborated with his son, Robert count of Mortain, in the founding of Grestain Abbey, but Robert contributed the lion's share of the endowment,[78] and when Herleve died and Herluin remarried, Duke William lost interest in the family. The almost stygian obscurity of Herluin's sons by his second marriage, Ralph and John of Conteville, contrasts dramatically with the fame and fortune of their two half-brothers.

[75] *Gesta Normannorum Ducum*, 119; many years later, Duke Robert Curthose granted Arques and Bures to Elias of St-Saens upon his marriage to Duke Robert's daughter: Orderic, iv. 182.
[76] Elisabeth M. C. Van Houts, 'The Origins of Herleva, Mother of William the Conqueror', *English Historical Review*, ci (1986), 399–404; cf. Eleanor Searle, 'Possible History', *Speculum*, lxi (1986), where it is suggested that Fulbert was in fact a ducal *cubicularius* to begin with. Even if so, the force of my argument would not be seriously reduced; David Bates, 'Notes sur l'aristocratie normande, 2.-Herluin de Conteville et sa famille', *Annales de Normandie*, xiii (1973), 21–38.
[77] Fauroux, no. 218; but see also LePrévost, *Eure*, iii. 301, where he appears as 'Herluinus vicecomes' at some point before the Conquest in a transaction with St-Pierre, Préaux.
[78] Bates, 'Notes-Herluin', 23–6; the *vicomte* of Conteville in later generations was responsible for a relatively small annual farm of 170 li.: Powicke, *Loss of Normandy*, 71.

His victory at Hastings provided William with an unparalleled opportunity to enrich his kinsmen and most intimate friends. Although the Domesday Class A magnate list does not perfectly reflect the Norman upper aristocracy of 1066, it nevertheless discloses the same policy of favouring kinsmen and the newly risen. In addition to the families already discussed (and excluding the Beaumonts and counts of Évreux), it includes the Clares, whose direct descent from Duke Richard I through his son Godfrey and Godfrey's son Gilbert count of Brionne was traced by Robert of Torigny and is fully confirmed by contemporary evidence;[79] and Count Alan of Brittany, whose grandmother was unarguably a daughter of Duke Richard I.[80] William of Warenne was newly risen, as we have seen, and Robert of Torigny's allegation that his mother was a niece of Gunnor[81] receives strong corroboration from a letter of Archbishop Anselm to Henry I of c. 1100–1 forbidding a marriage of potentially great political consequence between William II of Warenne and one of King Henry's natural daughters.[82] Anselm succeeded in blocking the marriage on the objection that the two were respectively fourth and sixth in descent from a single ancestor, and Lewis C. Loyd has demonstrated that Robert of Torigny's genealogy embodies precisely the degrees of affiliation to which Anselm objected.[83] Henry I's throne was at risk in 1101, and William of Warenne joined the coalition that almost cast him from it – suffering two years of exile as a result. With so much at stake, it is difficult to believe that Anselm could have been permitted to assert an affiliation that did not exist, or that William of Warenne, at such cost to himself, could have misremembered the identity of his own grandmother.[84]

If one includes Montgomery and Warenne, then seven of the eleven Domesday Class A magnates numbered among the Conqueror's kinsmen, and all six Normans among these seven were from newly risen lineages enriched by the ducal bounty. Four names remain: Eustace of Boulogne, Duke William's friend and ally, who owed his Anglo-Norman wealth to the Conquest settlement; Geoffrey bishop of Coutances, faithful attestor and devoted administrator, who ascended into the uppermost stratum only in England; Geoffrey de Mandeville, the invisible man, who clearly enjoyed a similar post-Conquest ascent; and Hugh of Avranches, earl of Chester, to whom I will now turn.

Hugh of Avranches is the only man among the top eight on the ship list for whom there is no evidence whatever of kinship with the ducal house, but his

[79] Orderic, iv. 206–8; Fauroux, nos. 4, 24, 48; Dudo, De Moribus, 289; Douglas, 'Earliest Norman Counts', 133–5.
[80] Douglas, William the Conqueror, 29, 267–8, 426; cf. Gesta Normannorum Ducum, 325.
[81] Ibid., 328.
[82] S. Anselmi Cantuariensis Archiepiscopi Opera Omnia, ed. F. S. Schmitt (6 vols., Stuttgart-Bad Cannstatt, 1968), v. 369–70, ep. 424; the letter must have been written September 1100–September 1101 or 1105–9; political circumstances make the earlier range the more likely: see C. Warren Hollister, 'The Anglo-Norman Civil War: 1101', EHR, lxxxviii (1973), 322 and n. 2.
[83] Loyd, 'Origins of Warenne', 108.
[84] It is unlikely but possible that Anselm was referring to a relationship between Henry I's and William of Warenne's Flemish mothers, whose families seem to have been related in some undiscoverable way: Early Yorkshire Charters, viii. 40–6.

family appears to have acquired great riches while serving the dukes as *vicomtes*. William of Jumièges informs us in a passing remark that Earl Hugh's grandfather, Thurstan Goz, was *vicomte* of the Hiémois *c*. 1017–25, preceding Roger I of Montgomery in that important office.[85] Thurstan's son, Richard Goz, became *vicomte* of Avranches *c*. 1055–6 and passed his office and lands to his son Hugh. Lucien Musset, in a meticulous study of the endowment of Hugh's abbey of St-Sever, suggests that the family's extensive landholdings in the Avranchin date only from the time of Richard Goz's assumption of the vicecomital office, which was itself probably a result of Duke William's confiscating the lands of William Werlenc count of Mortain.[86] The duke's half-brother Robert was the major beneficiary of William Werlenc's fall, but Richard Goz seems to have received a share of the spoils. Musset traces much of the St-Sever endowment to lands in the Avranchin, the Hiémois, and the Bessin – where the family may also have exercised official responsibilities.[87] Hugh's grants of lands in the Hiémois, where we happen to know that his grandfather was once *vicomte*, and at key strongholds on the northern and southern frontiers of the Avranchin such as might reasonably be entrusted to a *vicomte*, seem to reflect the activities of a family of ducal officials with shifting territorial responsibilites and sticky fingers, gathering wealth by transforming their vicecomital lands into personal holdings; or, as Musset expresses it, 'encrusting themselves in their circumscriptions'.[88] If Musset is correct in seeing in this evidence the tracks of an ascending family, then Hugh of Chester joins his fellows atop the ship list and among the Norman magnates of Domesday Class A as a relative *nouveau riche*.

But although all of the Norman families at the uppermost levels of the 1066 or Domesday aristocracies seem to be newly enriched, the same may not be true of families slightly lower down. The family of Nigel *vicomte* of the Cotentin, for example, whose ancestors are vividly described by Eleanor Searle as 'the greatest line of Cotentin war leaders', gives one the impression of being very old.[89] And the origins of the lords of Gournay seem lost in the

---

[85] *Gesta Normannorum Ducum*, 118; cf. 160, where Orderic identifies Thurstan's father as Ansfrid 'the Dane'; on Roger I of Montgomery's succession to the *vicomté* see Fauroux, no. 69.

[86] Lucien Musset, 'Les origines et le patrimoine de l'abbaye de Saint-Sever', in *La Normandie bénédictine*, 358.

[87] Ibid.

[88] Ibid., 365, and, more generally, 357–67; the process reminds one of the way in which Roger, ducal castellan of Ivry, endowed the abbey of Ivry with lands in his presumably temporary custody (Appendix C, no. 2); Roger of Beaumont seems to have been similarly generous to Bec: above, no. 71.

[89] Searle, 'Dudo', 135; see Léopold Delisle, *Histoire du château et des sires de Saint-Sauveur-le-Vicomte* (Valognes, 1867), 1–2; Delisle states that Nigel I was preceded as *vicomte* by a *Vicomte* Roger *ante* 996, but Roger is so titled only retrospectively, in a pancarte of *c*. 1136: ibid., pièces justificatives, 59. William of Jumièges (*Gesta Normannorum Ducum*, 76) reports that an English army invading the Cotentin *c*. 1000 was routed by warriors (*milites*) under the leadership of Nigel [I], whom William does not explicitly describe as a *vicomte* but who was clearly in charge of the district. Nigel II, *vicomte* of the Cotentin, founded the Benedictine abbey of St-Sauveur-le-Vicomte *c*. 1080: Besse, *Abbayes*, 155–6; cf. *La Normandie bénédictine*, 328–34; but the honour reported only 15 knights and a quota of 5 in 1172. The family was of no importance in Domesday England.

fog of Viking myth.[90] Yet even at the penultimate level, the model of wealthy old Norman families achieving visibility by turning linear must be applied with caution. A number of aristocratic families, for example, are known to have established their subsequent fortunes only after immigrating into Normandy. The earliest known immigrants, the Tosnys – another early abbey-founding family – acquired their Norman wealth in the later tenth century when the Frenchman Ralph of Tosny seized the advantage of having had a brother appointed archbishop of Rouen by carving a great estate out of the lands of the archbishopric and the abbey of St-Ouen, Rouen.[91] The Taissons, founders of the abbey of Fontenay, migrated into Normandy from Anjou in the early eleventh century. They began attesting ducal charters toward the end of Duke Richard II's reign and were enriched from ducal and ecclesiastical estates.[92] The Giroie, who united in marriage with the Grandmesnils and founded St-Evroul jointly with them, had migrated from Perche and were generously enriched by Richard II.[93] Fulk of Aunou, the contributor of 40 ships in 1066, was the son of another immigrant, Baudri 'the German', by his wife, a niece of Duke Richard I's grandson, Gilbert count of Brionne – or so Orderic plausibly reports, adding that Baudri had come from Germany to serve Duke Richard II.[94]

Others among the Domesday or 1066 middle aristocracy, like the uppermost group, can be shown to have acquired the centres of their later power from ducal or ecclesiastical lands during roughly the second quarter of the eleventh century. This is true of the Giffards, who rendered 30 ships and 100 knights in 1066, and whose genealogy – rightly or wrongly – is traced back by Robert of Torigny to a sister of Gunnor.[95] The family acquired Montivilliers under Duke Robert I; their great Norman *caput* of Longueville, originally ducal demesne, bounced for some years between the abbeys of Bourgueil, Fécamp, and Jumièges, and landed in Walter Giffard's hands

---

[90] Daniel Gurney, *The Record of the House of Gournay* (London, 1848); *Early Yorkshire Charters*, viii. 6–7.

[91] Lucien Musset, 'Aux origines d'une class dirigeante: les Tosny, grands barons normands du xe au xiiie siècle', *Francia*, v. 1977 (1978), 45–80; 'L'aristocratie normande', 78.

[92] Ibid., 81–2.

[93] Orderic, ii. 22–4, traces the family backwards from Giroie to his father Arnold the Fat of Courcerault (in Perche: canton Nocé, Orne), who himself was the son of Abbo the Breton. But see Jean-Marie Maillefer, 'Une famille aristocratique aux confins de la Normandie: Les Géré au xie siècle', *Autour du pouvoir ducal normand x^e-xiie siècles, Cahier des Annales de Normandie*, xvii (Caen, 1985), 175–9, expressing serious doubt that the family originated in Brittany as Orderic says.

[94] Orderic, ii. 82; cf. Robert of Torigny, in *Gesta Normannorum Ducum*, 329, where, in a characteristic lapse, Fulk is correctly associated with the ducal house but by the wrong genealogical route; these and several other immigrating nobles are conveniently discussed in Musset, 'L'aristocratie normande', 81–4.

[95] Robert of Torigny, in *Gesta Normannorum Ducum*, 324–5; the editor's criticism of this genealogy (325, n. 1) results from his own confusion between William of Arques (grandson of Goscelin *vicomte* of Rouen, whom Robert of Torigny intended) and William count of Arques: see White, 'Sisters and Nieces of Gunnor', 57–9; *Complete Peerage*, x. Appendix, 52 and n. (g), where the Gunnor connection, perhaps too rashly, is accepted as certain.

around the mid-eleventh century.[96] Similarly, the two chief centres of the Ferrers family, Ferrières-Saint-Hilaire and Chambrais, were originally among the ducal demesne lands that passed from Richard II to his wife Judith sometime between 996 and 1008.[97] William Crispin, a kinsman of the Domesday Class B magnate Milo Crispin and, more distantly, of Duke William, received from the duke the *vicomté* of the Vexin and the frontier stronghold of Neufles – the Crispins' subsequent Norman power base – which had earlier belonged to the archbishop of Rouen.[98] Roumare, the Norman *caput* of Gerald *dapifer* of the ship list and his descendants, the future earls of Lincoln, was almost certainly in Duke William's possession in 1035;[99] Odo of Champagne, future lord of Holderness, acquired his Norman 'county' of Aumale only in the 1050s or 1060s on his marriage to the duke's sister Adelaide, who had been given Aumale as a dower.[100] And the Domesday Class B magnate Roger Bigot, a smallholder from Calvados, seems to have risen to wealth only in England in the mid-1070s, partly on Odo of Bayeux's coat-tails, by acquiring some of the lands forfeited by the Breton, Ralph earl of East Anglia.[101]

It is doubtless true that the recipients of ducal benefactions and ministries in eleventh-century Normandy would usually have been men of some standing to begin with, as would those fortunate enough to marry sisters and nieces of Gunnor or other women of the ducal house. The fact that we know little or nothing of their families' pasts can very plausibly be explained by the shift to lineages and toponymics that undoubtedly was occurring in Normandy during the pre-Conquest decades. Such a shift might well disguise the possible antiquity of such families as the Gournays and Laigles, the *vicomtes* of

[96] Fauroux, nos. 14, 14 bis, 34, 36; Bates, *Normandy*, 102, 104; Thomas Stapleton, *Magni Rotuli Scaccarii Normanniae sub Regibus Angliae*, 2 vols. (London, 1840–4), i. civ.

[97] Fauroux, no. 11; Douglas, *William the Conqueror*, 89; Powicke, *Loss of Normandy*, 338.

[98] Judith Green, 'Lords of the Norman Vexin', *War and Government in the Middle Ages: Essays in Honour of J. O. Prestwich*, ed. John Gillingham and J. C. Holt (Woodbridge, 1984), 49–50; J. Armitage Robinson, *Gilbert Crispin, Abbot of Westminster* (Cambridge, 1911), 14, 17–18; William Crispin was the son of Gilbert Crispin and Gunnor, sister of Fulk of Aunou and daughter of Baudri the German and his wife, Gilbert of Brionne's niece; above, no. 94.

[99] Fauroux, no. 94 (1035–*c*. 1040): Duke William gives the greater part of the forest of Roumare (dep. Seine-Maritime, cant. Maromme) to Fécamp.

[100] Barbara English, *The Lords of Holderness, 1086–1260: A Study in Feudal Society* (Oxford, 1979), 10; *Complete Peerage*, i. 351–2; Douglas (1964), 380–1. As a dispossessed count of Champagne, Odo obviously represented an old and very wealthy family, but he owed his Norman and English wealth to his marriage to Adelaide and the Conqueror's consequent generosity. Adelaide had been married twice before, and in her second marriage (to Lambert count of Lens in Artois) she gave birth to the Countess Judith who, as widow of the luckless Waltheof earl of Huntingdon, occurs in Domesday Book as a landholder toward the top of Class B (£613).

[101] *Complete Peerage*, ix. 575–6; Bates, 'Odo, Bishop of Bayeux', 11, where the Lacys and Ports are also shown to be minor tenants of the bishop of Bayeux in Normandy: cf. *Red Book of the Exchequer*, ii. 646; Wightman, *The Lacy Family in England and Normandy*, 215–26. The Bigods owed ½ knight to the bishopric of Bayeux in 1133 and 2 knights to the duke in 1172: Keefe, *Feudal Assessments*, 152.

the Cotentin and Bessin,[102] and perhaps the lords of Montfort-sur-Risle, contributors of 50 ships and 60 knights in 1066, who clearly added to their wealth as a result of their vicecomital services[103] but cannot be proven from our fragmentary surviving records to have acquired most of their later holdings from the Church or the ducal family. One cannot expect, of course, to discover places like Montfort of Laigle in very early records, because the names probably came into being only when the families had built their castles; Fulbert, the first lord of Laigle, is said to have named his castle after an eagle whose nest was found while he was building it.[104]

Nor is it always possible to separate old families from new, given the constant process of aristocratic intermarriage. William fitz Osbern's ancestry can be traced back in the male line to his grandfather Arfast, Gunnor's brother, but his great wealth came to him, as David Bates has demonstrated, from his maternal grandfather Count Rodulf, stepson of William Longsword. Or again Giroie, a knight of Perche, whose celebrated prowess prompted a great Norman magnate named Heugon to invite him to Normandy to wed Heugon's daughter and heiress. Giroie accepted, but alas, Heugon and his daughter both died before the projected wedding. Giroie then appealed to Duke Richard who, recognising his knightly valour, granted him all of Heugon's lands to be held, Orderic reports, *haereditario iure*.[105] It may be doubted that Giroie's family can thus be categorised as old Norman by ducal fiat, but the story does further confirm the rôle of the Norman dukes in the making of their aristocracy. It also illustrates, as does the case of William fitz Osbern's father, the process of well-connected young knights enriching themselves by marrying heiresses of wealthy older families – even though, in Giroie's case, the marriage did not actually occur.

We can never hope to measure precisely the number of aristocratic families that were 'old' in 1066. But this prosopographical analysis has demonstrated

[102] Ranulf II, *vicomte* of the Bessin in 1066, was a grandson of Duke Richard III; Ranulf's mother was Richard III's daughter. The male line runs backward from Ranulf II to Ranulf I (also *vicomte* of the Bessin) to Anschitil (who attests as *vicomte* but without specifying a *vicomté*): Douglas (1964), 93 with references.

[103] Bates, *Normandy*, 117 and 142 n. 93; Douglas (1964), 88.

[104] Orderic, ii. 356. Douglas (*Domesday Monachorum*, 66) states that Hugh II of Montfort's grandfather, Thurstan, seems to have been holding some land at Pont-Authou on the Risle, five miles upstream from Montfort *c.* 1025 at roughly the time that his son Hugh I attested his first charter as *vicomte*. The charter in which Thurstan is said to have appeared is in *Chartes de l'abbaye de Jumièges v. 825 à 1204*, ed. J.-J. Vernier, 2 vols. (Rouen, 1916), i. 41 (no. xii); better edited by Fauroux, no. 36: in 1025 Richard confirms various gifts to Jumièges including property at Pont-Authou by a certain 'Stotringus' whom Douglas identifies as Thurstan 'of Bastenbourg'; 'Stotringus' (or 'Stostringus' in two later copies; original lost) does not occur elsewhere in the ducal *acta* as a variant of 'Thurstan'; it might possibly refer to a member of the family of Sor. The suffix 'engi' is not uncommon in the formation of Scandinavian names: cf. Orderic, in *Gesta Normannorum Ducum*, 165, in reference to 'Rodbertus et Avesgotus, filii Willelmi cognomine Sorengi . . .' A further complication is that *ante* 1041 Gilbert count of Brionne appears to have been in possession of Pont-Authou: Fauroux, no. 98. On Hugh's first attestation as *vicomte*, see Fauroux, no. 65 (1027–33): 'Hugo vicecomes, filius Turstingi.'

[105] Orderic, ii. 22; above, no. 93.

that the very greatest of the Norman families of 1066, like the uppermost Domesday aristocracy, represented lineages that had been recently and vastly enriched, and the same can be said of a considerable number of the second-level families. The greater Domesday tenants-in-chief, like the first families of Normandy in 1066, abounded in ducal kinsmen, and this should not surprise us. Since the days of Richard I, Norman dukes had been elevating their non-inheriting or smallholding kinsmen to countships and *vicomtés*, bishoprics and archbishoprics. Looking ahead, King Henry I would create vast appanages for his non-inheriting kin – his bastard son Robert earl of Gloucester, his cousin Brian fitz Count, and his nephews Stephen count of Boulogne and Mortain, and Henry bishop of Winchester and abbot of Glastonbury.[106] In the fourteenth century King Edward III would reshape the upper aristocracy by making dukes of his younger sons. But no future king would ever enjoy William the Conqueror's opportunity to create an English aristocracy in exactly the way that he chose. He seized his opportunity by enriching his kinsmen and *familiares*, most of whose families had already risen to wealth in the duke's service and had served him loyally in return.

---

[106] Hollister, 'Henry I and the Anglo-Norman Magnates', 93–107, 184–8.

APPENDIX A

The Greater Domesday Tenants-in-Chief: Corbett's Class A

Name	DB value	Demesne	Enfeoffed	Doubtful	Shires	1066 ships
1. Odo bp. of Bayeux	£3240	£812	£2417	£11	17	100
2. Roger of Montgomery	£2078	£1031	£1045	£2	12	60
3. Robert c. of Mortain	£1974	£833	£1121	£20	20	120
4. William fitz Osbern	£1750[1]	—	—	—	—	60
5. William of Warenne	£1140	£548	£541	£50	12	—
6. Alan c. in Brittany	£1120[2]	£652	£432	£36	12	—
7. Eustace c. of Boulogne	£915	£610	£299	£7	12	—
8. Hugh e. of Chester	£794[3]	£161	£611	£23	20	60
9. Richard fitz Gilbert	£794	£473	£313	£8	9	—
10. Geoffrey bp. of Coutances	£788	£229	£535	£23	13	—
11. Geoffrey de Mandeville	£740	£488	£241	£11	10	—

Values are approximate and rounded off to nearest £.

[1] W. J. Corbett's estimate: *Cambridge Medieval History*, v. 510–11.
[2] Plus waste lands worth £118 TRE.
[3] Plus waste lands worth £270 TRE.

APPENDIX B

Ship List (rearranged in order of ships contributed)

Name	Ships	Knights	Office	William of Poitiers' seven great lay lords[1]
1. Robert c. of Mortain	120	—	ct.	Robert c. of Mortain
2. Odo bp. of Bayeux	100	—	bp.	—
3. William c. of Évreux	80	—	ct.	Richard c. of Évreux
Subtotal:	300			
4. Hugh of Avranches	60	—	vct.	Hugh the Vicomte
5. Roger of Beaumont	60	—	vct.	Roger of Beaumont
6. Robert c. of Eu	60	—	ct.	Robert c. of Eu
7. Roger of Montgomery	60	—	vct.	Roger of Montgomery
8. William fitz Osbern	60	—	dap.[2]	William fitz Osbern
Total:	600			
9. Hugh of Montfort	50	60	vct.	
10. Fulk of Aunou	40	—	—	
11. Gerald dapifer	40	—	dap.	
12. Walter Giffard	30	100	—	
13. Nicholas ab. of St-Ouen	15	100	ab.	
14. Remigius alm. of Fécamp	1	20	—	
Grand Total:	776	280		

[1] For the purpose of clearer exposition I have rearranged the order in which these names appear. See Appendix E for the correct order.
[2] Titled 'Count of the Palace', c. 1060s: Bates, *Normandy*, 155.

APPENDIX C

Norman Non-Ducal Abbeys Founded ante 1075[1]

I. Founded by Families Represented in William of Poitiers' Great Seven.

Abbey (founding date)	Founder(s)
1. Grestain (c. 1050)	Robert c. of Mortain (w/father)
2. St-Sauveur, Évreux (c. 1055)	Richard c. of Évreux
3. St-Sever (c. 1070)	Hugh of Avranches
4. St-Pierre, Préaux (c. 1030)	Humphrey of Vieilles (Beaumont)
5. St-Léger, Préaux (c. 1050)	Humphrey of Vieilles (Beaumont)
6. Le Tréport (c. 1060)	Robert c. of Eu
7. St-Pierre-sur-Dives (c. 1045)	Robert c. of Eu with his mother Countess Lesceline
8. Notre-Dame-du-Pré, Lisieux (c. 1050)	Lesceline with her son Hugh bp. of Lisieux
9. Troarn (c. 1050)	Roger II of Montgomery
10. St-Martin, Sées (c. 1055)	Roger II of Montgomery
11. Almenèches (c. 1060)	Roger II of Montgomery
12. Lyre (c. 1050)	William fitz Osbern
13. Cormeilles (c. 1060)	William fitz Osbern

II. Founded by Families Not Represented in William of Poitiers' Great Seven.

Abbey (founding date)	Founder(s)	Comment
14. La Trinité-du-Mont, Rouen (c. 1030)	Goscelin vct. of Rouen with wife	This family's holdings can be shown to have declined significantly by 1066: above, n. 21.
15. St-Amand, Rouen (c. 1030–40)	Goscelin vct. of Rouen with wife	
16. Conches (c. 1035)	Roger of Tosny	Roger's s. & h., Ralph of Conches, occurs on Orderic's list of great Normans in 1066: see Appendix E.

[1] All data from Cassandra Potts, 'Norman Dukes and their Nobles: Monastic Patronage before the Conquest' (Seminar paper, UC Santa Barbara, 1985), Appendix 2.

17. Fontenay (c. 1050)	Ralph Taisson with his brother Erneis	Family in decline by 1060s: above, n. 22.
18. St-Evroul (1050)	Hugh & Robert of Grandmesnil with William & Robert sons of Giroie	Hugh of Grandmesnil appears on Orderic's list of great Normans in 1066 (Appendix E), but Orderic may be biased.
19. Ivry (c. 1071)	Roger of Ivry	Roger's uncle and antecedent, Hugh the Butler, appears on Orderic's list: Appendix E.[2]

[2] On this family see Douglas, *Domesday Monachorum*, 56–7; Round, *The King's Sergeants and Officers of State*, 140–1; *VCH, Berkshire*, 1: 290–1; *Buckingham*, 1: 237; *Oxford*, 1: 382–3; and *Complete Peerage*, viii. 208–11. As ducal castellan at Ivry, Roger appears to have endowed the abbey with lands not entirely his own. He had lost the custody of Ivry by the time of the Conqueror's death when it was in Roger of Beaumont's hands: Orderic, iv. 114; cf. ii. 358, where Roger of Ivry is the ducal castellan at Rouen c. 1077; the fact that Roger of Beaumont was *vicomte* of Rouen c. 1050 (Bates, *Normandy*, 118) suggests the possibility of an exchange of responsibilities; see also Robert of Torigny in *Gesta Normannorum Ducum*, 288; I. J. Sanders, *English Baronies* (Oxford, 1960), 9. Roger of Ivry held Domesday estates worth £278 in Oxfordshire, Gloucestershire, and four other counties. A fossil of his former butlership in the ducal household can be detected in Waleran of Ivry's notice in the 'Infeudationes militum' of 1172: 'i militem de pincernatu; et sibi iii milites et dimidium': *Red Book of the Exchequer*, iii. 640.

APPENDIX D

Honours with 50 or More Knights or Quotas of 20 or More in the Norman Inquest of 1172[1]

Holder, 1172	Knights (Quota)	Holder, 1066	Ships (Knights)
1. Hon. of Mortain	unknown (29.67)	Robert c. of Mortain	120
2. Bp. of Bayeux	120 (20)	Odo bp. of Bayeux	100
3. C. of Alençon	111 (20)[2]	Roger of Montgomery	60
4. Hon. of Giffard	99 or 102.9 (?)	Walter Giffard	30 (100)
5. E. of Leicester	98.5 (?)	William fitz Osbern	60
6. Bp. of Lisieux	43.33 (20)	Hugh bp. of Lisieux	unlisted[3]
7. Ld. of Tancarville[4]	94.75 (10)	—	—
8. C. of Meulan & Henry of Neubourg	78.6 or 88.6 (25)	Roger of Beaumont	60
9. C. of Évreux	58? (?)[5]	c. of Évreux	60
10. Hon. of Montfort & Coquainvilliers	55.5 (?)	Hugh of Montfort	50 (60)

[1] All data from Keefe, *Feudal Assessments*, Appendix I.

[2] Roger also held lands subsequently possessed by the earl of Arundel, who neglected to report in 1172.

[3] Hugh bishop of Lisieux was son of William count of Eu (natural son of Duke Richard I) and brother of Robert count of Eu of the ship list; Bishop Hugh was co-founder (with his mother Countess Lesceline) of the abbey of Notre-Dame-du-Pré, Lisieux: Appendix C.

[4] The Tancarvilles' high enfeoffment total reflects the enrichment of this ducal household family through two marriages to wealthy heiresses in successive generations: the Conqueror's chamberlain, Ralph of Tancarville, married the daughter and heiress of Eudes Stigand, founder of the priory of Ste-Barbe-en-Auge (Besse, *Abbayes*, 204–5); and their son and heir, William of Tancarville, acquired the Norman lands once possessed by Goscelin *vicomte* of Rouen (whom we have encountered as the founder of two abbeys) through his marriage to Goscelin's great-granddaughter, Maud of Arques (*Complete Peerage*, x. Appendix F: genealogical chart at p. 48). These alliances enabled William of Tancarville in Henry I's reign to transform the small collegiate church that his father had established at Bocherville around the time of the Conquest into the splendid abbey of St-Georges-de-Bocherville that stands to this day: ibid., 10, App. 52, Besse, *Abbayes*, 49–50; *Normandie romane: la haute-Normandie*, ed. Lucien Musset (Paris, 1974), 143–90; *Regesta*, ii. no. 1012, where the traditional founding date of 1114 is revised to 1112–13.

[5] See Keefe, *Feudal Assessments*, 242, no. 68.

| 11. E. of Chester | 52 (10)[6] | Hugh of Avranches | 60 |
| 12. Ld. of Tosny and Conches | 50 (?) | Ralph of Conches | unlisted |

Ship list honours not reporting in 1172: c. of Eu; c. of Évreux;[5] e of Arundel.[7]

---

[6] Note, however, that after 1120 the *vicomtés* of Avranches and Bayeux were combined and remained so in 1172: *Complete Peerage*, iii. 166–7.

[7] Of the remaining laymen on the ship list, Fulk of Aunou had enfeoffed 34.5 knights and owed 4, and Gerald *dapifer's* successor, William of Roumare, submitted an idiosyncratic return claiming a quota of 3 or 4 knights.

APPENDIX E

A Comparison of William of Poitiers' and Orderic's Lists of Outstanding Norman Laymen in 1066

William of Poitiers' List (148) (in correct order)	Orderic's List (ii. 140) (order in parentheses)
1. Robert c. of Mortain	Robert c. of Mortain (3)
2. Robert c. of Eu	Robert c. of Eu (2)
3. Richard c. of Évreux	Richard c. of Évreux (1)
4. Roger of Beaumont	Roger of Beaumont (10)
5. Roger of Montgomery	Roger of Montgomery (11)
6. William fitz Osbern	William fitz Osbern (5)
7. Hugh the vicomte [of Avranches]	—[1]
	Ralph of Conches (4)[2]
	William of Warenne (6)
	Hugh the Butler [of Ivry] (7)[3]
	Hugh of Grandmesnil (8)[4]
	Roger of Mowbray (9)[5]
	Baldwin and Richard fitz Gilbert (12–13)

[1] Orderic disliked Hugh of Avranches (ii. 260–2): 'Ipse terram suam cotidie deuastabat, et plus aucupibus ac uenatoribus quam terrae cultoribus uel coeli oratoribus applaudebat. Ventris ingluuiei nimis seruiebat, unde nimiae crassiciei pondere praegrauatus uix ire poterat. Carnalibus lenociniis immoderate inherebat – etc.' But cf. iii. 216 where Orderic describes Hugh as 'preeminent' among the Conqueror's magnates in Normandy.

[2] The fact that Ralph's father, Roger of Tosny, had founded the abbey of Conches c. 1035 (Appendix C), and the 50 knights reported on the honour in 1172, suggest that this family may have been among the wealthiest in Normandy in 1066 despite its absence from William of Poitiers' list and the ship list. Ralph of Conches's sister married William fitz Osbern.

[3] See Appendix C, n. 2.

[4] Co-founder of St-Evroul (Appendix C); the Grandmesnil honour owed 10 knights to the duke and had the service of 40 in 1172.

[5] Brother of the Class A Domesday landholder Geoffrey bishop of Coutances and father of Bishop Geoffrey's English heir, Robert of Mowbray earl of Northumberland: John LePatourel, 'Geoffrey of Montbray, Bishop of Coutances, 1049–1093', EHR, lix (1944), 133. Roger's Norman estates, forfeited by Robert of Mowbray in 1095 and afterwards granted to Nigel of Aubigny, are recorded in the Inquest of 1172 as owing the relatively modest quota of 5 knights from a similarly modest total of 11.39 knight's fees. See Complete Peerage, ix. 368, 372; Loyd, Anglo-Norman Families, 71; Gallia Christiana, xi. 'Instrumenta', col. 222 alludes to a kinship tie between Roger of Mowbray and Nigel vicomte of the Cotentin.

Taxation and the Economy

SALLY P. J. HARVEY

AS A MAJOR motive for the Domesday Survey, taxation has long held the centre stage. J. H. Round's study of 'Danegeld and the Finance of Domesday' in the 1886 commemoration volumes began with a quotation from a paper given 130 years before, which spoke of 'the inseparable connection between the Domesday Survey and Danegeld'.[1] Although V. H. Galbraith scorned the idea of a geld motive, he nevertheless granted the Domesday Survey a rôle in uncovering lands previously unhidated or untaxed by the shire authorities, and thought that the geld had been revived as an annual tax in the later years of William.[2] In this way, he admitted that geld had perennial importance and was not irrelevant to the making of the Domesday Inquiry.

We can now see that it is perfectly possible to give due weight to the novelty of Domesday Book as a feudal *valor*, at the same time as to continue to acknowledge the Survey's interest in fiscal assessments. Thanks to Galbraith, it is generally recognised that Domesday Book was neither a tax-recording nor a tax-accounting document. Indeed, both survive independently. Yet fiscal reassessment of a radical kind was attempted through the Domesday Inquiry, although, arguably, never fully implemented.[3] I propose now to seek from Domesday data the answer to why a fiscal reassessment was needed at all, when taxation in the eleventh century was obviously effective – if not over-effective – and to suggest that the seeking of information on estate values and even manorial data was germane in more than one respect to a reappraisal of assessment.

Round's discussion of danegeld included many of the essential questions about the levy and incidence of geld. But since then, the general picture has tended to become blurred by detailed studies of assessments in particular areas, whilst R. S. Hoyt's conclusions on the subject of exempt taxation in

---

[1] J. H. Round, 'Danegeld and the Finance of Domesday', *Domesday Studies*, i. 77–142.
[2] Galbraith (1961), 100–1, 42. That the countrywide geld was an annual institution rather than a frequent one in the later years of William I seems still unproven, as the direct evidence in Domesday Book relates to a borough context, and a separate borough levy is suggested by the Exeter evidence, DB, i. 264a, 100a.
[3] Harvey (1975), 186–9; (1985), 86–103.

Domesday Book do not hold generally good.[4] Recently, however, two careful studies of taxation have made the fiscal ground surrounding William I's reign much firmer. Both studies have drawn attention to the significant size of the sums raised by the geld: Dr Lawson for the reigns of Aethelred II and Cnut, taking the study to the fourth decade of the eleventh century; and Dr Green for the reigns of Rufus and Henry I and on into the 1160s.[5] Yet the subject is by no means exhausted, particularly in respect of the context of Domesday Book, and also of the evidence on geld that it contains. The studies of Lawson and Green indeed serve only to highlight the question. If the early eleventh-century impositions levied according to the Anglo-Saxon Chronicle have any reality – sums of the size of £21,000 in 1014 and £32,147 in 1041 (and even in 1018 of £82,500, on Cnut's accession: £72,000 on the country and £10,500 on London) – then, by 1086, the geld was indeed, as Dr Lawson has said, 'a mere shadow of its former self'.[6] Yet, if in 1086, it was already a shadow, it was taking an unconscionable time a-dying! It was still capable of considerable yield; about 10 per cent of the total revenue paid into the Exchequer (£2400) in 1129–30, and no less than 19 per cent of the money paid in 1155–6. Danegeld seems to have been levied annually at the normal rate of 2s a hide in Henry I's reign. There are also indications that it was, on occasion, imposed at a higher rate.[7] Even the taking of a feudal aid for the marriage of Henry I's daughter seems to have been levied, like a general geld, on hidage.[8]

Sums the size of £32,000 let alone £82,500 are very high indeed, bearing in mind that each penny of each pound was a silver coin, perhaps averaging in the region of 86.5 per cent fine.[9] The long-made distinction between a tributary levy and a levy for stipends of troops is necessary here: certainly the figure of £82,000 should be regarded as a maximum, only leviable exceptionally as tribute rather than routinely as taxation. But it is not an impossible figure. In Domesday Book the total value of the agricultural surplus handed over to maintain the ruling groups in 1085 adds up to something approaching £72,000.[10] Even so, there is a manifest difference between the tens of thousands of pounds of the years of Ethelred II and Cnut and the single thousands of Henry I's reign. Hence, the question that now demands attention is what happened to taxation in the interval – particularly in William's reign where we have the evidence of Domesday (at which time the

[4] R. S. Hoyt, *The Royal Demesne in English Constitutional History, 1066–1277* (Ithaca, New York, 1950), 25–36; cf. C. Hart, 'The Hidation of Northamptonshire', *English Local History Occasional Papers*, 2nd ser., 3 (Leicester, 1970), 23.

[5] M. K. Lawson, 'The Collection of Danegeld and Heregeld in the reigns of Aethelred II and Cnut', *EHR*, xcix (1984), 721–38; J. A. Green, 'The Last Century of Danegeld', *EHR*, xcvi (1981), 241–58.

[6] Lawson, 722, 726, 723.

[7] Green, 254, 242.

[8] T. H. Aston, 'Domesday Book', *The Oxford Magazine* (10 May 1962), 289.

[9] An average produced by H. Bertil Petersson, *Anglo-Saxon Currency* (Lund, 1969), 157, from figures by J. S. Forbes & D. B. Dalladay, 'Composition of English Silver Coins 870–1300', *British Numismatic Journal*, xxx (1961), 82–7.

[10] Darby (1977), 359.

fineness of coin was over 90 per cent)? And just how did taxation figure, or not figure, as a motive for the Domesday Inquiry?

Of central importance is to determine how closely the taxation changes of William's reign were related to the economy itself and the tax-bearing components of it. With regional distortions already visible in 1066, as Maitland has indicated, had taxation simply become outdated?[11] Radical alterations in geld liability certainly could and did take place without Domesday Book. In Northamptonshire, it was changed several times in the course of the eleventh century. On more than one occasion the subject of political reprisals and devastation in the 1060s, both before and after the Conquest, Northamptonshire received a radically reduced level of liability, from 3200 to 2600-odd hides, known to us first from the surviving Northamptonshire Geld Roll of the 1070s. This total was later radically reduced by just over half, effected proportionately within the hundreds, to the figure of 1250-odd hides recorded in Domesday Book.[12] Without the County Hidage and the Geld Roll, we should have known nothing of these changes as Maitland has said, since in Northamptonshire Domesday no hidage for King Edward's day is given. But they show that a more equitable regional redistribution of taxation was perfectly possible within the existing fiscal practices of assessment and levy.

Leaving aside any considerations of equity, assessment needs to take sufficient account of the balance of the economy to permit the continual successful levy of tax. There is an art of the fiscally possible. When the above changes took place, it is therefore arguable that they were generally intended to be geared to the changes in the economy or in tax-paying abilities. England was a wealthy country in the eleventh century;[13] but it was a wealth based largely on hard-won agricultural surpluses, and in William's reign much of the country had been devastated by warfare and the suppression of rebellion.

The question of the closeness of the tally between tax liability and returns from land has recently been subjected to painstaking statistical study for the Domesday county of Essex. The conclusion of this analysis by Drs MacDonald and Snooks is that, at the time of Domesday, taxation in the county was indeed broadly related to the annual values of land and 'the capacity to pay' of Domesday manors. Hence, they argue, the taxation system was aligned upon economic reality, albeit the smaller holdings were proportionally more heavily taxed than the larger.[14] This new approach to an old problem is welcome; even if it does not always yield new conclusions and even if the conclusions cannot be translated to other counties. Thus, without the benefit of computerised analysis, both Maitland and Vinogradoff long

[11] Maitland (1960), 530–1.

[12] F. Baring, 'The Pre-Domesday Hidation of Northamptonshire', *EHR*, xvii (1902), 470–9; Harvey (1985), 97; table in Hart, 'Northamptonshire', 38.

[13] P. H. Sawyer, 'The Wealth of England in the Eleventh Century', *TRHS*, 5th ser., xv (1965), 145–64.

[14] J. MacDonald and G. D. Snooks, 'How Artificial were the Tax Assessments of Domesday England?', *Econ. HR*, 2nd ser., xxxviii (1985), 352–72.

ago noticed that there was a general tendency throughout Domesday for a hide of land to be worth £1;[15] or, put another way, for land producing £1 of income to be assessed at one hide. Nor do these new findings invalidate arguments that an important motive for Domesday Book was to obtain an entirely new basis for fiscal reassessment, represented in the ploughland; the Geld Accounts for the south-west show that the fiscal system was by 1085 certainly unable to complete the levy of a 6s geld successfully. Thus, in Devon, geld was paid on 613 of its 1028 hides.[16]

The fact that smaller holdings were taxed more heavily than the larger is the simplified expression of already well-known circumstances of land-holding which affected taxation levels. There was at the time of Domesday, exemption for the 'demesnes' of the greatest landowners and for those who held in chief. Exactly what 'demesnes' meant in this context has not been agreed. Hoyt has argued, from study of the geld accounts of the south-west, that 'the manorial demesnes of manors held in demesne by the king and his tenants-in-chief' were exempt from geld.[17] We shall see below that manorial demesne seems to have been the minimum that was claimed elsewhere. Twelfth-century practice will not help here, for it was undoubtedly different. The concessions then were confined to individual tenants-in-chief, usually barons of the Exchequer,[18] whilst Henry I confined the specific concession of his Coronation Charter to 'the demesne ploughs' of serving knights (though some would interpret these as tenants by knight-service). In 1086, further distortions occurred through complete exemptions, which in several cases implied the right of landholders to levy geld for their own use, perhaps to redistribute the hides internally, as Battle Abbey did.[19] Even in cities liability often remained the same from 1066 to 1086, although tenements held by French burgesses were exempted also. Amongst those who no longer contributed to the geld burden of Shrewsbury were 43 French burgesses who seem to have been forgiven geld, and 39 burgesses which the earl gave to the Abbey 'who once paid geld with the others', implying that these tenements now paid their geld, but to the Abbey.[20] The corollary of these practices was that the smaller holdings of subtenants, freemen and villeins were indeed more heavily burdened, and many of the burgesses, as at Shrewsbury, were in a poor state. A direct enunciation of the extreme position is contained in Huntingdonshire Domesday for Hurstingstone Hundred.[21] There, it is said that the ploughs (or carucates) of the demesnes are exempt, but that the villeins and sokemen of the hundred pay geld according to the hides in the written record – an entry which implies that the assessment remained the same, but that the burden was redistributed.

[15] Maitland, 465; P. Vinogradoff, *English Society in the Eleventh Century* (Oxford, 1908), 383, 506–7.

[16] Harvey (1985); Finn, *Liber Exoniensis*, 105–8; F. Barlow, *William Rufus* (1983), 242.

[17] Hoyt, 56: cf. Round, 92–7.

[18] Green, 246–7.

[19] E. Searle, 'Hides and Virgates at Battle Abbey', *Econ. HR*, 2nd ser., xvi (1963), 290–300.

[20] Round, 122–6: DB, i. 252a.

[21] DB, i. 203a.

Thanks to work over the past two or three decades, it is now generally acknowledged that the importance of geld has survived Galbraith's attack; and that the new statistical and computerised methods of analysis will presumably assist us in the huge research task of relating our Domesday data about assessments to our data on the economy. Meanwhile, the large and long-posed question of what happened to the geld during William's reign and how it was related to the economy and to the prosperity of various classes remains open. And it remains one on which an opinion must be formed if we are to achieve a valid and comprehensive view of the motives for the Domesday undertaking.

What was William or what were his treasury officials trying to do when they juxtaposed two sets of data – the values of manors, the new achievement of the Domesday Inquiry, side by side with the existing data on hides? If fiscal reassessment was the aim, why bother to include some old assessments? The remarkable scope and rapid production of Domesday Book betrays both the strength and the stress of William's position in 1085. Which – strength or stress – is the more relevant to the question of taxation? The stability and strength of William's financial position is attested by the coinage of Type VIII, probably the last issue of his reign. This issue represents either the first type of a heavier new standard of 22.5 grains (rather than 21.5), or, more likely, the first type in which the full weight of the new standard introduced several years before had been consistently met.[22] The storm and stress of William's position is evidenced in the projected Danish invasion of 1085; in the troops that were raised in Normandy to counter it and were kept over winter in this country; in the need for William to take a 'mickle geld' of 6s on the hide in 1084 and, it is thought by some, to take another similar geld in 1086.[23]

Let us turn first to the economic picture in order to characterise a few changes in the direction of the prosperity of landholders during William's reign and to see whether taxation was geared appropriately to them, and so to judge whether Domesday Book had reason for a fiscal motive.

The general picture which Domesday Book gives is that, after a considerable fall in returns following revolutionary changes in landholding in the period 1065 to 1085 and consequent upon the laying waste of land, most profits from landholding recovered, and many indeed actually increased. How had the magnates and landholders achieved this increase in their annual incomes? One thing is clear. It was not from any extension or intensification of their own agricultural activities on the demesnes. Only one or two clear examples of dynamic management stand out, precisely because they are so exceptional.[24] Generally, however, the trend was towards fewer demesne

---

[22] Table of coin weights of William's reign, G. C. Brooke, *A Catalogue of English coins in the British Museum: the Norman Kings*, i (London, 1916), cliii; cf. P. Grierson, 'Sterling', *Anglo-Saxon Coins*, ed. R. H. M. Dolley, 266–83, esp. 275.

[23] Anglo-Saxon Chronicle, s.a. 1084; Galbraith (1961), 87–101, 223–30.

[24] S. P. J. Harvey, 'The Extent and Profitability of Demesne Agriculture in England in the later eleventh century', in T. H. Aston *et al.*, *Social Relations and Ideas: Essays in honour of R. H. Hilton* (Cambridge, 1983), 45–72.

ploughteams and, on the historical evidence available, towards a run–down of desmesne stock and arable.[25]

The advantages of large-scale demesne agriculture (by 'demesne' agriculture, I mean that a substantial proportion of a manor was kept in hand) lay in a full supply of basic foodstuffs for the lord and his household in the conditions of a sporadic and uncertain market. After the Norman Conquest there were fewer large secular landlords for whom this was a year-round concern. Only for ecclesiastical communities did this continue to remain a priority. On the other hand, large-scale demesne agriculture required considerable resources in manpower, both supervisory and servile. Whenever demesne agriculture declined, slavery declined with it; where such agriculture remained strong in Domesday, in the royal and ecclesiastical lands of the west and south-west, there slavery also remained strong. The supervisory class is largely a hidden class in Domesday Book; but we can see sufficient of the radmen or riding-men of the western counties and of the *geneat* of the treatise on estate management, the *Rectitudines Singularum Personarum*, to realise the import of their presence on the estates with a significant proportion of land in demesne.[26] Large-scale demesne agriculture was reliant on them and on other natives, given all the attendant problems of language, culture and trustworthiness which the newcomers had to face. Nor does the question of administration and management find its answer in slaves and riding-men alone.[27] Of the handful of lay estates which display an interest in demesne agriculture, two of the most prominent are the estates of Earl Roger of Montgomery and Richard Fitz Gilbert of Tonbridge and Clare. It is no coincidence that both these magnates were also known patrons of houses of secular clerks, whom we know were resident on sites of their great demesne enterprises.[28] There are indications that Roger's estate organised an annual account, and that Richard Fitz Gilbert's estates were run with reference to specific calculations of the relationship of stock to man-power and that Clare had already had a great demesne in the Anglo-Saxon period. Resident labour, from slaves and oxherds to the riding-men and the literate clerks, was vital to the continuance of demesne agriculture.[29] Against this background, and given the administrative effort required to make a success of large-scale demesne agriculture (foodstuffs could anyway be supplied by the requirement of rents and dues in kind), it is not surprising that the source of the rising incomes of the new landlords is to be sought elsewhere.

One lucrative option was to run down the demesne sectors of individual manors by renting out more land to small tenants. Making slaves into *bordarii* – smallholders of about 5–10 acres – was one form which this process took.[30]

[25] S. P. J. Harvey, 'Domesday England', in *Cambridge Agrarian History of England*, ii, ed. H. E. Hallam (Cambridge, forthcoming).

[26] Ibid., *EHD*, ii. 875.

[27] J. F. A Mason, 'The Officers and Clerks of the Norman Earls of Shropshire', *Transactions of the Shropshire Archaeological Society*, lvi (1957–60), 244–57; Harvey, *Agrarian History*.

[28] R. Mortimer, 'The Beginnings of the honour of Clare', *Anglo-Norman Studies; Proceedings of the Battle Conference*, iii, ed. R. A. Brown (1980), 129–30; Mason, esp. 256.

[29] Mason, 256; Harvey, *Agrarian History*.

[30] Maitland, 423; F. H. Baring, *Domesday Tables* (London, 1909), 178.

Leasing out whole manors was another option. The costs of providing supervision and management were, for the lessee, subsumed into the benefits of year-round residence. For the lessees of one or two manors it was thus a possibly profitable venture, or for Anglo-Saxons who had lost their own manor it was a possible way to continue to work what was formerly their own land. All the Domesday evidence indicates that leases in this period were not made for long terms; or, if they were, the annual payment could be varied. The dues of freeholders and sokemen could usually be raised to meet the high demands of the lessor. It was particularly easy for sheriffs or for large landholders who held whole hundreds with their manors for they held both assets and jurisdiction. In fact, manorial rights over the appendant land and other dues, largely hidden by the structure of Domesday, which usually values a manor as a whole, were the aspect of the manor which produced the real profits. Sometimes, however, contrasting values and assets will illustrate the point. On the substantial manor of Wells, the bishop's land in hand was worth £30, a holding of the canons was worth £12, and another holding of the bishop's men was worth £13. Each had six teams in demesne and comparable livestock, but the bishop's land had also 300 acres of meadow, as well as pasture, woodland and moorland attached. On Glastonbury Abbey lands in Dorset, Somerset and Wiltshire, knights and subtenants of the abbey possessed nearly 40 per cent of demesne teams and over 50 per cent of the peasants' teams on their lands.[31] Yet in value they held only one-fifth to one-quarter of the abbey's lands. Some of the demesnes' resources went to support large sheep flocks, but much of their products were disposed of in rents and sales. At Kirtlington, £8 came 'from meadow, pasture, pannage and other dues', and at Shipton under Wychwood, meadow, pannage, rent and other customary dues produced £12 17s.[32] Increases could also be imposed, on a smaller scale, on the dues which were attendant on pastures, grazing and woodland rights. In this way, for some years, many manors in the east and south-east of England could be made to pay, or 'render', more than they were worth. In a few such cases, Domesday Book records that such a render 'could not be borne'.[33] It was not the plight of the French reeve which was the jurors' concern, but that of the small freeholders of the manor, on the raising of whose rents the shire reeve, the local reeve or the manor's lessee relied.

In 1085, demesne agriculture, by comparison, could not in general offer such profits. Normally (leaving aside the special needs of the monastic houses and some exceptional estates of the west of England) only the smallest manors maintained a high proportion of demesne, often holding as many ploughteams in demesne as did the tenantry of the manor. A single group of holdings also stands out from the general picture; those of the riding-men usually consist of a high proportion of demesne or quite often of demesne entirely. The value of such a holding is not high; for instance, in one

---

[31] Harvey, 'Profitability of Demesne Agriculture', 50–2, 70–1.
[32] DB, i. 154b.
[33] E.g. DB, i. 2b, 40a–b.

Shropshire case, '3 radmen plus 8 slaves have 12½ ploughs' which were worth less than £5.[34] These returns cannot compare with what a manor of similar size with attached rents obtained. Nevertheless, such holdings – and also the smaller manors – show that, although the profits of these demesnes were not comparable to those derived from manorial dues, it was worthwhile for those with on-the-spot expertise and with limited resources and costs to maximise their demesnes.

Thus the raising from freeholders of hundredal and manorial dues up to the level of full-scale rents was much more readily profitable than demesne agriculture. But such policies held within them the seeds of their own downfall; they could not be other than short-lived; sooner or later they could only lead to diminishing returns. The retention in our abbreviated record of complaint by 'the English', men presumably of the vill or of the hundred, about the level of the return squeezed from the manor, is of the greatest interest here. It is not necessarily to be seen as a testimony to the disinterested character of the Domesday record-takers; but rather as a pointer to the royal interest. It was an established principle, from the non-hidation of some royal demesne onwards, that exemption from taxation rendered landlordly revenues more profitable. It was presumably generally also recognised that the converse was true, that over-milking of manorial revenues made royal taxation less profitable, indeed less possible.

In concluding this outline of the sourcees of profits from agriculture under the Norman landholders, some general trends can be identified which form the background for the levy of taxation in William's reign. There was the swing away from large-scale demesne agriculture, particularly on lay estates, with the concomitant build-up of pressure to raise dues from small free-holders to the level of full rents. On the other side of the picture, there were sufficient economic pressures for the holder of the small manor, as well as the freeholder, to maximise his small demesne. Here we should remember that there were, at the very least, twice the number of ploughteams – the weighty part of the working capital in agriculture – in the hands of tenants and peasants than there were in the hands of the lords. On the largest estates, the proportion was usually much greater. In Surrey, the demesnes supplied 262 of the county's ploughteams, whereas the men supplied 1011. In Middlesex, the demesnes supplied 135 to the peasants' 412.[35] Thus, at the very least, well over two-thirds of arable activity depended directly upon the peasantry and on the smallest agricultural units for continuing viability. Finally, there was the general upward trend of rents, leases and increments in the south and east. This took place against the background of a rising population, and of considerable competition between Norman newcomers anxious to take on land and Anglo-Saxons anxious to stay in some way on the tenurial ladder, even as rent-payers, or as custodians, officials, or lessees of the conquering group.

Now we turn to consider the changes in taxation which took place in the

[34] DB, i. 254a; Harvey, *Agrarian History*.
[35] Baring, 17, 85.

Conqueror's reign. The assessment unit of the eleventh century was the hide and in the north, in Domesday Book, the carucate. Unfortunately, Domesday's treatment of hidage and carucage is not nearly as comprehensive as its treatment of values. Some counties in Domesday Book, for instance Nottingham and Derbyshire, recorded only Edwardian hides or carucates for geld. Some counties recorded only present-day hides, as in Warwickshire. Only on the south-eastern circuit of Domesday Book, in Surrey, Sussex, Hampshire and Berkshire, are we consistently given hides for two dates, for 1066 and 1086, King Edward's day and 'now'. Kent, assessed in sulungs, has been reassessed only in part. These counties, as Round wrote long ago in his preliminary discussion, deserve to be looked at in more detail, to illustrate the manner and thereby the possible rationale in which the reductions of tax assessment took place: for reduction it is, in almost every case.[36] The clearest and most consistent principles emerge from Berkshire and Surrey. With these principles most of the remaining counties agree, but with a larger number of exceptions and divergencies.

In Berkshire, the neat and well-known five-hide unit or its multiples has been made completely misshapen. Reductions were sweeping, frequently halving, or even abolishing, assessment. In almost all of Berkshire and Surrey, concessions were confined to the manors kept in hand by tenants-in-chief and others who held of the king directly, their 'demesne manors' as they are often called. Yet, in several respects, they do not accord fully with any enunciated principle of demesne exemption. These reductions were made during William's reign on the lands of ecclesiastical houses as well as on the lands of lay lords. Had the principle of the exemption of ecclesiastical demesne asserted by the late *Leges Edwardi* really obtained, this would have been unnecessary.[37] Lands of the archbishop of Canterbury received considerable reductions late in William's reign, and the archbishopric could hardly have been by-passed had such exemptions of the Church obtained in Edward's and indeed Stigand's day. Exemptions were not confined to the demesne sector of manors directly held in chief, to the 'manorial demesne of the manors held in demesne' as Hoyt termed the principle. In fact, reductions were often extensive in size, and in some cases embraced the whole manor. Again, contrary to Hoyt's principle, beneficiaries were a very wide range of persons, including many Anglo-Saxons who survived as 'King's Thegns' and thus were unlikely to be tenants by knight-service. Exemptions were given according neither to vill nor to hundred, as in Northamptonshire and as in Cambridgeshire where reductions of about 40 per cent had taken place in six hundreds, but to tenancy;[38] they were extended to all manors not sub-tenanted. Thus in 19 out of 22 hundreds in Berkshire, the geld reduction was only partial. By contrast, all landholders, great or small (some 64 in Berkshire and all those of Surrey), experienced reductions in the assessment of the manors in which no subtenant was placed. The concessions applied not

---

[36] Round, 110–12.
[37] Quoted in Round, 83–4; cf. Hoyt, 56; Green, 246–7.
[38] C. Hart, 'The Hidation of Cambridgeshire', *English Local History Occasional Papers*, 2nd ser., 6 (Leicester, 1970), 26–30.

merely to the greatest landholders in Berkshire but also to great landholders who held only small lands in Berkshire, to minor tenants-in-chief, and to most of the king's thegns, and even to the king's serjeants in Berkshire (which was not true for the serjeants in all other counties). The difference in principle between the subtenanted manor and the demesne manor is high-lighted in a few cases in Berkshire, where a tenant-in-chief holds two manors in the same vill: the retained manor has had its hidage reduced in number, but the much less valuable manor with the subtenant has received no reduction. At West Hanney, held by Walter Giffard, the demesne manor fell from 14 to 7 hides, whilst no change occurred in the subtenanted manor. And at Ginge, held by the abbey of Abingdon, 10 hides were reduced to 2¼, whilst the manor which Rainald held remained at 2 hides.[39]

Let us look more closely at these sweeping reductions, to try to find out more about the principles which do hold good. Each of the counties of the south-east seem to have a slightly different character in this respect, perhaps reflecting the different shrieval authorities. Within Surrey there was more of a contrast between tenants-in-chief as to the extent of the reductions obtained than within Berkshire, which contrast underlines the tenurial basis for reduction rather than the hundredal. Several different levels of reduction seem to obtain in Surrey. Most blatant are the Surrey landholders whose assessment has been completely wiped away and who are now assessed for nothing. This is true for the count of Mortain's three manors, the single manor of St Wandrille and the single manor of Battle Abbey (this was to be expected from its charter).[40] Then there are the manors which, like most of the county, were fairly severely treated in King Edward's day and which now appear in 1086 as absurdly leniently treated. Many were holdings of the new magnates of the most influential sort, yet they also included lands of established ecclesiastical houses. The count and countess of Boulogne, Chertsey Abbey and St Peter's Winchester were amongst the most obvious. Richard of Tonbridge, exceptionally, gained huge rebates both for his demesne and for his tenanted estates. On a few estates, the reduction in rateable value was much needed. The archbishop of Canterbury's estates at Croydon and Mortlake, worth only £12 and £32 respectively in King Edward's day, were then assessed at 80 hides each; in 1086 Croydon was rated at 16¼ hides, and Mortlake, worth £38 then, paid geld in all for 33 hides.[41] (It remains quite likely, in view of the extraordinarily low Edwardian values of these large demesne estates, that supplies to the lord's household were not always calculated for the 1065 value. This may also be true of some of the smallest manors of 1086, although there is no means of telling if this were so.)

Turning to Sussex and Kent, the reductions in respect of certain tenants-in-chief were even more partial. These reductions may even have embalmed self-assertive refusals to pay geld. This seems to be true of the bishop of

[39] DB, i. 60a, 59b.
[40] DB, i. 34a.
[41] DB, i. 34a, 32a–34a.

Bayeux at least. The bishop's many subtenants in Kent also have very low sulung assessments in relation to their value. In Surrey no geld was paid on the Bayeux estate: one of the bishop's demesne manors was further said 'never to have paid geld since the bishop seized it'. This situation deserves to be compared with the bishop of Bayeux's lands in Hampshire, held by as influential a royal official as Hugh de Port, the 1066 assessment of which remained unchanged.[42]

In Sussex, it is interesting that the different administrative units there, the Rapes, have been either accorded different fiscal treatment or have themselves apportioned responsibility on different lines. The count of Mortain, William's other half-brother, was obviously placed – or had placed himself – in a similar category to that of Odo of Bayeux. Some of the count of Mortain's demesne manors (West Firle, Willingdon and Westburton) have become completely exempt, whether they were 48 hides, 50½, or 2 hides.[43] Earl Roger of Montgomery's present assessments of demesne manors were considerably reduced. On William of Warenne's estate, subtenants as well as William's own land experienced reductions, which, although substantial, were usually justifiable in terms of changed levels of value; yet, four of these manors now paid no geld at all.[44] William de Briouze's Rape received large reductions unjustified by the trends there in land values. For instance, Shoreham was in King Edward's day worth £25 and rated at 12 hides; in 1086 it was only rated at 5 hides and a ½ virgate, yet it was worth £35 and paying £50.[45] Again, the indications are that a general and generous concession has been differently administered according to the shire or sub-shire division; but, most of all, according to the will of the landholder (just such variations as may also be seen in the make-up of Domesday Book).

Thus, far from being aligned to the trends in agricultural profits and rents outlined earlier, the fiscal changes ran in precisely the opposite direction, giving the tenants-in-chief huge concessions which bore no relation to the demesne sector of their manors. True, in Berkshire and Surrey in King Edward's day there were more hides than £'s worth of revenue. There was thus a possible argument for a small reduction (if there was anything official in the hide per £ of revenue principle). It is also arguable that the hides in 1086 were perhaps a very approximate reflection, on one or two estates, of the lowest interim values and so the tenants-in-chief may have argued their case. The first three demesne manors of Earl Roger in Sussex suggest that this might have been the case. Singleton's value in Edward's day was £89, 'afterwards' of £57, and £93 and a mark of gold in 1086; its hidage had been 97½ and was now 47 hides. Binderton had a value of £5 TRE, afterwards £3, now £7; its hidage had been 7, and was now 3 hides. Hastings TRE had been worth £80, afterwards £60, and now £100; the hidage had been 80 and was now 48.[46] Yet it remains that reductions on demesne manors were such that

[42] DB, i. 31a, 46a–b.
[43] DB, i. 21a.
[44] DB, i. 23a, 26a–27b.
[45] DB, i. 28a.
[46] DB, i. 27b.

they bore no correspondence with current reality, and were even over-generous measured by the low interim values for the date at which the estate changed hands. Surrey, worth £1533, went from 1830 to 706 hides, and Berkshire, worth £2524, from 2473 to 1338,[47] whereas the rating of subtenanted manors remained on the heavy side. The hidage was in fact much better aligned to the values of land in 1065 than in 1086. It was not so much that the hides current in 1086 were 'out of date', but that recent concessions had been allowed to run riot and make nonsense of the assessment. More of the small freeholders' and villeins' surplus was being transferred to the holders of manors in raised rents and dues. At the same time the holders of manors were themselves being exempted from tax on their own lands and their decreasing demesne enterprises, thereby trans-ferring the weight of the tax burden to the freeholders and villeins. By 1086, tenants-in-chief in the south-east – what may be regarded as the heartland of William's power in England – had, almost universally, gained large reduc-tions in taxation on their lands, with correspondingly lower yields in taxation possible.

That the concessions made were indeed concessions to demesne manors in this circuit and not to the demesne sector of the manor, as Hoyt thought, is worth enlarging upon. The demesnes in the south-east, as represented in the demesne ploughs, were very much smaller than the scale of the reductions in tax assessments. Thus, the conclusion must be that either manorial demesne was not in fact the basis of the concession; or, that demesne agriculture had greatly declined; or, that the demesne had been grossly misrepresented. It is quite possible that all three played their part. In the south-eastern circuit, demesne hidage was not recorded separately. Perhaps the original require-ment to record the demesne stock and the ploughteams in the Domesday returns was in order to verify the extent of demesne activity, not only in respect of values but also in respect of fiscal exemptions. The twelfth-century document containing the stock of demesnes in the king's hands, the Roll of Ladies and of Heirs and Heiresses (*Rotuli de Dominabus et Pueris et Puellis*) shows that the record of stock was used to verify the claims of the value and activity of the demesne.[48]

Evidence from other circuits indicates that the size of the demesne claimed by tenants-in-chief was of import in the Domesday Survey. Such indications exist particularly clearly in Circuit III, Middlesex, Hertfordshire, Bucking-hamshire, Cambridgeshire and Bedfordshire. In these counties Domesday treats the hidage of demesne manors differently from the hidage of manors with subtenants. Subtenanted manors supply three categories of information – ploughs in demesne, total hides, and total ploughlands. Lands with no subtenant record the hides held in demesne also. A random example will illustrate the additional information given in these counties. 'The Count of Mortain holds Bledlow. It defends itself for 30 hides. There is land for 18

---

[47] Figures from Maitland, 464–5, and Darby (1977), 359.
[48] *Rotuli de Dominabus et Pueris et Puellis*, ed. J. H. Round (Pipe Roll Soc., xxxv, 1913).

ploughs. *In demesne 16 hides* and there are 4 ploughs there . . .'[49] In one case, the hides in demesne have even been supplemented by further information on unhidated ploughlands (*carrucatae terrae*) held in demesne. Despite the fact that the manor defended itself for 5 hides, the record declares it to be more extensive, but under-used. 'There is land for 8 ploughs besides these 5 hides'; one plough only is at work on the demesne, though there could be two more: a point reinforced by the further information that there are three ploughlands in demesne.[50] This separate information on the hides of the demesne manors held directly applies to the whole county of Buckinghamshire, except for the three royal manors. The same interest in demesne hides is also evident throughout the Domesday record of Middlesex and of Hertfordshire to include even three women holders of land, thus illustrating the point that the concessions did not apply strictly to tenants-in-chief by knight-service.[51] So consistently does the extra information tally with the lack of subtenant in these counties that it encourages the faith that subtenants are mentioned, not haphazardly in Domesday Book as usually inferred hitherto, but for a fiscal reason and wherever there was a subtenant, at least in these counties. However, the separate record of demesne does not obtain throughout Domesday Book: or even without exception in Circuit III. There is only some record of demesne in Bedfordshire; however, nine-tenths of Cambridgeshire does observe the 'no demesne hides if subtenanted' principle, the main exceptions being the royal lands. That there was such a principle is further indicated by the bishop of Rochester who appears with a tenant-in-chief's heading but no demesne hidage. Then the entry explains that he held this manor 'under Archbishop Lanfranc'.[52] The record of subtenants in Domesday may be more variable elsewhere, since Circuit III contains exceptionally well-ordered information and was probably the first to be completed.[53] The counties of the south-west also contain separate record of the hides of the demesne, but there is not the same distinction apparent between tenanted and untenanted land.

What did exemption – especially total exemption – mean in practice? Was it the privilege of being free from the general geld, or did it enable the exempted landholder to collect the geld for himself? Some landholders (all of them churches) are occasionally said clearly to have the privilege to collect the geld due for themselves. The bishop of Worcester had the geld in King Edward's day from Great Hampton. Finally, the monks of Bury St Edmunds received a quarter of the geld raised from its land: 'when £1 went from the town sixty pence went to the provision of the monks'.[54] Are these extraordinary notes in Domesday Book because they describe an extraordinary situation, or because the returns of these ecclesiastical houses were independently and carefully produced? From twelfth-century experience it would

---

[49] DB, i. 146a.
[50] DB, i. 151a.
[51] DB, i. 142b.
[52] DB, i. 190b.
[53] *Domesday Rebound*, 29–31; Galbraith (1961), 8, 203–4.
[54] DB, i. 174a; ii. 372a.

seem that the forgiveness of geld implied the right to levy geld or gelds for personal use, or at least so it was taken. It may well be that this practice was more common than Domesday Book indicates, for, another instance is recorded in the detailed Exeter Domesday where a manor held by the canons from the church of St Petroch is said never to have paid geld except to the church (*nisi ad opus ecclesiae*), whereas its counterpart entry in Great Domesday states simply that the manor 'never paid geld' (*numquam geldavit*). In the early twelfth century, some tenanted inland of Burton Abbey owed geld to the abbot.[55]

What is the significance of the uncovering in the course of the Domesday Inquiry of the extent of the exempt demesne? It was revealed in the south-east by noting the extent of the concessions received and in the counties of Circuit III by noting the demesne hides. The Kentish assessment list edited by Hoyt points to a date for concessions to Canterbury lands of 1085, just a few months earlier than Domesday Book.[56] It seems likely that the concessions for the rest of the south-east were of similar date; the tenurial pattern with which they so closely coincide suggests that they were recent. We know that they were short-lived, since they were abandoned and the 1066 figures copied into the later official abbreviations of Domesday Book.[57] Certainly, an abrogation of the concessions took place at some time between the survey and Henry I's reign. The Edwardian hidage was then made the basis for the levy of geld in these counties in the twelfth century.[58] It is tempting to see the uncovering of these in Robert of Hereford's well-known description of the Domesday Inquiry: 'Other investigators followed the first, and men were sent into provinces they did not know or where they themselves were unknown in order that they might be given the opportunity of checking the first survey and, if necessary, of denouncing its authors as guilty to the king. And the land was vexed with much violence arising from the collection of the king's taxes.'[59] When the hidage of 1086 was exempting a wide and loosely defined demesne, it was also exempting the valuable meadow, woodland and pasture rights attached: the flexible element in agriculture and the resources which enabled the arable to be exploited successfully, as, for instance, in the needs of oxen for meadow, hay and pastures. It is also tempting to see a carefully worded attempt to avoid a similar pitfall in Henry I's exemption from geld in his Coronation Charter of 'demesne ploughs' – not 'demesne' – of serving knights.

Let us now summarise our picture of the trends in the economy with those changes in assessment visible under William I. Whilst tenants-in-chief and royal lessees were exacting very much higher returns from freeholders and small tenants in William's reign than previously, they themselves paid very much less tax. On the lands of most of those who held directly from the king,

[55] DB, iv. f. 202, p. 183; cf. DB, i. 120b; *EHD*, ii. 889.
[56] R. S. Hoyt, 'A pre-Domesday Kentish Assessment list', *Early Medieval Miscellany* (*Pipe Roll Soc.*, lxxvi, 1960, new ser., xxxvi, 1962), 189–202.
[57] Public Record Office E.36/284; PRO E.164/1.
[58] Green, 244; Hart, 'Cambridgeshire', p. 27.
[59] W. H. Stevenson, *EHR*, xxii (1907), 74; also *EHD*, ii. 912.

either much reduced or no geld whatsoever was levied; or, they themselves were levying and consuming the geld. Thus, the small agriculturalist (the man we must remember who supplied more than two-thirds of the plough-teams of England), together with the subtenants of small manors with limited resources, had to bear the total brunt of the weight of taxation, at the same time as having much more of his surplus taken from him in rents and dues.

Hence, the Domesday Inquiry had a double motive for seeking information on the values of estates. Not only were the values useful in vacancies and wardship but also to see where the surpluses formerly produced by free-holders and sokemen were now going and how much revenue the tenants-in-chief were in fact receiving which was untaxed. Hence, there was good reason for seeking the values of King Edward's day. The separate information on demesne ploughs and indeed demesne livestock made it possible not only to verify the values stated but also to verify the actual extent of the demesne in relation to the exemption claimed. So the contributors to the first Survey could be denounced as guilty – just as Robert of Hereford had said.

It has been credibly argued that the sanction which enabled the levy of huge sums of taxation in the early part of the eleventh century was the principle that men had either to pay the geld due, or forfeit the land to the shire reeve, who might give it to whoever paid off the obligation.[60] This may well have been the process by which the many freeholders and soke-holders 'added to' royal and other manors during William's reign had lost their former autonomy, and were thereby placed in a position where a full rent could be demanded from them. If this were so, manorial lords who held in chief had no reason to object to high levels of taxation. But if the Domesday surveillance of demesne had a specific purpose, they had every reason to object to it and to Domesday Book.

It was, then, not so much the Edwardian hidage that was so out-of-date which caused the problems of William's reign, as the extensive exemptions obtained by tenants-in-chief in the course of the reign itself. This, together with the effects of rebellion and devastation in the early years of the reign, led to diminishing returns in the course of the Norman administration of the taxation system. The Domesday Survey, amongst other things, enabled officials to see just how the landlords were profiting at the expense of the national geld.

Yet the Domesday Survey may well have come too late to alter the situation radically. It seems to have coincided with a turning point in the rising curve of rents. A run of bad harvests and the attempt to levy more taxation for which William II was notorious may well have meant the end of the rental spiral. Even if we may expect as many as one in three harvests to be poor, the thirteen years 1086–98 inclusive had eight years of bad harvests and cattle plague mentioned in one chronicle, compared with only three or four in the previous thirteen years.[61]

[60] Lawson, 722.
[61] *Anglo-Saxon Chronicle*, ed. D. Whitelock, s.a. 1073–98.

The study of Aethelred's and Cnut's huge taxes has pointed out that England was a wealthy country and implied that such sums were not necessarily totally punitive.[62] But the heaviest were tributes levied via the taxation system, rather than taxation as such. Perhaps William the Conqueror hoped for tribute on a similar scale. But, wealthy as it was, England could not sustain tribute at those levels indefinitely. I conclude from the Domesday evidence that – at least as far as the agrarian structure was concerned – high levels of taxation had become incompatible with high returns for land-holding, that is returns as high as the level currently being demanded in 1085–6. The agricultural sector shows every sign of having reached the point where it was Either/Or: either the magnates' maintenance of such incomes, or successful taxation – a dilemma reinforced by the row of poor harvests starting in 1086 itself.

The case of Kent illustrates well the other side of the relationship between heavy taxation and the economy. Kent was less heavily manorialised than anywhere else in southern and midland England and had fewer ploughteams in demesne. It was, as Maitland said, very much underrated for tax, in King Edward's day and in 1086. Nevertheless in terms of profitability from landholding, it produced amongst the highest revenues for its landlords of any county, both absolutely and, more importantly, per man and per team recorded.[63] The small peasant unit here was allowed to assert its contribution to economic supply.

In a word, in Domesday Book, we can trace the results of a very lax attitude towards tenants-in-chief, and others who held of William I, which distorted the incidence of the geld, as also evidence of the attempt to work towards a distinctly over-ambitious correction of the situation. But by 1086, it seems as though large-scale demesne agriculture had already 'peaked', whilst rents and leases were approaching the stage of diminishing returns. And after more than ninety years of heavy taxation, William II's reign, unfortunately so lacking in fiscal or economic surveys, seems to see the working out of this conflict and the eventual and painful realisation of what was possible. Twelfth-century gelds, in reverting to King Edward's day assessments and to pardons for specific tenants-in-chief only for specific yields, probably constituted a more realistic levy from the agricultural sector.

---

[62] Lawson, 722.

[63] The highest, according to Maitland's tables, 464–67; amongst the highest, according to Darby (1977), 359.

Local Churches in Domesday Book and Before[1]

JOHN BLAIR

THE PARTICIPANTS AT the eighth-centenary celebrations would be truly astonished to see how much information Domesday Book has yielded during the last hundred years. While this has most obviously been achieved through analysis of the texts themselves, it is also thanks to a realisation that the study of Domesday communities cannot be confined to Domesday Book, but must explore the full range of written, topographical and archaeological sources for the world in which it was compiled. This has led in turn to another realisation: that Domesday records a landscape in a state of transformation. A generation ago it was still taken for granted that medieval villages and field-systems were a direct product of the Anglo-Saxon settlements: thus the basic fabric of the village community in the eighth century, the eleventh or the fourteenth was essentially the same. Now we know that common fields were products of a long and complex evolution, perhaps nowhere reaching anything like their final form until the tenth century. Peasant settlement, too, was dispersed and formless: regular villages with streets and plot-boundaries are currently ascribed to dates varying between the ninth and twelfth centuries, but not a single pre-Conquest example has yet been proved archaeologically. While the critical changes in settlement and manorial structure seem to centre on the tenth century, rural England of 1086 was still some way from the settled landscape familiar from later medieval estate records.[2]

As with villages and fields, so with the local church: there is probably no time at which it has developed so rapidly and so decisively as during the

---

[1] For comments on an earlier draft of this paper, I am very grateful to Mr Nigel Chapman, Dr Brian Golding, Dr R. K. Morris, Mr David Roffe, Dr Gervase Rosser, Dr Julia Smith and Dr Alan Thacker.

[2] An important analysis of the economic context of manorial structures is E. Miller, 'La Société Rurale en Angleterre (X^e–XIIe Siècles)', in *Settimane di Studio del Centro Italiano di Studi sull'Alto Medioevo*, xiii (Spoleto, 1966), 111–34. For changing villages, see C. Taylor, *Village and Farmstead* (London, 1983), 125–74; for changing field-systems, see papers in R. T. Rowley (ed.), *The Origins of Open Field Agriculture* (1981). Two recent studies which emphasise developments between the late ninth and eleventh centuries are P. Stafford, *The East Midlands in the Early Middle Ages* (Leicester, 1985), and J. Blair, *Landholding, Church and Settlement in Early Medieval Surrey* (Surrey Arch. Soc. forthcoming).

period between 1000 and 1150 for which the Domesday survey is the half-way mark. Both the main interest and the main problem of the Domesday record of local churches is that it describes a state of unparalleled flux. This is not the place to analyse the formulae of the church entries, or to comment circuit-by-circuit on the commissioners' recording policy. The data have been summarised successively by Page, Gifford, Darby and Morris,[3] and with the era of computer-based analysis just dawning it would be superfluous to develop their conclusions here. Rather, I shall suggest an institutional framework to which such analysis in the future can perhaps refer. As we grapple with the technical problems of Domesday Book, it is essential to remember that not only is the recorded data multi-layered and fluid, but so was the reality behind it.

For present purposes, suffice it to say that churches in Domesday Book can be classified as 'ordinary' or 'superior'. The second category includes a wide range of minster and collegiate churches, some ancient but others relatively new. These were not listed systematically, but a high proportion appear as holdings in their own right and many others can be identified from passing references.[4] The 'ordinary' churches, our concern here, have laconic entries which usually take the form *est ibi aecclesia, est ibi presbiter, est ibi aecclesia et presbiter*, or *presbiter habet* x *carucas*. The variations between these formulae, and in the incidence of church references, show some consistency by circuit and shire, but are also influenced by more localised and less obvious consequences of the data-collection process. In some cases the formulae seem to have been determined at the level of hundred or wapentake; in others there are discrepancies between churches on royal demesne and all others.[5] Perhaps more important, inclusion or omission seems often to be determined seigneurially. It can be shown that churches on manors of some tenants-in-chief, especially great ecclesiastical tenants such as Burton, Worcester and Shaftesbury, are consistently omitted, while others were exceptionally assiduous in returning churches of all ranks.[6]

Such shortcomings, which result purely and simply from the circum-

---

[3] W. Page, 'Some remarks on the churches of the Domesday survey', *Archaeologia*, lxvi (1915), 61–102; D. Gifford, 'The Parish in Domesday Book' (unpublished London PhD, 1952), 91–154; the church sections in the various regional volumes of *The Domesday Geography*, summarised in Darby (1977), 52–6; R. Morris, *The Church in British Archaeology* (Council for British Archaeology Research Rep., xlvii, 1983), 68–71. See also S. D. Keynes, '*Anglo-Saxon Architecture* and the historian' [part of review of Taylor & Taylor, *Anglo-Saxon Architecture*], *Anglo-Saxon England*, xiv (1985), 293–302.

[4] See J. Blair, 'Secular minster churches in Domesday Book', in *Domesday Reassessment*, 104–42.

[5] Mr D. Roffe (personal comment) notes that in the Five Boroughs and in Yorkshire *presbiter et ecclesia* is used in some wapentakes but plain *ecclesia* in others, and that in Lincolnshire also the evidence suggests 'different policies at the level of wapentake/hundred'. Cf. Blair, 'Secular Minsters in Domesday', 112, n. 15.

[6] The works listed in note 3 mostly stress variations by shire and hundred. Seigneurial determination of the church data is noted, however, by P. H. Hase, 'The Development of the Parish in Hampshire' (unpublished Cambridge PhD, 1975), and by Mr Roffe (personal comment), who sees it as the overriding determinant in the Danelaw shires. M. L. Faull takes a pessimistic view: M. L. Faull and S. A. Moorhouse (eds.), *West Yorkshire: an Archaeological Survey to AD 1500* (3 vols., Wakefield, 1981), i. 212–13.

stances of 1086, may prove the main determinants of inclusion or omission. But the form of the data may also be moulded by older and more funda- mental background factors, reflecting genuine regional contrasts in the number and status of local churches. If the basic aim was to include churches in so far as they were worth mentioning as assets, such contrasts must have influenced the principles which the various groups of commissioners adopted. Nobody would now dispute that the Domesday record of churches is highly incomplete, but there may be patterns in its incompleteness. Effective use of the data requires not only a closer analysis of how it was compiled, but also a better understanding of how the churches themselves came into being.

I

The only 'parochial system' of mid-Saxon England was one based on minster parishes: large territories, perhaps five to fifteen times the size of an average later medieval parish, served by teams of priests operating from central mother churches.[7] Within this framework, the provision of local churches progressed by slow stages. Subsidiary cult centres, controlled and served directly from the minsters, seem to have existed from the time of the Conversion,[8] and such purely subordinate satellite churches may have been common in the eighth and ninth centuries. The chronology of 'private' churches served by single, resident priests is much less clear. Here sources of native English origin before *c.* 950 are notably silent[9] – in contrast to Frankish texts of the early ninth century onwards, where the village priest with his *mansa* of land is a recurring and familiar figure.[10] Admittedly Bede shows

[7] See Blair, 'Secular minsters in Domesday' and other works cited ibid., 104–5, note 2; J. Blair, 'Minster churches in the landscape', in D. Hooke (ed.), *Anglo-Saxon Settlements* (Oxford, forthcoming); M. J. Franklin, 'The identification of minsters in the Midlands', *Anglo-Norman Studies*, vii (1985), 69–88; and several papers in J. Blair (ed.), *The Local Church in Transition: Minsters and Parish Churches 950–1200* (Oxford, forthcoming).

[8] Blair, 'Minsters in the landscape'.

[9] See my review of Morris (1983) in *Journal of the British Archaeological Association*, cxxxix (1986), 168–9. The 747 Clofesho synod, which does contain such references, is almost certainly Frankish-derived: see W. Levison, *England and the Continent in the Eighth Century* (Oxford, 1946), 86; Morris (1983), 50. J. Godfrey, 'The place of the double monastery in the Anglo-Saxon minster system', in G. Bonner (ed.), *Famulus Christi* (1976), 348, takes these provisions at face value. The so-called 'Excerptiones of Archbishop Egbert' have also misled (F. Seebohm, *The English Village Community* (2nd edn, 1883), 115, followed by several later writers): they are in fact much later than Egbert's time, and of purely Carolingian origin (Levison, 118). A passage in Theodore's Penitential (*Councils and Ecclesiastical Documents*, eds. A. W. Haddan and W. Stubbs (3 vols, Oxford, 1869–71), iii. 203), which has been taken to refer to private churches, almost certainly means merely that the laity must pay 'their [tithes] to churches' – presumably minsters: I am most grateful to Mrs S. Wood for pointing this out.

[10] For a general survey of the Frankish local church see P. Imbart de la Tour, *Les Paroisses Rurales du IVe au XIe Siècles* (Paris, 1900). For local churches in the ninth century, see also U. Stutz, 'The proprietary church as an element of medieval Germanic ecclesiastical law', in G. Barraclough (trans.), *Medieval Germany 911–1250* (Oxford, 1967), 35–70; R. McKitterick, *The Frankish Church and the Carolingian Reforms, 789–895* (1977), 64–79; J. F. Lemarignier, 'Encadrement religieux . . . , de Charles le Chauve aux derniers Carolingiens', in *Settimane di Studio del Centro Italiano di Studi sull'Alto Medioevo*, xxviii. 2 (Spoleto, 1982), 765–800.

Bishop John of Hexham (687–705) dedicating churches on the lands of two thegns,[11] but what sort of churches is unclear: the text would not be incompatible with, for example, the late seventh-century minsters founded by Mercian *principes*.

The contrast between England and the Frankish world is as marked in the archaeological as in the written record. We have nothing comparable to the rich seventh-century 'founder burials' in Swiss, Bavarian and Belgian churches.[12] The proliferating excavations of English parish churches are indeed revealing older phases in stone and timber – but not substantially older.[13] The first identifiable structural phase seems never to be significantly earlier than *c.* 900, and sometimes there is evidence that the church succeeded mid- to late-Saxon secular occupation. Thus at Raunds, Northants., settlement debris extending up to the late ninth century was overlain by a small church of *c.* 875 × 900, around which a cemetery was established in *c.* 925.[14] In most other cases, the first church is at least a generation or so later than at Raunds.[15] Probably it is too early to argue from negative evidence: Richard Morris's suggestion that abandoned mid- and late-Saxon settlements may contain churches has not yet been adequately explored.[16] But on present showing, the main period of local church-building coincided with the economic and topographical changes of the tenth and eleventh centuries.

Since, however, these changes were not confined to England, more local explanations must be sought for why the proliferation of English local churches was so long delayed. One reason may be that the minster system was more highly organised from the outset, and more successful in maintain-

[11] *Baedae Opera Historica*, ed. C. Plummer (2 vols., Oxford, 1896), i. 287–8.

[12] D. Bullough, 'Burial, community and belief in the early medieval west', in P. Wormald (ed.), *Ideal and Reality in Frankish and Anglo-Saxon Society* (Oxford, 1983), 196: 'Examples of fully-dressed burials with an ample range of precious objects *under* churches are now known from southern Belgium to Alamannian Switzerland.' I am grateful to Mr S. Burnell for further information about such burials and their contexts.

[13] The 'church-like' timber buildings on seventh-century rural sites at Chalton and Foxley are of very uncertain function: see T. Tatton-Brown in *Current Archaeology*, lx (February 1978), 30, and M. Millett in *Archaeological Journal*, cxli (1984), 185. I am grateful to Dr S. R. Bassett for the Chalton reference.

[14] I am grateful to Mr G. E. Cadman of the Northamptonshire Archaeology Unit for this summary of the current conclusions on Raunds. Two other cases with the first church probably just pre-900 are: *St. Pancras Winchester*: first phase in the late ninth century (D. Keen, *Survey of Medieval Winchester* (2 vols., Oxford, 1985), ii. 742); *Barton-on-Humber, Lincs.*: mid tenth-century church, over cemetery established in perhaps the ninth century (W. and K. Rodwell, 'St. Peter's church, Barton-upon-Humber', *Antiquaries Journal*, lxii (1982), 283–315).

[15] Three cases are: *Barrow-upon-Humber, Lincs.*: mid tenth-century church with associated burials (J. M. Boden and J. B. Whitwell, 'Barrow-upon-Humber', *Lincs. Hist. Arch.*, xiv (1979), 66–7, and further information kindly supplied by Mr Whitwell); *Asheldham, Essex*: first church (timber) probably late tenth or early eleventh century (P. J. Drury and W. J. Rodwell, 'Investigations at Asheldham, Essex', *Antiquaries Journal*, lviii (1978), 138–40); *St Mary's, Barton Bendish, Norfolk*: eleventh-century church and graveyard succeeding tenth-century cultivation (N. Batcock, 'The parish church in Norfolk in the 11th and 12th centuries', in Blair (ed.), *Local Church in Transition*).

[16] R. Morris, 'The church in the countryside: two lines of inquiry', in D. Hooke (ed.), *Medieval Villages* (Oxford, 1985), 55–9. There is also a need for excavations in churchyards to determine the presence or absence of earlier churches *near* but not *under* their successors.

ing its hold through the ninth and tenth centuries, than in the Frankish lands.[17] Tenth-century aristocratic wills suggest that old minsters were still the normal, accepted objects of parochial allegiance and conventional piety,[18] and it was only gradually that this allegiance and piety came to be more locally directed. The first founders of manorial churches were not necessarily hostile to the minsters, and their foundations were not necessarily contentious. It.is too often assumed that every lord who built a church did so as an act of separatist defiance, arrogating to it a 'parish' forcibly detached from the *parochia* of the old minster. The status of local churches in their communities, and their relationships to the minsters in whose *parochiae* they were founded, were various: not all had pretensions to independence, and only those which did need have proved a threat. If a thegn could have a priest in his household, why should he not give him a church?

Throughout the whole period from the tenth century to the twelfth, laymen's churches could evidently begin informally and acquire land and jurisdiction by stages. Non-royal testators who mention private priests and churches are all of the late tenth century onwards. Æthelflæd (962 × 991) leaves two hides each to 'Ælfwold my priest' and 'Æthelmær my priest', while Ælfhelm (975 × 1016) leaves land at Carlton and Gestingthorpe to his heirs 'except that which I grant to my priest'.[19] Some grants are specific to individual churches as well as to individual priests. Æthelric (961 × 995) leaves land at Bocking to Christ Church Canterbury 'except one hide which I give to the church for the priest who serves God there'.[20] The East Anglian Siflæd (*c*. 950 × 1050) directs in her first will that 'my church [at Marlingford] is to be free and Wulfmær my priest is to sing at it, he and his issue, so long as they are in holy orders, and free meadow to the church', and in her second will leaves 'to the *tūnkirke* in Marlingford five acres and one homestead and two acres of meadow and two waggonloads of wood'.[21] Between *c*. 1030 and the Conquest five more East Anglian wills, those of Thurketel, Thurstan, Wulfgyth, Eadwine and Ketel, make gifts of land to one or more churches which are in some cases specified as the *tūnkirke*.[22] Eadwine's is especially striking for what seems to be systematic endowment of churches on his numerous Norfolk manors:

> I grant the estate at Algarsthorpe to St Edmund's except ten acres which I give to the church there. And Leofric is to have the three acres which he occupies. And I grant the estate at Little Melton to St Benedict's, and ten acres to the church. . . . And ten acres south of the street to Bergh church. And ten acres north of the street to Apton church, and four acres to Holverstone church, and four acres to Blyford church and ten acres to Sparham church. . . . And after

---

[17] See, however, S. Reynolds, *Kingdoms and Communities in Western Europe 900–1300* (Oxford, 1984), 81–7, who argues that in the Frankish world, too, the supremacy of mother churches survived much later than has been supposed.

[18] J. Blair in introduction to Blair, *Local Church in Transition*.

[19] D. Whitelock, *Anglo-Saxon Wills* (Cambridge, 1930), Nos. 14, 13.

[20] Ibid., No. 16 (1).

[21] Ibid., Nos. 37–8.

[22] Ibid., Nos. 24, 31–4.

Ketel's death, the estate [at Thorpe] is to go to St Edmund's without controversy; and [that] at Melton to the church which Thurward owned; and the land which Edwin, Ecgferth's son, had, free to the church; and eight acres from the estate at Thorpe, to Ashwell church; and eight acres from the estate at Wreningham to the old church, and two acres to Fundenhall church, and two to Nayland church.[23]

Æthelgifu, a rich Hertfordshire lady of the 980s, leaves slaves and stock to four of her priests, and the language suggests that they are in some sense a household group: with the surplus after bequests to minsters 'one is to think about the vigils and [give it] to her priests'. On the other hand, 'the half-hide which Wineman possessed [is to be given] to the church, and Edwin the priest is to be freed, and he is to have the church for his lifetime on condition that he keep it in repair, and he is to be given a man'. The editors perceptively suggest that 'the priests, of whom Edwin was one, served the estates of Langford, Clifton and Stondon as one ecclesiastical institution with three churches if such existed at the time of the will'.[24]

The wills indicate two trends between 970 and 1066: a shift of emphasis from priests in minsters or household groups to priests in individual churches; and the granting of land to local churches already in existence. Between a proprietary minster and the churches on a landowner's various manors there may be not a sharp contrast, but a spectrum. A modest thegn might maintain in his household a priest who ministered in the adjoining church; equally, a great lord might build dispersed churches for the intermittent use of priests who normally lived together. In these circumstances the churches could be *ad hoc*, non-essential and perhaps sometimes short-lived; but the more firmly the priests' lives came to be based upon them, the more they would need permanent endowments. This may explain the numerous bequests to churches which, it must be assumed, had previously lacked separate means of support; certainly Æthelgifu's instruction that her priest was to 'have the church . . . on condition that he keep it in repair', and Siflaed's that 'my church is to be free', suggest that the arrangements had hitherto been informal. But the further we go beyond the year 1000, the more likely we are to find local churches with their own lands – and pretensions to their own parochial rights.

Here it must be pointed out that nearly all the surviving wills between 1000 and 1066 are East Anglian, and hence may be atypical. It has often been noted that many Danelaw churches were in multiple ownership by 1086, and that most of these had probably been endowed corporately.[25] Domesday Book makes this explicit at Stonham, Suffolk, where the church land had been given by nine free men for the good of their souls, and at Stifford, Essex,

---

[23] D. Whitelock's translation, ibid., 87–9. Cf. comment ibid., 199–201.
[24] *The will of Æthelgifu*, eds. D. Whitelock, N. Ker and Lord Rennell (Roxburghe Club, Oxford, 1968), 8, 74. It is worth stressing that as well as making these bequests, Æthelgifu was a munificent patron both of old minsters and of reformed monasteries.
[25] Lennard, *Rural England*, 290; F. M. Stenton, *Documents Illustrative of the Social and Economic History of the Danelaw* (1920), lxx–lxxi, lxxviii; Page, 85–8.

where the church had 30 acres given by the locals (*vicini*) in alms.[26] It is thus not impossible that Eadwine and the other testators were merely contributing to churches also endowed by others. The word *tūnkirke* might be taken to imply some communal or public status, though analogy with the standard place-name compound of *tūn* with late Anglo-Saxon proprietors' names would rather suggest the translation 'estate church'.[27] We can do little more than note that Æthelgifu, in Hertfordshire, made a land-grant to one of her churches, and suggest that the East Anglian wills record the local form of a general practice.

The foundation of new churches continued through the eleventh century and into the twelfth. As R. V. Lennard pointed out, the passing references to churches founded by lay lords and consecrated by notable bishops between 1066 and 1100 can only be the tip of the iceberg.[28] To quantify the church-building activities of Anglo-Norman lords requires detailed local studies, few of which have yet been attempted. But there are enough explicit references to make it quite clear that new churches continued to be founded in substantial numbers up to the 1140s, often on relatively small subinfeudated lay manors.[29] The Norman settlement failed to check, and may have stimulated, the spate of private church foundation, which continued into Henry I's reign unabated.

As the wills and other sources show, many eleventh-century local churches had their own priests. But this pattern was not universal: other churches, including at least some built by the lords on whose land they stood, were served by priests sent out from the minsters. In the best-attested case, at Milford in Hampshire,[30] a church was built in *c.* 1090 by the lord of the manor, who gave land to Christchurch minster in return for regular visits by a Christchurch priest to say mass. Such churches, 'seigneurial' in that they existed primarily for the convenience of a lord and his household, were in no sense independent. Alternatively, a group of minster-priests who had itinerated through a large *parochia* might themselves build dispersed churches for their own convenience.[31] The strong tendency for such 'centrally-served' churches to acquire resident priests during the twelfth century makes it hard to know how common they may have been in the eleventh, but traces are sufficiently widespread to suggest that they were far from exceptional. Foundations of this type represent the collaborative as against the separatist element in local church provision: they were extensions of minsters, just as other churches may have been extensions of lay households.

---

[26] DB, ii. 438a, 24b.

[27] For *tūn* in place-names meaning 'estate' rather than 'farm' or 'village', see for instance M. Gelling, *The Place-Names of Berkshire* (3 vols., EPNS, xlix–li, Cambridge, 1973–6), iii. 939–41.

[28] Lennard, 295–8.

[29] As argued in detail for Surrey by Blair, *Early Medieval Surrey*, ch. V. The current British Academy project to publish episcopal *acta* promises to bring to light much new twelfth-century evidence.

[30] Discussed in detail by P. H. Hase, 'The mother churches of Hampshire', in Blair, *Local Church in Transition*.

[31] Notably at Bromfield, Salop.: Blair, 'Secular minsters in Domesday', 128–31. Cf. the other cases noted ibid., 131, 139–41.

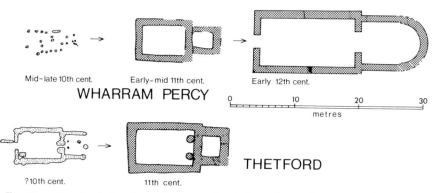

Mid–late 10th cent.   Early–mid 11th cent.   Early 12th cent.

WHARRAM PERCY

0   10   20   30
metres

?10th cent.   11th cent.   **THETFORD**

Fig. 1. Two local churches which were first built in the tenth century, and acquired a permanent form in the eleventh. (Wharram Percy after plans kindly supplied by Mr J. G. Hurst; Thetford after Medieval Archaeology *xv (1971), p. 131, by permission of Mr B. K. Davison and the Society for Medieval Archaeology.)*

II

Another source for the changing status of churches is the buildings themselves, whether standing or known through archaeology. While more parish churches must be excavated before it is possible to generalise with confidence, a pattern is already emerging.[32] Often there was a tenth- or early eleventh-century first phase in timber or stone, small and poorly built. The eleventh- or early twelfth-century phase was usually as simple, but larger, and of a structural quality which allowed it to stand as the nucleus for future additions (Fig. 1). In other words, during the eleventh century English rural churches seem to have crossed what students of domestic architecture call the 'vernacular threshold': the minimum level for widespread permanent survival.

The dating of standing 'Anglo-Saxon' churches cannot ignore the implications of this below-ground evidence. In about a half to two-thirds of English parish churches there can be identified a simple core, either a rectangular cell or a rectangular nave with square or apsidal chancel. This will probably have been classified as 'Saxon' or 'Norman', and thus included in or excluded from the Taylors' corpus, according to whether it displays Anglo-Saxon or Norman Romanesque building technology.[33] The two traditions are distinct enough in themselves: tall, narrow proportions, walls less than three feet thick, double-splayed windows, stripwork, 'long-and-short' quoins and a preference for very large blocks characterise English work; whereas Norman-trained masons built windows tapering in one direction only, and fine-jointed, regular stonework using relatively small blocks. But the chronological significance of these contrasts is doubtful. English technology

[32] It is made especially clear by the diagram in Morris (1983), 83, Fig. 24.
[33] H. M. and J. Taylor, *Anglo-Saxon Architecture* (3 vols., Cambridge, 1965-78).

272

(which should be distinguished from English architectural style) was simple, indeed almost vernacular, and could have co-existed over some generations with methods derived from the great Anglo-Norman building projects.[34] The more the volume of church-building had increased since *c.* 1000, the greater must have been the body of trained masons in 1066. The Conquest cannot have destroyed this growing pool of expertise.

It has indeed become clear that very many of the church buildings which we call 'Anglo-Saxon' were built well into the eleventh century. The Taylors list just over 400 churches, some 320 of which (that is, about four-fifths) they assign to 'Period C', 950–1100. Of these, a high proportion show details derived from Norman Romanesque of the 1020s onwards. Eric Fernie has recently proposed a 'school of minor churches, inhabiting the hundred years from the second quarter of the eleventh century to the second quarter of the twelfth, which is neither simply "Saxon" nor simply "Norman"', and suggests that 'half, if not the majority, of the surviving buildings commonly grouped under the label "Anglo-Saxon" belong in this category'.[35] Studies of the last ten years have shown that some notable churches, or even whole groups of churches, which used to be thought characteristically 'Anglo-Saxon' were probably built by English-trained masons during the half-century after 1066.[36] A remarkably large number of churches show a fusion of traditions: either Romanesque architectural ornament with English technology (Pl. VIIIa), or traditional English forms realised in the new Norman masonry (Pl. VIIIb). Just when the styles and techniques of Anglo-Saxon architecture were becoming obsolete, they were being used in more churches than ever before.

For Domesday scholars this poses obvious problems.[37] To take one example, Domesday Book says of Netheravon in Wiltshire that the church is 'waste and roofless so that it is almost collapsing'.[38] Since the west tower appears in the Taylors' corpus, it might be concluded that the commissioners can here be caught out in an unwonted flight of exaggeration. But the Netheravon tower (Fig. 2)[39] is essentially an 'overlap' building, Romanesque in many details if owing much to English traditions in its conception and execution. Given the Domesday comment, it is clear enough that the tower was built *c.* 1090 to replace the derelict church; but a standard *est ibi ecclesia* would have left no means of knowing whether the surviving fabric had recently been built in 1086, or whether it was built soon afterwards to replace the church then listed. The disappointing conclusion must be that only with the small number of standing 'Anglo-Saxon' churches definitely

[34] For this distinction between style and technology, and the architectural context of the eleventh-century churches, see R. Gem, 'The English parish church in the 11th and early 12th centuries: a great rebuilding?', in Blair, *Local Church in Transition.*
[35] E. Fernie, *The Architecture of the Anglo-Saxons* (1983), 171.
[36] For instance, R. Gem, 'The early Romanesque tower of Sompting church, Sussex', *Anglo-Norman Studies*, v (1983), 121–8; S. Heywood, 'The round towers of East Anglia', in Blair, *Local Church in Transition.*
[37] For the pitfalls of regarding Taylor & Taylor as a valid corpus of Anglo-Saxon churches against which the Domesday data can be measured, see Keynes, '*Anglo-Saxon Architecture* and the historian'.
[38] DB, i. 65a.
[39] Taylor & Taylor, i. 456–9.

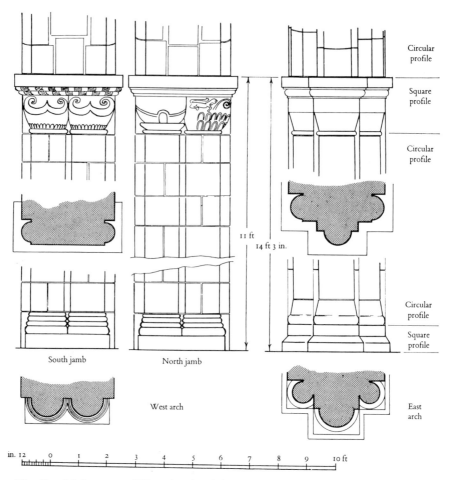

Fig. 2. *Netheravon, Wilts: details of the west tower, probably built immediately after the Domesday survey. (From H.M. and J.* Taylor, Anglo-Saxon Architecture I *(Cambridge, 1965), p. 457, by permission of Dr Taylor and Cambridge University Press.)*

earlier than the Taylors' 'Period C3', and in the small but growing number of cases where excavation has revealed the earlier phases, can we be confident on physical evidence that a church existed in the year of the Survey. Broad correlations are unlikely to be valid. Where there are many Domesday references but few standing 'Anglo-Saxon' buildings, later medieval enlargements could have destroyed the evidence; where there are few references but many buildings, most of the latter could post-date 1086. To take a less negative view, the 'Period C' churches are a remarkable phenomenon in themselves: Domesday England was, indeed, in Ralph Glaber's famous phrase, 'shaking off the robes of ages and putting on a white mantle of churches'.

III

I have tried to identify four developments in local church provision during the age of Domesday Book. First, the foundation of churches gathered momentum from soon after 900, continuing at a high level through the eleventh century and only slowing down in the early twelfth. Secondly, there was a tendency from about 1000 onwards for churches which may previously have existed somewhat informally to acquire permanent endowments, setting a pattern which was to be normal, indeed obligatory, by the twelfth century. Thirdly, an unknown proportion of local churches were served by minster-priests operating what would now be called 'team ministries', although this system probably declined fast after 1100. Fourthly, from *c.* 1050 onwards new churches were built, and old ones rebuilt, in a more permanent and imposing form, a change which may reflect a gradual progression of local churches at all levels towards greater permanence and stability.

These hidden influences must affect the Domesday data. It is conceivable that *aecclesia*, *presbiter* and *aecclesia et presbiter* are not mere vagaries of form but sometimes embody real differences, either between specific cases or between the patterns prevailing in different areas; while the occasional *aecclesia sine presbitero*[40] could record not a temporary deficiency but a normal arrangement. Churches served from minsters, and thus lacking priests of their own, may be ignored more often in *est ibi presbiter* areas than in those using *est ibi ecclesia*, where it can be demonstrated that at least some such cases are listed in the common form.[41]

Except for the abnormal 'Circuit D', some attempt at a systematic record of churches was evidently made in all areas surveyed. It is worth considering if omissions result at least partially from local circumstances influencing the conventions adopted at shire or hundred level, not simply from the vagaries of hundred jurors, lords and reeves, or from plain incompetence. If they do, the likely pattern is not hard to predict. Where most churches had attained a common level of self-sufficiency and independence by 1086, a higher proportion will tend to be listed: there would have been little to choose between them. But where the descending hierarchy of minster, independent church with priest, dependent church with priest and dependent church without priest remained important, churches towards the lower end of the scale are more likely to have been ignored. In all cases the churches without independent rights or endowments, and thus without value as property, are the least likely to appear; and these would have remained commonest where organisation remained most hierarchical. Thus it is in the sections of Domesday Book where 'superior' churches are most conspicuous that gross omission of humble churches is most likely.

---

[40] Darby (1977), 52.
[41] As at Greenham, Berks.: B. R. Kemp, 'The mother church of Thatcham', *Berkshire Archaeological Journal*, lxiii (1967–8), 17.

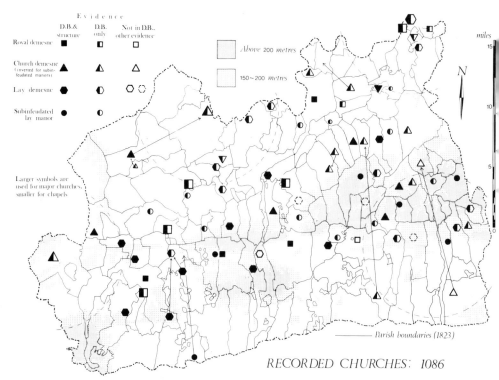

Fig. 3. Surrey churches recorded in Domesday Book. (From Blair, Early Medieval Surrey.)

These predictions cannot be properly tested until local bias and seigneurially determined omissions have been identified more clearly. But some broad patterns are already apparent.[42] In the south-western counties and in Wiltshire, 'superior' churches are numerous and conspicuous but lesser churches, which must have existed, are ignored completely;[43] whereas in Suffolk, where private church-holding flourished, 75 per cent of later parish churches are listed and the record must be almost complete.[44] Contrasts between Suffolk, Norfolk and Essex in the ratios of churches to manors must reflect different criteria adopted at shire level; but the criteria may themselves reflect different perceptions of the local church hierarchy within the areas surveyed. So the problems caused by genuine regional variation and by differing circumstances of compilation are interwoven: the first may have influenced the second, and the second certainly distorts our understanding of the first.

[42] These patterns were first systematically analysed by Gifford, 'Parish in Domesday Book'. Cf. map in Darby (1977), 54.
[43] Blair, 'Secular minsters in Domesday', 108, 112–13.
[44] Morris (1985), 53.

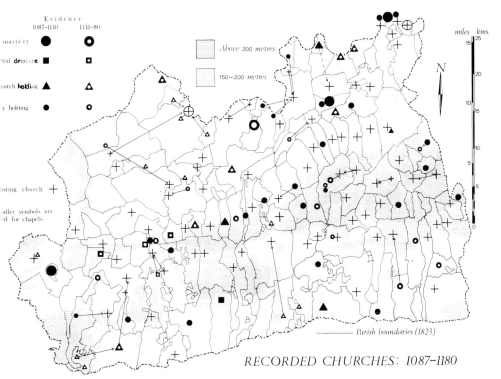

Fig. 4. Surrey churches first recorded between 1087 and 1180. (From Blair, Early Medieval Surrey.*)*

The case of Surrey provides a final example and suggests a way forward.[45] Its context raises little confidence in the data for churches: the same circuit included Kent, where the satellite surveys show that Exchequer Domesday omits more than half of all churches standing in 1086.[46] Yet there are grounds for thinking that the Surrey record is in fact extremely good. Internal evidence suggests a contrast within the circuit: the incidence of churches is weighted much more consistently in Surrey than in Kent towards valuable and populous manors. Nor does there seem to be any case of consistent seigneurial omission: no churches are listed on the main demesne estate of Chertsey Abbey, but since its outlying manors are abnormally 'well-churched' the contrast seems to be a genuine one, either in the distribution or in the status of the daughter churches. But the most telling argument for the Surrey

[45] This paragraph summarises an argument presented fully in Blair, *Early Medieval Surrey*, Ch. V.
[46] G. Ward, 'The lists of Saxon churches in the Textus Roffensis', *Archaeologia Cantiana*, xliv (1932), 39–59; G. Ward, 'The Lists of Saxon churches in the Domesday Monachorum and White Book of St Augustine', *Archaeologia Cantiana*, xlv (1933), 60–89; T. Tatton-Brown, 'The churches of Canterbury diocese in the 11th century', in Blair (ed.), *Local Church in Transition*.

data is its close consistency with the known eleventh-century geography. In areas of established settlement the thirteenth-century complement of churches is almost complete in the Domesday record (Fig. 3); gaps left to be filled by churches first recorded between 1086 and *c.* 1140 are mainly in those Wealden areas where charters show rapid growth of settlement during the same years, and in a strongly marked line of villages on the dip-slope of the North Downs which were probably at a formative stage in the late eleventh century (Fig. 4).[47] So consistent a pattern could scarcely have emerged if the Domesday listing was not at least some 80 per cent complete. Since mother-church rights were notably strong in Kent, but weak in Surrey,[48] the contrast between the Domesday data for the two counties accords with the present hypothesis.

When more minster *parochiae* have been reassembled, more of the early medieval landscape has been reconstructed, and patterns within the Domesday text have been better analysed, it should become possible to see if any real principles of selection underlie its record of churches. Local studies to provide the parochial and economic context will be needed more urgently once computers have brought the material into a manageable form. It will be important to remember that however much we improve our manipulation of the data, this complex and developing society can never be understood simply by examining its state during a few months in 1086. Even as the commissioners toured England, its regions were moving, through various stages and at various speeds, towards the parochial system which was to crystallise during the next century.

---

[47] For the context see Blair, *Early Medieval Surrey*, Ch. II.

[48] See the contrasting verdicts on eleventh-century minster organisation in the two counties in: Tatton-Brown, 'Churches of Canterbury Diocese', and Blair, *Early Medieval Surrey*, Ch. IV.

The Taxation of Moneyers
under Edward the Confessor and in 1086*

D. M. METCALF

IN 1901 W. J. Andrew published a wide-ranging article about the coins of Henry I, 502 pages in length.[1] This took up the entire annual volume of the Royal Numismatic Society's *Numismatic Chronicle*. In the course of the article Andrew passed in review and discussed fully the evidence of the Domesday Survey relating to moneyers. Apart from Ballard's succinct summary[2] his work remains the only detailed attempt to resolve the historical questions which it raises. In order to explain why payments by the moneyers are mentioned for only about one-fifth of the towns where coins are known to have been struck in the mid-1080s he evolved the theory, which is central to his monograph, that mints were operated in one of two ways. Either they were royal mints, held directly by the king, in which case the moneyers themselves were accountable directly to him for the payment of all fees, rents, and profits; or the mints were farmed to the burgesses or otherwise granted to a lord, in which case there would be no separate royal dues from the moneyers and therefore no occasion to mention them in the Survey. Most mints, he believed, were alienated in one of these ways. Andrew went on to argue that a lord could only exercise the privilege of striking coins when he was within his lordship. If he went abroad, minting had to stop. This in his view explained why some mints were continuously active whereas others seemed to work intermittently. He rejected the explanation that the patchy occurrence of the successive varieties was merely a reflection of a very low survival-rate and that the gaps might one day be filled. Much of his article is then taken up with an attempt to marry, town by town, the dates at which

*I am grateful to Dr Sally Harvey, Dr Pamela Nightingale, Miss Susan Reynolds, and Dr Ian Stewart, MP, each of whom read an earlier draft of this paper and offered numerous very helpful suggestions for improvements. Mr James Campbell made perceptive comments at the lecture, from which the final text has benefited.
[1] W. J. Andrew, 'A numismatic history of the reign of Henry I, 1100–1135', *Numismatic Chronicle* (hereafter *NC*)[4], i (1901), 1–515, 8 Pls.
[2] A. Ballard, *The Domesday Boroughs* (Oxford, 1904).

intermittent minting started and stopped, with the curriculum vitae of the local lord.

In the volume of the *Numismatic Chronicle* for the following year two members of the staff of the Public Record Office, C. G. Crump and C. Johnson, wrote a comment on Andrew's article, five pages long, which was quite exceptionally damaging.[3] They spoke scathingly of his theory that mints not directly in the king's hands could only work when their lord was in England. The number of existing coins was too small, they said, and the movements of the great barons too imperfectly known and their chronology often unascertainable for the theory to be capable of proof. They pointed out a selection of egregious errors which served to show, all too clearly, that Andrew had filled the greater part of his monograph with a cobweb of worthless argument. Sir John Evans and the other editors of the *Numismatic Chronicle* were of course much embarrassed. The psychological impact of the rebuttal on the English numismatic fraternity was profound and has, in a sense, lasted until quite recently. Andrew tendered his resignation from the Society, and it was eventually accepted. In 1903, however, after an almighty row, a certain number of Fellows transferred their allegiance to a new, rival society, the British Numismatic Society[4] – and that is why Britain, unlike other countries, to this day has two learned numismatic societies instead of one.

Crump and Johnson poured scorn on Andrew, but they did not actually disprove his hypothesis. To disprove that a baron had to be present in this country in order to exercise the privilege of minting, all that is necessary is to produce some coins that can be dated to periods when he was certainly abroad. The chronology of Henry I's coins has been extensively revised since Andrew wrote[5] and more material is available through the publication of the Stockholm collection.[6] Examples can now be offered from half a dozen mints which demolish his position.[7]

The suggestion that most mints were omitted from the Survey because they had been granted away is implausible. Complicated and various as

---

[3] C. G. Crump and C. Johnson, 'Notes on "A numismatic history of the reign of Henry I" by W. J. Andrew', *NC*[4], ii (1902), 372–7; 'Errata . . .', ibid., III (1903), 99.

[4] R. A. G. Carson, 'A history of the Royal Numismatic Society', *NC*[7], xvi (1976), xii–xv.

[5] G. C. Brooke, *A Catalogue of Coins in the British Museum. The Norman Kings* (2 vols., 1916) i. is a fundamental study. For a summary incorporating subsequent revisions, see M. Dolley, *The Norman Conquest and the English Coinage* (1966), 21–9, and, for a listing of mints and moneyers, J. J. North, *English Hammered Coinage, c. 600–1272* (2nd edn 1980), 155–62. Further revisions are being debated, which would have the effect of pushing most or all Henry I's types except xv progressively a little earlier. This would not affect the cases *contra* Andrew. See D. Walker, 'A possible monetary crisis in the early 1130's', *Seaby Coin and Medal Bulletin* (1984), 284–6; J. D. Gomm, 'Henry I chronology: the case for reappraisal', ibid. (1985), 105–7; D. Walker, 'Christmas 1124: end of Henry I Type XIV?', ibid., 232–3.

[6] C. E. Blunt and M. Dolley, 'Royal Coin Cabinet, Stockholm. Anglo-Norman Pennies', *SCBI*, xi (1969).

[7] Chester, Chichester, Gloucester, and Hastings afford useful proofs.

lordship and the exercise of power in towns were, it seems clear enough that a distinct majority of the mints were in towns where the king's interests were dominant or where revenues were shared between king and lord.[8] (Domesday Book does after all treat towns quite separately at the beginning of its account of each shire.) In all those towns where the king retained a substantial interest it is very difficult to believe, if moneying yielded a revenue, that the king had no share of it, even if Domesday Book is silent on the subject.

It is of course not in question that the king retained full authority over the design, weight-standard, and alloy of the coinage at all mints, and that it is only the way the revenues from minting accrued that is uncertain. These revenues were sometimes alienated by the king, both before and after the Conquest, in one of three ways. First, a bishop or an abbot might have a moneyer.[9] This was a venerable but restricted tradition going back to the eighth century if not earlier, and it did not become widespread. Secondly, the earl might have his third penny of the fees paid by a moneyer to the king, and presumably of any other customary payments similarly. This arrangement shows us that, bishop's moneyers aside, the king was prepared to regard revenues from the mints as part of the total royal revenues from towns, i.e. that mints or their moneyers were thought of as appertaining to towns. Thirdly, if the lordship of a town was granted completely to a tenant-in-chief, he received some if not all of the revenues connected with the mint.

Also by 1066, it appears that the burgesses might farm the customs of their town including certain annual payments due from the moneyers.

It is well known that William I continued the minting arrangements which had existed in the time of King Edward almost to the letter. The design of the coinage was still changed at intervals of two or three years, and moneyers were to be found in all large towns and in some smaller ones – and even in one or two places that could hardly be described as towns.[10] The relative importance of the various mints and the geographical pattern of monetary circulation also continued essentially unchanged.[11] William at first no doubt simply adopted the existing fiscal arrangements for drawing profit from the mints, in particular the fee which each moneyer paid for his new dies when the design was changed. But at a number of mints in towns which were farmed to the burgesses he appears to have raised the level of taxation very steeply, probably at a date before c. 1077 (by when, at the latest, the weight

[8] This emerges from the lists of boroughs in Ballard, op. cit. (note 21), 9f and 118–20 (not to be relied on for numismatic information), and from his text passim.

[9] The statement in Domesday Book that the bishop of Hereford had a moneyer and that the bishop of East Anglia was allowed to have one are among the most surprising evidence that the text affords, and they raise the difficult question whether other bishops were similarly privileged. In any case, it is virtually certain that not more than five per cent of the output of coinage was alienated in this way.

[10] The system is described in Dolley (1966).

[11] D. M. Metcalf, 'Continuity and change in English monetary history, c. 973–1086', British Numismatic Journal l (1980), 20–49; ibid., li (1981), 52–90, especially at 55 and 84–5.

of the sterling penny had been increased from what it was at the beginning of the reign, and stabilized).[12]

William did this by extending a practice that was already in existence before 1066, and which involved, coupled with the general farm of the town, another payment which looks like an annual farm of the mint. It has been interpreted in that way, but it would be more cautious and perhaps more accurate to describe it simply as a tax. The Domesday Book account of Huntingdon uses a phrase which seems to imply some quite radical change in the existing arrangements, when it says that King William 'laid the *geldum monete* on the town' – 'geldum monete posuit in burgo'. Now, *geldum monete* might be construed to mean 'a tax of money', a money tax as opposed to a tax in kind, but I think that this strains the obvious sense, namely that *geldum monete* means 'the tax of the mint'. Whereas moneyers had been taxed personally in respect of their office, William laid the tax of the mint on the town. Another construction of the phrase *geldum monete* which has been suggested sees in it a possible reference to the *monetagium*. There are difficulties, however, in converting the *monetagium* from a hearth tax into an urban tax. In any case, what King William actually did, as exemplified by the detailed evidence (to which we will have to return), could certainly be described as laying upon some towns a tax *de moneta*, which in some entries is specifically said to be payable by the moneyers. So unless we envisage the moneyers as the collectors of the *monetagium*, the interpretation falls. We may rest the case, therefore, on the details of payments in other towns, and accept the Huntingdon entry simply as providing a neat phrase which sums up a conclusion that has to be demonstrated elsewhere. William laid the tax of the mint on the town. If that is correct, it is crucial to the whole topic. It may be the only important change that he made in the arrangements for minting, which otherwise continued undisturbed.

The *monetagium*, to digress briefly, seems to have been in theory an extortion under threat, a kind of protection money. In practice it was just one more form of general taxation, and it was as totally unrelated to the work of the moneyers as the present-day tax on vehicles known as the Road Fund is unrelated in reality to the building or repair of roads.

Personal taxation of moneyers TRE; collective taxation of the moneyers of a town in 1086: that is the drift of what the Domesday Book entries tell us. There was a change of emphasis, but little or no innovation. But we are left

---

[12] The date *c.* 1077 refers to the introduction of the 'Sword' type, Type VI. P. Grierson, 'Sterling', in *Anglo-Saxon Coins*, ed. R. H. M. Dolley (1961), 266–83, at 274–5 claims that with this type the weight was increased from 21.5 to 22.5 grains. This proposition has recently been given further currency and support by P. Nightingale, who notes, however, following C. S. S. Lyon, that in practice the average weight of the heavier (i.e. later) coins was only about 1.39 g (21.5 gr.). Even this is optimistic. The well-preserved 'PAXS' coins in the Beauworth hoard, which are very carefully weight-adjusted, have a modal weight no higher than 21.3 gr. (1.38 g). It is difficult to collect up enough suitable material to calculate comparable modal values for, e.g. Types V and VI. Mr Lyon's careful statement, 'During the second half of his reign the standard is noticeably raised to about twenty-one per ounce (*c.* 21¼ grains)' is authoritative and is as far as one should go. In other words, the metrological evidence for any marked change in *c.* 1077, at the beginning of Type VI, as opposed to by *c.* 1077, is tenuous.

with severe problems of historical interpretation, which arise because we have to decide whether that is the whole story. Did all the mints pay a tax TRE as well as moneyers' fees, or only some? When William reassessed the tax on farmed towns, did the new tax of the mint include and supersede the fee payable when the design of the coinage was changed? That is the natural reading of the text, but is the text misleading? Was the traditional fee still payable by moneyers in other towns? Without comprehensive answers to these questions we cannot judge the total level of taxation on minting TRE, nor can we assess the scale of the changes that William made. It is impossible to answer the questions with certainty, or even adequately, but we can perhaps narrow the options by attempting to set minting arrangements into context in the evidence about taxation of the towns, and into the context, also, of what we can learn from the coins themselves.

Let us turn next to the coins. It may not be fully appreciated how scarce Norman coins are today in comparison with those of, for example, Æthelred II or Cnut – as of course they are also in comparison with coins of the thirteenth century. This may be partly because fewer were made, but it is mainly because fewer were any longer carried to Scandinavia, to turn up in hoards found there.[13] William's coins have had a very low survival rate – with the conspicuous exception of one particular issue, the eighth of his reign, about which we are extremely well informed because of an enormous hoard found in 1833 at Beauworth, five or six miles SE of Winchester, and consisting of upwards of 8,000 specimens almost exclusively of that type. They come from virtually every mint in England, and each coin, of course, carries the name of its moneyer.[14] The British Museum had their pick of the hoard, and carefully selected one of every variety that seemed in any way different.[15] Numismatists are disposed to believe that the 'PAXS' type, introduced perhaps in the autumn of 1083, was still current or had just been superseded at the time of the Domesday Inquisition in 1086. It is surprisingly difficult to offer any direct evidence for either the dates or the length of time that the type was current. The only clue seems to be a unique coin of the Cardiff mint of Type VI, found in the grounds of Cardiff castle, and which arguably was not minted before 1081. In any event, the correspondence of Type VIII with the Inquisition is close enough, and affords a most fortunate opportunity, of course, to compare what Domesday Book says about moneyers with the situation on the ground.

On that basis we can say that the English coinage at the time of the Inquisition was being produced at some 65 mints,[16] of which only 26 are

---

[13] The evidence that there was not a dramatic decline in output after 1066, relieved only sporadically, e.g. by the 'PAXS' type, is to be found in the statistics of stray finds, which are likely to be casual or accidental losses. They continue at much the same level as in the time of Edward the Confessor. See Metcalf, 'Continuity and change', 47.
[14] An invaluable account of the hoard was published by E. Hawkins in *Archaeologia*, xxvi, and is reprinted in R. Ruding, *Annals of the Coinage of Great Britain*, 3rd edn., i. (1840), 151–61.
[15] The museum acquired some 600 coins. Out of another sixty coins of the type without a formal Beauworth provenance, about fifty may well have come from the hoard.
[16] See North, op. cit. (note 5).

mentioned in Domesday. There were roughly 165 moneyers, whom we know by name, and those names are predominantly Old English (84 per cent) or Old Norse (12 per cent) with no sign of an increase in Continental Germanic, i.e. Norman names since the time of King Edward, even in towns where Norman burgesses are mentioned.[17] Had there been an influx of Norman names as old moneyers relinquished office and new men took over, one would have had to conclude that the Conqueror's men were infiltrating, for the change could hardly have been put down to new fashions in name-giving. Few men can have achieved the serious responsibilities of being a moneyer below the age of twenty; but in any case the question does not arise: the proportion of Continental Germanic names shows no increase. This has been seen by Oman as evidence that the towns suffered less dislocation from the Conquest than did the ownership of land,[18] and although his argument was sketchy it may be pointing in the right direction. If the king's approval was necessary for the licensing of a new moneyer (and we have no way of knowing whether such matters came to his attention), he could through the processes of natural wastage over twenty years have introduced a good many of his own nominees, without in any way depriving honest men of the enjoyment of office. But for obvious and sensible reasons moneying was a job that was kept within the family where possible, and it may have required a commercial background to make a success of it.

Although moneyers put their own name on their coins and were individually punishable, it seems that each town had a fixed establishment of moneyers, varying little over decades.[19] There were one-moneyer mints, two-moneyer mints, and so on up to a normal complement of seven at Canterbury and eight at London. Domesday Book implies that the sheriff or other authorities dealt with the moneyers of a town as a group for revenue purposes. In that sense at least we can speak of 'the mint', meaning the moneyers as a group. The Winchester material suggests, however, that moneyers might be working on separate premises.[20] Our idea of a mint as an institution with its own precincts is probably anachronistic until the middle of the twelfth century. It might be nearer the truth to say that each moneyer made coins on his own premises, upon demand, when customers came to his door.

[17] With the possible exception of Howard at Norwich. For the normalisation and interpretation of the moneyers' names, see V. Smart, *Cumulative Index of Volumes 1–20, SCBI*, xxviii (1981).

[18] C. Oman, *The Coinage of England* (1931, 1967), 80f.: 'The wealthy citizen-class in England did not suffer as did the land-holding families.'

[19] A. Freeman, *The Moneyer and the Mint in the Reign of Edward the Confessor, 1042–1066* (British Archaeological Reports, British Series, 145; Oxford, 1985), in a work of nearly 600 pages, has 'namierised' Edward's moneyers. For the Norman period, the evidence can be studied in the tables in Brooke, *Catalogue*, cxcvi–ccli. For the reign of William I it is summarised (or interpreted) in Dolley, *Norman Conquest*, 13f., and cf. Brooke, *Catalogue*, clxxxviii.

[20] The Winton Survey records, 'Et in mercato fuerunt v monete, que fuerunt diffacte precepto regis'. Even the Winchester material is not without its difficulties, however, because Winchester moneyers often shared the same obverse die, which they are rather unlikely to have done unless they were working on the same premises.

The 'PAXS' type was struck from upwards of 550 reverse dies, each capable of striking (let us say, at a conservative estimate) on average 10,000 coins, but that multiplier could be in error by quite a large factor. The 'best guess' that has been estimated statistically for the number of reverse dies is 880. If we make the calculation by a different route, by taking the proportion of dies in the Swedish collection that are not represented in the British Museum *Catalogue*, and increasing the total there by that proportion, the result is convergent.[21] We are perhaps speaking, then, of eight or nine million coins with a face value of £35,000 to £40,000. Some of the total was carried abroad and thus lost to the English currency, which was probably renewed quite thoroughly when the 'PAXS' type was introduced. With the exception of the rare coins minted in south Wales, all the dies were made centrally (in London), as we may judge from an analysis of their style, which is not susceptible of being interpreted in terms of more than one die-cutting centre.[22]

Notice that 880 dies is a small number when set against upwards of 8000 coins in the Beauworth hoard: the hoard was large enough to contain several specimens from every die that was ever used. Our knowledge of the 'PAXS' type ought therefore to be statistically more than 99 per cent complete, if it were not for two possible blind spots. First, the Beauworth hoard could have been concealed before the end of the issue of 'PAXS' coins, in which case there might be dies and even moneyers not represented in it.[23] Secondly, mints distant from Hampshire may be inadequately represented. Both these points are amenable to research.

Notice also the implications of the low survival rate of types other than 'PAXS'. Of the seventh type, the British Museum *Catalogue* has only thirty-five specimens – a wildly inadequate sample even to discover the number of mints.

[21] The *BM Catalogue* includes fewer obverse than reverse dies. If it were a random sample it would point towards a 2:1 die ratio. The Stockholm coins add more new obverse than reverse dies, which is contrary to what might have been expected, and shows that the British Museum chose 'varieties' (i.e. legend varieties) but did not attempt to choose a specimen of every different obverse die (the legends being the same). The Ashmolean Museum coins in *SCBI, Oxford* support the same argument. For the estimate of 880, see Metcalf, 'Continuity and change'.

[22] Brooke changed his mind about this, and therefore felt the need to discuss the problem at some length, *Catalogue*, cxxxv–cxl. Much work has subsequently been done on die-cutting styles and 'centres' in late Anglo-Saxon England, and students would now, I think, accept that the 'PAXS' dies emanate from a single centre, except, of course, for the Cardiff, St Davids, and (?) Abergavenny coins – which M. Dolley reattributed to the Welsh Marches, but which have now been firmly reinstated in G. C. Boon, *Welsh Hoards, 1979–1981* (Cardiff, 1986), 40 and 46–8, not omitting 66f., note 38. That the main die-cutting centre was in London and not, e.g. in Winchester is evidenced by the DB entry for Worcester. Half-a-dozen or more minor variations of style are recognisable in the plates of the BM *Catalogue* but none of them is limited to one region, with the possible or partial exception of Exeter coins.

[23] The mint of Guildford (moneyer Særic) was not represented among the coins acquired by the British Museum direct from the Beauworth hoard, but it is virtually certain that BM *Catalogue* 690 is from the hoard. At Malmesbury the Tamworth hoard adds Sæweard. At Stafford Godric is missing (the Beauworth hoard had only two specimens of this mint). The few Tamworth hoard coins that the museum acquired often share dies with Beauworth specimens – which must not be assumed, however, to have been selected rigorously as die-varieties.

In principle the coins of the 'PAXS' type give us a far more complete, exact and unbiased view of the work of the English mints than Domesday Book does. But on the administrative arrangements for controlling the moneyers and for collecting the profits they are inevitably silent. In that sense the coins and the text are complementary. The coins themselves could never tell us how minting was taxed. They can, arguably, be used to prove that what Domesday Book records is very incomplete. And they can give us a financial perspective, by providing quantitative statistics against which to form an impression of whether taxation was heavy or light, and whether it was equitable.

Andrew's strategy of matching the Domesday Book evidence against the evidence of the coins, borough by borough, was fallible because of the nature of Domesday Book. There was (as we can now appreciate) probably little occasion for information about the mints to be entered in the record. The Treasury may be presumed to have held other records, no longer surviving, which listed the king's dues and revenues, including those from the mints. The towns in many cases were omitted from the Domesday Inquisition because they had been surveyed separately or because the king's interests were not in dispute. At Winchester, that earlier survey has been tentatively dated on the evidence of the moneyers' names, which should of course correspond with those on the coins, to c. 1057.[24] Summaries abstracted from the earlier records were added to Domesday Book, and brief information about the mint was sometimes included in the summary.[25] Normally it was omitted. It is very difficult to believe that at those towns where it was omitted the mint yielded no revenue. The alternative seems to be that the abstracting was not consistent.

Unless one could show that the mints mentioned in Domesday Book are there for some special reason or reasons, and that these did not apply to the mints omitted, there is no progress to be made along that line.

The existing evidence is little enough. Moneyers are mentioned here and there in the text of Domesday Book as private individuals paying rent or occupying property, but about their official activities there are only a few hundred words. For twenty-six boroughs we have a sentence each or at most two or three sentences in the text. There are limits to what one can hope to do with so little. After checking each statement against the coins to make sure that it is not at variance with them we can compare the entries with each other for consistency. When we do that, it becomes evident that the same or similar administrative arrangements are variously described. The form of words varies, and at some boroughs it is fuller or more explicit than at others. Where there are apparent inconsistencies (and this is the nub of the problem) we have to decide, essentially by common sense, whether it is more probable that the inconsistencies are real, e.g. because particular local arrangements had been permitted to survive, or that the information in the text is

[24] *WS*, i. 9–10.
[25] Harvey (1971), 753–73, at 767–71.

deceptive, either because memory has played the witnesses false, or because those conducting the Survey did not grasp clearly what they were being told, or because the information has been misleadingly summarized. At Hereford, for example, but nowhere else, we are told that when the king came into the city, the moneyers were to make as many coins for him as he chose – that is, from the king's own silver – and they were also under obligation to accompany the sheriff on military expeditions into Wales. Whether they went as fighting men or as moneyers is not made clear. The latter seems distinctly possible, for we have a coin of Rufus struck at Rhyd-y-gors, the lowest fording-place of the Towy just below Carmarthen, and coins of the Conqueror attributable to Abergavenny, Cardiff and St Davids, all apparently by the same moneyer, Ælfwine de Turre.

What the first part of the Hereford entry means, no doubt, is that the moneyers were obliged to work for the king without fee, and this is perhaps a local peculiarity. Medieval moneyers could only work when customers brought bullion to them. The coins produced from the customer's silver were handed back to him, but the moneyer retained a fee of perhaps a shilling or eighteen pence in the pound to cover his working expenses and the king's profit. At Hereford the king appears (unusually) in the rôle of customer, but a customer to whom in special circumstances the moneyers have traditional obligations. The arrangement may have originated in the need to coin silver taken in tribute from the Welsh, or it may be merely to do with military needs on expeditions.

The basic financial arrangement before the Conquest, about which the text admits of no doubt, is that moneyers had to buy their new dies, and pay a flat fee, when the type was changed – that is, at an interval of either two or three years. The system is, again, described most fully in the entry for Hereford, where we read

> Seven moneyers were there. One of these was the bishop's moneyer. When the money was renewed each of them gave 18s. to receive dies: and at the end of one month from the day on which they returned each of them gave the king 20s. And similarly the bishop had 20s. from his moneyer.[26]

This seems to mean that each moneyer paid 18s for his pair of dies of the new design, and then had a month's grace, from the day he returned to Hereford, before he was required to pay the king's fee of 20s, presumably with the help of the profits he had accumulated by using the new die. The 18s was in respect of the cost of supplying the die, and could be seen as defraying the running costs of the die-cutting establishment, which was in London. The fee was presumably handed over locally, perhaps to the sheriff. The bishop's moneyer obtained his dies from London like everyone else, but paid his fee of 20s to the bishop. This interpretation of the text is buttressed by the entries for Worcester and for Shrewsbury (on the same circuit?) which speak

---

[26] DB, i. 179a.

specifically about payment at London and about buying the dies like the other moneyers of the country:

> In the city of Worcester King Edward had this custom. When the money was changed each moneyer gave 20s. at London to receive the dies of the coinage.[27]

And in Shrewsbury

> The king had three moneyers there, who, after they had bought the dies of the coinage like the other moneyers of the country, fifteen days later gave the king 20s. each. And this was done when the money was changed.[28]

It is, I think, the common-sense assumption that moneyers at all mints would have had to make similar if not identical payments for their dies, and one may suppose that at some stage when the system was set up or reformed they would all have been expected to pay the same fee of 20s, as a tax on moneying.

There are misunderstandings and discrepancies: the Worcester entry, perhaps describing a procedure not fully understood or remembered, perhaps on the basis of oral evidence by someone who was not a moneyer, telescopes the two stages. At Shrewsbury the period of grace is only a fortnight.

At the four Dorset boroughs, namely Bridport, Dorchester, Shaftesbury and Wareham, and nowhere else, a single concise formula is repeated at each: 'rendering to the king one mark of silver and 20s. when the money was changed'.[29] Two interpretations are possible. Either the mark of silver and the 20s were both payable when the money was changed, in which case the mark of silver is perhaps the payment for the die, loosely described as a payment to the king (cf. the inaccuracy at Worcester); or it is a separate and presumably annual tax, in which case the formula omits to mention that the dies had to be bought. Each moneyer paid a mark.

At Hereford, no tax is mentioned, possibly because the moneyers were under the obligation of expedition service in lieu. Was something similar true at Worcester and Shrewsbury, where again no tax is mentioned, or is the Domesday Book summary incomplete on this point? If the Dorset entries were all the evidence that moneyers at many mints paid a tax as well as a fee TRE, some doubt would remain.

There is also, however, the evidence of Colchester, where the town was farmed by the burgesses TRE for £15 5s 3d which included £4 from the moneyers; Ipswich, where the moneyers similarly paid £4 per annum for the mint; Huntingdon, where there used to be three moneyers paying 40s between the king and the earl, 'but now they are not'; and Chester, where there were seven moneyers who paid £7 to the king and earl, 'beyond their farm', when the money was changed. In the three southern Danelaw mints one can perhaps detect traces of a system of payments of £4 or £2, and it is possible that Colchester and Ipswich were four-moneyer mints and Huntingdon a two-moneyer mint, later upgraded to three moneyers during

[27] DB, i. 172a.
[28] DB, i. 252a.
[29] DB, i. 75a.

the reign of Edward. It is in any case certain that, if the mark of silver is a tax, the tax was assessed differently here and in the Dorset boroughs. If there was an annual tax and a triennial or biennial fee, both of 20s, the possibilities of confusion in the record are enhanced.

The twenty-shilling fee, which presumably applied to all or almost all moneyers in the time of King Edward, is otherwise mentioned in Domesday Book only at Lewes.

In practical terms a pair of dies which cost the moneyer 38s and a journey to London, plus an annual tax of up to 20s, could be used by him to produce thousands of coins before the dies wore out, provided that sufficient customers presented themselves at his door with silver to be coined. He will have charged them at a rate which was presumably standard at mints throughout the country. From what we know of later medieval charges, and the little we know of Carolingian practice, it might have been a shilling or 1s 6d in the pound, but we have no contemporary information on this point. At the figure of 10,000 coins, which has become common currency as a guess at the average output of a reverse die, a shilling charge would yield just over £2. Out of this the moneyer also had to pay for fuel, crucibles and staff before he began to make any profit for himself.

It begins to look, therefore, as if the work of the moneyers was heavily taxed without any question of the king collecting in addition a fee from each pound of silver minted. If the moneyer worked in his own premises any such fee would have been a voluntary tax, unless a second official of outstanding probity stood over him night and day.

If when the moneyers received their dies they had received not a pair but a set, consisting of two upper or reverse dies and one obverse, as was the standard practice later in the middle ages, our calculations of profitability would be materially altered. The evidence is, however, unambiguously of a die-ratio close to one-to-one.

Most moneyers used more than one pair of dies to strike the 'PAXS' type – at a smallish mint, three or four, but in London or Winchester each man might wear out as many as a dozen or more reverses in the three years – and this raises further practical questions. Did they have to buy these dies at 18s each, travelling to London to obtain them? If so should we expect to find signs, in the coins, that they thriftily went on using dies until they were excessively worn? Perhaps not: it was not the face of the die that wore out, but the end hit by the hammer flaked away until, like the stub of a pencil, the die was too short to hold comfortably. Could the prudent moneyer buy several dies at a time? (Might this explain why Beorhtweard, at Bristol, uses five different reverses with the same obverse – or why Æthelstan at Winchester similarly uses four reverses, having muled one of those four with an obsolete obverse of the preceding type?) Are we to imagine 160 moneyers, when the type was changed, queuing up at the workshop door while each told the die-sinker his name and town, to be punched into the almost complete die while he waited?

On a rough calculation using the figures of one shilling in the pound and 10,000 coins per die, it looks as if the break-even point into profitability would not have been reached until the moneyer had fully used a minimum of five or six dies within a three-year period. It may be that a shilling in the pound is too low a guess, or that the notional average of 10,000 coins per die is too low, and we may recall the well-documented annual averages of 14,000 to 20,000 per reverse die in the fourteenth century.

If 10,000 is anywhere near the mark, there will undoubtedly have been years when some moneyers, at mints where there was little demand, will have failed to recoup the costs of their office by striking coins. Being a moneyer may have brought them valuable business contacts, which made it worthwhile to sustain the loss. It is not clear whether they could escape their fee for some issues by opting out, and later opt in again. At a busy mint, on the other hand, if the tax was the same as elsewhere, being a moneyer was moderately profitable.

Royal revenue from the mints TRE will have depended on the number of moneyers in commission at each recoinage. Unless Domesday Book gives a distorted picture, it will have been at most about £160, once every two or three years, plus at most about the same annually in tax, much of the grand total being subject to the earl's third penny – on average, something of the order of £150 a year on a two-year cycle or £125 a year on a three-year cycle.

Total taxation (shared by the king and the earl) of £200–£250 a year may seem an implausibly low share of the profits from 800–1000 dies. That may be an overestimate of the number of dies in the later part of Edward's reign: close estimates cannot at present be worked out. (And the last type, current in 1065, would seem to have been struck from only two or three hundred dies.) Domesday Book is silent about the incidence of an annual tax TRE at the major mints of London, Lincoln, York and Canterbury, which between them used half or more of the national total of dies. If the king was aware of how profitable it was to be a busy moneyer, and taxed those mints more heavily, the national total for annual tax may have been rather greater than Domesday Book reveals. But that is mere speculation, based on the belief that Edward would not have neglected to take as much tax from the business of minting as it would bear.

Next let us turn to the other half of the evidence, the payments made by moneyers in 1086, the 'now' of the Domesday Book.

Only a single entry, for Lewes, indicates (apparently) that the fee when the types were changed was still payable. 'And for new money', the entry reads, '112s'). This is the single most difficult piece of Domesday evidence relating to the taxation of moneyers. In 1086 dies were still being cut centrally, and there can be virtually no doubt that moneyers had to obtain their dies from London in the same way as before. Presumably they had to pay for them. The question that is difficult to answer is whether at some mints, but not at others, the triennial fee to the king had been abolished or incorporated into some sort of composition fee. The figure of 112s does not suggest any obvious answers. Lewes in 1086 seems to have been a three-moneyer mint, and the text appears to be saying that each moneyer paid 112s, for it contrasts that figure 'now' with 20s from each moneyer TRE. Are we to believe that some mints continued under the old system, paying an increased fee when the money was changed, while other mints were excused? All we can say is that elsewhere there is no mention of the triennial fee among the taxes described.

Lewes apart, we find a dozen entries which describe payments relating to the mints 'now', i.e. in 1086. They are nearly all places where the borough paid a round sum compounding for all or most of its customs, plus another round sum for the mint.[30] The two payments are run together into a formula varying slightly from place to place, but in the general form, 'Now it pays £30 and £10 for the mint', or 'Now it returns £60 and from the mint the king has £20'. The standard figure for this supplementary payment in the farmed boroughs where it is recorded is £20, but in one case it is £10, in another £40, and in another £75. At Bath William held the borough and the mint rendered 100s – possibly another sub-multiple of £20, for Bath was only a two-moneyer mint. The still smaller mint of Malmesbury also rendered 100s, which was paid by the burgesses. The figures fall so much into a pattern that one may suppose there was a systematic purpose in imposing similar payments on boroughs and their mints as far apart as Ipswich, Leicester and Gloucester.

In one instance only, namely at Leicester, the payment is stated to be annual. That is, however, the natural reading of the text elsewhere, and that is how the text was construed by Andrew and by Ballard. It is supported by the entry for Colchester, referred to above, which records that the burgesses TRE farmed the borough of the king for £15 5s 3d which included the sum of £4 from the moneyers. That statement is circumstantial, and we must accept, therefore, that William's reform was not a novelty, but was simply the extension of an administrative practice that existed before the Conquest. What was new was the level of the exactions. The standard figure of £20, if charged annually, was a very heavy imposition, far in excess of the profitability of most if not all mints, on almost any reading of the evidence.

Lincoln, as we know with some certainty from Mossop's corpus, used only about 18 dies in the 'PAXS' type, but is said to pay £75, which works out at a probable average of £13 per die. If Domesday Book is reporting the results of the Inquisition, and not merely abstracting some earlier document, this was very rough justice; it suggests that the rates had been fixed before c. 1077, until when the mint had a much larger complement of moneyers – eight rather than two. (York similarly was cut back from a dozen moneyers to four in c. 1070.[31] What tax they paid is unfortunately not known.)

The mints paying £20 a year similarly each used, so far as we can judge, about twenty dies during the currency of the 'PAXS' type – a level of taxation of probably about £4 a die. Life can sometimes be very unfair, and it may have been apparent to one and all that this tax on the moneyers could not

---

[30] Bath, 100s, DB, i. 114a; Colchester and Maldon (together or severally?) £20, DB, i. 107b; Leicester, £20 a year *de xx in ora*, DB, i. 230a; Lincoln, £75, DB, i. 336b; Nottingham, £10, DB, i. 280a; Oxford(shire), £20 in pence *de xx in ora*; Thetford, £40, DB, i. 119a; Wallingford? (assessed at £60 but pays £80), DB, i. 56b.

[31] R. H. M. Dolley, 'A further die-link within the York mint in the so-called "Paxs" type of William I' *Numismatic Circular*, lxvii (1959), 227.

be derived from the profits of minting. And yet, it seems to have been on the moneyers rather than the burgesses in general that it fell. The payment at Leicester is 'from the moneyers' and at Ipswich it was 'the moneyers' who 'ought to pay £20'. If they were men of greater substance than the other burgesses, the king may have seen fit to tax them more heavily, knowing that they profited indirectly from holding office. But he did not always succeed in collecting the sum that he had in mind. At Ipswich again, the moneyers had fallen into arrears: 'in four years they have paid only £27'.

If we assume that Domesday Book is related in this respect to the numismatic evidence from *c*. 1074–7, the payments at Lincoln and elsewhere seem to be more or less in accordance with the numbers of moneyers then in office. Thetford, paying double the standard amount, was the only six-moneyer mint on the list. Gloucester, Ipswich and Oxford, paying £20, were four-moneyer mints. Nottingham, paying £10, was only a two-moneyer mint. The going rate, with exceptions, was £5 a year for each moneyer. (Going back for a moment to Lewes, we may note that perhaps the simplest explanation of the figure of 112*s* compared with 20*s* is that it is reporting, in a slightly confused way, a tax of £5 a year for each moneyer plus 12*s* a year or 36*s* over three years payable at the change of type.) If Colchester and Maldon paid £20 between them, rather than £20 each, it may be because both were two-moneyer mints in *c*. 1077 (although Colchester had risen to four by 1086, while the Maldon mint had by 1086 apparently fallen on thin times). Leicester, paying £20, seems to have been a one-moneyer mint, even though Domesday Book speaks of moneyers in the plural, and as it apparently used only two or three sets of dies was in any case grievously over-taxed in comparison with, for example, nearby Nottingham. At Oxford the tax is apparently laid on the shire rather than the borough; and at nearby Wallingford, which was assessed at £60 but paid £80, it is an obvious conjecture that the difference of £20 was in respect of the mint (and paid annually?).

At Leicester and at Oxford the payment of £20 is specified as being '*de xx in ora*'. Dr Nightingale has argued persuasively that this refers to a new and higher weight-standard introduced by William with his sixth coin type, in *c*. 1077.[32] Presumably the same requirement was laid on other boroughs, to pay in coins of good weight, even if it is not so specified in Domesday Book.

If the level of taxation recorded at Lincoln, Leicester, Thetford, Colchester, Ipswich, Oxford, and Gloucester was applied generally across the country,

---

[32] P. Nightingale, 'The evolution of weight standards and the creation of new monetary and commercial links in northern Europe from the tenth century to the twelfth century', *Econ. HR*, 2nd ser., xxxviii (1985), 192–209, at 201. The argument is further developed in P. Nightingale, 'The ora, the mark, and the mancus: weight-standards and the coinage in eleventh-century England', *NC*, cxliii (1983), 248–57. The evidence of the exact date at which the weight of the penny was increased is not, in my view, clear. See note 12 above. By *c*. 1077, twenty pennies weighing on average about 1.35 g would make up an ora weighing about 27 g. Perhaps *ad numerum de viginti in ora* does not mean literally by tale: the receiver, in other words, put a ten-ora weight in the scale, and the tax-payer poured in enough pennies to tip the balance. Twenty per ora should have been exactly right, and it saved time and trouble to put the onus on the tax-payer.

William was attempting to derive an income in excess of £750 a year, perhaps even in excess of £1000 a year, ostensibly from the profits of minting. That would be roughly a three- or fourfold increase in the level of taxation. It could, of course, have been recouped, and the moneyers might have been treated equitably, if William had sanctioned an increase in the customer's fee for each pound of silver minted. No information on that point survives. The moneyers certainly did not venture to make ends meet by tampering with the quality of the coins. Anyone who felt like complaining would do well to reflect that it might be even worse.

Lesser lords were more restrained. From the Taunton mint, which struck more coins than Bath or Malmesbury, the bishop of Winchester took a tax of 50s, while at Pevensey the earl of Mortain received only 20s.

Towns in Domesday Book[1]

SUSAN REYNOLDS

THE TITLE OF this paper is 'Towns in Domesday Book', not 'Boroughs in Domesday Book', and I shall start by arguing that the distinction is a significant one. It involves ideas as well as words. Although the usages of the words 'town' and 'borough' overlap, the range of their meanings is different and the ideas or concepts which they represent can be distinguished – and need to be if we are to make sense of Domesday. The word 'town' in modern British English is one which is normally used to describe a type of human settlement which is found in many different societies and periods. When we talk of a place as a town, or as urban, we normally, I think, assume without thinking about it that we are talking about a permanent human settlement in which a significant proportion of the population is engaged in non-agricultural occupations – characteristically in a variety of trades and industries and probably in some administrative, political and professional work too. A town therefore normally lives off the food of the surrounding countryside (though of course it may import some from further away) and supplies this countryside with other goods and services in return. Its functions as a market centre make it also a convenient centre for religious, administrative and legal purposes, though which of these functions came first in any particular case will vary. Because of the distinctive functions of towns their inhabitants normally regard themselves, and are regarded by outsiders, as a different sort of people. However deeply they are divided among themselves they tend to be united at least in regarding themselves as united in their urbanity against the country bumpkins around.

This may seem a loose definition and one which is rather remote from the problems of Domesday Book. I maintain, however, that 'town' in this loose sense is the best translation of *burgus* in Domesday. I shall come back to that shortly, but first I should like to emphasise that in so far as the definition is loose it is loose because the category itself, though immediately recognisable, is essentially one with a fuzzy edge. Many places may be hard to assign to one side or the other of the urban/rural boundary. In modern terms, is a place a town or a village if it has a handful of shops, one bank and maybe a jobbing

[1] I am grateful to Howard Clarke and Michael Metcalf for reading this paper and commenting on it to me.

builder and a pottery run by a drop-out from the rat-race as its only non-agricultural industries? With a few more shops, a chemist, several banks, and the pottery thriving to take on more staff it will slip over the boundary to urbanness. When it has a Boots it is right over: it is a town. With a Marks and Spencer it is not merely a town but a town which outranks other smaller towns round about. The looseness of the definition does not make it less useful. It is useful precisely because it is not cumbered with any of the characteristics of towns which derive from particular social and political circumstances. The concept represented in everyday use by the word town is therefore one which can be used comparatively when discussing different societies past and present. When we ask whether a particular society had towns we are asking a significant question and the answer will tell us something important about that society. The first necessity is to get clear what we mean by towns in general before we start to distinguish the different sorts of towns and the different characteristics which towns assumed in different societies and circumstances.

When we look at towns in different societies and different periods we are going to see a lot of different things. Physically – in size and buildings and so on – they have differed for many obvious reasons. At some times (like the middle ages) most towns were so small that to us they hardly look like towns at all. Still, if they fulfilled urban functions I would call them towns and we can use our knowledge of towns in general and our ideas about the essence of urbanness to analyse them. In different societies the essential functional and social distinctions between town and country may be marked in different ways: sometimes towns dominate the country, sometimes they are ruled separately. Privileges may be granted to them by some outside authority or acquired in other ways. But all these variations tell us about the circumstances in which towns live: they do not define towns as such. If we get bogged down in the merely local and occasional characteristics of urban life we make comparisons impossible and without comparisons with other societies we can make little sense of each. Charters, special tenures or rules of law, walls, market squares, mints, town halls, or insignia of independence do not define towns. They are characteristics of some towns in particular circumstances.

That is why I would rather talk about Domesday towns than Domesday boroughs. 'Borough' is a word which belongs in a particular society and implies particular legal and constitutional rules. Its connotations are particular, not general, and it is unsuitable for comparative use. *Burgus* in Domesday Book is traditionally translated 'borough', but 'borough' has since 1086 acquired constitutional and legal connotations which have changed as the constitutional and legal circumstances of English towns have changed. It is hard to realise and remember that, if one has been trained, as I was, in the old traditions of constitutional history, but I have to keep reminding myself. Our sort of history grew out of legal history – lawyer's history – and that tended to look for precision through definition, pinning words down like butterflies to stop the distracting flutter of changing usage, changing phenomena and changing ways of looking at them through the centuries. By talking of medieval towns as boroughs we skewer them on the constitutional preoccupations of later historians. The evidence that Domesday Book uses *burgus* in the sense implied by our use of the word borough – that is a place belonging to a recognised category defined by a consistently distinctive status – is to my mind unconvincing. The use of the Old English word *byrig, burh, burg*, etc. the Latin *burgus*, and the later 'borough' is no more of a guide to understanding the origin, development and changing nature of English towns than is the use of the word car and its cognates in tracing the history of vehicles powered by the internal combustion engine. As the objective phenomena – towns or cars – change, the ideas people have about them, and the rules which are made about them, change too, though often patchily and belatedly. Sometimes changes of objective phenomena and of ideas are reflected in changes of vocabulary, sometimes not. Words, concepts, and things all change, but they tend to change out of kilter. Each is a poor guide to the other.

Failure to realise or remember this accounts for a good many of the controversies which surround what are usually called the 'boroughs' of Domesday Book and indeed medieval 'boroughs' in general. I shall therefore start by trying to clear our minds of later associations and by setting the scene of towns, the vocabulary used about them and the ideas of them which that seems to reveal, all as I think it was in 1086. To start with things or objective phenomena: the settlements, and the activities, rights and customs of their inhabitants, irrespective of the particular words used to denote them. It is, I think, established that during the tenth and eleventh centuries there was an increasing number of settlements in England which, although very small by our standards, fulfilled urban functions. They were growing partly because the economy as a whole was growing, partly because royal government was promoting recourse to them for minting, trading, litigation and tax-paying. As a result – and here I move from things to words – people needed to refer to them in many contexts: economic, military, political and presumably also because they were rather obvious landmarks. Old English offered several words for the purpose, notably *byrig* (*burg, burga, burh*, etc.), *ceaster, port* and *wic*. These were traditionally rendered in Latin as *urbs, civitas* and *portus*, but other Latin words were available and sometimes used, and the OE glossaries suggest that the equivalents were never exact. Though *ceaster*, for instance, was normally rendered as *civitas*, someone who wanted to translate *cives* from Latin might use *burhware* or *portmen* instead of *ceasterwara*. By the eleventh century *urbs*, the traditional equivalent of *byrig*, was being varied or superseded by the vernacular-derived *burgus*, though we do not seem to have any record from before 1086 of the associated word *burgenses*, soon to be used all over northern Europe for townsmen.[2]

---

[2] For earlier usage and its implications: J. Campbell, 'Bede's words for places', in P. H. Sawyer, ed., *Names Words and Graves* (Leeds, 1979), 34–54. For tenth- and eleventh-century use see J. Tait, *The Medieval English Borough* (Manchester, 1936), 25–67, and review of F. W. Maitland, *Domesday Book and Beyond*, in *EHR*, xii (1897), 768–77. Tenth- and eleventh-century glossaries are also suggestive, though they show how words in classical or ecclesiastical sources would be translated rather than how to render vernacular words into Latin: R. P. Wülcker, ed., *Anglo-Saxon and Old English vocabularies* (London, 1884), for instance, does not include *burgus*. *Byrig*, rather than *burh*, seems to be the most commonly occurring form: A. di P. Healey and R. L. Venezky, *A Microfiche Concordance to Old English* (Toronto, 1980).

I have mentioned things (the growth of towns) and words. I come now to the ways that people thought about towns and what lay behind the words they used. Given that towns were growing, changing and developing new customs and new solidarities, and that a number of different words were available for converse about them, one might expect that usage would be shifting, variable and inconsistent. Even without those conditions it might well have been, because that is how it normally is in real life. In real life words do not have exact or consistent meanings, nor can they be relied on to have either a neat range of mutually exclusive uses or one core or primary meaning which is more right than others. Dictionary makers deduce meanings or senses from usage. They do not control usage. It varies from place to place, even from speaker to speaker, as well as from time to time. In normal converse we have a very high tolerance of inconsistencies and varieties of meaning: think of words like house or table. Less common words are often used without anyone having any clear idea what they mean: look at inflation or monetarism or parameters. Medievalists, even those who admit that the word *burgus* was used loosely in Domesday Book, commonly seem to assume that it and its cognates had a fundamentally constitutional sense, that it primarily denoted – that it *ought* to denote – places of a particular legal or constitutional status.[3] This is not only anachronistic. It is based on the surely mistaken idea that people were primarily thinking about the places they referred to as *byrigan* or *burgi* in constitutional terms and moreover that they were agreed about their constitutional and legal definitions. These assumptions ignore the usual way that words are used and the particular impossibility of achieving any uniformity or precision of legal usage in medieval conditions. Precise and consistent definition of terms is possible only in a legal system in which professional lawyers argue according to accepted rules and which has a system of appeals to a recognised authority which records and publishes its decisions. In the eleventh century and for centuries afterwards none of these conditions obtained. Law in the eleventh century was administered locally by assemblies of local people under royal or seignorial officials. Uniformity of usage was impossible.

Towns in particular were likely to develop their own peculiar customs: within a general framework of shared values they developed procedures for commercial litigation, rules of land tenure and cash rents which were all both convenient to traders and craftsmen and profitable to king and lords. New rules and customs were, as they always are, both the result and the cause of disputes, disputes which were resolved in different ways in different towns. Even if someone, like the king, for instance, had wanted to define the rights and obligations of towns and townsmen in general he could not have done so. Not only would it have been unthinkable for any king, even William the Conqueror, to override all local customs, but the climate of thought and the

---

[3] E.g. M. D. Lobel, *The commune of Bury St Edmunds* (Oxford, 1935), 3–15; Darby (1977), 289–90 (including references to 'burghal status', p. 290).

technology of communication made comprehensive codification impossible. When general decrees were issued they must often have been interpreted differently all over the country: writs and law codes had no interpretation clauses. To take an example from Domesday: the entries for three of the towns described at the heads of their counties in Circuit III begin with their hidages, while that of the fourth (Cambridge) says that it was a half-hundred but was never hidated. This looks like a different interpretation of words – perhaps of a question asked – rather than a difference of substance. The varying relationships of towns with the hundreds around them can likewise probably be best explained by the varying ways that the same general system of government and law developed in different places. To try to deduce a single original pattern behind arrangements that can only have developed as towns and custom developed is to indulge in the sort of hypothetical history that is associated rather with 'charter myths' or folk etymologies than with modern methods of scholarship.

To suppose therefore that every time that a place was referred to as a *burgus* or its inhabitants as *burgenses* it can be assumed to have had at least a lowest common denominator of status in common with other places referred to (at some time or another) as *burgi* is nonsensical. So it is to believe that because the word *ceaster* was generally used for the grander or more important towns, many of which had once been Roman and many of which were bishops' sees, everyone who used the word did so only after a quick bit of research on Roman Britain or cathedrals. The context of references to *byrigan* or *burgi*, *ceastra* or *civitates* varied and so the connotations attached to the words varied too. It was this background of colloquial usage, supplemented probably by an equally indeterminate range of current west French usage, which was in the minds of King William's clerks or those whose words they wrote down, when they encased *burgus* and *burgensis* in the amber of a legal record that soon seemed to bear the authority of a Last Judgement.

This, at least, is what I deduce, given the background, from the variety of ways that places which look to me like towns were referred to in Domesday Book. Sometimes they are called *civitates* but more often *burgi*, while their inhabitants are nearly always *burgenses* rather than *cives*.[4] Most of the places called *civitates* were also referred to as *burgi* or had inhabitants referred to as *burgenses*. Applied to such places the two words are generally used more or less indistinguishably, and where they are not the implied distinction looks *ad hoc* rather than a reflection of current usage.[5] Most of these towns were centres of county government, most were bishops' sees and most were of

---

[4] Shrewsbury and York are the only exceptions I have noticed. In both cases the expression *burgenses* is also used.

[5] E.g. Gloucester (DB, i. 162a): the phrase *in burgo civitatis* contrasts with references to *murus civitatis* at Chester (i. 262b) and cf. Hereford (i. 179a) where those living *in civitate* are contrasted with those outside the walls. That land at Chester *nunquam pertinuit ad manerium extra civitatem sed ad burgum pertinet* suggests that the words were in this context synonymous. See below, n. 39.

Roman origin, but the three categories do not coincide exactly.[6] Some places (including some of these) are on occasion also referred to simply as *villae*, Hereford (or part of Hereford) is once called Hereford port, and some places whose inhabitants are called *burgenses* are in this record themselves called *villae*. Sometimes, of course, the shape of sentences means that a place-name suffices and no common noun is needed.[7] *Burgus* and *civitas*, I conclude, are not words which the clerks of Domesday used to denote a legal or constitutional status. They are words used in Domesday, as in other sources of the time, to denote places that people would have noticed, without any fuss about definitions or qualifications, as different from the ordinary run of agricultural villages and hamlets – though of course all of them would have included some inhabitants who made their livings from agricultural or horticultural pursuits.

Towns presented a problem to the makers of Domesday. Not a problem of classification or definition because they were not, I submit, in the business of classification or definition, but a practical problem of recording the king's property and rights, and other people's property and rights after a period of many dispossessions and much destruction, especially in so far as that property and those rights gave rise to obligations to the king. Much as towns had grown in the previous couple of centuries they were an anomaly in a predominantly rural scene and they did not fit normal categories. The smaller market towns, which were managed by royal or seignorial reeves along with the rural estates in which they lay, were not too difficult. Information about them could be entered with that of the surrounding manor, generally in the form of a note of the income due from townspeople (*burgenses*) or traders (*mercatores*), or sometimes of the separate profit derived by the king or local lord from a market or tolls or mint.[8] Bigger places, where the king had extensive interests, and where the more important of his subjects were likely to have property and interests too, were what posed a problem, and it is not surprising that they were dealt with separately. This special treatment, by which most of those entered in Great Domesday ended up in gaps carefully left for them at the beginning of the county sections, was not, however, merely the result of an *ad hoc* decision by either the commissioners or the final

[6] J. H. Round's list (*VCH Essex*, i. 415) is better than Ballard's (*Domesday Boroughs* (Oxford, 1904) 5n.) or Darby's (1977, 364–8) though it lacks Stafford. My list is Canterbury, Chester, Chichester, Colchester, Exeter, Gloucester, Hereford, Leicester, Lincoln, Oxford, Rochester, Shrewsbury, Stafford (i. 247b), Winchester (i. 44a), Worcester, York; with Colchester and Rochester as the non-county towns; Colchester, Gloucester, Leicester, Oxford, Shrewsbury and Stafford as non-episcopal; and Hereford, Oxford, Shrewsbury and Stafford as non-Roman.

[7] E.g. Bury St Edmunds, known as 'Seynt Eadmundesbiri' or -'byri' by the mid-eleventh century (Whitelock, *Anglo-Saxon Wills*, 68, 72, 73, 183; Harmer, *Anglo-Saxon Writs*, nos. 8, 18) and was described in DB, ii. 372a as having been enlarged since 1066 in a way which implies a distinctively urban character: cf. Lobel, *Bury St Edmunds*, 3–15.

[8] Some omissions may be explicable by the absence of royal interests: e.g. St Albans; Hastings, Rye and possibly Winchelsea, where nearly all royal rights had passed to the lords of rapes; and perhaps Coventry.

scribe,[9] any more than it was the result of any distinctiveness as yet perceived in terms of a definable status. The towns with separate entries in both volumes are those which look as if they had, for one reason or another (generally size and complexity), become established as separate units of government under their respective sheriffs before 1066. In many cases there is evidence in Domesday that their sheriffs managed them, whether directly or through subordinates, as part of their general, county-wide duties, not as appendages of any single royal manor or group of manors.[10] I do not, incidentally, think that it is helpful to describe either these towns or those mentioned along with the king's lands as 'royal boroughs'. The expression *burgum* [*sic*] *regis* is, I think, used only once in Domesday and the division between royal and seignorial boroughs does not seem to me to fit the political ideas or the fiscal realities of the eleventh century.[11] Every part of the kingdom was under some degree of royal authority and the king would draw some degree of profit from every big or important town (except, in 1086, Chester and perhaps some of the Sussex towns), but as the king's political and fiscal interest would be greater in a bigger town, so would that of others. Royal and seignorial interests in towns were not mutually exclusive.

The real problem for the Domesday commissioners was that the dues and obligations owed by large towns were complicated, profitable and distinctive – which was why towns were administered separately. As Domesday itself tells us, towns produced some collective services and lump sums for the king but a good deal was raised from them by cash payments of various sorts from individual householders. Given all that we know about English government before 1066 it seems highly likely that some written records of these were available. Two sorts seem to me detectable. First, though in some cases the

[9] I differ here from V. H. Galbraith (1974), 152, and C. Stephenson, 'The composition and interpretation of Domesday Book', *Speculum*, xxii (1947), 12, but not, I infer, from G. H. Martin (1985), 158–9.

[10] The information, for instance, about Dover, Canterbury and Rochester in the introductory section of Kent is clearly attuned to royal rights and what the sheriff collected. The absence of any town at the beginning of Sussex may result from the fragmentation of royal rights among the rape lords. The four towns at the beginning of the Dorset section (and in the same position though a slightly different order in Exon Domesday) were presumably dealt with as a group by the sheriff. In Exon Domesday Barnstaple, Lydford, and Exeter, in that order, are at the end of the royal property in Devon, and Totnes is at the end of Juhel's. Though in Great Domesday Barnstaple and Lydford were put at the beginning of the king's land and Totnes at the beginning of Juhel's, they had presumably all been looked after by the sheriff in 1066 and all but Totnes still were in 1086. The renders of Oxford, Northampton, Leicester, Warwick, Worcester, Hereford and Chester were all, at least in part, combined with those of their counties. Nottingham and Derby were entered together at the beginning of Notts. since the two counties were run by one sheriff. In DB, ii. Colchester is after the *invasiones* for Essex; Norwich, Yarmouth and Thetford are together after the main section of the king's land (and before the escheats) in Norfolk; and Ipwich is at the end of the king's land in Suffolk. Dr Ann Williams has pointed out to me that the entry of, e.g. the bishop of Worcester's property in Worcester (DB, i. 173b) apart from the main entry confirms my hypothesis about the reason for the separate town entries.

[11] The Stamford entry (DB, i. 336b) begins by saying what geld the *burgum regis* gave TRE: presumably the intention was to distinguish the main (Lincs.) part of the town from the holdings of Queen Edith and Peterborough abbey, which were outside the county and shared most but not all of the common obligations.

customs set out in Domesday could have been reported only in oral testimony, the combination of detail in some entries with the survival of a report from Aethelred's reign about tolls and customs at London makes it seem possible that inquiries were made from time to time into customs and tolls owed in at least the larger towns, and that written records of these were kept.[12] Second, and more important, in most of the bigger towns there must have been lists of householders' dues, some of the others perhaps on the lines of the Winchester list of *c.* 1057 which can be detected from the Winchester survey of *c.* 1110.[13] But though some records of these kinds must have been available to the commissioners they can have been of only limited use. The relatively large and mobile populations of towns would at the best of times have made lists of householders complicated and have given them a built-in obsolescence, while any simplification through the substitution of lump sums would leave the record inadequate for the sort of verification that the Survey of 1086 was intended to achieve. The years between 1066 and 1086 had not been the best of times for most English towns and few lists can have been systematically revised or even annotated with any degree of thoroughness since the Conquest.[14]

Tentatively, I suggest that the Domesday commissioners' procedure for dealing with towns under shrieval control may have been something like this: the sheriff would produce the available records which would then be gone through in what were in principle county assemblies at which townspeople, along with at least some lords with urban properties, were present to give oral testimony to supplement, correct and bring the records up to date.[15] How separate these sessions were from those at which rural properties were dealt with is unclear.[16] Information provided by lords or hundred juries about urban property which owed rent to manors outside was not generally, if ever, incorporated into town entries, but whether inquiries into the two sorts of property were conducted together or separately the trouble of

[12] *Gesetze*, i. 232–6; for the date: P. Wormald, 'Aethelred the Lawmaker', in D. Hill, ed., *Ethelred the Unready* (Oxford, 1978), 62–3. The correction from *sunt* to *erant* in the Lewes customs (DB, i. 26a) might imply a direct copying from a pre-Conquest exemplar, but this is unlikely in the final text. The tense used of the immediately preceding customs varies but in this case the changed relation of earl and king made the tense important and the scribe may have realised this while writing.

[13] *WS*, i. 9–10, 407. The absence of information about 1086 might imply that the returns for DB had disappeared if they had ever been made, but cf. the Gloucester and Winchcomb surveys of *c.* 1100: A. S. Ellis, 'Domesday tenants of Gloucestershire', *Transactions of the Bristol and Gloucestershire Archaeological Society*, iv (1879–80), 91–3.

[14] Failure to mention new cathedrals in the towns to which sees had been recently moved might reflect a reliance on out-of-date lists (though see below, n. 24). The sheriff of Devon, on the other hand, may have had a list of current landowners with property in Exeter and Barnstaple: below, p. 303 and nn. 17, 18.

[15] The Nottingham and Derby entries and the arrangements of other towns listed in n. 10 suggest that the sessions were county rather than town ones.

[16] See the suggestion of Harvey (1975), 179.

correlating the two sorts of information would have been enormous.[17] In Devon the session to deal with towns under the sheriff may have been held early on as information about dependent town properties was added to that about rural estates but not vice versa, but that could be because the sheriff supplied the list direct. It need not imply that town and country sessions were totally separate.[18] I see no reason to suppose that the town sessions were not part of the main inquiry by the first set of commissioners in 1086.[19]

What the commissioners asked about has to be deduced from the surviving entries, but they suggest that it was not in principle all that different, *mutatis mutandis*, from what they asked about manorial property: namely, what dues were paid TRE, what are paid now and what is the town worth, and how do you account for any shortfalls since 1066?[20] Whether the resulting text was generally copied and cut and rearranged as much as Howard Clarke shows some of the non-urban returns to have been I do not know. All I can say is that the final scribe of Great Domesday certainly rearranged and abbreviated some of the material that he found in the provincial or circuit drafts.[21]

At any rate the result as we have it is, in my view, a lot more informative and systematic than is implied by the customary moans and wails about the 'borough entries'.[22] The arrangement of the material is certainly varied – as it is in the manorial entries too, and the amount of detail varies. Detail, of course, was affected by the recopying, but we have to recognise that even at the first stage the commissioners and their clerks did not deal with enough towns to get into the swing of them as they could with rural estates.[23] It must have been very confusing to correct and correlate material in the written lists (such as they were) with that produced orally. We know that townsmen, or their representatives, sometimes produced contradictory testimony, but they

[17] Lists of properties attached to manors appear in the relevant *Domesday Geographies*. Note, e.g. Wallingford: *Domesday Geography of South-East England*, 276–7. Lists in DB town entries of lords with urban properties do not follow the order either of the county lists of tenants in chief or (where these differ) of the entries of their holdings. The Devon list of urban properties (see n. 18) was not correlated with the manorial returns into which it was incorporated: see the different number of burgesses in Barnstaple attributed to Baldwin the sheriff in Exon Domesday, 123b, and DB, i. 102a. To judge from Inquisitio Eliensis (ICC, 120–1), information about Ely properties in Cambridge was cut down in recopying. Cf. Martin (1985), 155–6, on St Augustine's Canterbury material.

[18] In Exon Domesday it is always added at the end of the tenant's holding, but in DB it is sometimes at the beginning: references listed in Darby, *Domesday Geography of South-West England*, 281, 283.

[19] Following H. B. Clarke's suggestion about the nature of the two inquiries: Clarke (1985), 66.

[20] Information about *quando recepit* was often inapplicable to towns, but I have noted references, or possible allusions, to it or to *postea* for Dover, Rochester, Pevensey, Chichester(?), Wallingford, Wilton, Exeter(?), Hertford, Gloucester, Winchcombe, Chester, Nottingham and Maldon. This distribution does not run counter to that plotted by Darby (1977), 212.

[21] For Devon, above, n. 18; for Cambridge, n. 17. The gap left for Derby (DB, i. 272a) suggests that the scribe was rethinking his plan as he copied. In general, see Clarke (1985) and Martin (1985).

[22] E.g. Stephenson, 'Composition and Interpretation', 12; Darby (1977), 289.

[23] Though note similarities of towns dealt with in single counties (e.g. Dorset); of those in Circuits III and IV (except that at Warwick 1086 information is given first); and of Hereford, Shrewsbury and Chester.

may not have been much more reliable when they were united in placatory conciliation or mulish resentment. Their accounts of holdings which no longer paid the customs they had paid in King Edward's day must often have been presented in a disorganised way, for the information was complex, controversial, and covered a long and disturbed period. Nevertheless some of the lists which have been dismissed as confused are not too bad if one reckons that their point is not to give total numbers of burgesses or even of sums received, but to account for unpaid dues and give as good an idea as possible of what the king ought – in his servants' opinion – to be getting.[24]

Starting from this point of view, one important piece of information comes across loud and clear. There was a lot to be got out of townspeople, partly in services of various kinds but mostly in cash. Many, perhaps most, people who lived in towns had to pay rent.[25] In most of the bigger towns many paid their rent to the king but others were tenants of nobles, churches or other townsmen and paid it to them. Some paid no rent, as such, and it may well be that there were more of these than are revealed in a record concerned with obligations rather than with freedom from them.[26] Other obligations which townsmen in general were expected to owe (though some did not fulfil their obligations and others were for one reason or another more or less legitimately exempt) were tolls and other customary dues and services commonly subsumed under the words custom (consuetudo), customs, or all customs. These words might or might not cover military service or payments towards the military service of the town, and the tax which Domesday generally calls geld.

When we move from this level of generality things get difficult. The distinction between property rents (which often but not always seem to be

---

[24] Darby's condemnation e.g. of the Norwich entry (Domesday Geography of Eastern England (3rd edn, 1971), 139) seems to me unjustified. Round ('Domesday of Colchester', Antiquary, vi (1882), 56; VCH Essex, i. 417) was so busy worrying about Freeman's errors and the difference between Normans and English that he apparently failed to notice that the difference between the two lists of the Colchester entry is that one is of those paying custom and the other is of those not paying. One reason why new cathedrals are omitted (or perhaps subsumed in ecclesiastical estates nearby) may be that their urban tenants were exempt from custom.

[25] The units of property are described variously as mansurae, masurae, mansiones, hagae, or domus. Some entries use two or more of these words, some use none. Apart from a single reference in the Huntingdon entry, hagae seem to be referred to only in Circuit I. The hagae in Oxford are mentioned in the Berkshire section (i.e. in Circuit I): DB, i. 57b, 62. DB, i. 106b uses domus where Exon Domesday, 298, uses mansurae, so some of the variations come from copying rather than from varying local vocabularies. At Wallingford the same properties are referred to both as hagae and masurae (DB, i. 56b, 59b), but at Chichester (i. 23a) the number of houses is distinguished from the number of hagae. The need to make distinctions would depend on circumstances.

[26] At Wallingford (DB, i. 56b) some people had the gablum from their own houses and received penalties for certain offences committed in them. At Stamford (i. 336b) there were sokemen who held their lands in dominio and from whom the king received only penalties, heriot and toll. At Southampton (i. 52a) some had their houses free (quietas) or had had the customs from them granted to them by King William. In other places rent as such may or may not be included in 'customs'.

meant by the words *redditus, census* or *gablum*[27]) and the other dues (the customs) may have been clear enough when the rent was payable to another lord but customs went (as they more often did) to the king. It must, however, have been harder to maintain when both rent and customs (which were sometimes owed, like rents, annually, house by house) went to the king. There is no reason why the distinction between the king as king and the king as landlord should have been uniformly conceptualised in all towns.[28] Even if it had once been, it may well have become blurred since 1066 as increased sums were demanded and townspeople (especially the conquered English among them) had to muck in to make them up as best they could. This blurred distinction between the king as king and the king as lord may also help to explain the varying meanings which seem to attach to references to the king's *dominium* in the town entries. At Wareham, for instance, the houses *in dominio regis* excluded those belonging to the abbey of Saint Wandrille,[29] but at Hereford, where other lords certainly received payments from burgesses, the whole city was nevertheless referred to as *in dominio regis*. *Dominium* covered different sorts of lordship from property to government.

All the uncertainties which arise from ambiguous or inconsistent terminology (and I could cite many others) are very frustrating, especially if we want to use Domesday statistically, but I think that we should resist the illusory certainties of imposed definitions and resign ourselves to the impossibility of counting incomparable entities, or at least postpone counting until we are reasonably sure we understand what we are counting. All the town statistics are tricky. Even if we leave aside the horrid problem of multipliers, many entries do not give any total of burgesses or houses in 1086, or in 1066, or either. Some townspeople who paid rent (of some sort) to a lord other than the king were mentioned in the town entry, some were

---

[27] For varying uses of *census* see e.g. DB, i. 179a (Hereford entry); *gablum* seems to be a latinisation of *gafol* which was also used in the eleventh century (J. Earle and C. Plummer, eds., *Two Saxon Chronicles Parallel* (Oxford, 1892), i. 339) for the tax which seems to be called *geldum* in DB.

[28] J. H. Round, 'Danegeld and the finance of Domesday', in *Domesday Studies*, i. 77–142, maintained that the distinction was vital (and cf. *VCH Berks.*, i. 311). It is certainly clear in the examples he mentions but these do not include entries which refer simply to undifferentiated customs or in which other lords are not mentioned. He also said ('Danegeld and finance', 124) that 'custom' included all customary dues, but this vitiates his distinction since rent would normally be customary. At Worcester (DB, i. 172a) the king took no custom from individual houses except *census domorum sicut unicuique pertinebat*. The Winchester survey of *c.* 1100 calls *langabulum* and *brugabulum* customs: *WS*, i. 33, 44, 47. Cf. F. W. Maitland, *Township and Borough* (Cambridge, 1898), 48–9, 70–3, 185–6.

[29] But it is not clear whether it excluded houses not in the main entry which paid rent to other churches (listed in Darby, *Domesday Geography of South-West England*, 121). The *burgenses regii* at Colchester (DB, ii. 107) were presumably those who rendered custom, but there is no evidence that any burgesses had been exempt from it TRE (i. 104–7): those who were not 'royal burgesses' in 1086 seem therefore to be those who, rightly or wrongly, were not then contributing. Fewer lords probably got away with freedom from custom before 1066. Tait's argument from twelfth-century evidence for an original distinction between burgessland in custom and thegnland not in custom (*Medieval English Borough*, 88–96) seems to derive from the sort of 'hypothetical history' which I suggest above is dangerous.

mentioned under the rural manor where they paid it, some (but not many) were mentioned in both places. It seems fairly clear, moreover, that the sort of townspeople who were likely to be recorded were the sort who headed fully contributing households: how many that omitted, especially in the bigger towns, is anyone's guess.[30] All this makes it impossible to work out reliable totals of burgesses or money where none are specified and prompts doubts whether such totals as are given are very significant. Nonetheless the statistics are still suggestive and no one studying Domesday towns can fail to be grateful to the *Domesday Geographies* for their marshalling of the material. But statistics are not everything, and some of the uncertainties of terminology which frustrate us statistically are in themselves illuminating so far as, by reminding us how anachronistic is our desire for precision, they direct us to consider the uncertain conditions in which townspeople struggled to satisfy a rapacious government and the government struggled to maintain some modicum of custom and good order.

If we leave the obsessions with later legal technicalities and quantification which have bedevilled the study of Domesday towns – and the obsession with feudalism which has oddly bypassed some of the information about townsmen's military service – there is a lot of material still to be studied in the town entries. I shall pick out only one aspect that particularly interests me: namely the evidence of the collective activity of townspeople and their degree of collective organisation and independence. The corporate or unincorporated character of towns in 1066, their liberties or lack of liberties, and the effect on them of the Norman Conquest have been extensively discussed, but I think everyone, even Maitland and Tait (at both of whose names I nonetheless feel inclined to bow), has been so obsessed with looking for the origins of what came later that they have not looked hard enough at what Domesday says and implies about the situation in 1066.

Because English towns did not have charters of liberties before the Norman Conquest it does not mean that their inhabitants did not have any autonomy, did not promote their collective interests and did not bargain with the government. Charters were one method by which medieval kings and lords could recognise or increase or restrict local autonomy: they did not create it. All over Europe, even in Italy, they were rare before the twelfth century and became common then as a manifestation of the striking development of governmental control and above all of record-keeping at the time. Thanks to Domesday Book we can see that several towns had already won some collective privileges and can suspect that others may lie behind low hidages and quotas of tax and service. Though town dues were not generally yet consolidated in a single lump sum,[31] many of the smaller fixed

---

[30] The Norwich bordars (probably former burgesses) who paid no custom because of their poverty may be exceptional more in being mentioned than for any other reason. Cf. C. Dyer, 'Towns and cottages in 11th-century England', in H. Mayr-Harting and R. I. Moore, eds., *Studies in Medieval History presented to R. H. C. Davis* (London, 1985), 91–106.

[31] The idea of a 'borough farm' at this date may therefore be slightly misleading. Where the constituents of *firme* are mentioned they seem very various. In other cases it is impossible to know what was included or to be sure of the distinction between *firme* and other sums which

renders, like the precise definitions of procedures and penalties at law, probably reflect past disputes and concessions. Dover, the first entry in the book, is a case in point. Before 1066 the king had done a deal with the townspeople whereby they provided a fixed quota of naval service and ferries for his messengers and in return kept most of the profits of justice from the town.[32] At Colchester one annual sum was said to be paid by *tota civitas* and another by the royal burgesses, the burgesses were said to manage some land outside the walls for themselves, and they and the burgesses of Maldon made a joint payment for their mints.[33] This confusion of groups and categories, seen in the context of medieval law and collective activity, is testimony less to lack of what later lawyers would call corporate status than to the acceptance of communal values.[34] Collective responsibility and collective bargaining were also common enough for the news of a good deal to get around and be copied. Exeter had to pay geld only when London, Winchester, and York did so, while three smaller towns in Devon had jumped on the band-wagon by an agreement that they should jointly do the same amount of military service as Exeter did.[35]

The internal organisation through which towns withstood the demands of royal tax-collectors and the bullying of royal officials is obscure. Probably the main forum of activity was the town assembly, presided over though it was by a royal official, but at Dover and Canterbury, for instance, we know that there were town guilds which may have been conveniently free of outside supervision.[36] Either way, whether in assembly or guild, the lead is likely to have been taken by the more substantial townsmen, possibly in the persons of such lawmen or *judices* as are recorded at Cambridge, Chester, Lincoln, Stamford and York.[37] In some towns lawmen may, like the

---

were perhaps equally fixed. At Colchester (DB, ii. 107a) the payment for victualling of *solidarii* or *expeditio* was excluded from the farm because it was made only if the king took service (not, as Round inexplicably maintained (*VCH Essex*, i. 422) whether he did or not) and presumably because, like the payment made to the *milites* of Berkshire, it was for the men's own support. Money for victuals, etc., is also mentioned in the entries for Lewes, the Dorset towns, Malmesbury and Wallingford.

[32] Profits of justice from Michaelmas to St Andrew's day still went to the king. Though there is no proper entry for Romney a similar arrangement (not specifying the autumn exception) seems to have been made there (DB, i. 4b, 10b) and perhaps at others of the later Cinque Ports.

[33] DB, ii. 107a–b.

[34] This is further discussed in S. Reynolds, *Kingdoms and Communities in Western Europe, 900–1300* (Oxford, 1984), 12–38, 158–68.

[35] DB, i. 100a, 108b.

[36] DB, i. 1a, 3a; S. Reynolds, *English Medieval Towns* (Oxford, 1977), 82.

[37] Stenton (in *Lincolnshire Domesday* (Lincs. Rec. Soc., xix, 1924), xxix–xxx) thought that the Lincoln and Stamford lawmen, who were said to have sac and soc (in Stamford explicitly over their own houses and men) were by 1086 probably 'a group of privileged burgesses rather than the expert members of a borough moot'. Having peculiar independence over their own households however would not exclude them from also having wider authority in their towns: the first might be a corollary of the second. If they did not have any wider authority they would not have been significantly different from some one like Tochi son of Outi at Lincoln or the seventy-seven sokemen at Stamford. The constitutional developments of the twelfth and thirteenth centuries would explain the atrophy of the lawmen's position between 1086 and 1279 better than anything before 1086 could do.

aldermen of London, have been responsible for wards, but even where wards are recorded they may not have been.[38] To us an even bigger problem than the leadership of towns at this time may be the definition of their membership. Domesday shows that some at least of the larger towns had defined territorial boundaries, within which the common obligations were shared and to which common privileges and rules belonged. Sometimes the town's jurisdiction extended outside the walls, though at Hereford those living outside paid slightly lower rents than those inside.[39] Within the boundaries, however defined, those who normally ranked as full members of the community – those normally referred to as *burgenses* or *cives* – were probably the resident householders who contributed their share of the town's customs. Two 'normallys' and one 'probably' in that sentence cover a mass of doubts and variations, variations that grew with growing populations, the sufferings and disruptions of the years since the Conquest, and the varying ways that towns coped with the result. In so far as Domesday reveals uncertainties and anomalies of this sort it reveals the truth: medieval towns, even the most independent and most fully corporate (in later terms) seem to have lived in a permanent state of muddle and uncertainty about the qualifications and obligations of membership.[40]

When all is said and done the most important thing about the town entries in Domesday is that, apart from brief notes that hint at the presence of a whole mass of smaller market towns or near towns, it gives enough information about roughly fifty places to show that, small as were their populations by modern standards, and despite the presence of agricultural workers among them, they were genuine towns. The amount of their revenues (however imperfect the totals), even the complexity and confusion of their revenues, and the collective activity that helped to raise them are evidence of that. Even if Domesday records little about trades and crafts (and why should it record more?) it is nonsensical to see most of the *burgi* as anything but active communities of what must have been a predominantly non-agricultural character. Whether most of them were flourishing or growing in 1086 is another matter. In many cases their total obligations, however made up, had grown, but it would be naïve to take that as testimony to their prosperity. Many houses had been burnt or demolished, and though a few places, like the Channel ports, gained business from the link with Normandy, and in others Frenchmen had come to swell urban populations, a good many of these immigrants, like the French nobles and their followers who held town property, used their position as members or

---

[38] Wards were mentioned at Cambridge and Stamford, ferlings at Huntingdon and shires at York. A *senator* (presumably alderman) of London is referred to in the mid-eleventh century and wards early in the twelfth: S. Reynolds, 'Rulers of London in the Twelfth Century', *History*, lvii (1972), 339n.

[39] DB, i. 179a. The evidence does not support the contention (e.g. in Reynolds, *English Medieval Towns*, 97) that *civitas* normally meant the whole jurisdictional area as distinct from the walled *burgus*: above n. 5.

[40] Reynolds, *Kingdoms and Communities*, 184–8 (incidentally correcting Reynolds, *English Medieval Towns*, 125–6).

camp-followers of an occupying force to evade payment of the dues which their defeated neighbours owed.[41] Perhaps by 1086 things were beginning to settle down but few English towns can have been very confident or harmonious communities. In such circumstances even the absence of complaint can be significant. The statements that the burgesses of Yarmouth gave the sheriff a *gersuma* or gift of £4 and a hawk freely and out of friendship (*gratis et amicitia*) and that, while 166 houses at Lincoln had been destroyed to make way for the castle, seventy-four others were uninhabited not because of oppression by the sheriffs and their servants but because of misfortune, poverty and fire, must have been diplomatically and carefully made.[42]

Taken as a whole Domesday offers precious little support for the traditional assumption that the Norman Conquest marked a significant stage of English urban development. What it shows is a wide range of English towns battered by twenty years of war, oppression and dislocation, but some of them growing nevertheless. We know that the check to urban growth turned out to be temporary. I am tempted to deduce from Domesday that the one long-term effect of the Norman Conquest on towns was in so messing up the royal records of customs and dues and so breaking the local acceptance of them that it must have seemed all the more advisable to leave towns to run themselves and keep their own records. Domesday's information about TRE, however, shows that that tendency was already formed, and everywhere in Europe it became accentuated in the twelfth century: I am probably being unduly influenced, as one so often is, by the particular way that this extraordinary record happens to lay a particular sort of information before me.

I think the Domesday town entries are more informative and reveal more significant information than many commentators, including the authors of the *Domesday Geographies*, suggest. That is because they are weakest on what the *Geographies* are most interested in and best at other less quantifiable aspects. But I nevertheless agree that they are difficult, very difficult. They have been made more difficult by being read as if they were written in the technical jargon of later lawyers and as if their compilers were preoccupied by what later constitutional historians or demographers would be preoccupied by, but even if one frees oneself from these obsessions, they remain difficult. It is very hard to know what was in the minds of the clerks and their informants. And regrettably we have to face the fact that they were not interested in telling us all that we want to know.

---

[41] A clear case of non-contributing immigrants is Shrewsbury (DB, i. 52a) but the lists of non-contributors elsewhere (e.g. Cambridge, Colchester, Norwich) are also significant. At Nottingham the new settlement seems to have been made to contribute to the obligations of the old: the sheriff is referred to as *apponens eas* [i.e. thirteen new houses] *in censu veteris burgi*: DB, i. 280a.

[42] DB, ii. 118b; i. 336a.

Early Norman Winchester[1]

Martin Biddle

IN NOVEMBER 1086, if we are to believe the author of the *Carmen de Hastingae Proelio*, the leading citizens of Winchester surrendered their city without a struggle.[2] Having received Duke William's instruction to pay tribute, as others were doing, the *primates urbis* consulted with Queen Edith, in whose dower the city lay and who was apparently in residence, and ordered by her to conform, went out with gifts to meet their conquerors. It was a far cry from that day just sixty years before when the citizens, safe within their walls, had watched the Viking host pass by with the loot of fifty miles inland.[3]

What kind of city was this which the Normans found? Lying in the narrow valley of the River Itchen, surrounded by suburbs, it was above all an ancient place, already a millenium old. Girt by Roman walls, entered along the routes of Roman roads through five gates, all of Roman origin, it was a city from the Antique world, as in the twelfth century its legends were proud to claim. And yet within its Roman walls, the regular grid of streets to each side of High Street was of much more recent date, a planned creation of the later ninth century designed to apportion the walled area for permanent settlement while at the same time allowing movement on interior lines for the rapid reinforcement of any threatened part of the defences.[4]

[1] Much of the substance of this paper was first argued in detail by Derek Keene and myself in *WS*, i. 241–508, summarised on 470–88. A full list of Winchester Studies will be found, together with a bibliography of other recent work on Winchester, in Martin Biddle, 'The Study of Winchester. Archaeology and History in a British Town', *Proceedings of the British Academy*, lxix (1983), 93–135, at pp. 130–5.

[2] *The Carmen de Hastingae Proelio of Guy Bishop of Amiens*, ed. Catherine Morton and Hope Muntz (Oxford, 1972), 40–1. For discussion of the authorship, date and reliability of the *Carmen*, see R. H. C. Davis, 'The *Carmen de Hastingae Proelio*', *EHR*, xciii (1978), 241–61, and R. H. C. Davis, L. J. Engels *et al.*, 'The *Carmen de Hastingae Proelio*: a discussion', *Proceedings of the Battle Conference* (now *Anglo-Norman Studies*), ii (1979), 1–20. Whatever the outcome of this discussion, there is no evidence to suggest that Winchester, unlike Hampshire and neighbouring counties (see *WS*, i. 470, n. 1), was physically damaged by the actual events of the Conquest. The account in the *Carmen* may be substantially accurate.

[3] *Two of the Saxon Chronicles Parallel*, ed. C. Plummer, 2 vols. (Oxford, 1892–9; reprinted, 1952), i. s.a. 1006 (C, D, E, F).

[4] Biddle, 'The Study of Winchester', 125–6. See also, Martin Biddle and David Hill, 'Late Saxon Planned Towns', *Antiquaries Journal*, li (1971), 70–85, and *WS*, i. 277–82.

Although scarcely two centuries old, these new streets of the city were lined with houses and small churches, usually placed close together and already densely packed on High Street and even along some of the side streets.[5] A few of the houses, especially in High Street, were probably stone-built,[6] but most of them were timber, perhaps of more than one storey and no smaller in area than the stone houses.[7] There were several guildhalls,[8] and probably as many as thirty or more parish churches.[9] On the eve of the Conquest the city within the walls, with the exception of its public buildings, must have presented much the appearance it was to retain for the greater part of the Middle Ages. Street frontages were continuously built-up; much, perhaps most, of the encroachment that could reasonably be allowed on streets and open spaces had already taken place. The structural framework of the walled city was thus already well established by 1066, while outside the walls the built-up area of the suburbs, although still expanding, was probably nearing its maximum extent.[10] (Fig. 1.)

Dominating the lower buildings of the commercial and domestic city rose the great towers of the south-east quarter occupied by three monasteries of royal foundation – Old Minster, New Minster and Nunnaminster – and by two palaces, the bishop's residence at Wolvesey in the south-east angle of the Roman walls and the royal residence immediately west of Old Minster in the heart of the city.[11] It was this area, literally one-quarter of the walled city, which embodied the peculiar status of Winchester as the emerging capital city of the English.[12] And it was in this area that the greatest changes were to be worked in the decades following the Conquest.

These changes and the accompanying stability in the basic fabric of the inhabited city are an epitome of the Conquest. Appropriately, it was the construction of the castle at the beginning of 1067 which first made them felt. In obedience to the Conqueror's orders, William FitzOsbern, left in Winchester 'with a temporary command over the whole kingdom towards the north', began the construction of the castle some time between Christmas 1066 and February 1067.[13] An existing salient on the south-west of the Roman defences, occupying the highest ground within the walls, was cut off

---

[5] *WS*, i. 337–48.

[6] Ibid., 339–40, 346–8, Fig. 11.

[7] Ibid., 345–6, 348.

[8] Ibid., 335–6.

[9] Ibid., 329–35, 458–9. For further consideration of Winchester parish churches, see Derek Keene in *WS*, ii. 106–33, and idem, 'Introduction to the Parish Churches of Winchester', in *Bulletin of the CBA Churches Committee*, 23 (Winter, 1985), 1–9.

[10] For this summary, *WS*, i. 458.

[11] *WS*, i. 289–328.

[12] For an evaluation of Winchester's traditional claim to be the 'capital' of Anglo-Saxon England, and for the concept of an 'early capital' in the rise of such cities, see Martin Biddle, 'Winchester: the Development of an Early Medieval Capital', in H. Jankuhn, W. Schlesinger and H. Steuer (eds.), *Vor- und Frühformen der europäischen Stadt im Mittelalter* (Abh. der Akademie der Wissenschaften in Göttingen, Philog.-hist. Klasse, 3 Folge, 83), i (Göttingen, 1973), 229–61.

[13] Frank Barlow, '*Guenta*', *Antiquaries Journal*, xliv (1964), 217–19. For a new history of the castle, see now Martin Biddle and Beatrice Clayre, *Winchester Castle and the Great Hall* (Winchester, 1983).

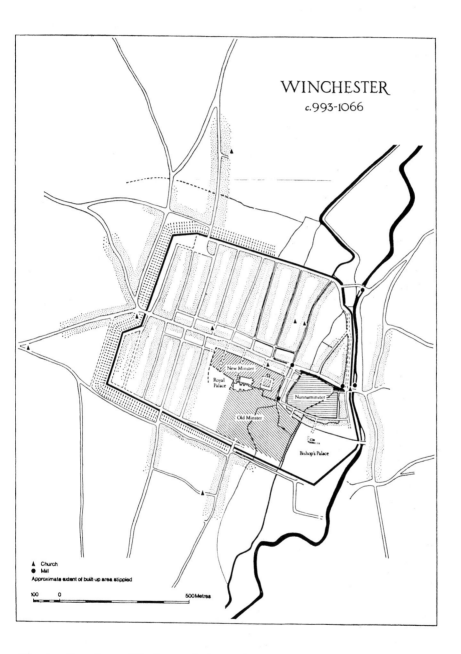

WINCHESTER
c.993-1066

New Minster

Royal Palace

Nunnaminster

Old Minster

Bishop's Palace

▲ Church
● Mill
Approximate extent of built-up area stippled

100   0   500 Metres

Fig. 1.   Late Saxon Winchester. Only parish churches known to be of pre-Conquest origin are shown.

313

from the rest of the city by digging a line of ditch and bank through the occupied area, destroying streets and houses.[14] Outside the walls, more houses and an external lane were destroyed in widening the city ditch to form the outer defences of the castle.[15] By Easter 1072, the castle enclosed a *capella regia* in which was held the council at which the primacy of Canterbury over York was discussed.[16] Thereafter the castle developed rapidly into one of the most powerful fortresses of the kingdom and by the mid-twelfth century (and probably by 1100) had within it 'that complex of halls, chambers and chapels which constituted a medieval palace'.[17] By 1135, when William of Pont de l'Arche, sheriff of Hampshire and Berkshire, custodian of the castle and of the treasure, delivered both to the new king, the treasury was clearly within the castle.[18] It was apparently there in 1111, on the evidence of an Abingdon Chronicle,[19] when a plea was made before the queen *apud Wintoniam in thesauro* and Domesday Book (*Liber de Thesauro*) was called in evidence,[20] in what seems to be the earliest appearance of the treasury as a court as well as a working office. The treasure was indeed probably already in the castle by 1100 when Henry rode within hours of William Rufus' death *ad arcem Guentoniae, ubi regalis thesaurus continebatur*.[21]

Here, then, in the castle, the storing of the treasure seems to have evolved in the years around 1100 both into a working office and into a court in which reference could be made to Domesday Book, the most important of its records. Here, too, before the mid-1120s, if we follow Professor Hollister,

> the exchequer process was coming into being, not as a separate office or ministry, but as a semi-annual audit of the sheriff's accounts. . . . The twelfth-century exchequer was not a department but an occasion. Its staff was the treasury staff; its records were treasury records; and its receipts went directly into the treasury. Henry I's administrators regularly conducted two exchequer audits concurrently, one in England (probably at Winchester), the other in Normandy (at Rouen or Caen).[22]

[14] *WS*, i. 302–5, cf. 486–7.

[15] *WS*, i. 303.

[16] Bishop and Chaplais, pl. xxix and opp.; cf. *WS*, i. 302 and n. 4.

[17] H. M. Colvin (ed.), *The History of the King's Works*, 6 vols. (1963–82), ii. 855.

[18] *Gesta Stephani*, ed. K. R. Potter and R. H. C. Davis (2nd ed., Oxford, 1976), Cap. 4 (p. 9); *The Historia Novella by William of Malmesbury*, ed. K. R. Potter (1955), Cap. 460, 463; cf. *WS*, i. 305. Robert of Torigny's claim (written late in the twelfth century: *Chronicles of the Reigns of Stephen, Henry II, and Richard I*, ed. Richard Howlett, 4 vols. (RS, 1884–9), iv. 129) that a great part of Henry's treasure, recently brought from England, was at the castle of Falaise on his death, appears to conflict with the evidence of the *Gesta* and the *Historia Novella* regarding the *ditissimum regis Henrici aerarium* (*Gesta*, Cap. 4) then at Winchester. Ordericus Vitalis (a contemporary witness) writes only of 'the treasure in the charge of Robert of Gloucester at Falaise', a reference probably to the Norman as distinct from the English treasure: Ordericus, vi. 449.

[19] *Chronicon Monasterii de Abingdon*, ed. J. Stevenson, 2 vols. (RS, 1858), ii. 116.

[20] *Regesta*, ii. no. 1000. For the text, see *Chronicon de Abingdon*, ii. 116.

[21] Ordericus, v. 290; cf. *WS*, i. 304. A later phrase in the same chapter (also p. 290) appears to confirm the view based on the phrase quoted that the treasure was not merely in Winchester but actually in the castle: *arx cum regalibus gazis filio regis Henrico reddita est*. For the earliest officials of the treasury in Winchester, see the valuable discussion by C. Warren Hollister, 'The Origins of the English Treasury', *EHR*, xciii (1978), 262–75.

[22] Hollister, 'English Treasury', 273.

Winchester Castle was probably thus the setting for the first appearance of two of the greatest offices of the Anglo-Norman state (Fig. 2).

The ancient palace lay by contrast in the city centre.[23] Its position, immediately adjacent to and perhaps in part actually overlying the Roman forum, hints at an origin in the sub-Roman period. But nothing certain is known of it until the last years of the Anglo-Saxon period. The treasure was probably kept there from at least the time of Cnut,[24] and in 1043 and 1053 it was the setting, with the adjacent cathedral, for the courts held at the Easter festival[25] (Fig. 1).

In c. 1070 the Conqueror extended the enclosure of the original palace north to High Street and doubled it in size, by taking in the New Minster cemetery, destroying twelve houses and five *monete*, and blocking a street *pro coquina regis*.[26] On this enlarged precinct he built a palace and hall (*palacium cum aula sua*) which Gerald the Welshman at the end of next century described (with no very obvious reason for exaggeration) as second neither in quality nor quantity to the palace at London (i.e. Westminster).[27] To what extent William demolished the buildings he found on the site – a complex probably centuries old – is not recorded. Perhaps he left them standing, as Rufus did at Westminster, for all the evidence implies that the new works were on the newly enclosed land. If this were so, Gerald's description is the more comprehensible, for in area covered at least (Winchester Palace in the twelfth century: more than 2 ha; Westminster in the fourteenth century: about 3.1 ha), he was not far out (Fig. 2).

Winchester, like London, now had two royal centres. There can have been no initial intention to abandon the old royal palace in favour of the castle, quite the opposite, but this was soon to happen. Already in 1072, perhaps because the king's new hall by the cathedral in the city centre was not yet finished, the Easter council was held in the castle.[28] But this must have been an exception, for the central fact about the royal connection with Winchester in the Norman period is that the city was the scene of the Easter crown-wearing in every year the court was in England, as far as we can tell, from 1068 until 1104. The only exception was in 1097, when Rufus was delayed by bad weather in the Channel.[29] The combination of church festival, the king's ceremonial appearance, and the accommodation and feasting of a vast

[23] For the palace, see *WS*, i. 289–302.
[24] Anglo-Saxon Chronicle, s.a. 1035 (C, D); cf. s.a. 1043 (D).
[25] Martin Biddle, 'Seasonal Festivals and Residence: Winchester, Westminster and Gloucester in the Tenth to Twelfth Centuries', *Anglo-Norman Studies*, viii (1986), 51–72, at Appendix D.
[26] *WS*, i. Survey **I**, **57–61** and **80–1**; cf. pp. 293–3.
[27] *domos regias apud Wintoniam . . . regiae Londoniensi non qualitate non quantitate secundas: Vita S. Remigii*, Cap. 27, in *Giraldi Cambrensis Opera*, ed. J. S. Brewer, J. F. Dimock and G. F. Warner, 8 vols. (*RS*, 1861–91), vii. 46; cf. *WS*, i. 294–5. For the palace at Westminster, see Colvin, *King's Works*, i. 14–17, 491–4, and Plan III; and for an outstanding painted reconstruction by W. T. Ball of the abbey and palace at the end of the eleventh century, see Richard Gem, 'The Romanesque Rebuilding of Westminster Abbey', *Proceedings of the Battle Conference* (now *Anglo-Norman Studies*), iii (1980), 33–60, at 48–9 (Fig. 5).
[28] See above, n. 16.
[29] Biddle, 'Seasonal Festivals', *passim*.

gathering required the proximity of church and residence. This need was precisely fulfilled at Winchester by the juxtaposition of cathedral and central palace, and it may have been much in William I's mind when he ordered the enlargement of the site and the building of a new hall. Likewise, when after 1104 Winchester ceased to be the setting for regular crown-wearings, the central palace fell into disuse and the focus of the royal house moved to the castle. A similar shift from open residence to castle occurs at just this time in the move from Old Windsor to Windsor (c. 1110).[30]

It is difficult now to remember that it was the Anglo-Saxon Old Minster which was the Conqueror's cathedral at Winchester, and the scene of his and his son's crown-wearings until 1093 (or possibly 1095).[31] Old Minster was over four centuries old when the Conqueror entered Winchester for perhaps the first time at Easter 1068.[32] It lay close beside the much younger church of New Minster, and was separated from the palace only by a small green, perhaps 30 m across, outside its west front. Immediately east of the green rose the great west-work, some 25 m square and 40 to 50 m in height, enclosing and surmounting the site of St Swithun's burial in 862. From here Old Minster stretched eastward for 76 m, its high altar surmounted by a second tower in several timber stages and hung with bells. As the see of one of the greatest of English dioceses, as a pilgrimage church, 'hung from end to end on either wall with the crutches and stools of those who had been healed there',[33] as the royal church *par excellence* of England, the burial-place of many kings and the scene of Edward the Confessor's coronation at Easter 1043, its very existence was a potent political statement, recognised in William's Easter crown-wearings, and soon to be replaced by the greatest of all the Norman churches of its age (Fig. 1).

The construction of the new cathedral began in 1079.[34] The works dedicated in 1093 included the greater and more elaborate parts of the church – crypt, ambulatory and eastern arm; the transepts, crossing and central tower; and the eastern third of the nave. Until then Old Minster, its cemetery, and perhaps its conventual buildings had prevented the laying out of the rest of the nave and the western tower(s), but with the demolition of Old Minster, following the removal of the feretory of St Swithun to the new cathedral on the feast of his translation, 15 July 1093, the way was clear. The

[30] Anglo-Saxon Chronicle, s.a. 1110 (E).

[31] The monks entered the first part of their new cathedral on 8 April 1093. This was presumably the day of its dedication (WS, i. 308), although I wonder now if the formal ceremony may not have been postponed until Easter on 17 April when Anselm was present. William, however, had been ill at Gloucester for much of Lent, and the court may not have gone to Winchester. In which case, the first crown-wearing in the present cathedral took place at Easter 1095. Biddle, 'Sesonal Festivals', 65–6 (Appendix B).

[32] For Old Minster, see Martin Biddle and Birthe Kjølbye-Biddle, *The Anglo-Saxon Minsters at Winchester* (WS, iv, i. forthcoming).

[33] *Ælfric: Lives of Three English Saints*, ed. G. I. Needham (1966), 79 [Life of Swithun, lines 359–61].

[34] See now Richard Gem, 'The Romanesque Cathedral of Winchester: Patron and Design in the Eleventh Century', *British Archaeological Association Conference Transactions*, vi. *Medieval Art and Architecture at Winchester Cathedral 1980* (1983), 1–11.

work may have been completed as early as 1098, or have lingered on into the early 1120s,[35] but it is reasonably certain that it was planned as a whole from the start in 1079. The north–south line of the west front is close to that of the west front of Old Minster, and the axes of the two churches, although different, converge in the palace area to the west, factors which suggest that the position of the west front of the new cathedral was approximately fixed from the start in relation to a pre-existing open space and the structures beyond it[36] (Fig. 2).

As completed (and probably as planned in 1079), the new Norman cathedral was 162 m (533 ft) in overall length, a little over twice as long as its predecessor, longer when planned than any other church in Western Christendom, and rivalling any structure built in the West since classical Antiquity.[37] Richard Gem has demonstrated how in general scale (as distinct from overall length) 'Winchester bears a comparison with the Vatican basilica of St Peter built by the Emperor Constantine and itself planned to an exceptional scale to rival the basilica of Trajan',[38] and has argued that Bishop Walkelin (1070–98), as the principal patron, knowing the scale of St Peter's, gave his master mason certain specific measurements to follow in working out his detailed plan.[39]

The other features of the new church are equally eclectic: influences from (or at least parallels to) Old Minster itself, the Romanesque architecture of Normandy, the Low Countries, the Meuse, Lorraine, the churches of the Pilgrimage group, and the Confessor's abbey church at Westminster have all been detected as reflecting 'a wide-ranging interest in formulae that are as much outside the Anglo-Norman tradition as they are within it'.[40]

The adoption of these influences in Winchester Gem sees as to 'be attributed firmly to the patron, Bishop Walkelin', with possible contributions from Prior Godfrey, a native of Cambrai, who was a monk at Winchester before becoming prior in 1082.[41] The comparison of Lanfranc's Canterbury with Walkelin's Winchester is illuminating: Canterbury 'was certainly a large building . . . but it was not ostentatiously so; it breathed something of the discipline of Le-Bec. At Walkelin's church on the other hand everything was immoderate – though not without unity'.[42] In this scale, in the deliberate emphasis on continuity as well as on innovation, in the close topographical relationship between the new church and the existing (and recently enlarged and rebuilt) royal residence, and perhaps also in the rivalry with the Confessor's Westminster which may be detected in the

---

[35] Gem, 'Winchester', 2; but cf. WS, i. 309.
[36] The actual overlapping of the two churches, and their relationship to the area of the royal palace to the west, are best shown in Martin Biddle, 'Felix Urbs Winthonia: Winchester in the Age of Monastic Reform', Tenth-Century Studies, ed. David Parsons (London and Chichester, 1975), 123–40, Fig. 4; cf. Fig. 3.
[37] WS, i. 310; cf. Gem, 'Winchester', 3.
[38] Gem, 'Winchester', 3.
[39] Ibid., 4.
[40] Ibid., 4–9.
[41] Ibid., 10.
[42] Ibid.

structure, there seems, however, to be more at work than the will of a diocesan bishop, however mighty. The new Norman cathedral at Winchester appears above all to embody, through the willing agency and influential direction of this bishop and prior, a political perception of the potential significance of Winchester the city and its royal as well as its ecclesiastical rôle in the moulding of the Anglo-Norman state. That the Conqueror himself played some part in directing the scale and concept and in initiating the work seems probable.[43] That this political perception was to prove baseless already in the first years of the next century, is irrelevant to the last decades of the eleventh. For the time being 'St Peter's new cathedral in Winchester should make a worthy comparison with the place of the Apostle's burial in Rome . . . in an overall conception which, while still reflecting both the political and ecclesiastical pretensions of the Anglo-Norman state, yet would have attained . . . to a sublimity that must have made it one of the most telling expressions of the high medieval religious mind.'[44]

Continuity between Old Minster and the new cathedral may be reflected in the eastern chapel and in the location and planning of the west front, but it is seen with greatest clarity outside the north door of the nave. Here, over the demolished west-work of Old Minster, a plaster surface was laid and a monument built to preserve the exact site and alignment of St Swithun's tomb. Even more remarkably the stone coffins which had stood around the saint's tomb on the floor of the west-work were also preserved in position in this memorial court.[45] The identity of those buried in these coffins is unknown, but they can scarcely be other than some of those kings and bishops whose remains, translated into the new cathedral in 1093–4, now rest in mortuary chests on the screen about the high altar.[46] The translation of the bodies of both secular and ecclesiastical rulers, the careful marking of the external places of their burial, and the preservation of their remains inside the new church, combine to show that great as was the supplanting of the old church by the new, there was in these actions little which sought to suppress the historical and dynastic traditions of the Anglo-Saxon past. To the contrary, we can see here the fact, perhaps even the sensing, of that continuity which is so prime a characteristic of the change from Anglo-Saxon to Norman Winchester.

Of the two other great monasteries which stood in the south-eastern quarter of the city little need be said here (Fig. 2). Nunnaminster retained its site. In the late eleventh or early twelfth century the piecemeal remodelling of its domestic buildings on Norman lines began, while the abbey church of St

---

[43] William II continued this support, by granting stone from the Isle of Wight (*Regesta*, ii. no. 412d), and by his grant in 1096 of a fair of three days at the church of St Giles on the eastern hill of Winchester (*Regesta*, i. no. 377). After his death in the New Forest, William was buried at Winchester, not necessarily as a convenience, but possibly because his grants made it particularly appropriate. The other Norman kings were all buried in abbeys of their own foundation. See *WS*, i. 472 and n. 5.

[44] Gem, 'Winchester', 10.

[45] *WS*, i. 311–12.

[46] For these chests and their contents, see John Vaughan, *Winchester Cathedral. Its Monuments and Memorials* (1919), 15–28.

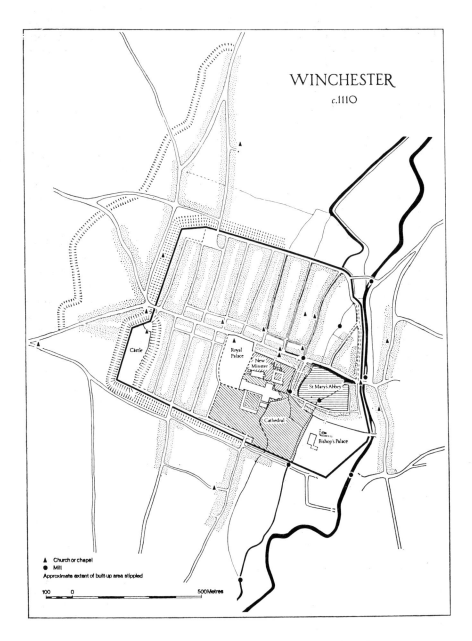

Fig. 2. Early Norman Winchester. Parish churches known to have been in existence by c. 1110 are shown. The castle chapel and the church of St Laurence, which may have originated as the chapel of the extended Norman royal palace, are also shown.

319

Mary was entirely rebuilt to a much larger plan and dedicated in 1108.[47] New Minster lost part of its site to the extension of the royal palace in 1069–70.[48] The remainder was extremely cramped. The domestic buildings, burnt down in 1065, were reconstructed east of the church on the basis of the former infirmary, but the solution was far from ideal.[49] About 1110, because of the restricted site, unhealthy conditions and *alia multa incommoda*, the monastery was moved to a new site at Hyde outside the north gate of the city, and the former site reverted to the cathedral priory to become part of the cathedral yard as it now is, and to be used for burial until the nineteenth century.

On the new site Henry I was in a real sense the founder of what became known as Hyde Abbey, for the migration took place on royal initiative and under strict royal control. The new buildings may have been well advanced by 1114 when the acquisition of the site and other lands was formally recognised,[50] but works probably went on for many years. The well-known capitals probably from the cloister arcade suggest that the cloister was not completed in stone until the later 1120s. They also show a dependence on the sculpture of Henry's own foundation of Reading Abbey which emphasises Henry's close involvement with Hyde.[51]

The bishop's residence at Wolvesey formed the fifth of the great enclosures in the south-eastern quarter of Winchester. Walkelin seems to have used the Anglo-Saxon hall and other buildings on the same site, for it was not until about 1110, and therefore in the episcopate of William Giffard, that reconstruction began.[52] The first new structure was a residential block containing the chambers designed to accommodate the bishop's private apartments, a function it continued to serve into the seventeenth century. The principal rooms were all raised to first-floor level on a solid substructure, and at this level there was a walled area, probably a garden. This looked westward over streams to the cathedral, a prospect which delights the eye today as much as it was surely meant to when the garden was first planted. Giffard's building was cased in squared stonework of high technical quality, closely similar to the ashlar of the central tower of the cathedral as rebuilt after the fall of 1107. It was also vast, 50 m (164 ft) from north to south and 24.4 m (80 ft) in width, the largest known non-monastic domestic structure of its date in England, apart from Westminster Hall. Fresh water was brought in by lead pipe from somewhere above the city, a service probably shared from the beginning with the cathedral.[53]

[47] *WS*, i. 321–3, 556. For the discovery and excavation of part of the nave of the abbey church, see *Find. The Newsletter of the Winchester Archaeological Rescue Group*, 25 (Sept. 1981), 3–4; 26 (Jan. 1982), 4–5; 29 (Jan. 1983), 2–4; and 31 (Sept. 1983), 4–6. See now also Kenneth Qualmann, 'Winchester – Nunnaminster', *Current Archaeology*, 102 (Nov. 1986), 204–7.
[48] See above, p. 315.
[49] *WS*, i. 313–17.
[50] *Regesta*, ii. no. 1070.
[51] George Zarnecki, in *English Romanesque Art 1066–1200*, Arts Council of Great Britain (1984), 172–3.
[52] *WS*, i. 323–8. See now also Martin Biddle, *Wolvesey*, Historic Buildings and Monuments Commission (1986).
[53] *WS*, i. 284.

From about 1130 onwards Henry of Blois, Giffard's successor in the see, continued the reconstruction. He demolished what was left of the pre-Conquest palace, adding first a two-storey chapel to Giffard's building and then a grand porch and next constructing a second large block to the east, separated from his predecessor's building by an open space which was soon to become a closed courtyard. Henry's new block contained a hall of public audience, suitable for his own position after his brother's accession to the throne in 1135 and his own appointment as administrator of the vacant archiepiscopal see the following year. The three legatine councils held at Winchester during Henry's years as papal legate, in 1139, 1141 and 1143, were probably all held in his new hall at Wolvesey.

Henry's works at Wolvesey continued for many years, gradually trans-forming the separate buildings into a defended courtyard house with much of the appearance of a castle. But already by 1138, before the works of fortification necessitated first by the threat and then by the reality of civil war, Wolvesey had become the very type of an early medieval palace on the grand scale. In the elaboration of its design and decoration, Wolvesey was fully the equal of contemporary royal and comptal palaces elsewhere, not least in France. The sculpture of the porch added by Henry to Giffard's west range c. 1135–8 recalls indeed the sculptures of the façade of Abbot Suger's great church at St Denis, consecrated in 1140,[54] and reminds us that the architecture of 'the first amateur of art of his age' was as exceptional as the manuscripts, enamels, jewellery, goldwork and statues which he com-missioned and collected so assiduously.[55]

The five great complexes in the south-eastern quarter of Winchester – the royal palace, the cathedral, New Minster (until c. 1110), Nunnaminster (St Mary's Abbey), and the bishop's palace at Wolvesey – mark this area out not only for the service of God but as a centre of the first order for royal ceremony and the emergence of administrative office. It is these buildings and all that they imply which are the basis of the popular claim that Winchester was the capital of England, in later Anglo-Saxon as well as in Norman times. However anachronistic such a claim, it crystallises an essential truth, the perception of which led the Normans to remake these buildings in their own fashion on the grandest scale (Fig. 2).

A comparison between the changes worked on the great buildings of church and state and those wrought on the ordinary fabric of the city reveals a notable contrast (cf. Figs. 1 and 2). If we compare the situation c. 1110, so far as we can reconstruct it, with that recovered for the pre-Conquest period, it is the essential continuity of the basic framework which is striking: the

[54] Zarnecki, in *English Romanesque Art*, 183; George Zarnecki, 'Henry of Blois as a Patron of Sculpture', *Art and Patronage in the English Romanesque*, ed. Sarah Macready and F. H. Thompson, Occasional Paper (New Series) viii, Society of Antiquaries (1986), 159–72, at pp. 160–2, pls. XLIV, XLV.
[55] David Knowles, *The Monastic Order in England*, 2nd edn. (Cambridge, 1966), 289–91; Zarnecki, 'Henry of Blois'; Neil Stratford, 'The "Henry of Blois Plaques" in the British Museum', *British Archaeological Association Conference Transactions*, vi. *Medieval Art and Architecture at Winchester Cathedral 1980* (1983), 28–37.

defences, gates and streets (apart from those closed for the construction of the castle and the enlargement of the royal palace) remain unchanged, as they do in the main today. The lesser churches seem also to display a basic continuity, but here the evidence is more difficult. Of the fifty-seven parish churches in the walled city and suburbs in the late thirteenth century, it seems probable that a substantial proportion, perhaps the majority, were founded before the Conquest.[56] But no more than ten or eleven are *known* to be of pre-Conquest date, four of these on archaeological evidence alone.[57] Striking examples of the discrepancy between first recorded mention and actual date of origin are provided by the churches of St Mary in Tanner Street and St Pancras, both first mentioned in 1172 and both shown by excavation to date from at least the early tenth century.[58] St Pancras indeed was already a transeptal church in two or even three pre-Conquest stages. There are presumably a number of post-Conquest foundations among the parish churches of the thirteenth-century,[59] but the relationship of the majority of the lesser churches to the patterns formed by the property boundaries around them suggests that they are in origin usually contemporary with the emergence of their surrounding tenements, and that is to say of pre-Conquest date.

Nor was the Conquest to result in any rapid change in the architectural fabric of these churches. None of the six surviving medieval parish churches shows any sign of alteration for a century after the Conquest.[60] Of the seven others which have been excavated, one was a twelfth-century foundation, and one was extended and another may have been added to or reconstructed in the late eleventh century.[61] There is nothing here to suggest that the Conquest had any particular effect on the lesser churches of the city. It is the later twelfth century, not the late eleventh, which saw a remarkable movement of reconstruction and extension: of the nine medieval churches which survived in whole or in part into the age of the topographical artist and ecclesiologist, and were then recorded (and three of these were to be demolished in the mid-nineteenth century), no fewer than six were remodelled in the decades immediately before 1200.[62]

Nor is there evidence for any notable change in the pattern or character of the city's housing stock in the decades following the Conquest. Trends

---

[56] *WS*, i. 329–35; cf. *WS*, ii. 106–13, Table 1 (pp. 134–5); Keene, 'Introduction'.
[57] *WS*, i. 329–30.
[58] *WS*, ii. 741–4, 761–3, Figs. 85, 89.
[59] E.g. St Mary in Brudene Street, on a property of the archdeacon of Winchester: *WS*, ii. 641. Some dedications, such as those to St Valery, St Leonard, St Nicholas or St Petroc, belong to the Norman period or later, but the churches were not necessarily founded in this period, for rededications were possible: *WS*, i. 330.
[60] St Bartholomew Hyde, St John in the Soke, St Lawrence, St Michael outside King's Gate, St Peter Chesil, St Swithun over King's Gate: *WS*, ii. Table 1 (pp. 134–5) and the refs. given there to the individual churches.
[61] St Mary in Brudene Street, see above, n. 59; St Peter in the Fleshshambles, *WS*, ii. 493–4; St Anastasius, *WS*, ii. 927.
[62] St Bartholomew Hyde, St John in the Soke, St Lawrence, as in n. 60; St Mary outside West Gate, St Maurice, and St Thomas (St Petroc), for which see *WS*, ii. 939–40, 538–40 and 881–3, respectively.

discernible or well established in the earlier part of the century, whether the subdivision of larger urban properties, the infilling of street frontages or of the rear parts of tenements, or encroachments on what little public space remained, can be followed without evident interruption, but perhaps with some diminution, over the next century.[63] There is no observable change in timber building technology until well into the thirteenth century, when earth-fast vertical posts began to be set first into sill-beams set on the ground and were then raised on stone dwarf walls.[64] Stone-built houses sometimes seem a characteristic of Norman towns, but surviving examples belong to the mid- or later twelfth century.[65] In fact stone houses were already appearing in Winchester in small numbers before the Conquest, especially in High Street and in the adjacent stretches of the richest side-streets.[66] A notable example surviving in St Thomas Street (Calpe Street), probably on a property held by a succession of moneyers between the reigns of Edward the Confessor and Stephen, is usually regarded as of twelfth-century date, but is probably earlier.[67] Although not pre-Conquest, it represents exactly both the social status and physical character of those *cellarii* in Winchester pillaged by the men of London in 1141.[68]

Even on the excavated tenements, where we have a precise knowledge of the development of the individual structures at ground level throughout the eleventh century, there is no sign of any specific change which might be attributed to the Conquest or the influences associated with it.[69] Steady, unfaltering, continuity seems to be the order of the day; even 'development' seems too strong a word.

Development seems, however, to be just what was taking place in the suburbs, a contrast which may suggest that it was only there that sufficient space for significant new building was still available, the walled area having long been fully built up. There were suburbs outside each of the city's five principal gates (East, North, West and South Gates, and King's Gate also in the southern wall) long before the Conquest.[70] They consisted essentially of single streets lined with properties, but both the east and west suburbs were larger and more complex. Very little is known of the early history of the eastern suburb, which lay in the soke, contained no royal properties, and is thus omitted from the survey of *c.* 1110 in the Winton Domesday.[71] The earlier stages of the west suburb are by contrast relatively well recorded. It seems to have been the most intensively occupied, and the most prosperous of the suburbs, and to have seen a considerable expansion of its built-up area

---

[63] *WS*, i. 280–2, 340–5, 349–86. For infilling in particular, see the evidence of the excavated properties in Lower Brook Street (Tanner Street), conveniently summarised in *WS*, ii. 758–67, and esp. Fig. 88.

[64] *WS*, i. 346.

[65] Margaret Wood, *The English Mediaeval House* (1965), 1–15.

[66] *WS*, i. 339–40, 346–8, Fig. 11; cf. *WS*, ii. 155–6, 165–7, 169–70, Fig. 10.

[67] *WS*, i. 346; for drawings and a plan of this house, see *VCH Hampshire*, v. (1912), 8–9.

[68] *Gesta Stephani*, Cap. 67.

[69] Summarised in *WS*, ii. 758–67; to be published in *WS*, v.

[70] *WS*, i. 260–8.

[71] *WS*, i. 244, 255–6, Fig. 4 (*c.* 1110), Fig. 5.

between TRE and 1148.[72] There were six churches, one at least as early as the tenth century, compared with only three in the east suburb, and outside King's Gate, and one in each of the other suburbs.[73] All this suggests that the western suburb was also the oldest and had seen the longest development, an observation which archaeology seems now to be confirming.[74] Whatever their individual history, however, all the suburbs seem to have reached their maximum extent and density of occupation in the twelfth century. Quite early in the century the boundary of the city liberty was defined around those parts of the western and northern suburbs which did not form part of the bishop's soke by the digging of a substantial ditch and bank.[75] The limits of the other suburbs, all apparently within the soke, were defined by bars and possibly by some kind of linear boundary.[76] In these limits, whether ditched or barred, we seem to see emerging the first signs of a physical outer boundary which might in time have crystallised as an actual line of defence as happened so often like an onion skin around many a continental town, and can be seen occasionally in England, most strikingly at Northampton.[77] This was not to be, for Winchester had reached its zenith and was henceforth to contract.[78]

The most striking single sign of economic development at Winchester in the aftermath of the Conquest is perhaps to be seen in the growth of St Giles's Fair on the eastern hill above the city.[79] In 1096 the king granted to the bishop a fair of three days on the eastern hill of Winchester, and in 1110, 1136 and 1155 this was extended successively to eight, fourteen and then sixteen days.[80] At first sight, this looks like an obvious index of the increasing importance of the fair, and hence of Winchester, as a centre for long-distance and especially international trade. This may be so, but we do not know that the grant of 1096 marks the origin of the fair as distinct from the alienation of its rights and profits over a period of three days, or that the subsequent grants represent more than a continuation of this practice at the expense of the Crown. The description of the regularly laid-out site of the fair in 1287 as *Nova Villa* might suggest a major reorganisation of the site at the height of its prosperity,[81] but it is not certain that the recorded extensions in the length of

---

[72] *WS*, i. 350–1, 356–8, 380–1, Table 12*a*, *b*.

[73] *WS*, i. Fig. 10.

[74] See, e.g. K. E. Qualmann, in David A. Hinton, Suzanne Keene and Kenneth E. Qualmann, 'The Winchester Reliquary', *Medieval Archaeology*, 25 (1981), 45–77, at pp. 47–50. These observations have been confirmed by subsequent excavations along Sussex Street. See also, Biddle, 'The Study of Winchester', 123–4.

[75] *WS*, i. 263–4, Fig. 26.

[76] *WS*, i. 264–5; cf. Figs. 5 and 10.

[77] Royal Commission on the Historical Monuments of England, *An Inventory of the Historical Monuments in the County of Northampton*, v. *Archaeological Sites and Churches in Northampton* (1985), 45–52, Figs. 7 and 8.

[78] For the start of Winchester's decline, see *WS*, i. 489–508. Dr Derek Keene's *Survey of Medieval Winchester (WS*, ii) can to some extent be seen as a commentary on its continuation (cf. *WS*, ii. 86–105).

[79] *WS*, i. 286–8, Fig. 8; cf. *WS*, ii. 1091–1132.

[80] *WS*, i. 286–8; see also above, n. 43.

[81] *WS*, i. 288; *WS*, ii. 1092; cf. Figs. 144–6.

the fair can be taken as a sign of greatly increased economic activity in the aftermath of the Conquest. The fair may be much older and have reached a high level of activity even before 1066.[82] That there was then some increase is perhaps probable, even likely, but its extent is difficult to gauge. Only constant archaeological observation and excavation may be able to solve this problem.

The effects of the Conquest on the physical fabric of Winchester may now be summarised:

1. essential continuity of form and function with little observable change in the basic fabric of defences, streets and houses;
2. major changes in architectural provision for the highest levels of royal and ecclesiastical activity, accompanied by an unprecedented expenditure on building sustained without interruption for over seventy years;
3. growth, expressed by the expansion of the suburbs and increased density of occupation in the walled area, and perhaps (but not certainly) in the increased length and importance of St Giles's Fair, all fuelled by the greatly increased investment of external wealth implied by the building programme in (2).

To what extent did these physical trends run parallel to changes in the society and population of the city in the century after the Conquest?

By 1070 all the great offices most closely associated with the city had passed or were about to pass into Norman hands: Walkelin became bishop in 1070 and his brother Simon was appointed prior of the cathedral monastery probably shortly afterwards; Riwallon was elected abbot of New Minster in 1072; and Beatrice became abbess of Nunnaminster before 1084.[83] Hugh of Port-en-Bessin was sheriff of Hampshire by c. 1070, and in 1096 was described as *vicarius* of Winchester.[84] Before c. 1100 the local justiciar in Winchester was Richard de Courcy.[85] And by 1105 at the latest the reeve of the city bore a Norman name, although this may mean no more than that his parents had named him in the new Norman fashion in the years immediately after 1066.[86]

The moneyers, however, present a different picture. Unlike those officials

---

[82] Cf. *WS*, ii. 1112. The construction of a bridge over the Itchen as early as ?859 (*WS*, i. 271–2), and the other evidence for the heavy use and early importance of the east–west route (now High Street) through the walled city (Biddle, 'The Study of Winchester', 120–1), may be an indication of the need for, and use of, a principal access to the fair site on the east hill.

[83] *Handbook of British Chronology*, ed. F. M. Powicke and E. B. Fryde (Royal Historical Society, 2nd ed., 1961), 258; *The Heads of Religious Houses in England and Wales 940–1216*, ed. D. Knowles, C. N. L. Brooke and V. C. M. London (Cambridge, 1972), under the respective houses.

[84] For the Port family, see J. H. Round in *VCH Hampshire*, i (1900), 423–4, 534; for Hugh *vicarius*, see *Regesta*, i. no. 379.

[85] Local justiciars were introduced by the Norman kings: H. A. Cronne, 'The office of local justiciar in England under the Norman Kings', *University of Birmingham Historical Journal*, vi (1958), 18–38. For Richard, see *WS*, i. **I, 45**, n. 4, and J. H. Round in *VCH Hampshire*, i (1900), 533.

[86] *WS*, i. 423–5, Table 46.

already mentioned, except perhaps the reeves, they were burgesses.[87] With other citizens of comparable wealth, they formed the highest rank in the social and economic hierarchy of the city, the highest rank, that is, of those whose interests were confined to the city and its commercial activities, unlike the royal officers who migrated with the court.[88] All those moneyers who struck coins for the Conqueror and for Rufus bore Old English names, and of the sixteen who struck for Henry I, eleven still bore English names, while three more may have been English, and only two (neither of whom struck before c. 1113) had names of continental Germanic (more specifically Old German) origin, names that were of essentially Norman fashion.[89] Continuity among the moneyers appears also in their succession from reign to reign, at least in so far as identity of name may be thought to indicate the same individuals: seven of the Conqueror's moneyers had struck previously for the Confessor and five for Harold II, and some of these may have continued into the reign of William II.[90] Even more striking perhaps is the evidence for the continuity of moneyers' interests in individual properties. In some instances this interest can be traced from TRE through c. 1110 to 1148 and beyond to properties held by men who were subsequently to strike coins for Henry II: two properties held by Anderbodus, a moneyer of the Confessor, demonstrate the continuity of moneying interests for the best part of a century.[91] In some cases one can show that this continuity 'arose from sons succeeding their fathers as moneyers, or at least from the retention of moneying in a single family'.[92] The moneyers may of course be a special case, an instance of continuity in administrative practice, rather than representative of any general continuity in tenure, but there are other factors which suggest the strength of English continuity at a relatively high level of urban society.

The problem is complicated by changes in name giving. The pattern revealed by the surveys in the Winton Domesday and in 1207 is clear enough:[93]

Estimated number of occurrences of personal names
of native and foreign origin in early medieval Winchester

	Native (%)	Foreign (%)
Survey I TRE	85.3	14.7
Survey I c. 1110	29.8	70.2
Survey II 1148	20.0	80.0
—　　1207	5.2	94.8

Here we have a trend which seems quite contrary to that shown by the moneyers, and which may reinforce the suspicion that they were a special case, for 55 of the 80 percentage points of change in personal names which

[87] Ibid., 421.
[88] Ibid., 444, 447, Fig. 24, Tables 50–2.
[89] Ibid., 476.
[90] Ibid., 413–15.
[91] Ibid., 416.
[92] Ibid., 416–19.
[93] Ibid., 183–7, Table 7, Figs. 1 and 2.

took place in the 150 years between TRE and 1207 occurred in the fifty years up to *c*. 1110, during which the composition of the moneyers, to judge from their names, changed not at all. But the contrast is not so stark as it might seem. One-third of the population still bore native names *c*. 1110; some families used 'foreign' names already before the Conquest (14.7 per cent TRE) and may have continued the practice; and there will be those who were born to English parents after the Conquest and yet were named for whatever social and personal reasons in the fashion of their conquerors.[94] By *c*. 1110 many of this third group will have been in their thirties or even older and will long have been part of the patterns of property holding recorded in Survey I. If the moneyers were a special group, therefore, it will have been in the strength of their adherence to English fashions, and we may wonder whether this may not have been a characteristic of the prosperous group of leading citizens to which they belonged and in which they may even have been pre-eminent.

It is difficult and perhaps impossible to reach any accurate estimate of the extent to which the change in personal names represents actual replacement of population rather than changes in fashion. But there are some ways to approach the question of the degree to which Englishmen and English families continued to hold (which of course is not necessarily to say that they themselves occupied) houses along the streets of Winchester between 1066 and *c*. 1110.

First, there is some evidence for continuity of tenure within the same family, and of this the moneyers provide some but not all of the evidence.[95] Even in those cases where a property was held by a Norman lord *c*. 1110, however, there will not of necessity have been a change of occupancy, and on the properties of the seven great fiefs, all technically in Norman hands by *c*. 1110,[96] continuity of English occupation seems as inherently likely as transfer to Norman families.

The problem of English survival can partly be gauged by looking at Norman replacement. By *c*. 1110 property-holders identifiable as being of Norman family had replaced Englishmen on about 19 per cent of the properties on the king's fief. This is a minimum figure: a further 42 per cent of property-holders on the king's fief had Norman names, and of these an unknown number will have been of Norman stock.[97] Thus, on the king's fief, the only one to which this test can be applied *c*. 1110,[98] the actual level of replacement of English property-holders by Normans in the fifty years since the Conquest must have been between 19 and 61 per cent.

It is easier to look at the direct evidence for English survival, however, for few Normans will have been given English names,[99] but the result will still

---

[94] Ibid., 189.
[95] Ibid., 409, 416–19, 445, 475.
[96] Ibid., 349–69; and cf. above, p. 325.
[97] *WS*, i. 475.
[98] Ibid., 350–3.
[99] Ibid., 475; for cases where English names seem to have been given to children of fathers with names of continental Germanic type, see ibid., 189.

be a minimum for we cannot tell how many Englishmen are concealed within the 42 per cent on the king's fief *c*. 1110 who bore foreign names. Nevertheless, of those who paid landgable on royal lands in Winchester *c*. 1110, 27 per cent had Anglo-Saxon (OE) names.[100] These include at least eight cases of sons succeeding their fathers, and two where an Englishman was succeeded by his wife.[101] The distribution of those with English names on the king's fief *c*. 1110 is perhaps significantly very uneven. There are very few in High Street and Gold Street (Southgate Street), two of the principal streets running to the city gates, but in the western suburb, and in some of the side-streets, there are notable concentrations of English names which in Bucchestret (Busket lane), on the north side of High Street, just inside East Gate, reach 61 per cent.[102]

There was, it seems clear, a considerable degree of continuity of tenure in Winchester in the decades after the Conquest. By *c*. 1110 English tenure (and thus perhaps English occupancy) of the greater streets was limited, but the English were not necessarily of lower status than before, as the moneyers and perhaps the reeves both show.[103]

To return then to our view of the city as a whole. Whatever the dislocation caused in the years immediately after the Conquest by the destruction of property for castle and palace, Winchester had prospered by *c*. 1110. This prosperity rested on an economic base already long established and highly developed before the Conquest, but it was fostered by the huge investment in construction which began already in 1067 and had not abated fifty years later, and by the expenditure of the Crown, reflected most particularly in the ceremonial of the Easter crown-wearings and in the large concourse which attended them.

Only with numbers and by comparison can we begin to appreciate what such a description actually means. How big was Winchester in the early twelfth century? What was its population? And how did it rank in relation to other places? Almost all the tests we can use are imprecise, especially so where the figures look most precise; the numbers are very rarely comparable even within the compass of one city, let alone for comparisons between one city and another. But the attempt must be made. Only by devising new quantifications and refining existing figures, both as to basis and quantity, can we hope to proceed from description to analysis, from analysis to explanation.

In the time of King Edward there may have been in Winchester about 1130 tenements.[104] By *c*. 1110, if the evidence of the king's fief can be extrapolated to the city and suburbs as a whole, this number may have risen by some 15

---

[100] Ibid., 475.

[101] Ibid.

[102] Ibid., 475–6.

[103] Ibid., 476; for the reeves, see ibid., 423–5, Table 46. From 1105 the reeves bore Norman names, but this does not necessarily imply they were of Norman birth, for they would have been of just that generation to whom, in the aftermath of the Conquest, English parents may have chosen to give Norman names: see above, p. 327.

[104] *WS*, i. 468, and n. 3.

per cent to about 1300 tenements.[105] This is perhaps the best index of size we have. It ought to be possible to use the number of parish churches in the same way, but their early history is rarely documented and we still know too little of their archaeology.[106] Square area is certainly some index, but the size of the walled area is no sure guide to the size or density of the occupied area, whether within the walls or without. In a city like Winchester, where the walls are of Roman date, and the walled area has been replanned in the ninth century, the walled area is as much an index of Romano-British or Alfredian urban expectations as a guide to Norman scale. The probable area of the various suburbs and of the site of St Giles's Fair add their own complications, but must be taken into account. By the later twelfth century, the picture may have been thus:[107]

	hectares	acres
The walled city	58.2	143.8
The suburbs		
North	19.6	48.4
South	49.2	121.6
East	21.1	52.1
West	20.7	51.1
Total	110.6	273.2
City and suburbs	168.8	417.0
The Fair	26.8	66.2
Total urban area	195.6	483.2

Perhaps most striking is the overall relationship of fair:walled city:suburbs at 1:2:4.

If we turn from estimates of properties and space to population, the problems are compounded. The application of the classic multiplier of 4.5 to the figure of 1300 tenements *c.* 1110, with an addition of 10 per cent for families in excess of the number of tenements, would suggest a population of about 6500.[108] But this will not do, for it is possible to suggest that in the early fifteenth century, when Winchester had been subject to more or less continuous economic decline for nearly three centuries and had suffered severely in the plagues of the fourteenth century, it still contained about 7750 persons.[109] From this a pre-plague population of between 10,000 and 12,000 can be suggested.[110] A population of at least 12,000 should probably

---

[105] Ibid., 481, and n. 6.
[106] See above, pp. 312 and 322, and cf. *WS*, i. 458–9, 485–6.
[107] Ibid., 484.
[108] Ibid., 440–1.
[109] Dr D. J. Keene's estimate in *WS*, ii. 366–7 which replaces the previous estimate of 6000 in *WS*, i. 440.
[110] *WS*, ii. 367–8.

therefore now be regarded as likely in the mid–twelfth century.[111] In which case, we must take a rather higher figure, say 13,000, for the period of the city's zenith early in the twelfth century when the number of tenements was some 200 more than it seems to have been in 1148.[112]

How then did Winchester with 1300 tenements in the early twelfth century rank by comparison with the other cities of the kingdom in terms of Domesday houses? It ranked second to London, equal with Norwich (1270), ahead of York (1181) and Lincoln (910), and far above Thetford (720) or Gloucester (508).[113] This is a ranking which is entirely consistent with that of the coinage, the most precise index of comparison we possess.[114] Moreover, both indices agree in seeing Winchester rise from fourth to second place in the period since the Conquest, a rise which is only partly due to Winchester's own development and must be accounted for in part at least by the decline of York and Lincoln consequent upon the devastation of the north early in the Conqueror's reign.[115]

The exact relationship of Winchester to London in terms of size and population cannot yet be stated. The point at which London surpassed Winchester in wealth and population lies somewhere in the middle of the tenth century. London produced about 24 per cent of the surviving coins of the period 973–1066, Winchester about 7 per cent.[116] This is still a crude guide, but if the production of coin is an index of commercial activity, London's bullion market in this period was some three times more active than Winchester. We do not yet possess figures to show how this relationship varied, if at all, in the half-century after the Conquest, when in relative terms from *c.* 1075 until well into Henry I's reign Winchester as a mint was second only to London.[117] But London seems to have had about twice as many churches in the twelfth century as Winchester, and in cities of this type, where multiple tiny parishes are themselves an index of population,[118] this figure provides another index of the relationship between the two cities, and one which agrees well enough with that of the coinage. In Norman England, Winchester was something like one–half to one–quarter the size of London, and with Lincoln, Norwich and York (but exceeding all three) formed the second rank of English towns.

The Norman Conquest wrought vast changes in the great buildings of state and church in Winchester, but did so in a context of essential stability in the basic urban fabric. Change and continuity in physical fabric were mirrored in the population of the city. Great investment in buildings and the

---

[111] This replaces the figure of 'in excess of' 8000 suggested in *WS*, i. 440.
[112] Cf. the estimate of tenements in *c.* 1110 (*WS*, i. 481, and n. 6) with that for 1148 (ibid., 468, and n. 3).
[113] Ibid., 485.
[114] Ibid.
[115] Ibid., 396–7, 468–9, 488; cf. David Hill, *An Atlas of Anglo-Saxon England* (Oxford, 1981), Figs. 222–3.
[116] *WS*, i. 468.
[117] Ibid., 397, 485.
[118] Ibid., 485–6, 498–9.

close bond between the city and the Crown brought Winchester in the decades after the Conquest to the zenith of its fortunes, perhaps above all as a ceremonial place. When the bond with the Crown failed early in the twelfth century, Winchester's long medieval decline began. The exceptional position of the Norman city was the result of the temporary enhancement of a political and emotional rôle which was in reality yielding to London long before the Conquest.

For forty years Winchester lived out its apogee on the brink of decline. Its greatest age had already passed when Geoffrey of Monmouth placed Arthur far back in its long history, and when Wace first wrote of the Round Table, but it was also in some sense to this great age, and to the ages which must (it seemed) have foreshadowed it, that Malory looked back when he saw Camelot in Winchester.[119]

[119] For this traditional 'history', see Martin Biddle (ed.), *King Arthur's Round Table* (forthcoming).
* A version of this paper was first given in the Upper Library of Christ Church in the Norman Conquest Special Subject of the Oxford Faculty of Modern History under the aegis of Mr J. E. H. Cowdrey and Dr J. F. A. Mason, to both of whom I am most grateful for their help and encouragement.

William of Saint-Calais and the Domesday Survey
Oxford, Trinity College, MS 28

(a) fo. 90r

(b) fo. 1r

(c) fo. 52v

(d) fo. 4r

Plate II

Hereford Cathedral Library, MS P.I.10

In hoc codice continentur hec.
1 Liber didimi de spu sco.
2 Dialoguf auguftini & orofu de fide. & de queftio
nib; quibufda ueterif teftamenta.
3 Difputatio auguftini contra felicianu hyreticu.
4 Epla B Auguftini ad probam de orando dm.
5 Sermo eide de lectione. Mulieref forte qs inuenies
6 Responfio eide ad dulctitu de octo queftionib;

(a) fo. 0v

de ueteri teftamento fup euf fide intellectuq;
doceamur. Nam & fupiuf prelocuti fum' in omnib;

(b) fo. 73r

guftif finib; cmmanda eft. Onif eni q b; amor & di
lectio debetur amplecae quauif maliof ppenfius
m aliof fufpenfiuf inclinet. puenit aut ufq; ad inimi
cof p q b; etia orare pcipim'. Ita nemo eft ingenere hu

(c) fo. 26r

MNIBVS
QUIDEM QUE DIUINA
sunt· cum reuerentia
& uehementi cura opor
tet animu intendere· mari
me aute hif que de sci spf di
uinitate dicuntur· prefertim cu

(d) fo. 1v

Plate III

Exon Domesday

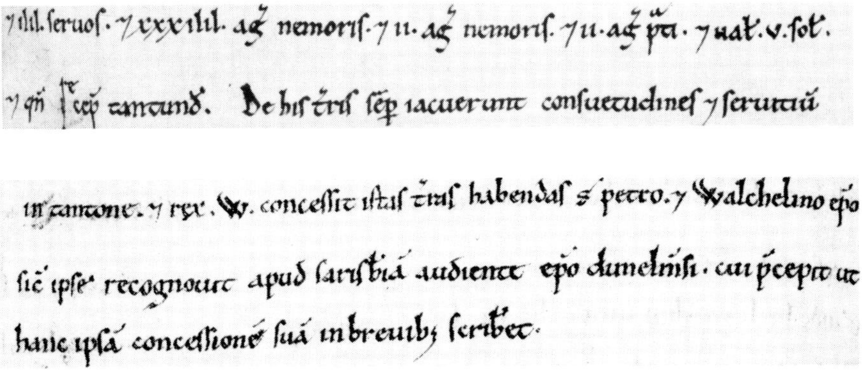

.ɪɪɪɪ. seruos. ⁊ xxxɪɪɪɪ. aǥ nemoris. ⁊ ɪɪ. aǥ nemoris. ⁊ ɪɪ. aǥ pᵃ. ⁊ ual. v. sol.

⁊ q̄ ꝼ ꞇꝛ̄ tantūd. De his ꞇꝛ̄s sep̄ iacuerunt consuetudines ⁊ seruitiu̅

in tantone. ⁊ rex .W. concessit istas ꞇꝛ̄s habendas ꝓ petro. ⁊ Walchelino ep̄o

sic ipse recognouiꞇ apud sarisbiã audiente ep̄o dunelmisi. cui p̄cepꞇ uꞇ

hanc ipsã concessione̅ suã in breuibꝫ scribeꞇ.

(b) fo. 175v

Great Domesday Book

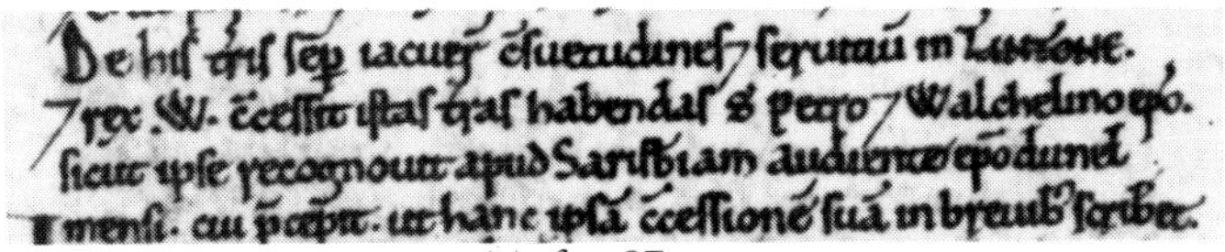

De his ꞇꝛ̄s sep̄ iacueꝛ c̄sueꞇudines ⁊ seruitiu̅ in Tantone.
⁊ rex .W. c̄cessiꞇ istas ꞇꝛ̄s habendas ꝓ peꞇro ⁊ Walchelino ep̄o.
sicut ipse recognouiꞇ apud Sarisbiam audience ep̄o dunel
̄mensi. cui p̄cepꞇ. uꞇ hanc ipsã c̄cessione̅ suã in breuibꝫ scribeꞇ.

(c) fo. 87v

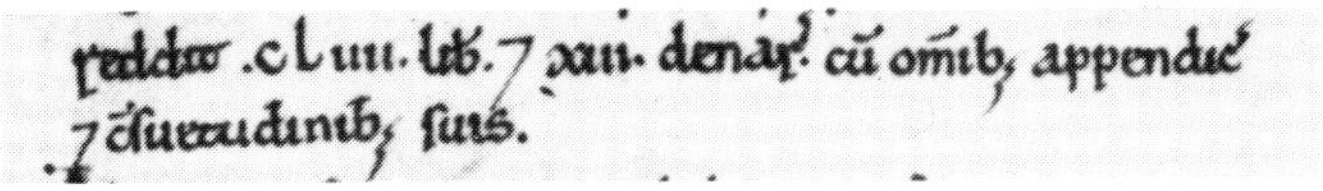

reddiꞇ .cl ɪɪɪɪ. lꝺ. ⁊ xɪɪ. denaꝝ. cū omibꝫ appendiꞇ
⁊ c̄sueꞇudinibꝫ suis.

(d) fo. 87v

Hiᵈ ɐ..ᵒ̣ᷓ̇uᷓꞇ.
.I. Rex Willelmus.
.II. Ep̄s de Execestre.
.III. Ecc̄lᵃ de Tauestoch.
.IIII. Ecc̄lᵉ aliquaꞇ s̄c̄oꝝ.

(e) fo. 120r

Ibi. ɪɪɪ. hide. h̄ꞇ ꞇꝛ̄a
.xxvɪɪ. TERRA Willelm̄.
Will̄s camerari
Ibi. ɪɪɪɪ. hide. In dn̄io
ibi. ɪɪɪɪ. serui. Uaꞇ
Te̅ W. ꞇ hasenepeꝛ

(f) fo. 167r

abb̄atisse Wiltuniensi. q̄ nunq̄ antea habuerat. postea
ū eas tenuiꞇ. Will̄s cūm dcā Quintone Suindone
⁊ cheurel que̅ erant tainlande. pᵒ t̄ꝛa de insula de Wꞇh.
que̅ p̄neꞇ ad firmã de Imblesberie.

(g) fo. 64v

beeltiia . ɪɪɪ . caꝛ. ⁊ in duabꝫ hane-
cheronis . ɪɪ . caꝛ. ⁊ in Laelum. x. b̄o

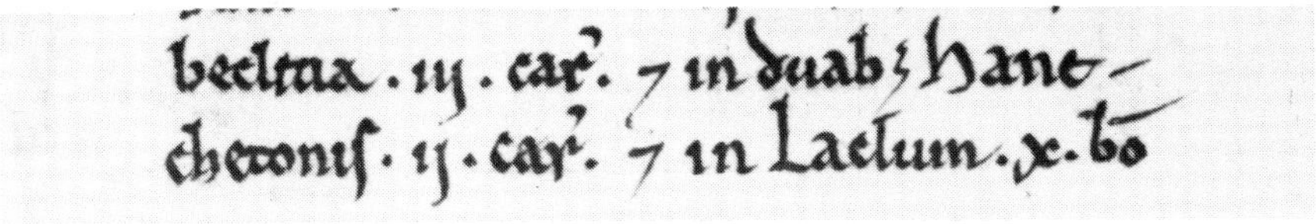

(h) fo. 333r

Plate IV

(a) Westminster Abbey Muniments XXIV

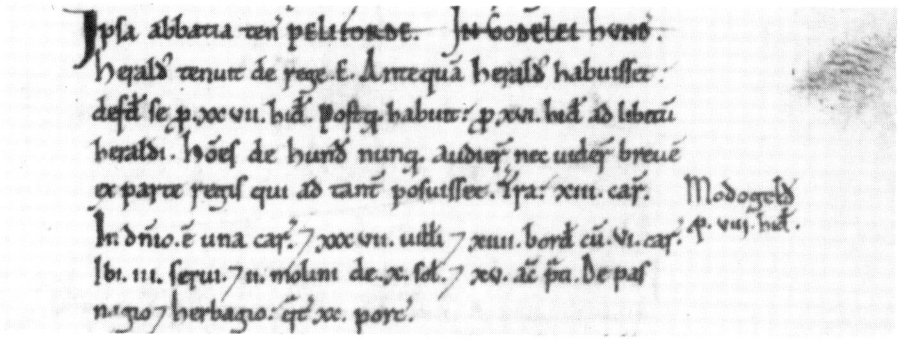

(b) Great Domesday Book, fo. 32r

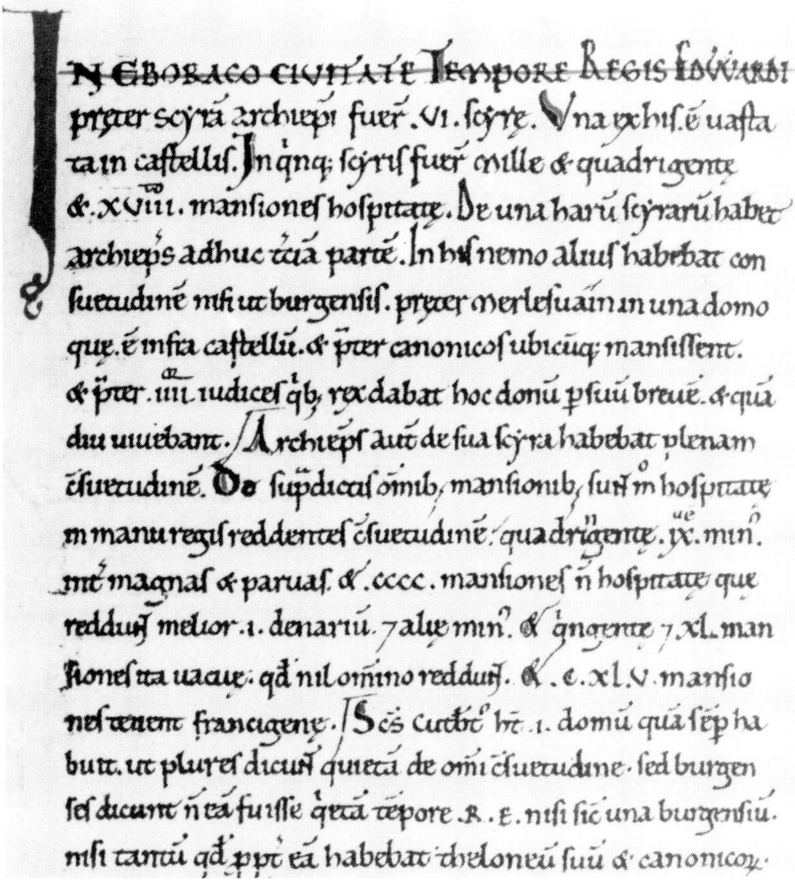

Plate V

The Domesday Manuscripts: Scribes and Scriptoria

(a) *Great Domesday Book, fo 298r, col. 1, lines 1–18: Scribe A*

(b) *Little Domesday Book, fo. 450r, foot: colophon (Scribe 7)*

Plate VI

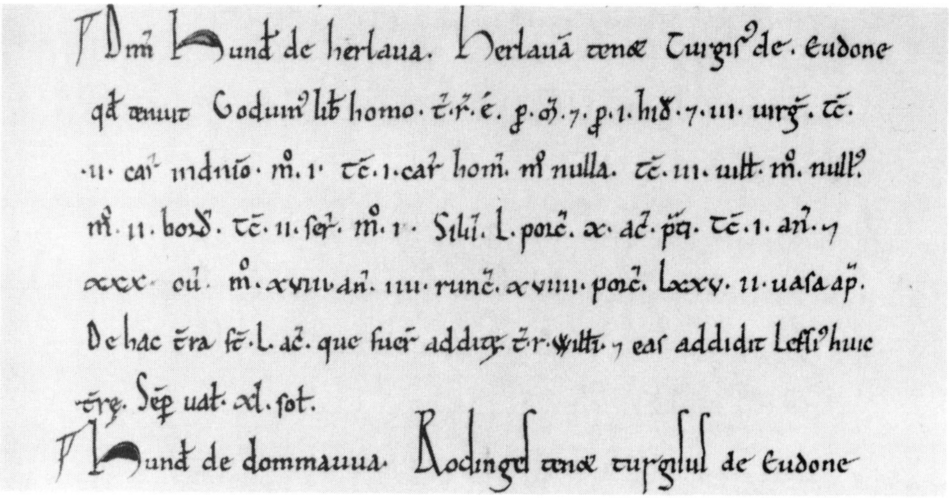

(a) Little Domesday Book, fo. 49r, lines 8–15: Scribe 1

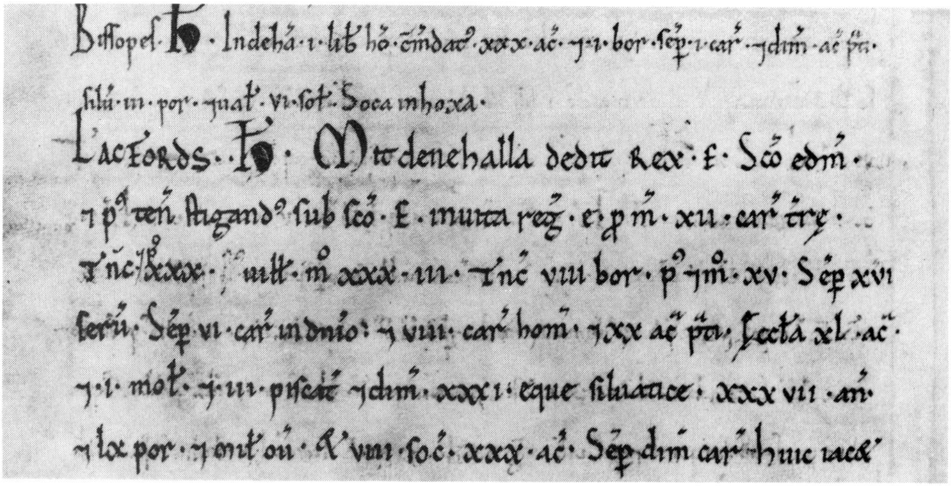

(b) Little Domesday Book, fo. 288v, lines 16–23: Scribe 2

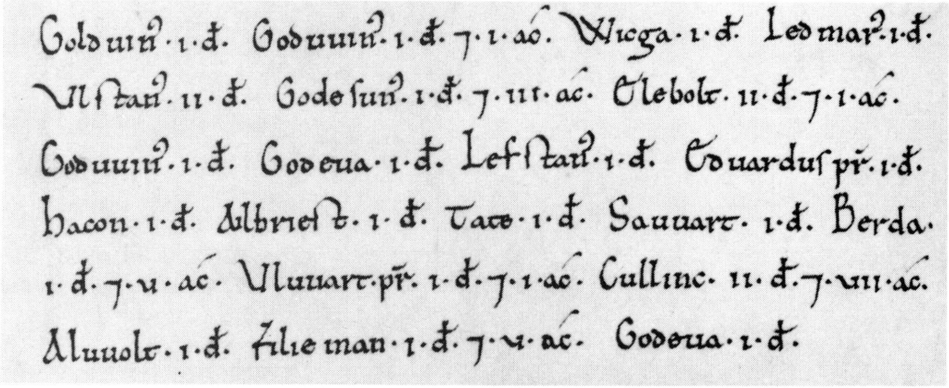

(c) Little Domesday Book, fo. 105r, lines 19–24 (slightly reduced): Scribe 3

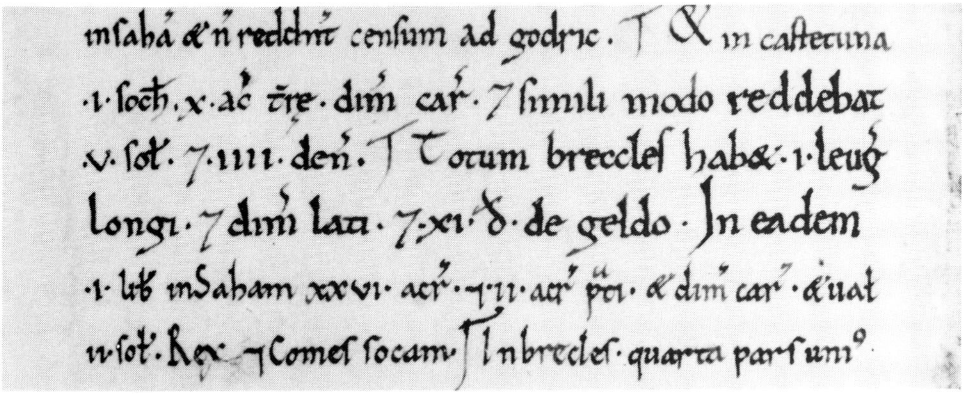

Plate VII

(a) Little Domesday Book, fo. 110v, lines 7–12: Scribes 2, 4

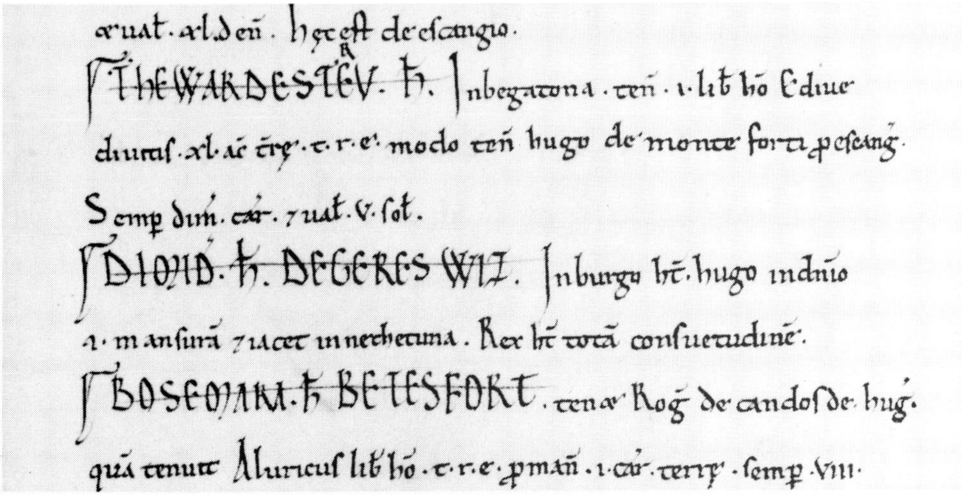

(b) Little Domesday Book, fo. 410r, lines 3–10: Scribe 5

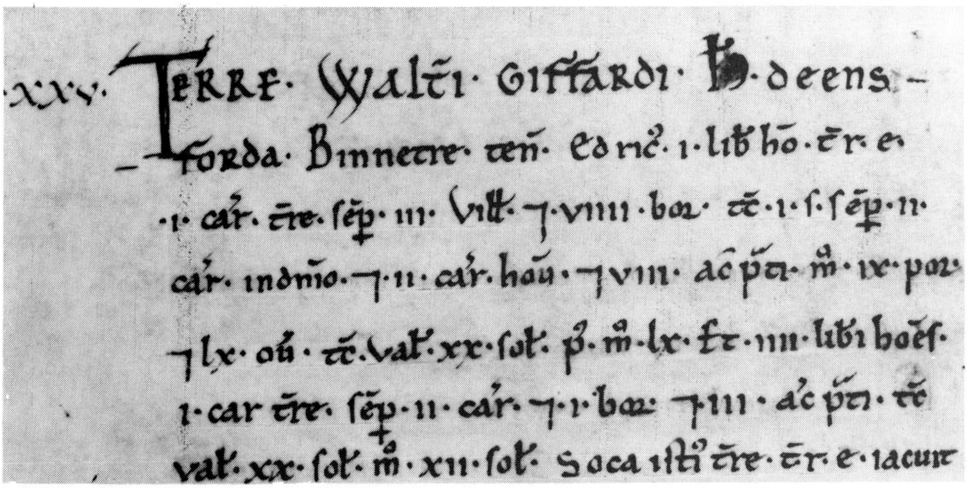

(c) Little Domesday Book, fo. 240r, lines 12–18: Scribe 6

Plate VII

Local Churches in Domesday Book and Before

Local church architecture in the age of Domesday Book.
(a) Doorhead at Tackley, Oxon: the mouldings are Norman in style, but the technique of cutting this piece from a single block of stone is in the English tradition (see R. Gem in Oxoniensia 1 (1985), pp. 41–2).
(b) Titchborne, Hants: here, by contrast, the style of the architecture is in the English tradition but the execution of the masonry in the Norman.

GENERAL INDEX

Abbrevatio of Domesday Book, 12
Abingdon (Berks.), 94, 258
Abington (Cambs.), 145n, 146
Abington Piggotts (Cambs.), 151
Abitot, Urse d', 166
Acle (Norf.), 60
Acquisition, of land, 59
Adalard, abbot of S. Bertin, 33
Adelaide, sister of William I, 239
Aelfwine, 'of Thetford', 210
Aethelred II, king of England, 3, 206,
    207, 210, 217, 250, 264, 302
Agaune, Hubert d', 34
Aigle, Gilbert de l', 44
Aix-en-Provence, 16
Alan, count of Brittany, 63, 220, 226
Alchin (Sussex), 186
Alençon, count of, 226
Alhampton (Somerset), 112
Allod, 19
Almenèsches, abbey of, 232
Alsace, 25
Alstonfield (Staffs.), 132
Amercements, 55
Ampton (Suffolk), 188
Andrew, W. J., 279, 280, 286
Anjou, Fulk, count of, 43
Annapes, 31
Anselm, archbishop of Canterbury, 7n,
    216, 236
Anselm, monk of Hautvillers, 20, 33
Antecessor, 24, 58
Arausio, see Orange
Archenfield (Heref.), 192, 194, 196
Arfast, bishop of Thetford, 95
    brother of Duchess Gunnor, 231
Armingford (Cambs.), 151
Arques, William of, 234
Arras, 34
Arras, abbey of S.-Vaast, 34
Arrington (Cambs.), 148, 150
Ashford (Derbys.), 111
Ashley (Cambs.), 145n

Ashmansworthy (Devon), 131
Ashmore (Dorset), 116
Ashurst (Sussex), 186
Aston, T., 140
Athelstan, king of England, 189
Ati's Cross (Clwyd), 190, 191
Aubigny, Nigel of, 229
Aunou, Fulk of, 222
Austria, 25
Autun, cathedral of, 36
Autun, priory of S.-Symphorien, 34
Avebury (Wilts.), 109
Avening (Glos.), 117
Axholme (Lincs.), 105

Badlesmere (Kent), 125
Badlingham (Cambs.), 149
Bagley woods (Berks.), 105
Baldwin, abbot of Bury St Edmunds, 7
Baldwin, sheriff of Devon, 228, 303n
Ballard, A., 11n, 279
Ballingham (Heref.), 195
Banbury (Oxon), manor of, 102
Bangor (Gwynedd), bishopric of, 184
Baring, F. H., 86n, 105, 109n, 139
Barlow, F., 6n, 7n, 204n, 210n, 216,
    218n
Barnstaple (Devon), 301n
Barrington (Cambs.), 150
Barton (Cambs.), 148, 150
Barton Regis (Glos.), 166
Bassingbourn (Cambs.), 151
Bates, D., 230, 231
Bath (Somerset), 71, 291, 293
Bathampton (Wilts.), 132
Battersea (Surrey), 207
Battle, abbey of, 3, 252, 258
Baudri the German, 238
Bavaria, 25, 30
Bayeux, Hugh, bishop of, 231, 259
    Odo, Bishop of, 60, 61, 69, 162, 215,
    220, 222, 231, 239, 259
    inquest of, 226n